Fireside Politics

Reconfiguring American Political History

Ronald P. Formisano, Paul Bourke,
Donald DeBats, and Paula M. Baker
SERIES EDITORS

Michael F. Holt
CONSULTANT

Washington County, Paul Bourke and Donald DeBats

Bennington and the Green Mountain Boys: The Emergence of Liberal Democracy in Vermont, 1760–1850, Robert E. Shalhope

An Army of Women: Gender and Power in Gilded Age Kansas, Michael Goldberg

Fireside Politics: Radio and Political Culture in the United States, 1920–1940, Douglas B. Craig

Fireside Politics

Radio and Political Culture in the United States, 1920–1940

Douglas B. Craig

The Johns Hopkins University Press | Baltimore and London

Printed in the United States of America on acid-free paper
2 4 6 8 9 7 5 3 1

The Johns Hopkins University Press
2715 North Charles Street
Baltimore, Maryland 21218-4363
www.press.jhu.edu

Library of Congress Cataloging-in-Publication Data
will be found at the end of this book.
A catalog record for this book is available
from the British Library.

ISBN 0-8018-6439-9

Contents

List of Maps, Illustrations, Figures, and Tables vii
Acknowledgments ix
Introduction xi
Abbreviations xix

Part I | Making the Medium, 1895–1940

1 *The Radio Age: The Growth of Radio Broadcasting, 1895–1940* 3

2 *Radio Advertising and Networks* 18

3 *Regulatory Models and the Radio Act of 1927* 36

4 *The Federal Radio Commission, 1927–1934* 59

5 *A New Deal for Radio? The Communications Act of 1934* 78

6 *The Federal Communications Commission and Radio, 1934–1940* 92

Part II | Radio and the Business of Politics, 1920–1940

7 *The Sellers: Stations, Networks, and Political Broadcasting* 113

8 *The Buyers: National Parties, Candidates, and Radio* 140

9 *The Product: Radio Politics and Campaigning* 167

10 *The Consumers: Radio, Audiences, and Voters* 186

Part III | Radio and Citizenship, 1920–1940

11 *Radio and the Problem of Citizenship* 205

12 *Radio at the Margins: Broadcasting and the Limits of Citizenship* 234

13 *Radio and the Politics of Good Taste* 258

Conclusion 279

Notes 285
Bibliography 329
Index 351

Maps, Illustrations, Figures, and Tables

Maps

1. Distribution of Radio Stations, March 1, 1923 10
2. NBC Networks, February 1928 31
3. Columbia Broadcasting System Network, February 1928 33
4. Radio Zones under the Radio Act of 1927 64
5. The "Radio States of America" 239

Illustrations

"Bridle Shy" 50
"Who's Elected?" 120
"Another Report to His Board of Directors" 125
The Champ 155
"A Tragedy of the Radio" 169
"Just a minute, dearie, until I shut off Herbert Hoover." 196

Figures

1. Radio Households and Set Production, 1922–1940 11
2. Radio Families, 1922–1940 12
3. Household Radio Ownership by Income Levels, 1935 14
4. Radio and Telephone Homes, 1920–1940 15
5. Rates of Growth of Selected Consumer Goods and Disposable Personal Income, 1920–1940 16
6. Advertising Expenditures by Medium, 1928–1939 26
7. Affiliated Stations and Total Stations, 1927–1940 34
8. Democratic and Republican Legislators on NBC, 1929–1935 138
9. NBC Billings, 1936 and 1940 Campaigns 165
10. Radio Listening by Sex, Age, and Education, 1940 216

11. Radio Program Preferences According to Reading Levels, 1940 217
12. Advertising Expenditures in Newspapers and on Radio, 1927–1940 224
13. Radio Listening by Sex, 1936 Winter Audiences 244
14. Color, Residence, and Ethnicity of Radio Families, 1930 252

Tables

1. Distribution of Radio Resources by Zone, 1927–1931 66
2. NBC Billings by Party, 1936 Campaign 136
3. Party Account Balances with NBC, November 20, 1936 136
4. Network Political Campaign Broadcasts, 1932 153
5. Subject Content of Federal Agencies' Network Programs, January–April 1937 158
6. *Radio and Amusement Guide* Ratings of Presidential Candidates' Air Personalities, 1932 173

Acknowledgments

Research for this book was supported by grants from the Australian Research Council, the Australian National University (ANU), and the Australian Academy of the Humanities. Sabbatical residences at the Institute of Governmental Studies at the University of California at Berkeley and the Department of History at the University of Sydney provided stimulating opportunities for research and writing.

I am grateful to the libraries and archives listed in the bibliography for access to their collections. I want also to acknowledge the help of Rod Stroud at the National Library of Australia, Catharine Heinz of the Broadcast Pioneers Library (as it then was), Fred Bauman and Edwin Matthias at the Manuscript Division and the Recorded Sound Reference Center of the Library of Congress, Mildred Mather, Dwight Miller, Shirley Sondergard, and Pat Wildenberg at the Herbert Hoover Presidential Library, Bill Beaudreau at the State Historical Society of Wisconsin, and—last but certainly not least—Lynn Ekfelt and Darlene Leonard of the Owen D. Young Library at St. Lawrence University.

Robert J. Brugger has been a tower of strength at Johns Hopkins University Press. His enthusiasm for this project has been both generous and sustained. I have also profited enormously from Marie Blanchard's and Julie McCarthy's editorial work, the anonymous reader's report, and the Cartography Unit of the Research School of Pacific and Asian Studies at ANU.

Family, colleagues, and friends read my drafts with care and wisdom. Andrew Craig in Kununurra, Barbara and Malcolm Crystal in Boston, Stephen Van Beek of San José State University and the Department of Transportation, Ian Hancock, Alison Kibler, and Fiona Paisley of the ANU, and Katie Holmes of La Trobe University all worked hard to improve my prose and tighten my thinking. John Hart, of the Department of Political Science at ANU, suggested the title of this book and has been an unfailing ally through good times and bad. Paul Bourke read an entire draft before his sudden death robbed us of a beloved friend and a generous and brilliant scholar. I feel honored to be the first holder of the Paul Bourke Fellowship at the Research School of Social Sciences at the ANU. Nelson and Linda Polsby and Ira and Martha Berlin were generous hosts and inspirational guests. Craig Mewett provided valuable research assistance for some of the material that appears in chapter 12. My colleagues in the Department of History in the Faculty of Arts and the History Program of the Research School of Social Sciences at ANU have also given me much support for many years.

In 1969, or thereabouts, my father built me a crystal radio set. Later improved by a single transistor powered by the battery from his dictating machine, that set gave me an early insight into the wonder of radio. It seemed miraculous to hear cricket broadcasts by day and Top 40 music by night through a piece of galena crystal. In 1999 my mother and father together read every word of two drafts of this book, painstakingly improving suspect syntax and weak logic. In between has been a lifetime of love, support, and good humour.

Introduction

This book explores radio's influence on interwar political institutions, debate, and theory. Radio emerged during the first two decades of the twentieth century in the wake of the telegraph and the telephone. Unlike its predecessors, however, radio's ability to transmit information instantaneously was not restrained by the need for poles, wires, or code. When station KDKA made the first scheduled broadcast on election night in November 1920, perhaps one household in 500 possessed radio equipment. Ten years later, 45 percent of America's 30 million families had at least one radio, and by 1940 radio had entered more than 80 percent of the nation's homes. "Of all the miracles this age has witnessed," a speaker at the World Radio Convention of 1938 declared, "radio is the most marvellous. It has taken sound, which moved with leaden feet, and given it to the wings of morning. We are now like Gods. We may speak to all mankind."[1]

Between the wars many Americans struggled to come to terms with radio's impact upon the ways in which they debated and formed public policy. The new medium presented as many challenges as promises to public life. Through it, citizens might become more enlightened about politics and policy, but they might as easily fall victim to propaganda. Few Americans doubted broadcasting's power to influence, and perhaps even form, political opinion, but this near unanimity made its destiny even more contentious. Throughout the 1920s, and with less frequency during the 1930s, many argued that broadcasting would finally create the ideal republic dreamed of by the ancient Greeks and envisioned by the leaders of the American Revolution. Through radio, world peace might be achieved by the free exchange of ideas across borders, and cultural standards would rise. Most important of all, New Dealer Harold Ickes argued in 1934, was radio's ability to educate listeners, for "a democracy will function more efficiently to the degree that the voters are informed and alert on public affairs."[2]

As broadcasting developed between 1920 and 1940, more skeptical views emerged about its sociopolitical destiny. A presidential committee on social trends in 1933 listed 150 social "effects" of radio and described it as second only in social importance to the automobile. But its effects were not all positive; radio increased the cost of campaigning and furthered the spread of propaganda and "rumors." Thanks to radio, the committee concluded, "greater possibilities for social manipulation, for ends that are selfish or socially desirable, have never existed." Hadley Cantril and Gordon Allport argued in 1935 that "the use of the radio should increase public enlightenment, encourage responsible citizenship, and enhance interest, intelligence, and tolerance among voters. This . . . depends of course upon an honest policy whereby the rights of the air are open to candidates of all parties, irrespective of their ability to pay or to confer favors upon broadcasting companies."[3]

Much of this book is taken up in describing the ways in which broadcasters, politicians, regulators, and listeners contested and formulated "an honest policy" for radio between 1920 and 1940. Broadcasters, and in particular the national networks, saw themselves as guardians of a booming industry. Although they proclaimed their commitment to public service, the networks' primary goal was to preserve and expand their businesses. To this end they argued for government regulation when it suited them—especially to "rationalize" the broadcast spectrum through a licensing system that enriched commercial broadcasters at the expense of nonprofit and local stations—but opposed it when it did not. Any attempt to use public policy or the public purse to weaken the economic, cultural, or political power of the major broadcasters was howled down as un-American by a broadcast industry that felt increasingly confident in claiming the privileges of the press while demanding the security of a governmental license.

Another powerful group occupied an even more ambiguous position within the debate over radio. The nation's political establishment, comprising elected politicians and appointees of the two major parties, tended to view radio as both a regulatory headache and a powerful weapon. Politicians' eagerness to use radio as a publicity and electioneering tool was exceeded only by their ignorance of its technical nature and demands. Although both major parties were convinced by 1928 of radio's usefulness in elections, presidents and legislators rarely ventured into the political and technical minefield of broadcast regulation. Only three times between the wars—in 1927, 1928, and 1934—did the Congress and the executive branch agree on new broadcasting regulation. Lawmakers were generally content to delegate control of radio first to the secretary of commerce, then to the Federal Radio Commission (FRC), and finally to the Federal Communications Commission (FCC).

Hemmed in by increasingly powerful lobby groups and hampered by their own ignorance, politicians tended to ride the radio wave rather than to channel it. The FRC and FCC, on the other hand, although endowed with almost unfettered licensing powers, soon manifested all the characteristics of capture by the industry they were supposed to control. The result, as Paul Lazarsfeld noted in 1942, was that "by and large, radio has so far been a conservative force in American life and has produced but few elements of social progress." The major broadcasters, anxious to maximize their audiences, had no interest in alienating them or their regulators by allowing "controversial" programming; audiences tended to listen to programs selectively but passively; legislators used radio without understanding it; and regulators preferred to talk about their powers rather than use them.[4] Consequently radio's potential to wreak a revolution on American political culture was severely curtailed by those who had most influence over its development.

Yet the idea of a "radio revolution" in American political life has been a durable feature of many histories of broadcasting. Until quite recently radio history languished in the shadow of a much larger historiography of television. Historians, sociologists, and media theorists of the 1960s and 1970s privileged the visual media—TV and the movies—above radio and the telegraph as areas worthy of detailed analysis and cultural theory.[5] Early accounts of radio tended to veer between triumphalism and technological determinism. Although few radio historians have matched the reductionism of Marshall McLuhan's claim in 1964—"that Hitler came into political existence at all is directly owing to radio and public-address systems"—many have followed some way in his determinist footsteps. J. Fred McDonald argued in 1979 that radio "inevitably reflected" an American culture of "commercial democracy" made up of "millions of relatively free-and-equal, middle class citizens." It could not have done otherwise, he concluded, because radio simply played to American tastes and mirrored American values.[6]

Recent work by Michele Hilmes, Robert McChesney, Philip Rosen, and Susan Smulyan has reconfigured radio history toward a more searching inquiry into the social, political, and cultural meanings of broadcasting. Taken together, these historians have looked behind what Hilmes has called "the mask that U.S. commercial media have created for themselves: as a naturally arising, consensus-shaped, and unproblematic reflection of a pluralistic society, rather than the conflicting, tension-ridden site of the ruthless exercise of cultural hegemony."[7] As a result, radio and its industry now seem less heroic but also more firmly rooted in their cultural and social context. We now know much more about the rise of the "American system" of broadcasting, the failure of reformers to achieve their vision of radio as an educative and culturally uplifting force, and the ways in which major broadcasters and their regulators excluded marginal or subversive voices. Instead of a radio revolution, Hilmes, McChesney, Rosen, and Smulyan, all suggest that the new medium's potential for social change was subverted by what McChesney described as the "dominant paradigm" of "the profit-motivated, network-dominated, and advertising-supported basis of U.S. broadcasting" that successfully silenced its critics as un-American.[8]

Other scholars have approached mass media from a behavioral perspective. Joshua Meyrowitz and John B. Thompson have argued that instantaneous communication, and especially television, have fundamentally reordered our conception of "publicness" from its traditional meaning of shared space toward a new and mediated nondialogical communication which is not localized in either space or time. Individuals can now receive messages, symbols, and images from the world beyond their own experiential horizons. This new form of social interaction has profound consequences for our identification and engagement with social structures, which have always depended upon exchange of information and symbols of community and common purpose. The telegraph, radio, and television, Meyrowitz concludes, have altered the "'situational geography' of social life." Because we can now hear the sounds and see the sights of previously hidden places, we have lost our old sense of place, and of "the distinctions between here and there, live and mediated, and personal and public."[9]

Analyses of program content have echoed this emphasis upon informational and symbolic exchange. Richard Ely, Pamela Grundy, and Margaret McFadden have shown that radio sent coded sociocultural messages to their listeners. Programs such as *Amos'n'Andy*, *The Jack Benny Show*, and hillbilly musical features mediated experiences of racism, economic depression, and regional dislocation in ways that legitimated individual experience while buttressing the values and institutions that had created those difficulties. Rather than a creature and mirror of American culture, radio was instead used to shape audiences' consciousness and social outlook in ways that suited the interests of those who controlled it.[10]

Although structuralists and behavioralists emphasize the impact of cultural-political context upon radio's development, surprisingly little attention has been paid to interactions between radio and political culture. Historians have noted that the first radio broadcast in 1920 was of election results, and they have hypothesized the effects of radio in strengthening the power of the presidency, in furthering political and policy information and education, and in changing the style and substance of political debate and campaigns, but we do not as yet have a detailed study of radio's role in interwar political culture.[11]

This book is dedicated to that task. By examining network records, congressional materials, regulatory reports, papers of prominent politicians and broadcasters, newspapers, periodicals, and the works of interwar social scientists, I have tried to present as broad a cross section of views on interwar radio as possible. The volume of sources available to historians of radio is daunting, and I make no claim to have exhausted them. My analysis focuses upon networks as the most influential broadcasters; my treatment of local and unaffiliated stations is more cursory and more reliant on previously published research. Preferring to emphasize the institutional dynamics of radio broadcasting, I have not ventured into content analysis of political programming or advertising between the wars. With the exception of works dealing with Franklin Roosevelt, this field remains undeservedly neglected.[12]

By using the term *political culture* I have attempted to use broad definitions of politics and political life to include not only the distribution and exercise of power but also ideas of what and who the political nation was. This is in keeping with modern usage of the term, as in David Farber's recent description: "the historically contingent practices and beliefs that give legitimacy to political structures and political authority to individuals and 'interests,' and which, in turn, political actors use creatively to affect public policy or, more generally, public life."[13] Although much of this book is concerned with the political process—legislation, regulation, and electoral contests—I also examine the rhetoric and reality of radio's impact upon conceptions of citizenship and community. In taking this approach I hope to go some way in bridging the gap between the structuralist and behavioral schools of media history. I have also paid attention to contemporary views on the impact of broadcasting on individuals—as both voters and citizens—and on the sociopolitical community.

I have ended my study in 1940 in the belief that the onset of World War II radically altered both the political culture of the United States and radio's role within it. The impingement of total war upon political institutions and debate, notions of citizenship, and freedom of expression created new forces in political culture, and in broadcasting, that deserve separate study.[14] I have also made some comparisons between American interwar radio and those of other democracies, including Australia, Canada, and Great Britain. Radio was championed as an annihilator of distance and as the most powerful unifying force in the world. It therefore seems appropriate to cross national boundaries, and even hemispheres, to examine its effects on public life.

International comparisons and emphasis upon political culture provide new perspectives on the development of American broadcasting. Recent historians have been very critical of the "American system," seeing it as a triumph of commercial greed over reformist vision. Yet that triumph was not complete; throughout the interwar period commercial broadcasters remained very nervous about the possibility of tighter regulation. An examination of the political culture of radio also clarifies the extent to which alternative visions of broadcasting—mostly involving varying degrees of public ownership or control—were either politically possible or socially desirable. In a political culture that venerated free enterprise and freedom of speech, and in an immediate context of antiregulation and negative statism during the 1920s, it is hard to imagine that radio could have developed in ways that diverged markedly from those assumptions. It is also difficult to find demonstrably superior performances in political broadcasting in any comparable nation during the interwar period. American broadcasters, and their legislators and regulators, were not paragons of inclusiveness, but the system they created gave listeners greater amounts, and arguably greater variety, of political programming than that provided to Australians, Britons, and Canadians.

In the following pages I also argue that the idea of a radio revolution in American political culture between the wars has been both exaggerated and simplified. The impact of broadcasting upon the ways in which Americans made public policy, contested elections, and defined citizenship was much less dramatic, and much subtler, than the hopes and fears of the 1920s and 1930s envisaged. Above all, I argue that the existing political culture, through its most influential actors, integrated radio into existing patterns and structures of behavior and power, and used it to its advantage. This process of integration operated even in the realms of political debate and electoral contest, areas long assumed to have been revolutionized by radio.[15]

But this is not to say that radio left no imprint upon interwar political culture. The new medium prompted subtle, but very significant, alterations to the ways in which Americans conducted public business and conceived of their community during the 1920s and 1930s. It brought forth new regulatory principles and institutions; politicians were forced to rethink the ways in which they communicated with their constituents, and all Americans had to adjust to the emergence of a new medium of cultural and political communication. Radio was far more than simply another industry within a burgeoning consumer economy; it brought with it powerful hopes for a new age of education, enlightenment, and engagement. Although these hopes were ultimately disappointed, the ways in which the political culture subsumed what

I call radio exceptionalism—the belief that radio was a very different medium to its predecessors and one possessed of a special destiny—tells us a great deal about community, citizenship, and politics in interwar America.

This book is organized into three parts. Part one introduces readers to the formation of a national radio audience and covers the development of broadcasting into its commercialized and networked form. I then sharpen my focus upon political culture by detailing the ways in which the new industry was regulated between 1920 and 1940. Part two discusses radio's role in electoral contests and government publicity between 1920 and 1940. Treating political broadcasting and advertising as a business, I examine the attitudes of broadcasters, political parties, and voters to it, as well as presenting those of contemporary social scientists and commentators. The chapters that make up part three broaden the discussion of political culture beyond the confines of public policy and elections. Here I examine contemporary rhetoric and reality concerning radio's impact upon the nature, and limits, of citizenship and community in order to show the ways in which radio worked within the geographic, racial, gendered, and cultural boundaries of interwar society.

These parts are unified by a number of key concepts: radio exceptionalism, listener sovereignty, and radio citizenship. The idea that listeners were sovereign over radio programming persisted throughout the interwar period, and proved to be very useful to broadcasters. Its resonance to the republican concept of popular sovereignty makes it particularly amenable as an organizing theme for a discussion of radio and political culture. The idea of a radio citizenship also coursed through interwar debate over broadcasting. Many broadcasters and social analysts argued that radio would create a new age of citizenship, in which all Americans could become better informed about, and more engaged in, the ways in which their society functioned. Taken together these themes illuminate the broader story of the ways in which radio's communicative and educational potential was recognized, and then co-opted, by the nation's corporate and political elites between the wars.

Abbreviations

AAA	Agricultural Adjustment Administration
AAAA	American Association of Advertising Agencies
ABC	Australian Broadcasting Company (1928–30)
	Australian Broadcasting Commission (1930–)
AC	Alternating current
ACLU	American Civil Liberties Union
AIPO	American Institute of Public Opinion
AM	Amplitude modulation
ANPA	American Newspaper Publishers Association
AP	Associated Press
ASCAP	American Society of Composers, Authors, and Publishers
AT&T	American Telephone and Telegraph
BBC	British Broadcasting Company (1922–26)
	British Broadcasting Corporation (1926–)
BBD&O	Batten, Barton, Durstine, and Osborn
CAB	Cooperative Analysis of Broadcasting
CBC	Canadian Broadcasting Commission
CBS	Columbia Broadcasting System
CNS	Columbia News Service
CPA	Communist Party of America
CPI	Committee for Public Information
CRBC	Canadian Radio Broadcasting Commission
DC	Direct current
DNC	Democratic National Committee
EPIC	End Poverty in California
FCC	Federal Communications Commission
FM	Frequency modulation
FRC	Federal Radio Commission
FREC	Federal Radio Education Committee
FTC	Federal Trade Commission

GEC	General Electric Company
ICC	Interstate Commerce Commission
kW	Kilowatt
MBS	Mutual Broadcasting System
MPPDA	Motion Pictures Producers and Distributors Association
NAACP	National Association for the Advancement of Colored People
NAB	National Association of Broadcasters
NACRE	National Advisory Council on Radio in Education
NBC	National Broadcasting Company
NCER	National Committee for Education by Radio
NRA	National Recovery Administration
RCA	Radio Corporation of America
REA	Rural Electrification Administration
RNC	Republican National Committee
TVA	Tennessee Valley Authority
UP	United Press
W	Watt
WPA	Works Progress Administration

Part I

Making the Medium, 1895–1940

For the first time in history the problem of free speech becomes an administrative problem.

— MORRIS ERNST, 1926

1

The Radio Age

The Growth of Radio Broadcasting, 1895–1940

When James Rorty looked back in 1934 on the beginnings of the radio age, he remarked that "radio broadcasting came into the world like a child born too soon and bearing the birthmark of a world culture which may never be achieved." Radio had emerged amidst high hopes of a new age of enlightenment and communication. Yet it had become a shabby and neglected child, left out on the streets because neither art nor education had the resources or the wit to adopt her. Eventually she had been picked up by businessmen and put to work selling "gargles, and gadgets, toothpaste and stocks and bonds."[1]

Rorty's judgment was too harsh. In fact, scientists, inventors, businessmen, politicians, and many listeners had all struggled to see radio fulfill its promise as the new century's preeminent medium of mass communication. First hypothesized in James Clerk Maxwell's theory of electromagnetism, the existence of radio waves capable of carrying signals at the speed of light had been proved by Heinrich Hertz in 1887 and then put to practical use by Guglielmo Marconi in 1895. By 1901 Marconi had succeeded in transmitting radio messages across the Atlantic Ocean, and soon radio proved itself as a lifesaver for mariners—including passengers on the *Titanic* in 1912—and as a coordinator of fleets and armies during World War I.

Marconi's great achievement was to show that radio telegraphy—the transmission of code without the use of wires—was both technically feasible and practically useful. Seeing radio as an improvement upon the telegraph, Marconi thought it best suited for point-to-point transmission—the sending of messages to a single specified receiver—rather than broadcasting to an unspecified number of receivers. But new visions of radio began to impinge upon

Marconi's point-to-point paradigm in the early years of the twentieth century. The most significant of these was radio telephony, by which the human voice, rather than coded messages, could be transmitted.

Successful radio telephony required new technological advances. The first radio transmitters produced short, discontinuous bursts of radio waves which varied in wavelength. Although these "spark" transmitters could send bursts of code, they were incapable of transmitting the continuous waves required to carry the undulations of the human voice. Reginald Fessenden, a Canadian-born inventor, persuaded the General Electric Company (GEC) in 1905 to produce a continuous wave transmitter, called the Alexanderson alternator. Combining this with his own receiving technology, Fessenden made the first radio transmission of the human voice on December 24, 1906. That triumph marked the beginning of radio telephony and thus of the radio age as we understand it today.[2]

Fessenden's achievement was soon complemented by the work of Lee de Forest, an Iowa electrical engineer. In 1907 de Forest patented his audion vacuum tube, which solved one of the great problems of early radio: that of rectifying and amplifying radio signals. Radio waves oscillate up and down; radio receivers must rectify them into a one-directional stream in order to convert the waves back into sounds. By improving an earlier tube designed by John Ambrose Fleming, de Forest's audion tube both rectified radio waves and significantly amplified them. This allowed receivers not only to pick up the human voice and music but also to make those signals loud enough to be heard easily through earphones and—later—loudspeakers. Although it took many years to perfect, the audion tube marked the birth of electronics, and made the modern domestic radio receiver technically feasible.[3]

Radio: Hobby and Industry, 1906–1918

The work of Marconi, Fessenden, and de Forest inspired many Americans to explore the mysterious world of radio after 1906. Before 1920, however, this required a high degree of skill and understanding of code and electrical componentry. Receiving sets had to be put together from a mixture of manufactured parts and homemade ingenuity. Nevertheless, many thousands of radio enthusiasts assembled primitive crystal receiving sets with the help of an increasing number of periodicals and books. These amateur radio enthusiasts considered themselves to be the advance guard of the radio revolution, and by 1912 there were more than 120 radio clubs across the United States.[4] Wealthier amateurs even tried their hands at constructing home transmitters, creating a two-way traffic in radio messages that was independent of commercial radio operations such as American Marconi. The majority of amateurs, though, were content to spend their evening hours, when reception was best, scanning the airwaves for whatever signals they could detect.

Others were busy trying to make money from radio. The American Marconi Company quickly assumed a dominant position in the young radio industry, focusing upon ship-to-shore and transoceanic radio telegraphic service. The commercial and safety advantages of maritime point-to-point radio communication were obvious, and organizations such as the United Fruit Company were quick to use it to manage their fleets more efficiently. The U.S. Navy also adopted radio after 1900, but in ways that unsettled the emerging commercial contours of the industry. The navy refused to deal with American Marconi on that company's usual terms, which involved leasing of sets with trained Marconi operators. Instead it took advantage of chaotic competition within the young industry by copying and improving patented equipment without authorization. Not surprisingly, relations between American Marconi (as well as other radio manufacturers) and the navy were soon strained.[5]

Radio remained a largely unregulated industry until 1912. By then growing numbers of amateurs, commercial operators, and naval stations had caused interference and congestion of wavelengths. The Congress responded by passing the Radio Act of 1912, which appropriated the airwaves as public property, to be temporarily allocated to individuals or corporations through a licensing regime. All nongovernmental operators required licenses from the secretary of commerce, and the president was empowered to close down or take over radio equipment "in time of war or public peril or disaster." Regulations under the act established a spectrum of wavelengths for radio transmissions. The largest and most desirable segment of the spectrum was reserved for government purposes. Commercial operations were also given generous allocations, but amateurs were pushed down to the least desirable end of the spectrum. Other regulations outlawed the Marconi practice of noninterconnection, which had barred the exchange of radio messages between it and other commercial operators.

The outbreak of World War I in August 1914 created a powerful new dynamic in the development of radio in the United States. Radio quickly became embroiled in the complexities of American neutrality between August 1914 and April 1917. With its undersea cables cut, Germany relied heavily on radio telegraphy to communicate with its American interests. Two powerful German-owned radio transmitters at Tuckerton, New Jersey, and Sayville,

New York, were capable of trans-Atlantic transmissions, and they came under suspicion of unneutral activities almost as soon as the war broke out. At first the Wilson administration was content to censor German radio traffic, but by the end of 1915 both Tuckerton and Sayville were under complete navy control.[6] The navy strengthened its hold over American radio after the United States' declaration of war in April 1917. Almost immediately President Wilson used his power under the Radio Act to place all private radio stations under naval control. The navy then ordered amateurs to cease operations and to dismantle their sets, beginning a period of enforced silence that would last until September 1919.

Although the navy's primary purpose in controlling radio was to ensure that its radio operations were properly equipped and staffed, it also made some attempt at broadcasting. News transmissions were beamed at France and the Low Countries from Tuckerton, and a radio "home news" service for U.S. troops began, in which newspaper columns were read out over the airwaves and then transformed into print for distribution at the front. Radio also played a role at the end of the war; Woodrow Wilson's Fourteen Points were broadcast to Europe in 1918, and on October 12 of that year the German parliament transmitted a request via radio to the United States for an armistice.

Postwar Maneuvering and the Formation of RCA

Radio had impinged lightly upon American political culture and institutions before 1918. The Radio Act of 1912 enjoyed smooth passage through Congress, and it provoked little sustained criticism after its enactment. The industry's emphasis upon radio telegraphy rather than telephony in the prewar years meant that the enormous communicative potential of the new medium was still more imagined than real. Although Americans were aware of the importance of radio in maritime and military affairs, and were exposed to some of its romance and mystery through periodicals and newspapers, it had yet to affect their lives and perceptions in concrete ways. All this was to change after 1918.

Radio became politicized when it was caught up in wider debates over the role of government in postwar society. The catalyst for this struggle was Josephus Daniels, Secretary of the Navy, who was determined to achieve permanent government control of American radio.[7] In December 1918 Daniels told a congressional hearing that the war had shown that radio communication was most effective when it was under government control. The American

Marconi Company, he thought, was inherently British in its loyalties. Permanent naval control of all radio operations would ensure that this vital form of modern communication would be safe from foreign domination.[8]

Daniels failed to persuade Congress, which was anxious to roll back the wartime powers of the federal government. Many in Congress and industry were also disturbed by the prospect of permanent government control of a formerly private enterprise. George Davis, general manager of the United Fruit Company's radio operations, warned, "We have just fought a great war to make the world safe for democracy, but if legislation such as this is to be an outcome of the war, the United States will have been made unsafe for business." GEC, through its vice-president Owen D. Young, also attacked Daniels's scheme as un-American.[9]

Although Daniels lost his battle for government-controlled radio, even his opponents acknowledged that radio should continue to develop under American control. The cutting of the German cables in 1914 had shown that the United States was ill-equipped to communicate independently with the outside world. The British now enjoyed a monopoly of oceanic cable facilities, but radio promised a worldwide communication network that bypassed this monopoly. It therefore assumed a vital role in furthering the United States' new position in world politics and commerce.[10]

While doing public battle with GEC over federal ownership, the navy was also engaged in secret negotiations with it to delay the sale of Alexanderson alternators to American Marconi. Admiral William Bullard, Director of Naval Communications, put the case to Young and other GEC executives that the proposed sale would "fix in British hands a substantial monopoly of world communications" at this "critical period of the history of radio." Young remembered that Bullard ended his presentation by appealing to them "as patriotic American citizens not to make the transfer." GEC agreed to buy out British Marconi's patents and shares in American Marconi.[11] GEC then incorporated the Radio Corporation of America (RCA), 59 percent owned by GEC and capitalized at $12 million, in October 1919. RCA's charter provided for a maximum of 20 percent foreign ownership and an American board of directors.

RCA consolidated its position through a series of patent agreements between 1919 and 1922. RCA began its corporate life with GEC radio patents as well as those belonging to American Marconi. RCA and GEC then agreed with Western Electric (a subsidiary of AT&T), Westinghouse, United Fruit, and other smaller firms over the next three years to share their radio patents and markets. GEC and Westinghouse were allowed to manufacture radio equipment, which would then be sold through RCA. In a move that would soon prove crucial to its future, RCA also won the right to operate radio telephony stations.[12]

RCA's initial commercial mission focused upon transmission of point-to-point commercial messages in competition with undersea cables and the overland telegraph. Very soon, however, the company also began to see the potential of radio broadcasting within the United States. RCA's general manager, David Sarnoff, wrote to Owen Young at the beginning of 1920, "I have had in mind a plan . . . which would make radio a 'household utility' in the same sense as a piano or phonograph." Noting that it was now possible to transmit music and to manufacture domestic receiving sets at a reasonable price, Sarnoff argued that RCA could become a radio broadcaster as well as a point-to-point transmitter. Concerts, baseball scores, lectures, and other important events could now be transmitted into people's homes. Even if only 7 percent of America's 15 million families bought a "radio music box" at $75 each, RCA stood to make $75 million in sales.[13]

The formation of RCA, the end of wartime radio control, and advances in radio technology all contributed to the birth of domestic broadcasting. RCA was interested in new markets, and the prominence of GEC executives in its ranks created a more conducive atmosphere for expansion beyond the old Marconi company's focus upon marine telegraphy. The potential market for broadcasting was also liberated by the lifting of the wartime ban on amateur radio receiving in September 1919. In June 1920 RCA's board of directors authorized Sarnoff to explore further the possibility of making and selling "radio music boxes."

Other companies moved in the same direction even more quickly. The Westinghouse Company, GEC's major rival in electrical manufacturing, applied for a license from the Department of Commerce to begin regular programming from its Pittsburgh headquarters. That license was granted on October 27, 1920, and a week later station KDKA made radio history by transmitting progress reports of the Harding-Cox presidential election results. Although other stations have vied for the title of America's first radio broadcaster, KDKA's program on November 4, 1920 is widely recognized as the nation's first scheduled radio broadcast.[14] Westinghouse had thus stolen a march on RCA, allowing it to force itself into the radio pool established by GEC when it formed RCA.

The Radio Boom: Stations and Broadcasters

Despite its importance to the history of radio, KDKA's first broadcast did not begin the radio boom of the 1920s. It was not mentioned in the *New York Times*'s election coverage, and neither set sales nor broadcast licenses boomed in 1921. A postwar economic slump depressed consumer income and confidence, and the radio industry had not yet transformed its products into easily accessible consumer goods. Only nine new stations began operating in the first six months of 1921, although one of those was RCA's WJY in New York. Improving economic conditions at the end of 1921 and the appearance of complete sets that required little home assembly created the first signs of a radio boom. As more consumers bought radios, more stations rushed on to the airwaves. Newspapers began to devote attention to radio, providing information about programs, set construction, and improving reception. Suddenly radio became a fad, and one of the major beneficiaries of the economic good times after 1921.[15]

In January 1922 there were 30 broadcasting stations on air; 12 months later there were 556. The total number of stations hovered around 600 between 1929 and 1936, as federal regulation brought order to the radio boom. Below this superficial stability, however, lay great volatility. Hundreds of small and undercapitalized broadcasters entered the market, eager to join the boom but ill-equipped to stay with it. During 1922, 642 new stations began broadcasting, while 94 disappeared. In 1923, 298 station closures easily outnumbered 249 new entries. The early broadcasters were predominantly radio and electrical manufacturers and dealers. In February 1923 nearly 40 percent of the 576 stations on air belonged to this group; educational institutions (13%) and newspapers (12%) were also well represented.[16]

Map 1 shows the geographical distribution of the 578 stations that were operational in March 1923. Every state except Mississippi had at least one station, and 39 had more than three. Station power varied immensely, from RCA's 50kW stations in New York down to the 100W local stations run by amateurs, colleges, or stores. Although their location became a hot political issue at the end of the 1920s, stations sprang up haphazardly in the early years of the decade.

The radio industry enjoyed a production boom during the 1920s. Figure 1 shows that growth in the number of radio households continued at a rate that defied the Depression.

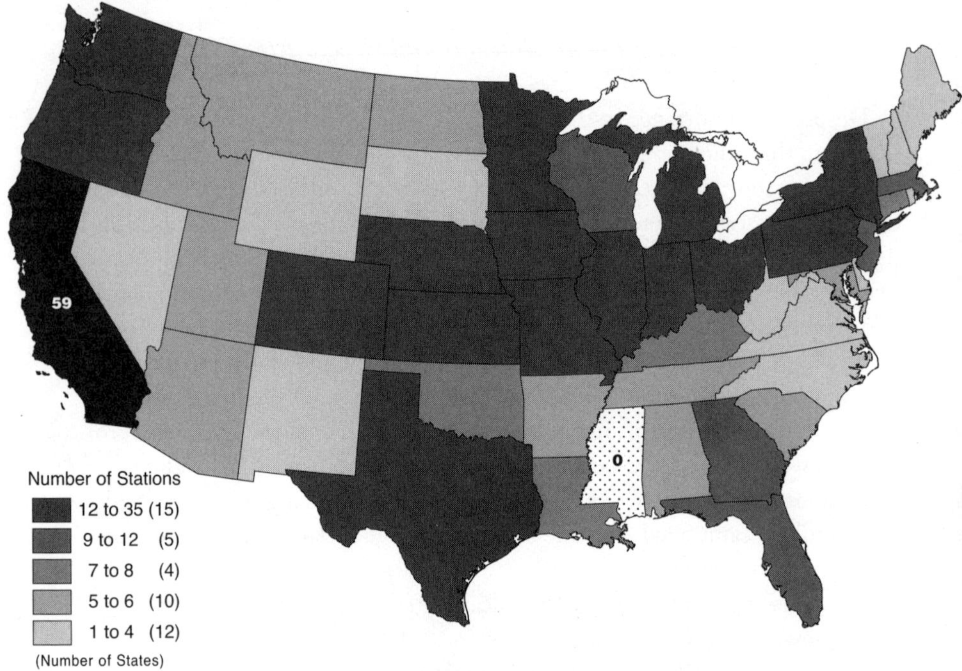

Map 1. Distribution of Radio Stations, March 1, 1923.
Source: Mapped from data in National Archives and Records Administration, RG 173, entry 1, file 1179, box 101.

By 1924 sales of radio equipment were double those of sporting goods and three quarters of those of the much older phonograph industry. The radio manufacturing industry now had about 2,000 manufacturers, 31,000 retailers, and more than 30 radio periodicals, all contributing to an industry worth $450 million per year in sales. Three years later, at the beginning of 1929, radio sales had reached $650 million and sets in use had nearly doubled to 9 million.[17]

Crystal sets, the cheapest type of radio to produce, sold in kit form during the 1920s for as little as $2, but their sales declined sharply with the arrival of valve sets. These offered great advantages, including the power to run loudspeakers, which made group listening possible. With the crystal set also disappeared many small manufacturers who had neither the plant nor the patents to keep up with the large firms. In 1922 RCA sold a range of radio sets that cost from $18 to $350. Valves usually cost extra, at about $5 each. Prices continued to fall; in 1925 the cheapest valve set was the Crosley Pup, which could be had for about $10, plus valves. In 1927 the first AC power sets came on to the market, relieving customers of the need to store and recharge batteries. By the end of the 1920s wealthy customers could pay up to $2,000 for the very best radios, elegantly housed in fine wooden cabinets and providing excellent output through advanced loudspeakers. Less privileged buyers could spend $150 for a set that provided performance and sound quality far superior to sets manufactured only three years earlier.[18]

Although the purchase of a radio represented a significant financial outlay for most urban workers, installment purchase plans lessened the immediate burden. Dealers began to offer installment plans in 1925, and by 1929 80 percent of radio sales were on credit. Car sets appeared in 1928, but their diffusion was initially slow because of the downturn in the automobile industry after 1930. Only 108,000 car radios were sold in 1930, and a mere 34,000 in 1931. By 1940, however, more than a quarter of America's cars were equipped with radios.[19]

The Formation of a Mass Radio Audience

"Let the day's troubles sink with the sun," ran a radio manufacturer's advertisement in 1923, "then turn on your Tuska Radio, and be whisked around the world. In those precious hours between work and sleep, you live in Radio Fairyland, where you are master of distance and ruler of a host of entertain-

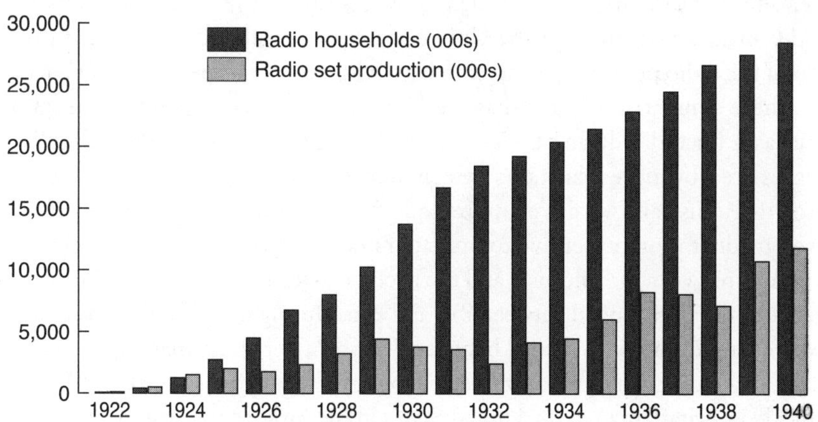

Figure 1. Radio Households and Set Production, 1922–1940.
Source: Graph constructed from data in *Historical Statistics of the United States*, 2:796.

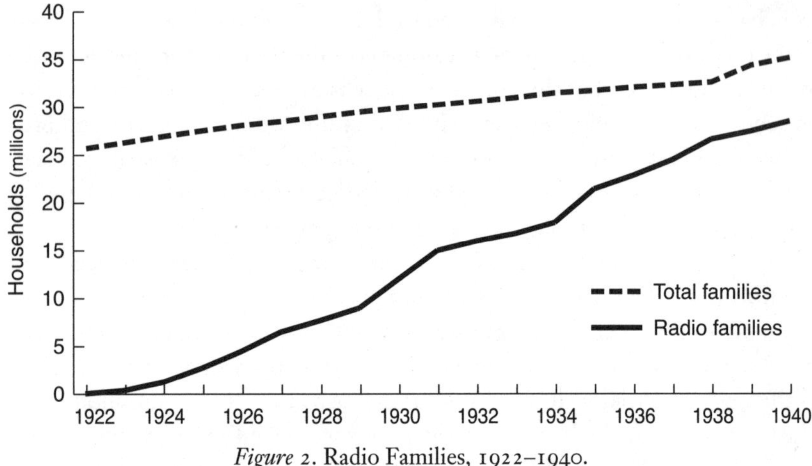

Figure 2. Radio Families, 1922–1940.

Source: Graph constructed from data in *Historical Statistics of the United States,* 2:796, and Roosevelt Papers, PPF 853.

ers." In 1922 only 0.2 percent of American households contained a radio; five years later nearly a quarter did. By 1930, 45.8 percent of American homes were equipped with radio, and by 1940 that figure had risen to more than 80 percent.[20]

In 1926 Senator Clarence Dill of Washington State noted that the United States, with just 6 percent of the world's population, owned 80 percent of the world's radios. In 1934 the United States' 147.9 radios per 1,000 persons were well ahead of Britain's 133.4, Sweden's 108.1, Australia's 78.1, Germany's 77.4, and Canada's 73.5. By 1938 the United States had displaced Denmark at the top of the radio per capita ownership lists, with 204 radios per 1,000 persons.

These comparisons show that the United States was not alone in its enthusiasm for radio during the 1920s. In Britain the number of listening licenses grew by more than 3,000 percent between 1922 and 1924, and rates of growth in Australia were even more explosive. Their licensing systems, however, made it more expensive to operate radios. In Britain listeners paid ten shillings per year for a license, and the average price for medium-quality sets between the wars ranged between £15 and £30. During this period most semiskilled English workers earned between £2 and £4 per week, making the purchase of a radio set a significant financial outlay. Although radio diffused more quickly in Britain than in the United States in the early 1920s, American radio households grew more rapidly after 1926. By 1937, 82 percent of American homes had radios, compared to 69 percent of British households. Three factors promoted faster growth of radio ownership in the United States: installation of electricity in homes was more rapid, installment plans for radio buyers came earlier, and Americans enjoyed higher levels of disposable income during the 1920s.[21]

Radio's progress in the United States, however, was not as all-conquering as its enthusiasts suggested. When diffusion figures are examined on a geographical basis, it is clear that radio ownership was closely correlated to both wealth and geography. In 1930, for example, the four wealthiest areas of the nation—the Middle Atlantic, the Pacific, New England, and the East North Central—were also the top four radio-owning areas. Nine of the richest ten states in the nation had the highest percentage of radio families, while eight of the poorest ten states occupied the bottom of the rankings. In 1930 the preponderance of radio families lived in the Northeast and East North Central, with the Pacific Coast also well represented. The old Confederacy, and in particular the Deep South—the poorest part of the country—languished well behind the rest of the nation. Nationally, 45.8 percent of all households owned a radio, but the average ownership rate in the 11 Confederate states was 11.9 percent, and that of the Deep South was only 9.7 percent. The *New York Times* concluded in 1932 that northern farmers, "followed at a decent interval" by urban professionals and "skilled mechanics," were the nation's foremost radio owners; radio's "favorite habitat seems to be with the average four-member family in middle-class homes in middle-size cities."[22]

By 1936, despite the Depression, all areas of the United States had made great strides in radio ownership. By then 74 percent of the nation's homes contained a radio, and all areas of the country had seen their rates grow by at least 10 percent per year since 1930. In 1936 radio ownership had grown to 87.5 percent in New England, 88.2 percent in the Middle Atlantic states, 84.5 percent on the Pacific Coast, and 80.9 percent in the East North Central states. Growth in radio ownership between 1930 and 1936 was highest in the South, with rises of 223 percent in the South Atlantic, 283 percent in the East South Central, and 248 percent in the West South Central states. Yet the southern third of the nation still lagged behind the rest of the country. The average across the old Confederacy was 48 percent of households in 1936, while in the Deep South it was 44.5 percent, far behind the national average.[23]

Across the nation radio ownership correlated to household income levels throughout the interwar period. Predictably, the poorest households were least likely to contain radios, although even they had a radio ownership rate of more than 50 percent in 1935. Figure 3 shows radio ownership by household income in 1935, plotted against a national average of 74 percent.

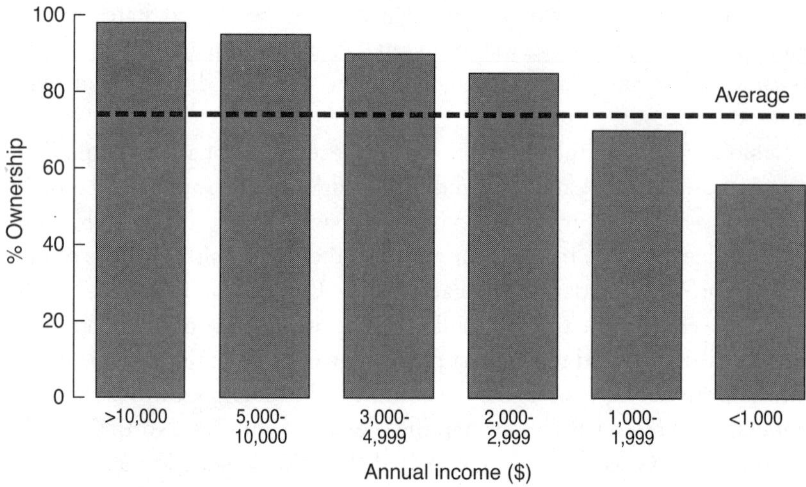

Figure 3. Household Radio Ownership by Income Levels, 1935.
Source: Graph constructed from data in Herman S. Hettinger and Walter J. Neff, *Practical Radio Advertising*, p. 41.

Radio ownership during the interwar period was not exclusively a product of income levels. The attractiveness of radio ownership also depended upon availability of good reception, AC power, and stations. The South lacked all these factors, but in the West North Central states farmers who enjoyed good reception bought more radios than their income levels might otherwise have suggested. Ownership rates in the West North Central thus were higher than in the Mountain states, where reception was poorer and stations fewer, despite the average higher per capita income of the latter region.[24]

Radio as a Consumer Durable, 1920–1940

Although radio was thought of as a fad during the early 1920s, it quickly proved to be a durable part of the consumer economy. During the interwar years Americans placed a high priority upon the purchase of a radio. They also showed their attachment to their radios by holding on to them during the hard times of the Depression.

The radio boom occurred in the context of a wider communications revolution after 1900. The total number of items per capita of first class mail rose by 70 percent between 1900 and 1930, and per capita use of telegraph facilities jumped more than 60 percent during the same period. In 1900 there were more than 1.3 million telephones, or 18 per thousand people. That proportion grew to 163.6 in 1930, and total phone calls per capita per year also jumped, from 64 in 1902 to 246 in 1927.[25]

Impressive as these figures were, telephone diffusion rates after 1920 still lagged behind radio. Despite the telephone's 44-year head start, radio took only ten years to overtake it within American homes (see fig. 4). The gap between the number of radio homes and telephone homes increased during the Depression. Telephone subscriptions dropped markedly, from 42 percent of homes in 1929 to 31 percent in 1933. Thereafter telephone penetration increased, but even in 1940 it was well below the 1929 figure. Radio diffusion proved much less sensitive to the Depression, although its rate of increase did lessen.

Many factors contributed to radio's higher diffusion rate. Telephone service remained expensive through the 1920s, although costs declined significantly in real terms after 1900. Consequently telephone subscription rates were closely related to economic status during the 1920s. In Robert and Helen Lynd's study of Muncie, Indiana, in 1924, for instance, they found that all 40 of the town's "business class" families had phones, compared with only 55 percent of workers' houses.[26] Radio ownership was more appealing to many poorer Americans because it required only one outlay for the purchase of a set, and then minimal ongoing costs for electrical power or battery charging. The low running costs of a radio set probably encouraged families to hold

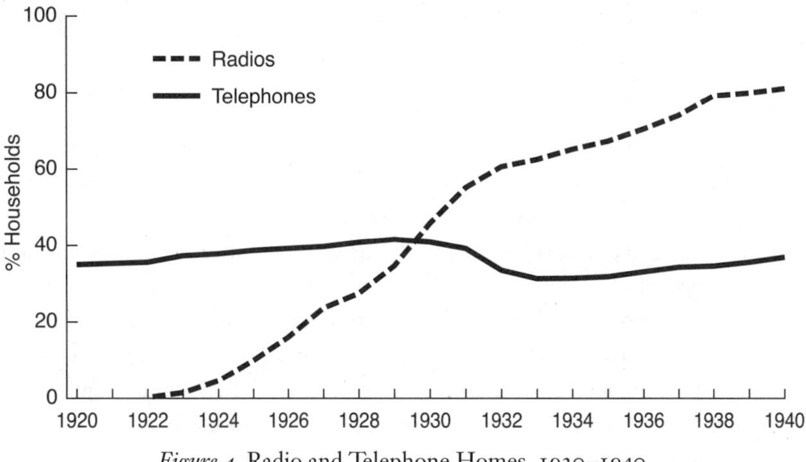

Figure 4. Radio and Telephone Homes, 1920–1940.

Source: Graph constructed from data in *Historical Statistics of the United States,* 1:43, and 2:783, 796.

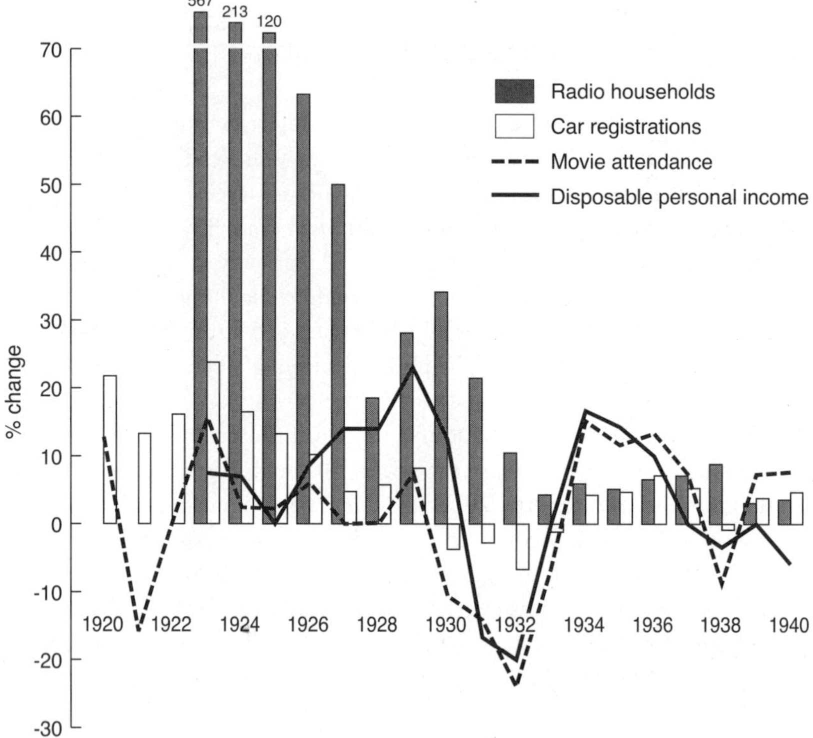

Figure 5. Rates of Growth of Selected Consumer Goods and Disposable Personal Income, 1920–1940.

Source: Graph constructed from data in *Historical Statistics of the United States,* 1:242, 2:783,796.

on to them even as they ceased to subscribe to their phone system during the Depression. There was little point in selling an almost worthless used radio set, and radio listening may well have been seen as a cheap alternative to a family outing to the movies. Average weekly movie attendance dropped by a third between 1930 and 1932, while the proportion of radio homes jumped from 45 percent to 60 percent in the same period.[27]

Figure 5 compares radio's growth rate in comparison with those of other communication and leisure goods and changes in disposable income. It shows that radio far outpaced any other rival for consumers' discretionary spending. Radio's growth rate after 1928 fell back to levels closer to those of other leisure and communication goods, although it still remained above those for automobile registrations and telephone households for the whole interwar period. In 1932, for example, the number of radio homes grew by 10 percent, while car registrations dropped by 6.7 percent, movie attendance by 20 percent, and telephone households by 5.7 percent.

Many families joined the radio audience at the same time that car registrations and the number of telephone households were shrinking. It is not possible to tell whether the same families bought a radio set as they divested themselves of cars and phones. What is clear, however, is that many Americans placed a very high priority upon entering the radio age, and that a large number of them were prepared to sacrifice other material aspirations in order to do so. Radio growth was fastest in the poorer southern sections of the nation during the Depression. Across the nation as a whole, the radio industry could point to the simple fact that radio households grew by more than 14 percent between 1930 and 1933 while disposable personal income fell by nearly 43 percent.[28] Radio was as close to Depression-proof as any industry in the economy.

By 1940 radio broadcasting had established itself as the preeminent communication medium in the United States. It had transformed itself from a fad of the Jazz Age into a household necessity that held attraction for increasing numbers of Americans even when incomes plummeted and jobs evaporated in the 1930s. As more and more Americans bought radios, questions about radio programming, and in particular the means by which the industry could sustain itself, became increasingly pressing. The young industry was forced to address fundamental questions about what it broadcast and, even more importantly, who was to pay for those programs.

2

Radio Advertising and Networks

A wide variety of organizations owned the first broadcasting stations. Of the corporate broadcasters, radio and electrical manufacturers had the most obvious interest in fostering broadcasting. Stations such as Westinghouse's KDKA gave people who bought radios something to listen to. Other early broadcasters used their stations to publicize their products or services, and many businesses were attracted by the thought of being identified with an exciting new technology. Although early stations did not earn revenue through the sale of advertising time, they were not purely altruistic creations. Quite apart from boosting sales for radio sets, radio stations were also perceived as effective forms of goodwill advertising.

By the middle of 1924, however, broadcasters were under pressure from their growing number of listeners, who demanded more programs and more sophisticated content. By then Americans had spent more than $200 million on radio sets, and they expected more than scratchy broadcasts of amateur musicians for a couple of hours each evening. Provision of high-quality programming was frequently beyond the means of the first broadcasters. Radio performers, as well, began to pressure broadcasters to pay them for their work. Stations offered performers no payment, only the expectation that their radio appearances would increase their phonograph sales and concert audiences. The result was that, as E. C. Mills of the American Society of Composers, Authors, and Publishers (ASCAP) noted at the beginning of 1924, radio programming depended on "the charitable inclinations of publicity hungry artists and musicians."[1]

Mills and ASCAP declared in February 1924 that the era of free radio performances was over. The promised boom in phonograph sales had not occurred; in fact record sales had suffered a precipitous decline since the advent of broadcasting. Radio, ASCAP declared, was a competitor rather than a complement to the phonograph and theater, and would henceforth have to pay its way. Royalty and talent payments added significantly to overhead costs, and they contributed to the closure of many stations. More than 180 stations disappeared from the radio spectrum during the first eight months of 1924. Time was running out for the old-style broadcasters, who found themselves paying more and more for only indirect economic return.

The Beginnings of Commercial Broadcasting

At the beginning of 1922 AT&T announced that it planned to establish a new radio station, WBAY in New York City, dedicated to the principle of "toll broadcasting." AT&T would run the station but would not provide programming for it. Instead, companies could produce programs and have them broadcast on WBAY for a fee of $50 per fifteen minutes. The idea of toll broadcasting owed much to AT&T's core telephone business, which was based on the principle that originators of calls should pay for them, and that the role of telephone companies was to provide only the infrastructure for communication rather than the content of messages.

WBAY, soon renamed WEAF, began broadcasting on July 25, 1922, but toll broadcasting proved to be a failure. No company acceptable to AT&T wanted to provide its own programs. WEAF did not run its first advertisement until August 28, by which time the station had resorted to its own programming to prevent an embarrassing silence on its frequency. Total revenue from advertising during the station's first two months of operation was only $550.[2] The business community was still unsure about the possibilities of the new medium and still intimidated by the technical novelty of preparing radio advertisements. Advertising texts and handbooks of the mid-1920s remained noncommittal about radio advertising's future. Yet AT&T persisted with the WEAF idea, and by the end of 1924 had assembled a web of stations linked by its phone lines. This offered advertisers access to millions of American homes via 13 stations stretching across the northeast of the country for $2,600 per hour.[3]

In August 1923 AT&T achieved another industry first, in the form of a sponsored series of shows. The Happiness Candy Company took over an existing WEAF program starring Billy Jones and Ernie Hare. Jones and Hare then became the "Happiness Boys," but they did not engage in direct advertising. Instead their program was laced with frequent references to their name and an announcement at the beginning and end of the show as to the company's support. Even this indirect advertising offended some listeners, who considered it to be a desecration of radio's bright promise. By late 1923, however, it was clear that shows like "The Happiness Boys" were the most obvious way out of the problem caused by listeners' demands for better programming and station operators' limited reserves of capital and performing talent. By this time RCA had also established its own chain of commercial stations, which earned revenue from sponsored shows such as "The National Biscuit Company Band," "The Wanamaker Organ Recital," and "The Royal Typewriter Salon Orchestra."

The Debate over Commercial Broadcasting

At the beginning of 1925 William Harkness, Assistant Vice-President of AT&T, announced that radio's development now lay in the hands of two groups of broadcasters: those who used radio to sell advertising time and those who used it to encourage sales of radio equipment. The *New York Times* responded, "It is just a little disquietening [*sic*] to learn that this miracle of the ages is in the hands . . . of those who view it as a purely 'commercial proposition.'" The only hope for radio, it concluded, was that advertisers would behave with "enlightened self interest" by providing listeners with culture as well as advertisements.[4] Although Harkness would eventually be proved correct, debate still raged as to how to pay for broadcasting.

Much of this argument centered upon the desirability of radio advertising. Lee de Forest, self-proclaimed "father of radio," condemned it as "nauseating and vulgar," and as "nothing less than an act of vandalism." Listeners, de Forest argued, had a right to hear good programming and would soon rise up and demand satisfactory service from stations. Although it was sympathetic to de Forest's complaint, the *New York Times* questioned his notion that radio listeners had rights. Purchasers of radio sets had no guarantees that they would receive high-quality programming, and they were consequently at the mercy of the broadcasters. This represented an early critique of the idea of listener sovereignty that would later be so important to the rhetoric surrounding radio programming.[5]

Those who were concerned by radio advertising advocated a variety of other ways of paying for broadcasting. David Sarnoff suggested that each set sold attract a levy to be accumulated in a fund to support broadcasting. He later argued that RCA be allowed to set up a series of "superpower" stations which could blanket the nation with programs. The editor of *Radio Broadcast*, soon to become the industry's most influential periodical, thought that wealthy individuals should endow radio stations as well as art galleries and libraries, on the logic that "a properly conducted radio broadcasting station can do at least as great an educational work" as these. Voluntary listener contributions were also suggested, despite doubts that enough listeners would donate money for entertainment that was ostensibly free.[6]

Some brave souls advocated municipal funding of radio stations. The City of New York made a start in this direction with the establishment in 1924 of WNYC. Yet such visions sat uncomfortably with both the First Amendment tradition of noninterference with speech and the press and the more recent antistatist and antitax fervor of the 1920s. The idea of municipal ownership of radio stations, Gleason Archer declared in 1938, was evidence only of "the mental fog in which thoughtful observers of the radio scene were then groping" in their desire to avoid capitulation to advertisers.[7]

The debate over funding of radio, and its eventual resolution in favor of the commercial broadcasters, has been explored by Susan Smulyan and Robert McChesney. Opponents of radio advertising found it difficult to coalesce behind an option that was attractive to listeners and policy makers, and their attacks upon advertisements were often tinged by cultural elitism. Proponents of commercial advertising, such as RCA and AT&T, were extremely powerful within the young industry, making it more difficult to halt the drift to commercialism.[8]

From the listener's perspective, radio advertising offered the great attraction of being the least financially intrusive of all funding schemes. Advertising gave to radio the illusion of being free because it required no direct payment from listeners. "No one wants a direct public tax and everyone wants the best there is," E. H. Jewett of AT&T told the press in September 1925. "The only way to reconcile these faraway poles is to bring in advertising. Then the public can have the quality it craves; the station can pay its way and the advertiser can have the publicity over the air." One National Broadcasting Company (NBC) listener in 1928 encapsulated this argument when he wrote to the network to congratulate it on its programs: "Why don't we have to pay for this? I can't believe that it's given to us." Critics of advertising found it hard to publicize their counter-message that listeners and consumers paid the full cost of 'free' radio through higher prices on the items they bought.[9]

Advertisers themselves were divided over the benefits of radio advertising. Often their attitudes depended upon their degree of loyalty to print media. *Printers' Ink*, the main journal of the print advertisers, objected strongly to the WEAF experiment. The problem with radio advertising was that it forced advertising material upon listeners without giving them the option to ignore it. Magazine readers could turn the page if they did not want to read an advertisement; radio listeners could only turn off their radios. Radio advertisers also had to remember that "the family circle is not a public place, and advertising has no business intruding there unless it is invited."[10]

Other advertisers were undecided about radio's potential. The most prominent advertising and publicity agents of the early 1920s, Ivy Lee and Edward Bernays, were slow to recognize the potential of the new medium. Lee, in his 1925 work on publicity, did not mention radio at all, and Bernays's *Crystallizing Public Opinion*, published in 1923, mentioned it only in passing. George Harrison Phelps, who owned an advertising agency in Detroit, on the other hand, did recognize the potential of radio advertising, but was ambivalent about it. Phelps conceded that radio offered an extremely attractive opportunity for any advertiser. It could deliver an audience of perhaps 20 million people at very reasonable cost, and already the new medium had become "the greatest influence for the betterment of civilization since the automobile." Yet Phelps feared that "Radio Broadcasting would suffer almost immediate annihilation if even subtle advertising were permitted to become a part of it."[11]

Over time, however, radio attracted more supporters within the advertising industry. By 1928 it had become an accepted medium of mass advertising, with sponsors and advertising agencies now confident that it not only boosted sales but also improved the public image of sponsoring companies. An increasing number of books on radio advertising appeared after 1925, all of which spoke glowingly about the new medium's potential to sway consumers' choices. Early anxieties about radio's intrusiveness gave way to a less apologetic conception that it was this quality that made radio such a valuable advertising medium. Radio, Frank Arnold declared in a 1933 advertising manual, was "the only medium where a blind man is just as good a prospect as the man with two good eyes!" Advertisers had long sought to reach people in their homes, where they were most receptive to sales pitches. Now radio, "utilizing the very air we breathe," could enter every home in the nation "through doors and windows, no matter how tightly barred."[12]

Radio broadcasters also adopted this new unapologetic tone. Stations and networks aggressively promoted the effectiveness of radio advertising to their sponsors.[13] Edgar Kobak, head of NBC's sales division, circulated a memo to his staff at the end of January 1936 urging them to redouble their efforts. Kobak began by noting that radio advertising by A&P supermarkets had "much to do" with his wife's decision to buy groceries there, and then generalized the task of selling radio time into a process of quasi-sexual conquest:

> A&P can't afford to send salesmen to see us each week and if they did they wouldn't get in very often—but their radio program is always welcome. Stress these selling advantages in your sales work. The people on whom you call are all salesminded—they have radios—they understand the advantage of relaxing the buyer before driving home the friendly sales message. But . . . they like to be urged and coaxed. They are just like the girls you used to urge and coax. . . . When you wanted that girl to say "Yes"—did you call daily or once a month? Well—if you want to be a successful time salesman, start making daily calls.[14]

The Nature of Radio Advertising

Sensitive to the debate over the commercialization of the air, advertisers in the 1920s were careful to avoid giving their critics more ammunition. Many paid homage to the idea of radio exceptionalism, and they declared they would not treat radio audiences as if they were readers of tabloid newspapers. Edward Bernays often reminded his advertising colleagues of the power of listener sovereignty, for "with the turn of the dial we can be obliterated." Early radio advertisements, in Roland Marchand's phrase, were marked by a "mystique of gentility" and a level of restraint that betrayed a fear of audience backlash.[15]

This was especially true for advertisements carried by the national networks. Advertisements during the 1920s were indirect, designed not so much to sell particular goods but to create goodwill for the advertiser's brand. NBC banned mention of price in its advertisements during the 1920s and refused to carry commercials for a long list of products including deodorants, patent medicines, and laxatives. American radio homes, in which children could listen to programs as easily as adults, were to be spared such vulgarities. This attitude persisted among some station managements until the late 1930s. When Station WQXR began operating in New York in 1936, it promised to accept advertising only under strict conditions. Products had to be advertised in a factual and informative, rather than "exaggerated or blatant," manner. Those that were "obnoxious or offensive" to WQXR's generally affluent and well-educated audience were banished from its programs.[16]

The typical network radio advertisement of the 1920s took the form of sponsorship of a 30-minute program. In April 1928 the Lambert Company sponsored the "Carnival of Music" on NBC. The opening announcement introduced the musicians and also the fact that their performance was sponsored by Lambert, makers of Listerine mouthwash and shaving cream. As was common during the 1920s, when audience measurement techniques were still in their infancy, listeners were encouraged to contact the sponsors by mail. The entire commercial message was short and restrained:

> With the playing of selections from Rubinstein's Ballet, the curtain is drawn on the Carnival of Music. In presenting the Carnival the Lambert Pharmacal Company of St. Louis, Missouri, acquaint you with their Listerine Shaving Cream. The Shaving Cream that has much to bring you of smoothness and coolness and speed in your daily shaving. New as it is, your druggist has it.
>
> The Lambert Pharmacal Company welcome comments on the program. Address your letters or cards: Listerine, L-I-S-T-E-R-I-N-E, Listerine, St. Louis, Missouri, or to the station to which you are listening.[17]

Local and non-network stations sold time for shorter and more direct advertisements, called "spots," from 1925. By 1928 the one-minute advertisement had become a standard unit of broadcast time on local stations. The use of spot advertising increased markedly during the 1930s, as the development of recording techniques allowed advertising agencies to carry the same messages to audiences across the country.

Early sponsors of radio programs tended to be firms that sold products to a broad cross section of the radio audience. Advertisements for toiletries, cigars, food products, and candy dominated the airwaves after 1926. In 1935 Herman Hettinger estimated that "convenience goods" made up 80 percent of national network advertising. Food, beverages, and confectionary accounted for a third of that category; the remainder consisted of cosmetics, car accessories, pharmaceuticals, and tobacco products.[18] In her study of the commercialization of radio Susan Smulyan argues that the first radio advertisers tended to be middle-sized firms faced with declining market share for their products. With the exception of national grocery chains such as A&P, early network advertisers tended to be manufacturers rather than retailers. The networks' national audience and the sponsorship form of advertising were better suited to promote brand identification and loyalty than to directing customers to specific stores. Retailers tended to choose local stations for their advertising in order to address their potential customers directly. In 1934 retailers bought about 40 percent of all advertising time on local stations.[19]

The nature of broadcasting changed in other ways after 1930. Large advertising agencies such as Batten, Barton, Durstine, and Osborn (BBD&O)

took a larger role, usually undertaking all the production for a sponsored program.[20] With each passing year radio advertising became more important to advertising agencies and broadcasters. The average number of commercial hours broadcast on the key stations of the NBC and CBS networks rose from 14 per week in 1927 to 35 in 1930. In 1927 advertisers spent more than $3.8 million dollars on network radio advertising; that figure increased almost seven times to $26.8 million in 1930, and reached $39.1 million by the end of 1932.[21]

Earlier inhibitions about intrusive advertising began to lessen as advertisers and radio operators grew more confident about public reaction to commercial radio but less sure about their own economic futures. Radio advertisements became more insistent as companies, hit hard by the Depression, strove to maintain sales. The early 1930s saw the emergence of what Roland Marchand has called "advertising in overalls": short, sharp, and arresting advertisements that abandoned the old reluctance to mention prices.[22] Stations also weakened many of their rules concerning the goods they would advertise and the format of advertisements. Although the Depression did not affect radio advertising revenues as severely as in the newspaper and magazine sectors (see fig. 6), broadcasters' declining incomes made them receptive to their clients' demands for more assertive copy. Even the genteel sponsorship model became more strident after 1930. In a 30-minute program sponsored by Maxwell House Coffee on NBC at the end of April 1931, for example, the announcer repeated the sponsor's name 23 times during his introductions to the musical performances, mentioned its manufacturer, General Foods Corporation, twice, and gave four homilies about the product. The eight musical performances during the show were hurriedly squeezed into this torrent of sales talk, brand names, and "news."[23]

By the end of the 1930s radio advertising had shaken off the shackles of radio exceptionalism and self-abnegation to become a powerful force. Figure 6 charts the growth of radio advertising relative to expenditures in other media after 1927. These amounts, which include both network and local radio stations, show that radio advertising had become the second largest advertising medium by expenditure within fifteen years of the first advertisement on WEAF in 1922. Although newspapers maintained their dominance over the advertising market, radio expenditure equaled that of magazines by 1937, and exceeded it by nearly $20 million by 1939. Radio advertising did undergo a relatively small downturn during the Depression, but this paled in comparison to those experienced by its two main rivals. After a 13 percent drop in 1933, radio advertising bounced back 38 percent in 1935 and continued to

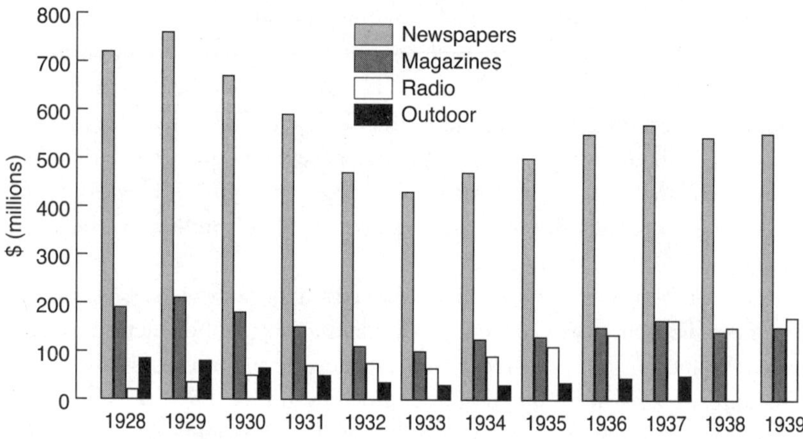

Figure 6. Advertising Expenditures by Medium, 1928–1939.

Source: Graph constructed from data in Warren B. Dygert, *Radio as an Advertising Medium,* p. 7, and Paul F. Peter, "The American Listener in 1940," p. 6.

grow strongly until another brief decline in 1938. Newspaper advertising expenditures, on the other hand, dropped by 43 percent between 1929 and 1933 and failed to recover to their 1929 levels during the rest of the decade.[24]

The networks, which had captured 51 percent of all radio advertising expenditure by 1936, did particularly well during the Depression. Their share of the national advertising dollar nearly tripled, from 5.3 to 15 cents between 1930 and 1936, while that of the newspapers remained almost static at 45 and 44 cents for those years. Radio's success hit magazine advertising particularly hard, because the two media were in direct competition for the attention of families at home. Magazines lost 20.5 percent of their advertising revenues between 1928 and 1937, and 15.5 percent of their share of the advertising dollar between 1930 and 1936.[25]

By 1940 broadcast advertisers could feel well satisfied with their efforts to establish radio as an advertising medium. Advertisers had been convinced of the cost-effectiveness of spots and program sponsorship, and large numbers of listeners wrote letters or sent in product labels in return for some benefit. NBC received over two million letters from listeners in 1930, and in 1931 an offer of a free bottle of mouthwash in return for two empty toothpaste cartons elicited 40 sacks of mail within 24 hours.[26] In 1929 NBC claimed that only one in 500 letters sent to it by the public contained "unfavorable criticism," although some complainants may have written directly to sponsors.

Even those who did complain often acknowledged the power of radio advertising. Edna Henrichs wrote to NBC in February 1935 about its "obnoxious and offensive" advertising for Listerine. The Saturday opera series was once sponsored by Lucky Strike, she wrote, and "I can't remember that the company ever made itself offensive." Because of that restraint, "[all] last year I smoked Lucky Strike cigarettes because I was grateful to the company."[27]

By the late 1930s radio advertisers also seemed to have succeeded in convincing many listeners that radio advertisements made broadcasting "free." An American Institute of Public Opinion (AIPO) survey of listeners in 1938 found that 47 percent of listeners considered that the amount of time dedicated to advertising on the air was "about right," and 17 percent had no opinion. Only 36 percent of respondents agreed that "too much" time went to advertising. The survey then asked participants how much they would be prepared to pay in order to eradicate advertising from radio. A full 79 percent refused to pay anything at all, while only 5 percent agreed to pay $5 per year. On this evidence, at least, most Americans seemed to accept Orestes Caldwell's proposition in 1931 that "you, the radio audience, demand variety and you get it without paying a dime."[28] By that time the "American system" of broadcasting funded by advertising was largely secure from effective criticism or reform.

Interconnection and the Idea of Radio Networks

Early broadcasters experimented with a variety of ways to connect stations. To some extent this was made necessary by AT&T's refusal before November 1924 to make its telephone lines permanently available to its radio rivals. David Sarnoff responded to this restriction by advocating the use of "superpower," but this only served to highlight the advantages of true networking. Without connection between transmitters there was no way to send the same program from each at the same time. Sarnoff dropped the idea once RCA came to an agreement with AT&T over use of its telephone wires.[29] Another possibility was to connect stations by shortwave transmission rather than wires. KDKA experimented with this after 1923, but found that it was too expensive and technically demanding to be attractive for domestic networking. Shortwave transmission later became the favored means of overseas broadcasting because of its superior long-range performance. GEC in the United States and the British Broadcasting Corporation (BBC) pioneered research in shortwave broadcasting that would culminate in worldwide broadcasts during the late 1930s.

Most radio experts agreed that wired interconnection, using AT&T's national telephone system, was the simplest way to connect radio stations. In January 1923 AT&T provided the first demonstration of networking by feeding a program from WEAF in New York to WMAC in Boston. By October 1924 AT&T had created a permanent link between WEAF and five other stations, stretching from WJAR in Providence, Rhode Island, to WCAP in Washington, D.C. AT&T went even further for special events. A Defense Test Day broadcast in 1925 went from WEAF to 18 stations over a 19,000-mile web of phone lines, encompassing Boston, San Francisco, Minneapolis, and Dallas.

By the middle of 1924 AT&T had developed its networking facilities and techniques sufficiently to announce the creation of the National Broadcasting System. This was an extension of the older WEAF network, now extended to include 16 stations. The National Broadcasting System covered the Northeast, parts of the Midwest, and the area surrounding Dallas, Texas. It was specifically directed at advertisers who sought access to a large proportion of the nation's homes at times when "the fathers and mothers of the nation . . . are gathered in their living rooms with minds at ease and in the condition most receptive to new ideas and suggestions." The 16 stations covered 65 percent of America's radio homes, 54 percent of its population, and 73 percent of its total personal net income.[30]

The Formation of the National Broadcasting Company

AT&T's efforts in networking made a truly national radio audience possible. Yet by 1925 it had begun to rethink its involvement in radio broadcasting. At the beginning of 1924 the Federal Trade Commission (FTC) issued a complaint against the eight companies involved in the radio patent pool, including RCA and AT&T, charging them with restraint of competition in the radio industry. Already battling public and congressional hostility over its telephone operations, AT&T saw radio as an unwanted diversion that could expose it to more public dislike and regulation.[31]

Pressures within the patent pool and cross-licensing agreements also propelled AT&T out of broadcasting. Originally AT&T had claimed that the 1919 agreements had given it exclusive rights to conduct toll broadcasting. This exclusion was contested by RCA, GEC, and Westinghouse, who eventually forced the matter to arbitration in 1925. AT&T lost both the argument over exclusivity and its remaining enthusiasm for radio broadcasting. In July 1926 it sold its flagship station WEAF to RCA for $1 million, and promised to stay out of radio broadcasting for eight years. In return it received exclusive rights to provide wire interconnection for the RCA group's broadcast stations.

For its part RCA became more interested in radio broadcasting and networking. In 1922 David Sarnoff advocated the creation of a "National Radio Broadcasting Company," composed of the stations owned by Westinghouse and GEC, to provide high-quality programming to listeners across the nation. "I feel that such a company will ultimately be regarded as a public institution," he wrote in June 1922. "Also, it would remove from the public mind, the thought that those who are doing broadcasting today are doing so because of a profit to themselves. In other words it removes the broadcasting company itself from the atmosphere of being a commercial institution."[32]

Improvements in networking techniques, developments within the radio patent pool, and the triumph of radio broadcasting between 1922 and 1926 enabled Sarnoff and RCA to give these ideas substance. By the time that RCA purchased WEAF from AT&T, Sarnoff and other RCA executives had decided that the new broadcaster would be funded from the sale of advertising time. Availability of AT&T's telephone lines also enabled RCA to run as a permanently connected network rather than as a series of superpower stations. Following the purchase of WEAF, Westinghouse, GEC, and RCA agreed to create the National Broadcasting Company (NBC). RCA held 50 percent of NBC's shares, GEC 30 percent, and Westinghouse 20 percent. The heart of the new network was in New York City, where NBC operated AT&T's former stations WEAF and WJZ.[33]

NBC operated primarily as a provider of programs to affiliated stations through its wire connections leased from AT&T. Generating transmissions through WEAF and WJZ, NBC provided two types of programs. The first were sustaining programs, produced by NBC without commercial sponsorship. In 1929 these were sold to affiliated stations for $45 per hour for evening programs and $22.50 per hour for daytime features. NBC also broadcast commercial programs, sponsored by advertisers. NBC paid affiliated stations $50 per evening hour and $25 per daytime hour to rebroadcast these programs.[34] Although NBC began by producing commercial programs itself, by 1929 nearly half were produced by advertising agencies.

This arrangement served simultaneously the interests of NBC, advertisers, and affiliated stations. NBC's revenue came from the sale of advertising time in the form of commercial programming. By providing affiliates with a reliable and inexpensive roster of sustaining programs, the network could increase its national audience and make itself more attractive to advertisers.

Over time NBC produced fewer sustaining programs, which cost it money, and instead broadcast more commercial programming, which brought in revenue. Advertisers secured larger audiences through NBC's increasing number of affiliates, while affiliated stations received programs at subsidized prices to fill their schedules. NBC affiliates during the late 1920s were free to pick and choose from both sustaining and commercial programming, and to provide their own local features at times that they saw fit.

NBC first broadcast on November 15, 1926. The new network began its programming to 19 stations by switching between symphony music from New York, opera from Chicago, and Will Rogers in Independence, Kansas. This broadcast, intended to be a showcase to audiences, advertisers, and potential affiliates, was in fact unrepresentative of the network's subsequent activity, which was to centralize programming in New York and then diffuse it to the radio periphery. Although most observers welcomed the advent of networked radio, others were more cautious. The *Brooklyn Eagle* editorialized that it represented "an unprecedented power in the shaping of public opinion. A narrow policy, a cheap policy or a propaganda policy might do great harm before it could be checked or controlled." The new network tried to allay these fears by stressing its commitment to public service and by announcing that its programming would be monitored by an advisory council of 12 prominent Americans representing "various shades of public opinion."[35]

NBC grew very quickly. Within a year it had increased its number of affiliates from 19 to 48, and by the beginning of 1928 it offered advertisers the choice of two networks: the "Red" based upon WEAF and the "Blue" built upon WJZ (see map 2). By August 1929 NBC used 21,000 miles of telegraph wire and 29,000 miles of telephone wire to connect its 65 affiliates.[36] Despite its claims, however, NBC did not offer a truly national audience to its advertisers. Even by combining its two networks, NBC could offer blanket coverage only of the Northeast. Coverage was spotty in Appalachia and along the West Coast, and nonexistent in vast areas of the West and South.

Like the National Broadcasting System before it, NBC offered coverage only of a majority of radio homes in the wealthiest consumer markets. This reflected the new network's true function as an advertising medium, as distinct from its public rationale as a conduit of national information and education. NBC charged advertisers dearly for access to its network; in February 1928 rates were set at $3,770 per hour for the Red network and $2,800 per hour for the Blue. Ten years later, despite competition from two other national networks, NBC charged advertisers $8,400 per hour for the slightly expanded Red network. Supplementary stations to cover the smaller markets of

Map 2. NBC Networks, February 1928.
Source: "Radio Broadcast Advertising," *McCann Digest*, Feb. 1, 1928, in NBC MSS, file 646.

the Midwest, Southwest, and West Coast each cost several hundred dollars an hour more.[37]

Despite these prices, sponsors were quick to subscribe. Listeners heard programs paid for by Palmolive, General Motors, the American Tobacco Company, GEC, and Standard Oil. In 1927, its first full year of operation, NBC had 77 advertisers, who spent an average of $49,000 each on program sponsorship. Nine years later 150 advertisers spent an average of more than $200,000 each on the network. By then NBC boasted 89 affiliated stations, a work force of 1,929, and a potential listening audience of 92 million Americans.[38]

In 1929 Manton Davis, RCA's vice-president and general attorney, told a congressional committee that "the operation of a good radio station was like raising a family of children—there was a great deal of satisfaction in it, but no profit."[39] Although NBC's three core stations did run deficits, the financial position of the network as a whole was rosier than Davis suggested. Advertising and sales income reached $21 million in 1932. From this revenue, and despite heavy investment in new facilities, the network recorded net profits of more than $2.3 million in 1931, and just over $1 million in 1932.[40] NBC's profits were folded into RCA's consolidated balance sheet, adding to that company's stellar performance during the 1920s. In 1921 RCA's gross income was less than $4.2 million, but eight years later it had grown to over $182 million. RCA's rapid growth, the *New York Times* observed in July 1925, "has constituted an industrial romance almost without parallel." Although it did not declare a dividend on its common stock until the late 1930s, RCA's shareholders enjoyed large capital gains during the late 1920s. Radio common stock sold for $32 in 1926, and for $549 amidst the heady speculation of 1929. During the Depression, RCA's common stock price sank to $2.50 in 1932 before recovering somewhat to $5 by September 1934. By that time NBC's performance had also improved sufficiently to deliver a net profit of more than $2.2 million in 1933.[41]

The Contagion of Networking

Two other national radio networks emerged between 1927 and 1940. NBC's first competitor arose from the unlikely combination of a phonograph company and a cigar manufacturer. In 1927 the Columbia Phonograph Corporation, anxious to secure a stake in an industry that had decimated phonograph sales, bought into United Independent Broadcasters. Renamed the Columbia Phonograph Broadcasting System, the new network went on air in September 1927 with 16 affiliates. It lost $100,000 in its first month, prompting the phonograph company to abandon it. Again renamed, the Columbia Broadcasting System (CBS) lurched from crisis to crisis until it was rescued by William S. Paley, the young vice-president of his family's Congress Cigar Company. Enthused by the possibilities of radio advertising, Paley persuaded his family in September 1928 to buy 50.3 percent of CBS's stock for $300,000. He then set out to create a radio empire.[42]

CBS had only 16 employees when Paley purchased it. He expanded his network by offering affiliates more generous terms than they received from NBC. Paley guaranteed stations 20 hours of commercial programming per week and sustaining programs at no cost. CBS quickly enrolled stations across the Northeast and parts of the Midwest. In February 1928 CBS transmitted to 17 stations, with an associated network in the North Pacific area (see map 3).

CBS's generous terms quickly attracted affiliate stations. That generosity, however, was balanced by its insistence that affiliates not preempt network

Map 3. Columbia Broadcasting System Network, February 1928.
Source: "Radio Broadcast Advertising," *McCann Digest*, Feb. 1, 1928, in NBC MSS, file 646.

commercial time. CBS could then offer advertisers a full national network whenever they sponsored programs. NBC, on the other hand, charged affiliates for sustaining programs, but allowed them to pick and choose among commercial programs. NBC advertisers thus could not be assured that all affiliates would air their shows. By 1934 CBS had 100 affiliates, and its corporate performance soon outshone NBC's. In 1932 CBS earned a net profit of over $1.9 million from gross sales of $13.8 million, while NBC could manage a profit of just over $1 million from almost double that figure.[43]

One other national network emerged during the 1930s. The Mutual Broadcasting System (MBS), organized in September 1934, operated on yet another basis from those of NBC and CBS. MBS was owned by its affiliated stations and produced no programming itself. Sustaining programs came from affiliates, while advertising agencies produced all sponsored material. MBS grew very quickly, beginning with four stations in 1934 and ending the decade with 116. Most of MBS's stations were low-powered, and the new network remained a distant third in audience size and revenues. Its total network time sales rose from $1.1 million in 1935 to $3.6 million in 1940.[44]

The National Networks in Action

NBC and the other networks were very sensitive to charges that they dominated American radio. Preferring to portray themselves as loose agglomerations of local stations rather than as centralized advertising media, the networks argued that their operations strengthened local affiliates by offering them excellent programming without limiting expression of regional differences and attitudes. Nevertheless, the networks swallowed up an increasing percentage of the nation's total number of stations, from 21 percent in 1930 to 59 percent in 1940 (see fig. 7). This trend rapidly accelerated through the 1940s to a peak of 97 percent in 1947.

The networks' control over the radio industry by 1940 extended well beyond their percentage of stations. Affiliates tended to be more powerful and more profitable than independent stations, and could reach many more listeners. Constituting 37 percent of all radio stations in 1936, NBC, CBS, and MBS affiliates commanded nearly 93 percent of the nation's total transmission power and almost 50 percent of radio advertising revenue. In 1938 the average net broadcasting revenue of affiliated stations was $58,130, compared to $4,139 for independent stations.[45]

The prominence of networks within broadcasting in the 1930s introduced strong elements of institutional stability to the industry. In many ways the net-

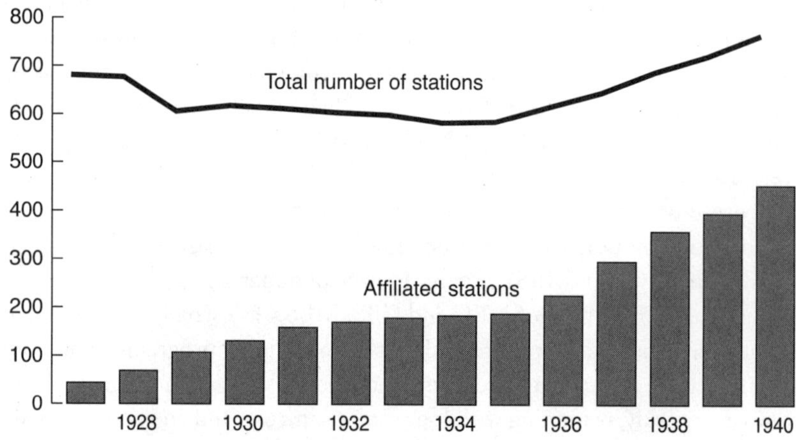

Figure 7. Affiliated Stations and Total Stations, 1927–1940.

Source: Graph constructed from data in Christopher H. Sterling and John M. Kitross, *Stay Tuned: A Concise History of American Broadcasting*, p. 512.

works replaced earlier forms of industrial self-regulation such as the cross-licensing agreements forged between 1919 and 1922. Those agreements, already weakened by AT&T's withdrawal in 1926, were finally extinguished in 1932 as a result of federal antitrust litigation. After six years of deliberation the Justice Department took up the FTC charges of 1924, and demanded an end to the patent pool and the complete separation of RCA from its founding companies.[46] By this time, however, there was no chance that the radio industry would return to its early days of anarchic competition and patent theft. The 1919 agreements had ensured that the industry had developed to maturity under a stable cartel of manufacturers, which now had no interest in resuming their old warfare.

The power of the national networks quickly manifested itself in other organizations developed by the industry during the 1920s. Foremost among these was the National Association of Broadcasters (NAB), founded in 1923 by 54 broadcasters to combat ASCAP's campaign to levy copyright fees upon music performed over radio. The NAB quickly became the broadcast industry's most important representative body, and soon reflected the new balance of power within it. It became more a protector of networks and their advertisers than an advocate for all broadcasters, large and small alike.[47]

By 1940 the broadcasting industry had consolidated into a stable industry dominated by the new networks and their large capital bases—wealthy advertisers and organizational expertise. Independent stations, on the other hand, continued the pattern of the 1920s, serving local interests and supported by local advertisers, religious and educational institutions, or groups of latter-day amateurs. Invariably lower powered and less profitable than affiliated broadcasters, they were increasingly marginalized within a system more and more geared toward the interests of the networks. Independent stations found it extremely difficult to further their interests within governmental regulatory organizations and representative bodies when those interests ran contrary to the aspirations of the national networks or their affiliates.

3

Regulatory Models and the Radio Act of 1927

Broadcasting posed a number of challenges to accepted notions of governance and regulation in the United States. Although it appeared to be inherently interstate in its scope, radio also promised to have profound effects upon local communities and individual sensibilities. It also raised questions about freedom of speech, equality of access, and acceptable limits of private control over public information. Exploration of contemporary perceptions and practice of regulation sheds light on the ways in which federal policy makers and their constituents saw the role of the state in regulating this new medium. Many of the great issues confronting policy makers of the 1920s were encapsulated by radio broadcasting, and their faltering steps toward effective federal regulation illuminate many facets of political culture between the wars.

The Regulatory Regime of 1912

The Radio Act of 1912 had been passed to regulate point-to-point transmissions. Because radio was then seen in terms of its maritime and telegraphic uses, the Department of Commerce was entrusted with its regulation. One of the purposes of the act was to encourage the use of radio to further maritime safety and to provide competition to the monopoly control of the telegraph by the Western Union Company. Consequently the Radio Act of 1912 directed the secretary of commerce to issue broadcast licenses upon application. There was no provision for the denial of such requests.

This open-ended regulatory regime was effective as long as radio remained a small-scale industry. The radio boom after 1920 placed enormous stress upon a system designed to cater to a small group of radio telegraphers and amateur broadcasters, and by 1926 regulators faced the task of fitting 528 stations into 89 channels. They did so by sharing broadcast hours, restricting some stations to low power, and maximizing the geographic separation of broadcasters assigned to the same wavelength. Because of the need to ration wavelengths, traditional American ideas of nonintervention by the state in the dissemination of opinion, established in the context of print media and embodied in the First Amendment, were inappropriate.[1]

These technical imperatives toward regulation were complemented by political and social factors revolving around radio exceptionalism. The new medium grew amidst a combination of high hopes and dark fears of its power to affect public opinion. Individual newspapers or magazines could prosper or wither according to their attractiveness to readers, who could make voluntary choices among them. Radio, on the other hand, had uniquely intrusive properties; its programs could enter all households and be heard by all members of the family. Regulation was as necessary to prevent radio from becoming a vehicle of propaganda, obscenity, and manipulation as it was to prevent interference. This confluence of technical necessity and social concern made radio regulation a powerful political issue throughout the 1920s and 1930s. Six regulatory models were available to the radio industry and its policy makers as they grappled with these issues.

Six Models of Radio Regulation

Voluntary Self-Regulation

Some radio enthusiasts, represented by the Radio League of America, argued during the 1920s that radio should be exempt from all regulation. Harking back to the days when radio was a hobby pursued by pioneering individuals rather than a burgeoning industry increasingly dominated by commercialism, opponents of radio regulation based their arguments on two premises. The first was that radio broadcasting was a form of speech, rather than a vehicle of commerce, and thus qualified for First Amendment protection. To the amateurs radio was best seen as a "magazine of the air," and thus analogous to the print media.[2]

The Radio League also tried to exploit a wider unease with the whole concept of governmental regulation. "It would seem today," its secretary C. Arthur Wood declared in November 1926, "as if every new discovery that comes as a gift to the human race must at once be taken by Congress to be fitted with a special uniform before it can become a servant of the people."

Instead, the league suggested that the new industry be left to regulate itself through a "Court of Arbitration" funded by levies upon broadcasters, manufacturers, and listeners and overseen by the Radio League itself.[3]

This version of radio laissez-faire, however, had few supporters by the mid-1920s. The league's conception of radio broadcasting as a form of speech rather than an item of commerce ran contrary to the emerging jurisprudence of radio regulation, and its vision of a self-regulating industry was mocked by the overcrowding of the radio spectrum after 1922.[4] Although the league expressed its own form of radio exceptionalism, as well as a version of antiregulatory sentiment that resonated through much of the political rhetoric of the 1920s, it was powerless in the face of more powerful stakeholders in the broadcasting industry. The amateurs had been marginalized by the advent of broadcasting, and their vision of radio as a participatory hobby of enthusiasts seemed anachronistic to an industry made up of professional broadcasters and millions of listeners.

Private Monopoly

An equally unpopular regulatory solution came from AT&T during its brief enthusiasm for broadcasting. At the beginning of 1922 Henry Thayer, president of AT&T, wrote to Secretary of Commerce Herbert Hoover with the suggestion that his company be given a monopoly over broadcasting. Believing that AT&T had exclusive rights to conduct toll broadcasting under the 1919 cross-licensing agreements, and pointing out that only his company could provide wire connections between stations, Thayer argued that AT&T faced a choice. It could either sell equipment to all parties who desired it, ultimately creating overcrowding within the broadcasting band, or it could take over the field itself by establishing stations "throughout the United States . . . which would be available for the uses of the general public." These stations would be connected by AT&T lines to create a national network. "This would result," Thayer promised, "in broadcasting being available to everyone and at a cost very much less than if it were necessary for everyone to own and operate his own broadcasting equipment." Thayer concluded by asking Hoover to assign to his company exclusive possession of the nation's available frequencies.[5]

Hoover's radio advisers responded carefully to AT&T's suggestion, and their caution was well placed.[6] Although technically attractive, AT&T's proposal was politically impossible. Broadcasting had already attracted a large number of companies, and all of them would have fought against Thayer's idea. The Bell company was also the least likely recipient of monopoly control over radio. It had already consolidated its control over the nation's telephone system, amidst much bad publicity. Even an administration as friendly to business as Warren Harding's could not have countenanced handing over yet another medium to AT&T's tender mercies. Hoover quietly buried Thayer's proposal, and the subsequent antitrust investigations by the FTC, congressional hostility, and industry lobbying made any further attempt to create a governmentally sanctioned private monopoly unthinkable.[7]

Public Control: The British Model

A much more popular model of radio regulation throughout the 1920s and 1930s envisaged varying degrees of public ownership and control of broadcast facilities. The movement for public control sprang from four sources: radio exceptionalism, disillusion with commercial broadcasting, the memory of wartime control of radio, and, most importantly, the example of the BBC after 1923.

Advocates of public ownership of radio stations argued that broadcasting's potential for public education made it too precious to surrender to the profit motive of private operators. Radio promised to transcend region, class, and prejudice to create a unified national audience and culture. At the same time as they championed its ability to redefine political and social discourse, however, many reformers also feared radio and its potential. The possibilities of propaganda and manipulation seemed very real at a time when millions of Americans seemed to fall under radio's spell. Those who saw the state, and in particular the federal government, as a beneficent force of social progress argued that radio's power to do good or evil in American society made its control by government a national priority. For many of these reformers the British model of broadcast regulation seemed to be the way of the future.

The early days of British radio were similar to the American experience. Guglielmo Marconi incorporated his Marconi Company there in 1897, and it quickly assumed a dominant position over British radio. The Wireless Telegraphy Act of 1904, the first piece of radio legislation in the world, vested control of the industry in the postmaster general and mandated the licensing of radio listeners and receivers. This began the British tradition of levying license fees upon all radio listeners, which proved to be the foundation of a distinctive "British system" of broadcasting for the entire interwar period. The British public first heard broadcast programming on June 15, 1920, when the most famous opera singer of the day, Dame Nellie Melba, sang a selection of arias. Regular programming began two years later.

At the beginning of 1922 British policy makers looked hard at the American experience to plan their own broadcasting future. Their first conclusion was that unrestrained development of broadcasting led to chaos. Rather than risk a repetition of the American experience, the postmaster general encouraged the six largest radio manufacturers to devise a broadcasting system that would avoid wavelength congestion and endless patent litigation. The companies agreed to create the BBC, and the postmaster general agreed to give it a monopoly over broadcasting and to pay it half of the revenues from listener license fees. The BBC was incorporated on October 18, 1922, and began broadcasting less than a month later.[8]

Although the BBC was born from a desire to regulate British broadcasting and to provide its founding companies with a ready market for their products, it quickly assumed a more overt cultural mission. Again the American experience was instructive. As American broadcasters, denied license fee revenue from their listeners, moved toward full commercialism, British regulators determined to take a different path. Because the BBC was a governmentally sanctioned private monopoly, it owed obligations not only to the government, which licensed it, but also to its listeners, who paid for it through their license fees. Chief among these obligations was to provide public service, which by 1923 had come to mean a strong element of cultural uplift.

This tendency became more pronounced after the accession of John Reith as the BBC's managing director in November 1923. Reith was adamant that radio should not follow the path of the cinema, which he thought had forsaken its enormous educative potential in favor of commercial gain. Instead, he committed his young company to three objectives. The BBC would operate within its means; yet it would not operate on the basis of profit; it would provide national coverage under unified control; and it would produce programs of the highest cultural standards that would educate as well as entertain listeners of all socioeconomic backgrounds and educational attainments. Reith was an adept, if authoritarian, executive who succeeded in winning the BBC's independence from both its founding companies and the government. After reviews in 1923 and 1926, the BBC was transformed into the publicly owned British Broadcasting Corporation, to hold an exclusive broadcasting license for an initial period of ten years and to be overseen by five governors.

Many American radio reformers cast envious eyes over the British model throughout the interwar period. During the first years of the 1920s, while commercial broadcasting was still in its infancy, the idea of public control along the lines of the "British system" seemed within the realm of political possibility. But growth and capitalization in American broadcasting occurred so quickly that attempts to alter radically its control and ownership soon faced enormous barriers. Even at the beginning of 1925, only four years after KDKA's first broadcast, the *New York Times* described a congressional resolution calling for the nationalization of all radio patents and the creation of a publicly owned broadcasting system as "truly startling." Existing radio patents were already so numerous and so valuable that their acquisition would bankrupt the Treasury and alienate some of the most powerful corporations in the nation.[9]

With the consolidation of broadcasting after 1926 into a stable industry dominated by national networks, calls for outright nationalization became increasingly infused with resignation and radicalism rather than political reality. In 1931 the *Nation* used the announcement of NBC's 1930 turnover of $22 million to reiterate its admiration for the British system, which put radio "under social control for civilized purposes . . . [and] does not reduce the whole art to the mental level of thirteen-year-olds." The American situation was very different, because "we permitted the creation of a great private vested interest in the air." Now the American listener "must hear chiefly what makes for advertisers' profits, and must stiffen his sales resistance against tooth paste, soap, and shaving cream. . . . And all this," the editors noted sadly, "seems more or less inevitable to us."[10]

American proponents of the British model were howled down by a powerful coalition of interests who extolled the virtues of what suddenly became known as the "American system" of privately owned broadcasting.[11] The argument against the British model focused upon two points. The first was that government-controlled broadcasting represented a dangerous extension of state power that ran against the American political tradition of a free marketplace of ideas. On one level, this argument took the familiar form of opposition to further taxation. Radio license fees, the broadcasters argued, were a needless imposition upon listeners, who now received their programming for nothing. American public opinion would not stand for this sort of tax, which would involve inspection of people's homes by snooping federal agents.[12]

The industry's argument against governmental intrusion also went to the heart of American traditions of limited government and freedom of expression. "We absolutely must not fall into the illusion that when we import a British institution we can also simultaneously import the fourteen centuries of British psychological and academic development which underlie that institution," the NAB warned in 1933. The British could tolerate radio licenses because of their deep trust in public officials and a complex web of understandings about the proper exercise of state power. Such would not be the case in America. "Think what will happen in America should the United States Government have control of the radio industry! The handling of the 'noble experiment' gives one a pretty good idea as to what will happen. Political parsons will choose our programs for us. . . . There will be no freedom of speech, no variety of entertainment. Taxation will go on the up and up."[13]

The second group of arguments used to assail the British model clustered around variety of programming. In 1925, the *New York Times* reported, London had one radio station compared to New York City's 14. Worse still, Americans were warned, the BBC used its monopoly power to broadcast what it thought people needed, rather than what they actually wanted. The result, according to the American radio commentator William Hard, was that British radio labored under hours of boring programming, with lectures, classical music, and "elevating talks" of "multitudinousness and magnitudinousness" dominating the airwaves.[14] American listeners, on the other hand, could choose between 500 stations broadcasting music, talks, political speeches, and educational material to suit all tastes and interests. Far from being an exercise in involuntary cultural uplift, American radio reflected the swirling cultural and regional diversity of its society.[15]

Although the idea of nationalized broadcasting would again be advocated by some New Dealers in the early 1930s, the battle for the elimination of commercial broadcasting was lost almost before it began. The political culture that venerated First Amendment freedoms and private enterprise did not allow radio exceptionalism to extend as far as the adoption of the British model. Battles over the public ownership of media had periodically flared up, notably over Samuel Morse's offer to sell his telegraph patents to the federal government in 1838, the Populists' proposals during the 1890s to nationalize the telegraph system, AT&T's dominance over the nation's telephone system in the early years of the twentieth century, and federal control of the railroads after World War I.[16] Those battles had all been resolved in favor of regulatory models that combined private ownership and public regulation; it was inconceivable that control of radio broadcasting, against a backdrop of 1920s normalcy, could have broken that mold.

Public Control: The Australian and Canadian Models

Those who sought a more politically feasible way of achieving a degree of public control of broadcasting could look to two other continental-size democracies for inspiration. Across the Pacific Ocean, Australia pioneered between 1924 and 1929 a hybrid form of broadcasting that promised to combine the benefits of the British and American models. Like most other developed nations, Australia joined the radio age with enthusiasm. Its wide open spaces and good listening conditions encouraged a strong amateur constituency to compete as fiercely for long distance reception (DX) records as their American colleagues. Scheduled broadcasting began in November 1923, and by 1934 Australians ranked fifth in the world in rates of radio ownership.

Broadcasting began on a "sealed set" system, in which radio sets could receive only one station. Listeners paid license fees to the postmaster general and to the station to which their set was tuned. This system proved unpopular, and was replaced in 1924 with a single license fee and unsealed sets. Until 1929 all radio stations were privately owned, although they were divided into two groups. Class A stations ran no advertising, but were funded from license fee revenues, while class B stations derived their income solely from advertising.[17] Responding to listener complaints about the technical and programming quality of the class A stations, and influenced by the British example, the federal government announced in 1928 that it would take over all class A stations and seek tenders for their operation as the Australian Broadcasting Company (ABC). The tender documents incorporated requirements that the successful bidder "shall do all in his power to cultivate a public desire for transmissions of educational items, musical items of merit, and generally for all items and subjects which tend to elevate the mind," and at the same time "cater for the reasonable tastes of the community as a whole."[18]

As the Depression reduced license revenues after 1929, the ABC found it difficult to provide service to Australia's far-flung population. The government then created the Australian Broadcasting Commission, again modeled on the post-1926 BBC. Class B stations were left to continue commercial broadcasting, garnering perhaps 80 percent of the listening audience during the first half of the 1930s, and developing into a combination of networked and independent stations similar to the United States'. The Australian broadcasting system maintained this dual form of ownership throughout the interwar period, and retains it still.

Canadian broadcasting followed a similar path to a hybrid broadcasting system during the late 1920s. Faced with the same problem of reaching listeners across enormous distances and with the additional pressures of numerous American stations just across the border, the Canadian parliament created the Canadian Radio Broadcasting Commission in 1932 to provide national broadcasting in competition with commercial stations. Transformed into the Canadian Broadcasting Commission (CBC) in 1936, the new body derived its revenue from license fees, and in return operated commercial-free broadcasting under a mandate to foster Canadian culture and national unity.

In a departure from the British and Australian models, the CBC shared national wire networks with commercial stations, and also acted as the regulatory body for all broadcasters.[19]

The ABC and CBC operated in competition with commercial broadcasters as yardstick enterprises, pressuring privately operated stations to improve their service and programming. All three public control models also introduced a new perspective on listener sovereignty. Whereas American broadcasters insisted that listeners were sovereign through their power to choose between numerous stations, Canadians and Australians argued that their models provided another dimension to listener empowerment. Listeners were no longer merely passive consumers of programming but also "owners" of their broadcasting system because their license fees funded the BBC, ABC, and CBC. Because listeners paid the piper, they were, as one Australian radio executive put it at the end of the 1920s, "entitled to call the tune to some extent."[20]

The Australian model received some favorable American press during the 1930s, and the geographically adjacent Canadian model attracted much more attention. The hybrid model became the favored approach of those who despaired of the ability of commercial broadcasters either to respond to the demands of their listeners or to improve the quality of their programs.[21] Hiram L. Jome advocated the adoption of the Australian model as early as 1925, with the federal government operating a series of superpower "Group A" stations, funded through a sales tax levied on the sale of radio sets and scattered throughout the nation in a synchronized network. Nine years later Jerome Kerwin proposed that the federal government take over a number of frequencies and conduct broadcasting without advertisements to demonstrate the power of radio to promote public welfare. Because a license fee system would be politically impossible, Kerwin argued, governmental radio should be funded from the federal treasury. The cost might be as high as $100 million, he warned, but "this expenditure in the interest of defense, education, and control in behalf of the people would be fully justified."[22]

The possibility of an American hybrid model had also been aired long before the Australian or Canadian systems existed. At the end of World War I the fate of radio stations constructed by the navy, the Department of Commerce, the Post Office, and the Department of Agriculture since 1912 attracted much attention. By 1922 these departments had built more than 30 stations across the nation to assist in military communications, weather reporting, and crop reports. Attempts in Congress early in the 1920s to allow these stations to compete with private broadcasters were defeated as an attack on private enterprise, but the federal government continued throughout the interwar period to broadcast from its own stations to the armed forces, seafarers, aviators, and farmers.[23] Tightly restricted by a suspicious Congress anxious to avoid any hint of competition with private broadcasters, governmental broadcasting struggled to find a meaningful place within the broadcast spectrum, and certainly never achieved the prominence hoped for it by some reformers. Its very existence, however, continued to inspire those who wished to restructure American broadcasting.[24]

Hooverian Associationalism, 1921–1926

Broadcasting was born on the same night that Warren Harding became president, sweeping to power on a series of vague commitments to return the country to "normalcy" after eight years of Wilsonian progressivism and wartime statism. In practice normalcy came to mean a disavowal of assertive federal regulation of industry. Instead, Harding and his successor Calvin Coolidge encouraged self-regulation and benign federal oversight over business. Herbert Hoover, who served as secretary of commerce under both men before his own election to the presidency in 1928, was pivotal in this policy.

Herbert Hoover brought some strong convictions to his work as secretary of commerce during the 1920s. Chief among these was the concept of associationalism, a variant of progressive corporatism that envisaged industrial, governmental, and community organizations as partnerships between private and public interest groups. Believing in the power of enlightened self-interest, Hoover argued that the role of government was to assist industrial self-regulation along principles of harmonious competition rather than to replace internal industry associations with external and coercive bureaucracies.[25]

As an infant industry in need of stabilization and rationalization, broadcasting occupied a great deal of Hoover's attention. He was a firm believer in radio's potential to become an important instrument of national consensus. As radio's chief regulator between 1921 and 1927, the secretary never ceased to remind broadcasters of their social responsibilities. In keeping with his associationalist bent, he argued that all groups interested in broadcasting—broadcasters, listeners, amateurs and the federal government—had complementary rather than conflicting interests in its development. He tended to view broadcasting through the prism of a free but socially responsible market, which possessed its own regulatory mechanisms based on a combination of self-interest and social responsibility.[26]

The Radio Act of 1912 vested in the secretary of commerce regulatory power over radio, but that power was significantly limited by the statute's loose drafting. As secretary, Hoover had no power to deny broadcast licenses, and even the allocation of frequencies and broadcast hours rested on thin legal ice. In the absence of judicial determination of the extent of his powers, Hoover continued to allocate frequencies to all applicants. In doing so he constructed a regulatory house of cards that depended upon the acquiescence of the industry for the sake of regulatory order. This form of regulation, more exhortatory than substantive, could last only as long as the radio spectrum could fit new entrants and only until a disgruntled licensee successfully litigated the issue.

Eager to postpone radio chaos for as long as possible, and motivated by his view that effective regulation rested upon cooperation rather than coercion, Hoover grew increasingly dependent upon the industry and its major players to give legitimacy to his regulatory regime. The result, as Philip Rosen has argued, was that radio regulation before 1927 became an intricate web of mutual needs spun in a legal twilight. Hoover needed broadcasters' acquiescence in his extralegal regulation, while the industry needed Hoover's associationalism to ward off the chaos that would surely come in the absence of any regulation at all.[27]

One result of this ambivalence was that Hoover ceded to the broadcasters almost all control over program content. Preferring to keep to the less controversial business of ordering the broadcast spectrum, Hoover chose not to enter the minefield of regulating broadcasters' behavior. Although the Department of Commerce urged broadcasters to avoid "transmission of all political, religious, labor or class propaganda, which would tend to engender factional controversy and strife," it took no action against transgressors. This restraint was in keeping with Hoover's benign view of New Era business ethics, and with his belief that radio listeners could be safely left to weed out unacceptable programs and stations.[28]

Nowhere was Hoover's reluctance to confront the industry over its behavior more obvious than in the case of advertising. During the early 1920s he frequently argued that the bright promise of radio would be dimmed if it were used for direct advertising. Yet the secretary put forward no alternatives to the rising tide of commercialism because of his opposition to monopoly broadcasting and license fees. Recognizing this problem in early 1924, he recommended to Congress that nothing be done to regulate advertising until "further experience" produced a viable and politically acceptable alternative.[29] Later that year he told radio broadcasters, "I believe that the quickest way to kill broadcasting would be to use it for direct advertising," and he suggested to them that they form an organization to fund "programs of national events" without recourse to advertising. Within two years of Hoover's warnings against advertising, however, it had become an essential part of the "American system" of broadcasting without further public complaint from its chief regulator.[30]

Hoover's most important associationalist instruments in regulating radio were the National Radio Conferences, four in all, that he called between 1922 and 1925. These conferences brought together representatives of the industry to advise Hoover on their preferred solutions to the problems of overcrowding, funding, and regulation. Industry conferences were Hoover's favorite way of putting his associationalist ideas into practice, and he used them within the radio, aviation, and housing industries during the 1920s. The radio conferences were also reminiscent of the Unemployment Conference of 1921, which Hoover persuaded President Harding to convene, and anticipatory of the post–Wall Street crash conferences of 1930 called to discuss unemployment and industrial production.[31] Hoover described the radio conferences as "experiment[s] in industrial self-government," which allowed "listeners, the broadcasters, the manufacturers, and the marine and other services to agree among themselves as to the manner in which radio activities are to be conducted."[32]

The radio conferences became progressively larger and more ambitious. The first, held in Washington early in 1922, had 15 official delegates and 24 observers representing amateurs, government departments, broadcasters, and manufacturers. Secretary Hoover presided over the conference, describing himself as "the special representative of the American small boy" and relaying his amateur radio enthusiasms. The first conference confined itself to making recommendations about the appropriate division of the radio spectrum. The second and third conferences, held in March 1923 and October 1924, focused upon issues arising from station overcrowding and interference. They called upon Hoover to open more wavelengths to private broadcasters and to institute a thoroughgoing scheme of wavelength and time-sharing to squeeze more broadcasters into the spectrum.[33]

Convened at the end of 1925, the fourth and final radio conference was forced to address the rapidly worsening problem of interference and overcrowding. Already there were 600 stations on air, with another 200 license applications lying on Hoover's desk. Although Hoover urged delegates to propose government action only in areas in which self-regulation had failed, the conference concluded that a complete reorganization was necessary to save the industry. Accordingly it recommended that the secretary be given new legislative powers to allocate licenses only to technically competent stations that served the public interest. These new powers, the conference declared, should be coercive and sweeping, and enacted as soon as possible. Only in the areas of interconnection, censorship, and advertising did the delegates reaffirm their faith in the workings of the free market and of broadcasters' social consciences.[34] In so doing the conference had also declared an end to the era of associationalist self-government of broadcasting.

The Collapse of Associationalism

Associationalism served many functions between 1921 and 1926. It was partially successful in postponing the inevitable through its arrangements to limit station overcrowding. By bringing together representatives of the broadcasting and radio manufacturing industries, the radio conferences also assisted in the creation of an industrial interest group that had direct access to federal regulators. In conjunction with the growing influence of organizations such as the NAB, Hooverian associationalism set in place a close and often closed cooperation between regulators and broadcasters that would persist long after 1926. Associationalism also began a tradition of minimalist broadcast regulation that would continue as a feature of the "American system" under the FRC after 1927 and the FCC after 1934.

Time and the pace of radio's industrial development, however, inexorably led to the collapse of Hoover's regulatory model. By the middle of 1925 industry leaders had grown impatient with associationalist substitutes for legislative action, and in December 1925 Station WJAZ in Chicago, owned by the Zenith Radio Corporation, finally called Hoover's bluff.[35] Unhappy with its frequency allocation and hours of operation, WJAZ simply changed its frequency and preempted a wavelength reserved for Canadian broadcasters. In the ensuing case Judge James H. Wilkerson of the U.S. District Court of Northern Illinois confirmed and extended the conclusions of the earlier decision in *Hoover* v. *Intercity Radio Company* (1922) that the secretary of commerce had no power to stipulate conditions in broadcast licenses; in fact he had no power to refuse or amend a license at all.[36] Wilkerson held that applicants for broadcast licenses could specify their own wavelengths, thereby negating Hoover's careful schemes that had squeezed 600 stations into 89 channels. After a brief period of uneasy calm, more than 250 new stations started broadcasting on frequencies and at power and hours of their choice. The airwaves, in Morris Ernst's phrase, became "an ethereal Fifth Avenue and Forty-second Street at rush hour."[37]

The Zenith litigation provides a clear example of the pressures exerted by sections of the broadcasting industry for new regulatory forms after 1925. The president of Zenith Radio Corporation, Eugene McDonald, was outspoken in his desire for an independent radio commission, and saw his litigation as a way to demolish Hoover's regulatory house of cards.[38] Hoover himself was privately pleased that pressure on Congress to create a new regulatory regime would now become irresistible. Until new legislation was passed, he told listeners and broadcasters in July 1926, the industry would have to proceed on the basis of "voluntary self-regulation" and new broadcasters would have to "proceed entirely at their own risk." Senator Clarence Dill, the Senate's foremost authority on radio matters, described Hoover's statement as "almost an invitation to broadcasters to do their worst."[39]

Congress Responds

Congress did not ignore radio regulation while Secretary Hoover and the broadcasters struggled to breathe life into the moribund structure bequeathed by the Radio Act of 1912, but a number of factors militated against swift congressional action on radio during the 1920s. Although most lawmakers who were interested in radio agreed that new legislation was required, they disagreed over its proper form. Democrats worried that new regulatory powers would be used by the Republican administration for partisan ends; Hoover's rivals objected to his elevation into a "radio czar," and many lawmakers objected to the creation of more federal regulatory bodies.[40]

Congress was also hampered by disagreements over the proper basis of federal radio control. Some reformers argued that radio should be treated as a public utility. Broadcasting was destined to become so powerful an agent of national communication and unity that it deserved recognition as being something more than a business conducted for private profit.[41] Regulation of public utilities had developed from the 1870s on the basis of two principles: that the federal government should set prices and standards of service, and that the public should receive unrestricted access to them. The key concept here was that of the "common carrier," in which utility owners were required to allow access to all who were prepared to pay for the privilege. Regulation of radio in this way seemed to its proponents to promise the most effective way of combining private ownership with public control. It also had the advantage of following a familiar regulatory theory that had emerged through the long struggle to evolve effective federal control of railroads, the

"Bridle Shy." O. R. Williams expresses skepticism, common in the 1920s, that Congress was capable of properly regulating radio—the new marvel of the age. *New York American*, May 1926, in the *Literary Digest*, May 22, 1926. Reproduced from the collections of the National Library of Australia.

telegraph, and telephones. The first three national radio conferences declared that radio should be regulated as a public utility, but they did not specifically endorse the extension of common carrier principles to broadcasting.

The public utility approach did not, however, prevail in congressional debate over new radio legislation. It attracted increasingly strong opposition during the mid-1920s from broadcasters, who argued that public utility and common carrier status would remove their ability to provide programming worthy of listeners' attention. Federal control of radio as a public utility, they argued, would also inevitably lead to censorship and contravention of the First Amendment.[42] The networks argued that they should be free of programming restrictions and of requirements to provide access to their facilities to anyone prepared to pay the necessary fee. The key to good broadcasting, they argued, was to provide a balance of programs that appealed to the widest audience. More privately, they also feared that public utility status would undercut the whole commercial rationale of broadcasting. Listeners would soon tire of unplanned programming, and their defection from radio would ruin every commercial broadcaster in the nation.[43]

Transformation of private broadcasters into common carriers also struck many less self-interested parties as being impracticable. Throwing the ether open to the public seemed to invite chaos, vulgarity, eccentricity, and even subversion onto the air. Broadcasting a radio program was a much more complex task than placing a phone call, mailing a package, or buying a railroad ticket. Opponents of public utility theory in radio regulation also enlisted the powerful weapon of radio exceptionalism to their cause. Radio, they argued, was far more than a utilitarian communications conduit. It was a powerful and unique instrument of social education that should be allowed to develop differently from the public utilities.[44] Behind this argument lay the broadcasters' determination to ensure that they could broadcast what they wanted, and could sell time at rates they saw fit, free from public utility obligations. New forms of radio regulation must come, the industry agreed, but only those that buttressed broadcasters' control.

Executive Regulation: The White Bill

Discussion within Congress and the radio community over the appropriate form of regulation after 1922 quickly settled around two proposals. The first, championed by Republican representative Wallace H. White of Maine, became the House of Representatives' preferred solution. Between 1921 and 1925 White introduced a succession of bills to regulate radio along the lines suggested by Hoover and the national radio conferences, all based on the principle that radio regulation should continue to be conducted by the Department of Commerce. The House passed a version of White's bill in January 1923, but it was buried in the Senate. White tried again in 1924, but this time his bill failed to reach a vote. Congress, more interested in tariff reform, placed a low priority upon radio legislation until the Zenith decision forced its hand. White then introduced a new version of his bill, which passed the House in March 1926.

The White bill conformed closely to the recommendations made by the fourth national radio conference. His proposals continued the regulatory structure set up by the Radio Act of 1912, but with significant augmentation of the secretary of commerce's powers. The secretary was empowered to grant, or deny, licenses according to the "public interest, convenience or necessity." The bill made it clear that a broadcast license vested no permanent proprietary rights in a licensee; the airwaves remained the property of the people. Broadcast licenses were to be issued for five years, after which stations would have to reapply for another term. The secretary was also granted sweeping powers to regulate frequencies, broadcast power, hours of operation, and the location of transmitters.[45]

White justified his regulatory scheme by echoing the Republicans' 1920s catchphrase of smaller and less intrusive government. "I dislike tremendously to see another independent commission set up," he told a Californian correspondent in December 1926.[46] As a Republican, White was also comfortable with the continuation and strengthening of Hoover's powers. He was close to Hoover, and the two men worked together harmoniously in their radio endeavors. For his part Hoover lent his strong support to White's bill. Calvin Coolidge also approved of White's proposals, and hinted that he would veto any rival bill that created a separate bureaucracy for regulating radio.[47] Anticipating arguments that his proposal vested too much power in the secretary of commerce, White pointed to a number of protections. First, the "public interest, convenience or necessity" formula provided both guidance to and restraint of the secretary. The bill also created a bipartisan radio committee that would provide advice to the secretary and a forum of appeal, and, third, the court of appeals in the District of Columbia was given jurisdiction to hear appeals on matters of law.[48]

Despite White's claims that his proposed legislation differed radically from the framework established in 1912, his bill tended to integrate radio regulation as much as possible into existing institutions and legislation. His bill was silent on censorship of broadcasts, reflecting White's desire to let First Amendment principles operate over the new medium. He also avoided detailed provisions against monopoly control over broadcasting; instead his bill declared that existing antimonopoly laws such as the Clayton Anti-Trust Act of 1914 and the Federal Trade Commission Act of 1914 would apply to radio broadcasting.[49] The overall tone of White's bill was moderate and instrumentalist; his bill sought to provide solutions to problems that had emerged with the 1912 act rather than to provide a thoroughgoing reformation of broadcast regulation.

Regulation by Commission: The Dill Bill

The Senate passed its own radio bill, drafted by Clarence Dill of Washington, in July 1926. The two proposals differed fundamentally in their conception of the proper regulatory structure for radio. Dill proposed an independent radio commission rather than an increase in the secretary of commerce's powers. This radio commission was to be a permanent body charged with full responsibility for radio and composed of members drawn from both political parties and from all areas of the country. Congress should not burden the Department of Commerce with radio regulation, Dill argued at the end of 1926, because the industry's problems were so complex as to require specialized and sustained attention from experts. This would ensure that radio regulation did not become the plaything of political appointees and the partisan political process.[50]

Dill's bill also differed from White's in several other ways. Broadcast licenses were to be issued for two-year periods rather than White's five, and the Senate version was more explicit in its protections against monopoly. Of great significance to Dill were provisions dealing with political advertising. Early versions of the Senate bill included a requirement that all candidates for political office be given equal access to the airwaves, and that in this respect radio licensees would be deemed to be common carriers. This provision attracted a great deal of criticism from broadcasters, one of whom noted that "a common carrier is obliged to take whatever is offered, whether it be Republican or Democrat, white or black, drunk or sober." This section was later watered down to allow stations to choose whether to accept political advertising. If they did, they were then obliged to treat all candidates equally.[51] Dill also drafted a specific prohibition against censorship of broadcasts except in cases of obscenity, profanity, and slander. Overall, Dill's proposal manifested a less trusting attitude toward regulators and broadcasters than that embodied in White's proposals.

Although it is clear that supporters of the Dill bill considered "one man control" of radio to be unsound in principle and dangerous in practice, partisanship also played a role in their opposition to White's proposals. Joseph T. Robinson, Democratic minority leader in the Senate, argued in April 1926 that it was unconscionable to vest control over broadcasting in an executive department that was answerable to the president. No single person, and certainly not a politician, should have control over such a powerful medium of public information and persuasion. The temptation to use that power for electoral gain, he thought, would be too great to resist.[52] Democrats and some Republicans had more immediate reasons to oppose executive regulation of radio. It was an open secret that Herbert Hoover wished to succeed Calvin Coolidge to the presidency, and Dill and his Democratic colleagues refused to strengthen his control over a powerful electioneering medium. Hoover's Republican rivals, such as Senators William Borah of Idaho, George Norris of Nebraska, and James Watson of Indiana, were also uneasy with Hoover's proposed new powers. The result was that the congress remained deadlocked over radio regulation throughout 1926.[53]

Extracongressional Debate

Congress's halting progress toward a new radio bill attracted attention from all elements of the radio community. Thousands of listeners, encouraged by broadcasters, wrote to their representatives demanding prompt action to prevent radio chaos after the Zenith decision. Industry journals such as *Radio Retailing* followed congressional discussions very carefully, and threw their support behind White's proposal as the simplest and cheapest means of radio regulation. RCA had supported White's proposals since 1923, and it and NBC continued to do so into 1927.[54] The 1926 convention of the Radio Manufacturers' Association did not formally commit itself to either of the two bills, but press reports made it clear that a majority of delegates favored White's proposal. The Senate bill's provision for political advertising attracted particular opposition, with several broadcasters complaining that it pushed "freedom of the ether a little too far," and that it was tantamount to "legislation compelling Democratic newspapers to print front page editorials indorsing [*sic*] the Republican party and vice versa."[55]

Wallace White preserved many newspaper editorials in his personal papers, and these reveal a strong degree of support for his bill. Many editors echoed White's opposition to the creation of yet another commission. "Just now," the Bluefield, West Virginia, *Telegraph* argued, "the tendency of the best thought in America is toward abolishing most of the commissions we now have, rather than creating new ones." To the *Telegraph*, radio was a "business preposition [*sic*]"and therefore belonged in the department of commerce. In Joliet, Illinois, the *Herald News* saw the conflict between the two bills in terms of senatorial dignity rather than lofty principle. The White bill worried some senators because it left open the possibility that "they might be required to submit their political speeches to the department of commerce to be edited by Scetary [*sic*] Hoover. A maddening situation, of course. No senator can be eloquent with an administration hand over his mouth."[56]

White did not have universal support. Within the industry Eugene McDonald, whose Zenith litigation had precipitated the collapse of radio regulation in 1926, lent fervent support to the Senate bill. McDonald wrote to all representatives and senators soon after the Zenith decision to warn them of the dangers of the White bill. The whole purpose of his litigation, he told them, was to show that "one man control" of radio was "most dangerous and contrary to the principles of our Republican form of Government."[57] Norman Thomas supported the Dill plan for similar reasons. He told a radio audience in May 1926 that the Senate bill removed from broadcasters the "terrible fear of offending the Cabinet officer from whom they get their license or the Administration of which he is part. . . . Mr Hoover might be an angel from heaven and lean over backward to avoid any sort of censorship of radio stations," Thomas argued, "but think it over. Would you take a chance of criticising tonight the policies of a man from whom you may desperately want something tomorrow?"[58]

The Politics of Passage

Although the House passed White's bill on March 15, 1926, it attracted considerable criticism, particularly in its failure to protect political broadcasting. Representative Ewin Davis, a Democrat from Tennessee, put this objection in stark terms to his colleagues, all of whom faced elections at the end of the year. As the bill stood, Davis argued, broadcasters were under no obligation to provide equal service to all. "They can permit one candidate to be heard through their broadcasting stations and refuse to grant the same privilege to his opponent. They can charge one man an exorbitant price and permit another man to broadcast free." Thomas Blanton from Texas used a similar tactic to argue for an amendment that allowed for prosecution of criminal slander over the airwaves. "We are all to go home soon to our primaries," he reminded his colleagues. "The night before the primary in your State some of your enemies could induce somebody in some other State . . . to make derogatory statements about you in such a way that it might absolutely ruin you in the . . . primary or election, and they would be absolutely impervious to punishment. . . . Do you want to take chances on that?"[59]

In the Senate some Republicans, including Hiram Bingham of Connecticut, railed against the proliferation of commissions and their inflation of the cost of government.[60] Dill was also quizzed about the protections offered by his bill to political candidates and discussion. Senators Tom Heflin of Alabama and Albert Cummins of Iowa argued that the bill's equal treatment of candidates should be extended to cover all discussions of public matters so that both sides of issues could be heard. Dill expressed his general agreement, but argued that "the opposition . . . was so strong in the minds of many that it seemed to me wise not to put it in the bill at this time." The Senate debate was relatively brief and generally supportive. Dill had marshaled a powerful coalition composed of leading Democrats and anti-Hoover Republicans, which passed his bill on July 2, 1926.[61] After a lengthy conference process the new Radio Act received President Coolidge's signature on February 23, 1927.

The Radio Act of 1927 showed clear signs of compromise between the Senate and House bills. Dill won his independent radio commission, but with a one-year sunset clause; after that period the FRC was to revert to the advisory and appellate role originally favored by White. Section 1 of the act reflected White's and Dill's determination to see that broadcasting licenses were privileges rather than rights, to be issued and withdrawn on the basis of public interest. Thus broadcast licenses were to be renewable for a maximum of three years, and the FRC was given powers to determine the fitness of broadcasters to begin or to continue broadcasting on the basis of "public interest, convenience or necessity." This formulation represented a small victory for those who had pushed for radio broadcasting to be regulated as a public utility. Although the precise wording was unique in federal statutes, it was common in state laws regulating utilities and was reminiscent of the 1920 federal Transportation Act's formulation of "the present or future public convenience." The phrase was left undefined in the Radio Act so as to give the FRC maximum latitude in interpreting it.[62]

The new act also vested power in the FRC and then the secretary of commerce to regulate radio licenses so as to avoid the chaos of 1922–26. Section 2 divided the United States into five geographic zones, and the president was empowered to appoint a commissioner from each with the advice and consent of the Senate. The FRC was authorized under section 4 to assign wavelengths, prescribe the location, power, and hours of operation of broadcast stations, and to promulgate regulations pursuant to its statutory powers. Section 6 of the new act reiterated the 1912 act's authorization to the president to take over any broadcasting station in the event of war or "a state of public peril." Section 13 incorporated a compromise between the Senate and House bills by directing the FRC to deny or revoke a license to any person or organization that had been convicted under antitrust laws. The FRC's powers were tempered by section 16, which provided for judicial review of its decisions. Dill's provision concerning political candidates became section 18, but with a proviso that incorporated White's concern that the FRC be denied censorship powers. At the insistence of the Senate, section 30 preserved a role for government stations by authorizing them to transmit, at "just and reasonable rates," press messages between American newspapers and foreign countries, and private commercial messages between the continental United States and Alaska.[63]

In its major features the 1927 act reflected a familiar pattern of federal regulation and statecraft. The legislators were careful to divide power over radio licensing between the FRC, the secretary of commerce, and the courts, and that of appointment to the FRC between the president and the Senate. The act also responded to fears that the FRC might become a rogue commission by its sunset clause, and by the requirement in section 3 that no more than three of the five commissioners could be members of the same political party. These provisions incorporated not only a general concern to divide power so as to limit the possibilities of its abuse but also reflected a more specific purpose to protect radio from manipulation by selfish or sinister forces.[64]

American broadcasters reacted to the 1927 act with a general sense of relief. Although they had not succeeded in forcing the passage of the White bill, they had achieved their goal of new regulatory legislation that could resolve the chaos within their industry. The broadcasters' intensive lobbying had also removed or softened some of the most objectionable features of Dill's proposals. They had escaped public utility and common carrier status, and the antimonopoly provisions of section 13 were much narrower than those that Dill had sought. With the exception of an innocuous requirement in section 19 to identify all advertising and sponsorship, the 1927 act presented no challenge to commercial broadcasting, and the FRC was not given power to regulate advertising rates. Overall, as Joseph P. McKerns argues, the 1927 act "provided for the regulation of radio in a manner least objectionable to the industry."[65]

The new radio act received a generally favorable reception in the press. Senator Dill's announcement that the new legislation would be the Magna Carta of radio listeners was reinforced by newspaper editorials across the country. "To the man in the street," the *Washington Post* believed, "[the act] constitutes the most important legislation of the session," and "millions of listeners-in will remember the Sixty-ninth Congress as the one which cleared the air." Complaints that the new legislation inadequately protected free speech and the access of noncommercial groups to the airwaves were largely lost in this chorus of relief and praise.[66]

The story of the Radio Act of 1927 simultaneously challenges the detail but confirms the substance of Gabriel Kolko's theory of business regulation. Focusing upon the period between 1900 and 1916, Kolko argued that regulation was generally instigated by the industries themselves to eradicate unwanted competition. Although Kolko argued that business groups preferred control by commission to executive regulation, and despite the fact that broadcasters' calls for a new radio act were backed by many of their listeners tired of interference and frequency jumping, radio regulation in the mid-1920s otherwise corresponds to his conception of industrial governance during the Progressive Era. The major broadcasters did indeed seek regulation to "escape from burdensome state regulation, to stabilize conditions within an industry, . . . [and] to create a buffer against a hostile public and opportunistic politicians."[67] In creating the FRC in 1927, the Congress had also created a new site on which interest groups would struggle to gain control of regulatory structures and processes.

4

The Federal Radio Commission, 1927–1934

Republican Representative Grant M. Hudson of Michigan voted reluctantly for the Radio Act of 1927. He objected to the creation of another commission, because "we are now . . . hobbled and controlled by bureaus and commissions. . . . Is there to be no end? Are we to come to the point where 50 per cent of the population will be laboring to support the other 50 per cent in Federal and State Government activities?" Hudson was unconvinced that the FRC would disappear after a year. "The commission will be as tenacious of life as the proverbial cat."[1]

Hudson's last warning was prescient: the FRC operated for seven years, not one. The story of the FRC and its persistence reveals much about the interplay between the broadcasting industry and its regulatory structure. Although the industry did not receive the executive regulation that it had sought, the Radio Act and the FRC almost immediately won its strong approval. The FRC never escaped the confines of this close relationship to the industry it was supposed to control. If Congress expected that the FRC would act as an independent and impartial defender of the airwaves against the selfish interests of the broadcasters, it would be sorely disappointed. Far from replacing the cozy alliance between broadcasters and regulators that had marked Hooverian associationalism, the FRC in many ways continued that tradition. The result was that commercial broadcasters quickly learned that they had very little to fear from their watchdog.

Examination of the FRC's major activities also demonstrates the degree to which radio regulation remained closely tied to the interwar political process. Although it enjoyed the legislative trappings of independence, the FRC and its members largely failed to translate that legal form into reality. Some commissioners did not even try to distance themselves from the administration that had appointed them, and all recognized that radio regulation could never be divorced from the interests and interference of politicians. Radio seemed so important to interwar society, and so important to political communication, that successive Congresses and presidents found it impossible to resist the temptation to intervene in its control. Largely unrestrained by judicial review, and closely allied with the increasingly powerful networks, the FRC remained very much a political animal.

The FRC Digs In

The beginnings of the FRC were not auspicious. The Senate confirmed only three of the president's nominees to the commission, Chairman Admiral Bullard, Eugene Sykes, and John F. Dillon, before it adjourned in March 1927. Orestes Caldwell and Henry A. Bellows then received recess appointments without salary.[2] In the rush of business at the end of the session the Congress also neglected to appropriate funds for its new commission. To make matters worse the FRC lost three of its commissioners before Congress could remedy its neglect; Dillon and Chairman Bullard died in October and November 1927, and Bellows—still unpaid—resigned in disgust at the end of 1927. They were replaced by Sam Pickard of Kansas, Harold Lafount of Utah, and Judge Ira Robinson of West Virginia. The FRC therefore had no appropriation and only one confirmed commissioner until March 1928, when the Senate finally confirmed Robinson, Caldwell, Pickard, and Lafount. An amendment to a bill, approved on March 23, 1928, also gave the commission its first appropriation and the commissioners their first paychecks.

It soon became clear that the one-year sunset clause would have to be extended if the FRC was to finish its work. The commission's beginning had been too shaky, and its tasks too great, for it to have been able to hand over a stabilized broadcasting industry to the Department of Commerce in such a short time. After much haggling, Congress authorized an extension of another year, but also legislated to end all the commissioners' appointments in February 1929. The passage of the Davis Amendment, to be discussed later, largely negated the work that the FRC had done in reorganizing broadcast licenses, and forced it to start again. This required another extension in March 1929, but this time, at least, the Congress did not quibble.[3] Perhaps embarrassed by its repeated interference with the FRC's tenure and personnel, the Congress finally put the FRC on a permanent footing in December 1929.

A number of factors combined to make the FRC an orphan on Capitol Hill. It had been forced upon the House through the conference process, and it remained vulnerable to congressional undermining. Many legislators were suspicious that the FRC might entrench itself as the permanent regulator of broadcasting, and others remembered their fears that it would inexorably grow in size, function, and expense. The FRC's annual reports revealed a steady growth in its personnel, from 57 in September 1928 to 90 in 1929, and finally to 237 in 1933. Its appropriations also grew rapidly, from $52,000 in 1928, to $295,440 in 1930 and $872,000 in 1933.[4] Such growth did not endear the FRC to its critics.

Despite its legislative protections and prohibitions against partisanship, the FRC remained firmly enmeshed in political machinations between 1927 and 1934. It quickly gained a reputation for being amenable to political pressure, especially when the pressure emanated from the White House and influential members of Congress. This was particularly the case during the commission's early years, as it staggered along with few political friends, uncertain tenure, and one-year extensions.[5] Listeners, urged by radio stations, continued to write in large numbers to their representatives, complaining about the broadcast power, frequency, or operating hours of their favorite stations. Senators and representatives also worked hard to assist their local broadcasters, for no politician wanted to be on the wrong side of such powerful opinion formers.

The proper extent of congressional communication with the FRC was discussed during a Senate Interstate Commerce Committee hearing at the end of 1929. Members of the committee first questioned FRC chairman Robinson about the effect of letters from the Hill in license deliberations. Robinson replied that they "naturally" influenced the commissioners in their work, for "who can . . . disregard the judgment of a United States Senator?" When pushed by the committee's chairman, Senator Couzens, Robinson agreed that it was "almost as reprehensible" for a member of Congress to write to the FRC in order to influence a decision as it would be to write to a court with the same purpose. Other senators begged to differ. Key Pittman of Nevada saw no problem in legislators seeking information from the FRC about the progress of a constituent's license application.[6]

Pittman's position better reflected political reality. The FRC received an almost constant flow of letters and phone calls from legislators and from the White House. In November 1930, for example, Mark W. Woods, Treasurer of the United States, wrote to Walter Newton, Secretary to President Hoover, about a station in Shenandoah, Iowa. According to Woods the station's owner,

Earl May, was a staunch supporter of the administration and had used his station during the recent congressional elections "to address his radio audience and urge support to the administration and to the necessity for the return of a Republican Congress. Results in Iowa are no doubt attributable in a large measure to Mr May's support." The FRC had recently reduced Mr. May's broadcast power and changed his frequency. "Inasmuch as Mr May has already conferred a distinct benefit on the administration," Woods argued, "it would seem that it would be appropriate to take steps to assign a better wave length to his station."[7]

As the Depression weakened the political prospects of the Hoover administration, its nervousness regarding radio seemed to increase. At the end of 1931 Republican representative James Strong wrote to Walter Newton about Dr. John Brinkley, whose station had been shut down by the FRC for medical fraud. Brinkley ran for governor of Kansas in 1930, and had come third as a write-in candidate. He then moved his station just across the Mexican border and resumed broadcasting. Strong advised Newton that Brinkley's Mexican operations should not be interfered with, for fear that he would run against the administration in 1932 and "lose us Kansas." No direct response to Strong's request remains in Hoover's presidential papers, although a week later Secretary of State Henry Stimson cabled the Mexico City embassy that the State Department had no objection to Brinkley's operations in Mexico, but that it would monitor his programming closely.[8]

The blurring of the FRC's political independence became even more pronounced after Franklin Roosevelt assumed the presidency in March 1933. Roosevelt appointed Herbert Pettey, who had run the Democratic radio campaign in the election of 1932, as secretary of the FRC. Pettey operated as a liaison between the commission and the administration, working primarily through his former boss Louis Howe. Pettey had few scruples about the FRC's quasi-judicial functions and confidentiality. In October 1933 he wrote to Howe to warn him about a FRC hearing on a wavelength dispute between a CBS station, WPG Atlantic City, and WLWL, operated by the Paulist Brothers of New York City. After "conferring with various members of the Commission without referring to any action such as I am now taking in writing to you," Pettey told Howe that it was clear that WLWL would lose. Howe should tell its supporters, including Senator Wagner of New York and party boss Ed Flynn, that they should not invest any political capital into the Paulists' lost cause. The administration should also take a "hands off" approach to this matter because CBS had so far been very cooperative with the Roosevelt administration.[9]

The FRC in Action: The Davis Amendment

Representative Ewin Davis, Democrat of Tennessee, was a fierce southerner and vociferous critic of the FRC. He was particularly worried that the commission, too eager to please NBC and other New York broadcasters, continued to deny the South its fair share of broadcast licenses. He told the House in 1928 that the FRC had "utterly disregarded" the requirement in section 9 of the Radio Act to provide "fair, efficient, and equitable radio service" to each of the "different States and communities." He therefore proposed a much stronger replacement for section 9, requiring the commission to allocate broadcasting licenses and conditions equally across the five radio zones established under the act, and to the states within those zones according to their populations (see map 4). This, Davis argued, was "entirely fair," because four of the five zones were substantially equal in their populations, while the fifth zone, covering the western states, Alaska, and Hawaii, was physically far larger than any other zone. So far, Davis declared, the FRC had treated southerners and westerners as second-class radio citizens.[10]

Congressman Emanuel Celler of New York opposed Davis's amendment as an exercise in cultural envy and radio jealousy. If radio facilities in the first zone were cut back to provide more licenses for the hinterland, Celler argued, the nation's cultural life would be diminished. New York City was not the home of network and commercial broadcasting for nothing; it was the cultural center of the nation. The South, on the other hand, could scarcely be described as a cultural dynamo, and its radio industry was held back by its large numbers of poor blacks and isolated farmers. Davis responded with barely concealed contempt. "New York is a great city and has as good as citizens as may be found anywhere; the same is true with respect to the citizenship in the third zone. . . . It is true that we have a considerable number of negroes with us, but they all speak and understand the English language and they are all American citizens and loyal to their country."[11]

Other southerners and westerners rose to support the amendment, often to express resentment against what they saw as the cultural imperialism of the Northeast, and it passed the House on a strongly sectional vote. Ninety-two percent of congressmen from the old Confederacy, and 75 percent from the western zone, voted yea, while 75 percent of representatives from the first radio zone voted against the amendment. Midwestern voting split, allowing the amendment to pass comfortably. It became law when President Coolidge signed the FRC extension bill on March 28, 1928.[12]

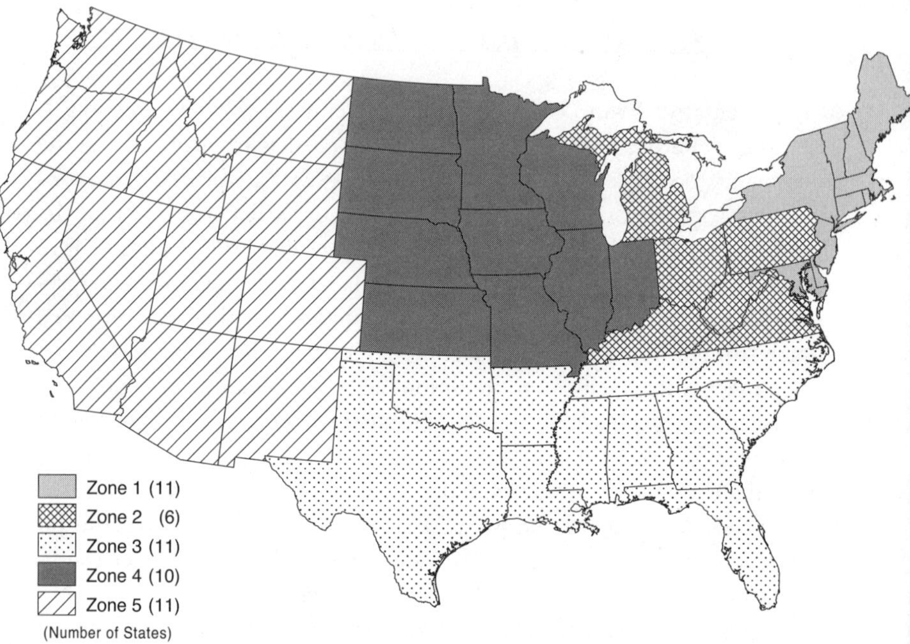

Map 4. Radio Zones under the Radio Act of 1927.

The passage of the Davis Amendment represented a significant congressional intervention into the broadcasting industry. Because broadcasting was illegal without a license, the new regional distribution requirement was an attempt to control the development, and not simply the conduct, of an entire industry. It was tantamount, as some critics at the time pointed out, to Congress legislating equality of railroad mileage across the nation.[13] That such a measure could pass Congress, and receive approval from the most fervently pro-business president of the twentieth century, was a remarkable testament to the power of radio exceptionalism and of anti-metropolitan sentiment.

Radio inequality was often in the eye of the beholder. In 1927, the year before the passage of the Davis Amendment, radio stations were distributed more or less equally across the nation, with only the fourth zone, encompassing the West North Central states, claiming more than its fair share. In terms of station wattage, however, the first zone, including New York and New England, was significantly overendowed. Distribution of the most powerful stations again favored the fourth zone. If, on the other hand, radio resources are compared to population, the fifth zone, with only 8.6 percent of the nation's people, was overrepresented in all categories. If those facilities are correlated to each zone's share of the nation's radio sets, however, the supposedly deprived southern zone ranked second in terms of access to stations. Thus, depending on the criterion, at least three "winners" and "losers" could be identified in the distribution of radio facilities. Certainly the case that the first zone was grossly overprovided seems to have been much less compelling than Davis had his fellow congressmen believe.

The FRC thus faced a daunting task in interpreting and implementing the Davis Amendment. Realizing that zonal equality could only be achieved by reducing the total number of stations, the FRC took the opportunity to eliminate those that it considered to be nonviable. In May 1928 the commission notified 164 stations, nearly a quarter of the national total, to show cause why their licenses should not be canceled. These stations, usually low-powered, underfunded, and not for profit, operated predominantly in the first, second, and fourth zones. None operated in the southern, or third, zone. By July 1928, 109 stations had lost their licenses, giving the commissioners some room to maneuver toward geographical equality.[14] Under the terms of the amendment the FRC was to achieve equality in allocation of licenses, station power, broadcasting wavelengths, and hours of operation across the five zones, and then to apportion radio resources within zones proportionate to each state's population. Additional factors, such as the land area of zones, had to be taken into account in allocating high-power "clear channels" and station wattage. The result was an intricate apportioning process that occupied most of the FRC's energy and resources for the rest of its life.

In June 1930 the commission unveiled its formula for more precise calculation of radio equality. This took into account variables such as station power, hours of broadcast, and shared frequencies to arrive at a single measure for each broadcast station. A five-kilowatt station operating during daylight hours on a shared frequency, for example, represented 1.5 "units of value." Each zone was allocated a total of 80 units, to be distributed among stations as the FRC saw fit.[15] Yet radio equality remained an elusive goal. As seen in table 1, none of the five zones in 1930 or 1931 achieved the magic figure of 80 units; and they still exhibited large variations in their provision of radio stations. Eventually the FRC, the industry, and Congress tired of this pursuit of radio perfection; although the Davis Amendment became section 307(b) in the Communications Act of 1934, it was repealed in 1936. Davis and his fellow agitators did take comfort, however, in the apportionment given to the South, Midwest, and West. As table 1 shows, these zones remained well above their

Table 1. Distribution of Radio Resources by Zone, 1927–1931.

	Zone 1	Zone 2	Zone 3	Zone 4	Zone 5
Land area (% of total)	3.6	6.9	21.3	18.4	49.7
Population (% of total 1927)	22.7	22.7	23.1	22.8	8.6
Radio sets (% of total 1927)	24.2	21.0	16.0	25.0	13.0
Stations (% of total 1927)	19.7	16.4	14.6	30.7	18.7
Total power (% of total 1927)	37.0	17.7	7.8	27.3	10.2
Stations 1kW+ (% of total 1927)	21.0	12.0	7.0	46.0	14.0
FRC Quota June 1930 (+/–% over zone share; 80 units)	–5.8	–10.7	+9.2	+16.1	+13.8
FRC Quota Jan. 1931 (+/–% over zone share; 80 units)	–6.0	–12.0	+11.0	+21.0	+16.0
FRC Quota June 1933 (+/–% over zone share ; 80 units)	–6.0	–8.0	+20.0	+26.0	+20.0

SOURCES: Rows 1, 2, 4, 5, and 6: *Congressional Record,* House, 70th Cong., 1st sess., 1928, 69, pt. 4:3981. Row 3: p. 3989. Row 7: FRC, Fourth Annual Report, 1930, p. 59. Row 8: Laurence F. Schmeckebier, *The Federal Radio Commission,* p. 49.

quotas between 1930 and 1933, at the expense of the first and second zones. The squeaky wheels of southern and western radio interests appear to have received some grease.

The FRC and Its "Appalling Responsibility"

Federal Radio Commissioner Henry Bellows addressed the League of Women Voters in Washington two months after the passage of the Radio Act of 1927. He told his audience that the commission had been given enormous power to define and enforce the licensing criteria of public interest, necessity, or convenience. "It is a rather appalling responsibility. How shall we measure the conflicting claims of grand opera and religious services, of market reports and direct advertising, of jazz orchestras and lectures on the diseases of hogs?" Fortunately, Bellows went on to say, the FRC could rely on millions of listeners, whose power over broadcasters was even greater than that of the commission. The FRC was prohibited from censoring programs, and so it was up to listeners to tell stations what they should or should not broadcast, and to determine "whether this potent agency . . . shall degenerate into a mere plaything or develop into one of the greatest forces in the molding of our entire civilization."[16]

The FRC's primary task was to license broadcasting stations. Its determination, subject to an appeal to the courts on matters of law, decided whether a licensee was operating in the public convenience, interest, or necessity, and thus whether it could continue to broadcast.[17] As the FRC's engineering standards became more rigorous, large numbers of low-budget stations were denied licenses because of the state of their equipment or the technical quality of their signal. The commission's engineering rules were neutrally expressed and made no distinction between commercial and noncommercial stations, but their effect was to discriminate against the latter. One FRC regulation made it obligatory for "full time" stations to broadcast for 17 hours a day. Stations operated by churches, universities, or other nonprofit groups found it much more difficult to satisfy this rule than did commercial stations with their greater revenue flows and larger staffs of technically proficient employees.[18]

The trend against noncommercial broadcasters was also a product of the FRC's interpretation of "public convenience, interest, or necessity." The commissioners refused to provide a definition of this phrase, but they did publicize "a few general principles" about it in August 1928. The interests of listeners were superior to those of broadcasters, and therefore the highest technical standards of broadcasting had to be enforced. Stations were also required to operate on regular broadcast schedules, and to maintain exactly their assigned frequency. The commission also announced that it would take into account an applicant's "character, . . . financial responsibility, . . . and past record," in determining whether to grant or renew a license.[19]

The FRC declared that broadcasters should serve the broadest possible audiences rather than what they considered to be special interest groups. The FRC took a licensee's programming into account in its deliberations, maintaining that the entire listening public within a station's operating radius was entitled to service from that station. If a station's programming was intended for, or appealed to, only a portion of the audience, then the FRC considered that the balance of potential listeners were victims of discrimination. Although explaining that "this does not mean that every individual is entitled to his exact preference in program items," the FRC insisted that all stations offer "a well-rounded program in which . . . music of both classical and lighter grades, religion, education, important public events, discussions of public questions, weather, market reports and news and matters of interest to all members of the family find a place."[20]

These requirements were a tall order for cash-strapped stations without network affiliation. The FRC consistently held that commercial stations, which had a vested interest in maximizing their audience in order to sell advertising time, were the most likely to satisfy them. Stations run by religious denominations and universities had smaller audiences in mind and thus deserved less favorable treatment.[21] The plight of noncommercial stations after 1927 was worsened by their own organizational and financial fragility. Dependent upon parent institutions or listeners for financial support, these broadcasters usually operated on a knife edge, and their failure rates were high. Of the 202 educational stations licensed between 1921 and 1937, 164 either surrendered their licenses or sold them to commercial interests. Of these, 30 percent failed within their first year of operation, and two-thirds did not reach their third birthdays. Many university stations began operations with high hopes of bringing education to the masses, but soon faltered as broadcasting costs increased, audiences diminished, and professors demonstrated that lecture-hall brilliance did not always translate into good radio technique. These problems were quickly reflected in an unfavorable allocation of frequency or broadcast times, sending many of these stations into a downward spiral to oblivion.[22]

Many church-operated stations also succumbed to the weight of FRC regulatory policy. These stations tended to be even more vulnerable than those run by universities, because they usually relied upon volunteer labor and listener or congregation subscriptions. The FRC closely monitored religious stations for any signs of sectarianism, of which it took an extremely dim view. The result of all these factors was that noncommercial stations, already in decline, suffered a precipitous drop in their share of the spectrum after the establishment of the FRC in 1927. In 1926 noncommercial stations represented 28 percent of all broadcast licensees; three years later their share had fallen to just 8.6 percent. This decline continued to decline through the 1930s to 4.8 percent in 1940.[23]

The noncommercial stations' loss was often the networks' gain, and the FRC came under increasing criticism for favoritism toward the "chains." These concerns became prominent during the debate over the FRC's second extension at the beginning of 1929. WCFL, a farmer-labor station operated by the Chicago Federation of Labor, charged that the FRC had allowed the radio trust to broadcast on seven of the 40 cleared channels that afforded exclusive broadcasting privileges to high-powered transmitters. Through its network, NBC also controlled programming on over 50 of the best broadcasting frequencies across the nation. WCFL went on to argue that the commission had given preferential treatment to other powerful corporate concerns, including CBS, major metropolitan newspapers, and Samuel Insull's power conglomerate. Three hundred and fifty other "private business concerns" and 30 local chambers of commerce had also received broadcast licenses since 1927. Yet the commission had repeatedly denied WCFL's application for a cleared channel and 50 kW, and had instead limited it to 1,500 watts and daytime transmission only. "In view of the fact that workingmen and women do not return from their work until after six o'clock in the evening," WCFL argued, "it is manifest that the limitation put upon the Station . . . practically destroys its usefulness." Because radio was "the most effective means known to man for influencing public opinion," the FRC's bias toward the radio trust and "Organized Capital" had profound implications for the health of American democracy and political debate.[24]

In Congress the FRC's critics focused on its treatment of the networks in the allocation of the 40 cleared channels. In an often testy exchange between Orestes Caldwell and Congressman Charles Abernethy of North Carolina during the House hearings on the extension bill in 1929, Caldwell confirmed that virtually half of these channels had been assigned to NBC and CBS stations. When asked how such preponderance corresponded to the "public convenience, interest, or necessity," Caldwell combined the FRC's policy of favoring stations that appealed to the broadest audience with the notion of listener sovereignty to create a perfectly circular argument. Cleared channels were awarded to "the most popular stations in each community," Caldwell declared, "and in every case those stations assigned a cleared channel have been the stations which without question are the most popular and the stations rendering the greatest service." The fact that a station might be affiliated to either NBC or CBS was not relevant.[25]

Those who accused the FRC of being too solicitous of networks could point to a pattern of behavior on the part of the commissioners. Although section 4(h) of the Radio Act empowered the FRC to make special regulations for "chain broadcasting," none were actually implemented. Under pressure from antimonopolists, the commission did promulgate General Order No. 43 in September 1928, which banned the broadcast of the same program on more than one station in any 300-mile radius. This was never enforced, however, and was quietly rescinded a year later.[26] Thenceforth the networks had little to fear from their regulators. Relations were also strengthened by the close links between the FRC and the NAB, and a "revolving door" between the networks and the commission. Commissioners Bellows and Pickard left the FRC to become vice-presidents of CBS in 1927 and 1929 respectively. Robert McChesney argues that the close links between the FRC, CBS, NBC, and the NAB contrasted starkly with the commission's "near total lack of contact" with noncommercial broadcasters. The FRC quickly came to see itself as the defender, rather than the regulator, of the existing system of commercialized and networked broadcasting and its major participants.[27]

By 1931 Clarence Dill, who had fought so hard to create the FRC in 1927, had lost all patience with it. The commission had sold out to RCA and the radio trust, he argued, by ignoring its obligations under the act to deny licenses to companies found guilty of monopolistic practices. He called for a new radio commission, this time "composed of big men truly representing the public."[28] New and more sweeping regulatory proposals became common on Capitol Hill. These targeted levels of advertising, the growing power of the networks, and the FRC as major radio problems demanding tighter legislative control. Many also included provisions to reserve a proportion of broadcast channels for noncommercial, governmental, and labor broadcasters.[29] These proposals all failed to pass, but they provided the inspiration for the Wagner-Hatfield amendment that is discussed in the next chapter.

These criticisms came together during a debate over a Senate resolution proposed by James Couzens of Michigan in January 1932. Pushed by strong pressure from religious and educational broadcasters, the Couzens resolution directed the FRC to report to the Senate on seven questions, most of which focused on the amount of advertising on radio and the feasibility of plans to reduce or eliminate it.[30] Clarence Dill, in a supportive amendment, added eight more questions, all of which were pointed inquiries as to the fate of educational stations under FRC regulation. Dill's final question asked the FRC whether it believed that "educational programs can be safely left to the voluntary gift of the use of facilities by commercial stations." The resolution passed on the voices, and the FRC set to work.

The FRC formally responded to the Couzens-Dill resolution in June 1932. Its report was very sympathetic to the interests of commercial broadcasters, and seldom has a regulatory body responded to a hostile Senate resolution with such a defiant defense of the status quo. The FRC concluded that commercial stations broadcast an average of 6.05 hours of advertisements per week, and that any reduction would adversely affect station revenue and therefore program quality. Total investment in commercial broadcasting had reached $48 million, and controls on advertising "would be wholly contrary to the spirit of American competition and would immediately paralyze the industry." The commission recommended instead that listener sovereignty should control radio advertising. If stations overadvertised they would lose listeners to stations that showed more restraint. The FRC reiterated the industry's line in its rejection of government operation of broadcasting stations. Outright appropriation, although popular overseas, was ill-suited to American geographic, cultural, and economic traditions. The cost of setting up a parallel system of public broadcasting along the Australian model would cost at least $220 million in the first year. The FRC did not explain why it would cost the federal government more than four times the total investment in private broadcasting to set up a parallel system, but the very size of its estimate would have resonated strongly against the backdrop of the Depression.

The commission's report also included a strong defense of the networks, praising them as the most efficient means of providing quality programming to virtually all listeners. Turning to Dill's eight questions on educational broadcasting, the FRC denied that it discriminated against them. Educational stations had declined to 5.5 percent of the national total because of a lack of public demand for their programs. The commission was not concerned about this, because nearly 98 percent of commercial stations reported that they offered their facilities to local educational institutions. Educational programming was thus safe in the care of commercial radio.[31]

The FRC's support of commercial stations and networks did not succeed in silencing either its own critics or those of radio advertising, and it was forced to concede at the end of 1932 that radio advertising was still on probation. Harold Lafount told the NAB's annual meeting in November 1932 that broadcasters were in danger of "selling their birthright for a mess of pottage" through "overcommercialism." Unless the industry mended its ways, Lafount predicted, Congress would soon buckle under the pressure of an irate public demanding greater regulation.[32] Lafount's speech was a friendly warning that portrayed the Congress, rather than the FRC, as the stern watchdog of American broadcasting. The NAB's members, having read the commission's latest defense of their interests and their conduct, knew that they had friends in the FRC.

The FRC and Free Speech

Although the FRC was content to let listener sovereignty determine the amount of advertising on radio, it was much more interventionist toward program and advertising content. Between 1927 and 1934 the commission actively shaped the nature of radio programming through its licensing powers, while consistently denying that this constituted censorship. Such denials were for good reason; section 29 of the Radio Act of 1927 forbade censorship of radio communications, with the usual exceptions for obscenity and profanity. The FRC's statements about its role always acknowledged this legislative requirement to respect free speech, and it invoked listener sovereignty as the only censor of the airwaves. "There is no censorship except public good will," FRC Commissioner Orestes Caldwell told a House of Representatives committee at the beginning of 1929, "and that is the best germicide I know of."[33]

Behind these statements lay a very different reality. At the same time as it prohibited the FRC from censoring stations, the Congress had also empowered it to deny licenses on the undefined basis of "public convenience, interest, or necessity." Successive commissioners exercised their licensing powers in ways that, indirectly but successfully, weakened the prohibition against censorship. Arthur W. Scharfeld, attorney for the FRC, noted in 1930 that the FRC had been given "complete control" over broadcasting, and that this included the ability to prevent the advertisement of fraudulent or dangerous products. Although the FRC "cannot set itself up as an arbiter of morals and good taste," it could act to protect listeners from exploitation. Scharfeld made no mention of section 29 at all.[34]

The FRC's determination to stamp out abuses led it to ban quack doctors and fortune tellers from the air. It then progressively broadened its interpretation of the public interest to encompass moral as well as physical dangers to the listening millions. Lottery information was banned, as were other forms of advertising found to be in "bad taste." At the beginning of 1934 the FRC issued a warning to broadcasters that it would take a dim view of any station that accepted liquor advertising. Although national prohibition had ended in 1933, the commission reminded stations that "millions of listeners throughout the United States do not use intoxicating liquors," and that "many children of both users and nonusers are part of the listening public." The FRC warned that any stations accepting liquor business would be required to show cause why "their continued operation will serve public interest, convenience and necessity."[35]

The FRC evolved its own definitions of freedom of speech and censorship which allowed it great latitude to control program content despite section 29. In doing so the commission undermined the same doctrine of listener sovereignty that it had so often used to avoid forms of regulation that it did not approve of. The FRC denied that entertainment programs and advertising deserved as much freedom of expression as political or religious programming. The radio audience, the commissioners argued, was composed of Americans of all ages and sensibilities, who had no protection other than the FRC. Listeners were "powerless to prevent the ether waves carrying . . . unwelcome messages from entering the walls of their homes. . . . The commission is unable to see that that guaranty of freedom of speech has anything to do with entertainment programs as such."[36]

The FRC was not alone in its reluctance to extend full freedom of speech to radio. The idea that radio was inherently different from print media, and thus subject to different rules regarding freedom of expression, was common.

In 1940 C. B. Rose listed a number of characteristics that "distinguished" freedom of the air from freedom of the press, all of which tended to entitle radio to less liberty. Rose argued that the size of radio audiences and the greater impact of the spoken word over written text meant that radio possessed much greater power to affect popular opinion. In addition it was much harder to provide equal facilities for rebuttal of falsehoods, and the scarcity of frequencies meant that radio would always have to be regulated. Radio audiences of a given program also tended to be far more diverse than readers of newspaper articles, including "illiterates and semi-illiterates." Finally, radio required closer supervision because of its susceptibility to manipulation and propaganda. The same type of reasoning had also led to censorship of motion pictures by state governments after 1910 and to the refusal of the U.S. Supreme Court to extend First Amendment freedom to movies in 1915.[37]

By limiting its actions to retrospective examinations during license renewal procedures of a station's output, the FRC argued that it escaped the prior restraint test of censorship established by the Supreme Court in 1931.[38] At the same time, however, the commission developed guidelines on acceptable programming standards that were taken into account when it decided whether to renew a broadcaster's license.[39] The FRC then published these guidelines, thus surely engaging in prior restraint. If licensees knew that broadcast of liquor advertisements or atheist speeches would endanger their licenses, they would be discouraged from broadcasting such material. Even FRC Commissioner James Hanley recognized that this situation "puts the commission much in the attitude of a spider sitting in its web waiting for some prey on which to pounce."

The FRC refused to license stations that spread what it judged to be propaganda, sectarianism, or subversion. Hanley argued in 1934 that "programs should be of wide appeal so that they will foster good-will and cooperation among all classes of our people and not stir social, political or religious strife or antagonisms."[40] The FRC's actions against a number of stations revealed the limits of its tolerance for free speech on radio. Dr. John Brinkley, whose run for governor of Kansas caused the Hoover administration so much concern in 1930, operated Station KFKB from Milford, Kansas. Dr. Brinkley received his medical "qualifications" from the Eclectic Medical University of Missouri, and in 1923 he established KFKB. His most popular program was "Medical Question Box," in which he diagnosed listeners' complaints and prescribed treatment from his own range of medicines. By 1930 KFKB had been upgraded to five kW, broadcast for 15 hours per day, and had a staff of 25.

Brinkley's speciality was to offer a cure for impotence by transplanting goat prostate glands into his patients. KFKB became Brinkley's chief form of publicity, broadcasting advertisements that attracted patients to Milford from all parts of the country:

> And now about wives. Don't get the impression that women are icebergs and are content with impotent husbands. I know of more families where the devil is to pay in fusses and temperamental sprees all due to the husband not being able to function properly. Many and many times, wives come to me and say, "Doctor, my husband is no good . . . "
>
> Now this operation, which I call "Compound Operation," consists of adding a new artery and nerve to the patient's own sex glands . . . which act as a charger. . . . My batting average is high. That is what counts. Well, what is my average? Oh, about 90 to 95 per cent! How's that?[41]

The American Medical Association had attempted since 1924 to have Brinkley's medical license revoked, and in May 1930 the FRC added its weight to the anti-Brinkley cause. It canceled KFKB's broadcasting license, on the grounds that its impotence advertisements were indecent, and the Medical Question Box programs were hazards to public health. Unsuccessful in his campaign for governor, Brinkley left for Mexico, where his 100 kW station XER continued to broadcast to America's impotent until 1941.[42]

Despite its protestations that political and religious broadcasting deserved greater protection than advertising or entertainment programs, the FRC was also prepared to use its powers to limit or silence stations that disseminated "propaganda." Radical and labor stations received particular attention. The example of WCFL, operated by the Chicago Federation of Labor, has already been noted. In 1928 WEVD, operated by the Debs Memorial Radio Fund to propagate socialism, had to fight hard to save its license. "If WEVD is taken off the air," its operators declared, "the people of the nation can truly recognize that radio . . . is nothing but a tool to be used by the powerful against any form of disagreement, or any species of protest."[43] The FRC renewed WEVD's license, but assigned it a less desirable shared wavelength with a warning that stations which were "the mouthpiece of a substantial political or religious minority" must conduct themselves "with due regard for the opinion of others."

Other stations were not so lucky. In denying a license in 1928 to the House of David, a religious sect, the commission took the opportunity to announce its policy that "a broadcasting station engaged in general public service has, ordinarily, a claim to preference over a propaganda station."[44] Three years later the FRC reasserted its policy against "propaganda" by deleting KGEF, a Los Angeles station run by the Trinity Methodist Church and its fiery Reverend Bob Shuler, because it incited religious intolerance and attacked public officials in an "unsubstantiated and irresponsible" way, and because Shuler had two convictions for contempt.[45] After loud complaints from Catholic listeners, the FRC also moved against WHAP ("We Hold America Protestant") in New York after it broadcast a barrage of anti-Catholic material during Al Smith's presidential campaign in 1928.[46]

In 1935 Louis Caldwell, former general counsel of the FRC, argued that the commission had illegally circumscribed freedom of expression on radio. Operating from the assumption that freedom in radio should be as wide as the freedom of the press, he explained that, instead, "a broadcasting station can be put out of existence . . . for the oral dissemination of language which, if printed in a newspaper, is protected by the First Amendment." Caldwell described the FRC's protestations that license revocation on the basis of past conduct did not constitute censorship as "a glaring fiction" that "puts a terrific strain on intellectual integrity." The fact was that the FRC used its power to interpret "public convenience, interest, or necessity" to ride roughshod over section 29 and to create a "hostile inquisition."[47]

The FRC in Court

The FRC enjoyed great latitude because of a series of supportive decisions by the federal courts between 1927 and 1934.[48] This was by no means inevitable; as Don Le Duc and Thomas McCain have argued, the Radio Act of 1927 was legally adventurous and vulnerable to judicial review. By granting the FRC power to deny licenses on an undefined standard of "public convenience, interest, or necessity," and by categorizing radio broadcasts as a form of interstate commerce, Congress gave the commission power to bar citizens from such commerce. This risked judicial disapproval under the protections of interstate commerce established by the U.S. Supreme Court in *Hammer* v. *Dagenhart* (1918).[49] The FRC also combined judicial and administrative functions in its power to determine public interest. In the Radio Act of 1927 Congress had effectively given an administrative body carte blanche to control entry into and conduct within an entire industry.

Fortunately for the commission, federal courts seemed as influenced by radio exceptionalism as were legislators and regulators. Of 41 cases collated by Le Duc and McCain, the FRC's decisions and powers were affirmed in 36, and the five reverses involved only minor procedural or factual issues.[50] On all major questions concerning radio regulation the courts accepted that the need to ration frequencies required the delegation of broad discretionary powers to the FRC. Broadcasters possessed no rights to their wavelength that were superior to the regulatory power of the Congress over interstate commerce.[51] The federal courts also excluded the states from jurisdiction over radio broadcasts and upheld the FRC's authority to take an applicant's character, financial resources, and past record into account when allocating licenses. The commission's refusal to be bound by the rules of evidence in its hearings also received judicial approval in 1929, and in 1933 the Supreme Court upheld the FRC's contention that its factual investigations were conclusive. Most significantly, the courts did not qualify the FRC's discretion to define "public convenience, interest, or necessity," and held that the onus of satisfying these criteria lay on the applicant. Although the Supreme Court held that the test "is not to be interpreted as setting up a standard so indefinite as to confer an unlimited power," it upheld the commission's sole right to make this determination as a question of fact.[52]

Having upheld the commission's power to revoke licenses, the courts remained untroubled by free speech issues in their radio decisions. This was in keeping with their less than stellar record on protection of free speech during the 1920s, particularly in the new media of motion pictures and radio.[53] Typical of the courts' attitude toward radio and free speech was the decision of the Court of Appeals of the District of Columbia in *Trinity Methodist Church* v. *FRC* in 1932. This arose from an appeal by Bob Shuler against the revocation of his license, but the court upheld the FRC in the strongest terms:

> If it be considered that one in possession of a permit to broadcast in interstate commerce may . . . offend the religious sensibilities of thousands, inspire political distrust and civic discord, or offend youth and innocence . . . then this great science instead of a boon, will become a scourge. This is neither censorship nor previous restraint, nor is it a whittling away of the rights guaranteed by the first amendment. . . . Appellant may continue to indulge his strictures upon the characters of men in public office. He may just as freely as ever criticize religious practices of which he does not approve . . . but he many not . . . demand . . . the continued use of an instrumentality of commerce for such purposes.[54]

The result of these decisions was that the FRC could take full advantage of its powers not only to rationalize the airwaves but also to cleanse them as they saw fit. "No ardent supporter of federal broadcast regulation could have asked for more in 1927," Le Duc and McCain concluded, and "few would have expected as much."[55]

The FRC under Fire

By 1934 the FRC had proved to be far more than a neutral and independent traffic cop of the airwaves. Assisted by the judiciary, it used its enormous power to mold the industry along principles that venerated high technical standards and which discouraged cultural elitism, propaganda, and controversy. These policies dovetailed with the aspirations of commercial broadcasters and networks to create an alliance between the regulated and the regulators which swept all before it. Religious zealots, quack doctors, local broadcasters, educational broadcasters, and labor activists found their competing visions of the destiny of radio broadcasting overwhelmed by the FRC and its powerful friends. The result was that control of the most powerful instrument of communication since the printing press was firmly centered in Washington and New York, and conducted by a regulatory body which never escaped its Hooverian associationalist origins, assumptions, and weaknesses.

5

A New Deal for Radio?

The Communications Act of 1934

At the end of January 1933 Eugene Coltrane of the National Committee on Education by Radio (NCER) wrote Senator William Borah, one of the FRC's most vehement critics, an eight-page letter "on the general subject of radio." Coltrane put forward a sweeping indictment of the ways in which broadcasting had degenerated under the FRC. Unspecified "evil influences" had infiltrated the airwaves; advertisements had become more direct and frequent, and "as a rule, very poor programs go with cheap advertising"; noncommercial broadcasters were in danger of extinction, and "if the present system of radio is to be continued, there is a real danger of chain monopolies." The only hope was for Congress to undertake a "scientific, accurate, impartial, and complete study" of radio and its problems so that a new plan for its future could be developed.[1] Radio, after six years of FRC control, needed a new deal.

The FRC came under attack from a number of sources, each representing noisy coalitions of varying degrees of influence. Those who felt that radio had not fulfilled its early promise in civic education focused their criticism upon the FRC, and calls for a rethinking of the regulatory structure created by the Radio Act of 1927 became louder after the commission's response to the Couzens-Dill resolution of 1932. Those who believed in radio's potential to inform political debate in an impartial way were dismayed by the broadcasters' seeming surrender to the early New Deal, and many broadcasters feared for their positions as temporary licensees of a public asset. The result of these anxieties was that broadcasting policy was drawn into the wider debate over the definition of the state that coursed through Franklin Roosevelt's first administration. By assisting the early New Deal, commercial broadcasters hoped to protect their industry from its attentions, while critics of the "American system" of broadcasting worked to apply the New Deal's reassessment of the proper role of state action to a broadcasting system that had betrayed its early promise.

Radio and the Early New Deal

The broadcasting industry, and especially the networks, gave the early New Deal almost united support. The economic crisis of 1932–1933 generated a chorus of demands that the nation suspend its usual forms of political debate and conflict in favor of a new discourse of national unity and cooperation. This was particularly true during the banking crisis in the months following Roosevelt's election. Saving the banks required a return of business and consumer confidence, and that required an act of national unity and faith. Roosevelt himself used this sense of national crisis to develop popular support for the emergency economic measures of his first Hundred Days, and radio broadcasting played an important role in that process. Stations across the country cooperated not only by providing the president with airtime on demand but also by silencing dissident voices.

Both NBC and CBS rushed to the new president's side after his inauguration in March 1933. The election of 1932, bringing Democrats to national power for the first time in radio broadcasting's history, caused some in the industry to perform some hasty political repositioning. This was particularly true of the two national networks. Political commentators generally agreed that Hoover's defeat would work to NBC's disadvantage, for it had strong Republican connections and had enjoyed close relations with both the Coolidge and Hoover administrations. In 1928 James Harbord, chairman of the board of NBC's parent company RCA, had taken leave to campaign for Hoover, and in 1932 he had published a pamphlet through the Republican National Committee which criticized FDR's alleged tolerance of corruption in New York State. NBC was further embarrassed by gossip that its president, Merlin Aylesworth, was a fervent Republican who had threatened to leave the country if FDR was elected. Rumor had it that a network representative had visited the new president to deny this allegation, but that Roosevelt accepted the denial "to the accompaniment of a hilarity that did not altogether allay anxiety."[2]

CBS, on the other hand, benefited from the change in administrations. The young network had been in NBC's shadow during the Hoover years, and William Paley had cultivated a distinctly liberal image for it. Although Paley's personal political affiliation was unclear, his second wife was a prominent Democrat. Henry Bellows, formerly of the FRC before his appointment as a CBS vice-president in 1929, described himself not only as a "lifelong Democrat" but also as a friend of FDR's from their Harvard days and a member of the "For Roosevelt before Chicago" club. On March 6, 1933, Bellows wrote to White House secretary Stephen Early to offer the "entire facilities of Columbia" to the president "at any hour, day or night, when he may want them during this emergency."[3] "Furthermore," Bellows publicly announced, "as a matter of public policy during the present emergency, we will limit broadcasts of . . . discussions of public questions by ascertaining that such programs are not contrary to the policies of the United States Government." NBC rushed to follow suit.[4]

The networks were as good as their word for most of 1933, broadcasting the president's fireside chats and giving airtime to members of his cabinet virtually on demand. NBC broadcast over 12 hours of speeches by administration figures during Roosevelt's first week as president but gave the Republicans no time at all.[5] This support for banking policy spilled over into support for all the new administration's recovery policies. In May 1933, for example, NBC station WBZ Boston wrote to the Massachusetts branch of the American Legion to warn it about radio speeches criticizing the impact of the Economy Act upon military pensions. Citing NBC's editorial policy, WBZ's manager told the Legion, "We believe that any utterance on the radio that tends to disturb the national confidence in its President is a disservice to the people themselves and is hence inimical to the national welfare. . . . As a great and powerful agency for the service of the public, these stations cannot become a party to attacks on the national security."[6]

Stations and networks were encouraged in this attitude by less than subtle hints from one of their regulators. In August 1933, Commissioner Harold Lafount issued a press statement that implied a threat to revoke stations' licenses if they failed to provide the National Industrial Recovery Act with wholehearted support. Lafount, a Republican, announced that it was the patriotic duty of broadcasters to refuse to sell airtime to advertisers who did not abide by their National Recovery Administration (NRA) codes. Lafount repeated the familiar FRC line that it had no power to censor broadcasts but that it reserved the right to take program content into account when deciding whether to renew licenses:

> The success of the recovery drive, it is generally conceded, depends on team work on the part of the whole nation—the buyers as well as the producers. Many are called

upon to make sacrifices for the common good and those who refuse to play the game deserve, and undoubtedly will receive, the odium of true Americans.

It is to be hoped that radio stations, using valuable facilities loaned to them temporarily by the Government, will not unwittingly be placed in embarrassing positions because of the greed or lack of patriotism on the part of a few unscrupulous advertisers.[7]

These statements sent a strong signal to broadcasters that their livelihoods depended upon their loyalty to government policy. Although Lafount was careful to stress that he was expressing a personal opinion, his call for voluntary censorship seemed to carry the imprimatur of the FRC, and few licensees could have missed his pointed remark that their broadcast wavelength was a temporary loan by the government.

The broadcasters responded enthusiastically. By the middle of 1934 the NRA alone had received approximately $2 million worth of free airtime, and the Department of Agriculture, the Public Works Administration, and the Reconstruction Finance Commission also received significant amounts of free publicity. The Democrats also won the lion's share of free airtime for speeches. During 1933 FDR spoke 20 times over NBC's network, and his cabinet spoke 107 times between them. NBC also paid Louis Howe, FDR's closest adviser, $900 per week to give its listeners an inside view of Washington affairs, and even Eleanor Roosevelt earned $4,000 for hosting NBC broadcasts during 1934.[8]

During this time few Republicans could be heard by American radio listeners; some GOP leaders complained that they received less than 10 percent of the Democrats' airtime. This imbalance was caused by a number of factors. The dramatic events of 1933 created strong demand for news and explanations of policy from the administration. The flood of legislation passed during 1933 generated a great deal of coverage, and FDR's skills as a radio speaker made his addresses very popular. The GOP, well aware that the political tide had turned against them, contributed to their comparative absence from the airwaves by making few requests for airtime.[9]

By the end of 1933 some in the broadcasting industry were rethinking their policies of self-censorship and New Deal boosterism. The crises of the winter of 1932–33 had receded, and network executives began to regret what they now saw as an overreaction to calls for national unity. Broadcasters also felt increasingly self-conscious about the apparent disparity between radio's subservience to the New Deal and the press's more robust attitudes toward federal policy.[10] In October 1933 Frank Mullen, NBC's director of agricultural programs, wrote to network vice-president Niles Trammell that the Agricultural Adjustment Act (AAA) and the NRA were increasingly unpopular among some business and farm groups, and he predicted that 1934 would witness much stronger opposition to the New Deal. It was now time, Mullen thought, that NBC rethink its policy of presenting only the administration's point of view: "We certainly do not want to create in the minds of the public the impression that we are operating in the interests of the Administration exclusively, as this trend will lead to government ownership faster than anything else we can do. I have a feeling that like the press we will command more respect from the Administration if we retain and foster the policy of presenting opposing arguments."[11]

Mullen's call was reinforced by a rising tide of criticism of the role of radio in the political culture of the early New Deal. Newspaper editorials were quick to pounce on what they saw as radio's surrender of objectivity and independence as further evidence that the new medium, which had become a powerful competitor for advertising revenue, was fundamentally inferior to print as a purveyor of news and opinion. The *New York Herald Tribune*, as rabidly anti–New Deal as the networks were pro-administration, claimed in May 1934 that radio broadcasting had become "the spokesman for the New Deal and largely restricted to government propaganda." Challenged by the FRC to provide "any facts or other material" to substantiate these assertions, the paper's editor, Ogden Reid, pointed to Lafount's 1933 statement, and then ran a series of articles in June 1934 condemning radio's failure to stand up both to the administration and the FRC.[12]

The *Herald Tribune* argued that radio regulation since 1927 had created a "tendency of the radio broadcasting industry to serve as hand-maiden and drummer boy to whatever administration happens to be in power in Washington." Because licensees faced "a possible death sentence" every six months from the FRC, which was made up of political appointees, they tended to avoid any risk of displeasing their regulators. Lafount's warning, the *Herald Tribune* thought, had been a "word to the wise" that had resulted in a torrent of pro-administration radio addresses, all paid for by the broadcasters. The chief villain was Herbert Pettey, installed as secretary of the FRC soon after Roosevelt's victory. Far from fulfilling his duties independently, Pettey had instead acted as the chief liaison between the administration and the broadcasters. Most pernicious of all, the *Herald Tribune* argued, was the degree of self-censorship by broadcasters. While newspapers ran "reams of arguments" both for and against the New Deal in the second half of 1933, the national networks had persisted in their policy of supporting the administration. Although the newspaper conceded that radio had become a hostage to political favoritism and partisan interference during the Republican administrations of the 1920s, it maintained that Roosevelt and the New Dealers had markedly intensified these influences. Caught between FRC pressure and broadcasters' timidity, the future of radio as a genuinely free educative and informative medium looked dim indeed.[13]

Toward a New Communications Policy

Concerns about the ability of broadcasters to protect radio from political favoritism dovetailed with reformers' determination that it be allowed to fulfill its educative and informative potential, creating new pressure for radio reform in the early 1930s. There were also political influences at work. Philip Rosen argues that the new Democratic administration, well aware of the power of radio in politics, hoped that the incumbent FRC commissioners would resign after the election of 1932 so that the new president could install his own appointees. When it became clear that the commissioners would see out their legislated terms, Roosevelt began to consider the possibility of replacing the FRC, and its existing personnel, with a new body of his own devising.

It is likely that the commission's past record of closeness to Hoover had not escaped FDR. Although Roosevelt was able to appoint two new commissioners, James Hanley and Eugene Sykes, soon after his inauguration, the politician in the president doubtless felt nervous that such a powerful medium lay in the hands of a body mostly appointed by his predecessor. Yet FDR could not escape Hoover's legacy of radio regulation, for his suggestions for radio reform followed closely ideas that the former president had urged during the last years of the 1920s. Like so much of the New Deal, FDR's communications policy owed more to the New Era than he cared to admit.

The origins of the New Deal's communications policy lay in President Hoover's view that public administration should be arranged along rational and efficient lines. With the establishment of the FRC, and the perpetuation of its licensing powers in 1929, control of radio broadcasting continued to be divided across departmental lines. Although the FRC held the lion's share of radio regulation, it still depended upon the Department of Commerce for its fieldwork and inspection operations. The Interstate Commerce Commission (ICC) also held some residual power over interstate radio telegraphy. Hoover had urged Congress to unify radio regulation and to bring all electronic media—radio, cables, telephones, and telegraphs—under a single regulatory authority.[14]

Hoover's early allies included both Senator James Couzens of Michigan and David Sarnoff. Couzens prepared a bill to unify all media under a new agency, and his Senate Interstate Commerce Committee held hearings to examine it at the end of 1929. Sarnoff, by then executive vice-president of RCA, gave his full support to Couzens's bill. Complaining that bodies such as the FTC had interfered with RCA's legitimate attempts to create a monopoly over American international cable and wireless traffic, Sarnoff argued that a unified communications policy would allow his company to achieve this patriotic purpose. This testimony elicited a strong response from Clarence Dill, who had long fought against monopolies in utilities and communications. "What you really want," an indignant Dill told Sarnoff, "is not government control, but government support of what RCA, as a privately owned and operated company, might do."[15]

Testimony such as Sarnoff's convinced many of the committee's members that full unification was premature. As an interim measure, unification of all radio regulation under the aegis of the FRC seemed a sensible step, and Dill introduced a bill to this effect in 1930. At this stage congressional action on radio reform became embroiled over educational broadcasting and advertising.[16] Growing impatient, Hoover created the Committee to Investigate the Duplication of Government Communications Facilities, which concluded that the FRC should assume control over all radio regulation. Accordingly Hoover issued an executive order in July 1932 that transferred the Radio Division of the Department of Commerce to the FRC.

The path to full communications unification, however, became cluttered by intervening events. Radio reformers, still smarting from the FRC's response to the Couzens-Dill resolution, began to campaign for a reallocation of licenses to guarantee a stronger presence for nonprofit and educational broadcasters. The ACLU called for a new inquiry into broadcasting after reviewing the FRC's performance on freedom of speech and its favoritism toward the networks.[17] The debate over a new communications policy thus became mingled with broader conflicts over the future of broadcasting. These developments appear to have caused broadcasters to rethink their earlier support of a unified regulatory regime. The departure of Hoover and the Republicans from power in Washington led to some nervousness among industry leaders, who doubted that the new administration would be as sympathetic to their interests as Hoover had been. Industry leaders also became nervous that a shake-up of radio regulation might provide an opportunity for reformers to force through their ideas for entrenching nonprofit broadcasting at the expense of commercial stations.

In April 1933 Alfred McCosker, President of the NAB, wrote to FDR and Postmaster General James Farley to outline the industry's concerns about reports that "drastic changes" were to be made to radio regulation. "All broadcasting interests," McCosker argued, "assumed that the President was more or less satisfied with the organic set up of the Commission and that nothing would be done to change it." McCosker also attempted to trade on the broadcasters' support for the New Deal to save it from unwelcome change. "It has been my ambition as well as that of others to coordinate the broadcasting industry with the new administration in order that it would be responsive to the needs of President Roosevelt and act as a unit in carrying out his policies. My task would be more difficult if there is any major change contemplated particularly when there does not seem to be any compelling reasons for a change." As a fall-back position, McCosker argued that, if reform had to come, the current "administrative machinery" for radio should be "kept in the hands of those who during the past six years have been familiar with it."[18]

President Roosevelt, keen to streamline the federal regulatory structure, persisted with the idea of a single communications regulator. Secretary of Commerce Daniel Roper led a committee, which included Clarence Dill and Congressman Sam Rayburn, to recommend the best way forward toward coordinating oversight of radio, telephones, cables, and the telegraph.[19] The Roper committee's deliberations quickly centered upon how far the New Deal would extend to communications in general and radio in particular. This debate soon assumed its customary form, with industry leaders, urging minimal change to existing regulatory forms, arrayed against reformers who were determined that the New Deal would indeed come to radio.

As educators and broadcasters rehearsed their arguments to the Roper committee, former secretary of the navy Josephus Daniels tried one last time to realize his old dream of government control of radio. Daniels occupied a special place in the president's affections, having been his mentor during the Wilson years. The president had appointed his old boss to be ambassador to Mexico, and from there Daniels wrote to FDR that the Roper committee should place radio not only under one regulatory umbrella but also under public ownership. "There is no more reason why other communications should be privately owned than the mails. Radio and telephone are as important parts of communications as the mail was when Benjamin Franklin was Postmaster General." FDR directed Roper to examine Daniels's suggestion seriously, sending the commercial broadcasters into a frenzy of lobbying against it.[20]

It is unlikely, however, that the president took the idea of public ownership to heart. Even Daniels recognized that there were more pressing issues occupying FDR's attention, and that there was no point "digging up more snakes than you can kill promptly, and the controllers of the telegraph and telephone and radio and cable are powerful." Apart from Daniels and Adolph Berle, few people of influence within the administration argued for such a frontal challenge to a politically powerful industry. Louis Howe, the president's chief political adviser, was uninterested in broadcasting reform, and the networks' enthusiastic support endeared them to an administration already battered by a much more hostile press.[21]

The Roper committee firmly and unanimously rejected Daniels's plan, arguing that it would ruin the American system of broadcasting which had served audiences so well since 1920. A major fight with broadcasters would be needlessly destructive to the close relationship between the administration and the industry, and imposition of listener levies would be deeply unpopular during the Depression. Instead, Roper and his colleagues argued in Hooverian terms that all communications should come under a single regulator in the interests of convenience, economy, and efficiency.[22] The committee's recommendations affirmed almost to the letter its initial brief from the president, and corresponded closely to the broadcasting industry's fallback plan. Most importantly, the committee's work finally laid to rest the ghost of public ownership. Although the industry did not gain the affirmation of the status quo that it had desired, it had succeeded in ensuring that the reformers won nothing of their agenda at all.

Congress and the Communications Bill of 1934

President Roosevelt's special message to Congress on February 26, 1934, was a model of simplicity and logic. "I have long felt that for the sake of clarity and effectiveness the relationship of the Federal government to certain services known as utilities should be divided into three fields—transportation, power and communications." The ICC had control over federal transportation policy, and the Federal Power Commission provided oversight over electric power. What was needed now was a single body vested with all powers to regulate cables, telegraphs, telephones, and radio.

The president's message was quickly followed by the announcement that Clarence Dill and Sam Rayburn, who had served on the Roper committee and were chairmen of the Senate and House interstate commerce committees, had formulated a bill incorporating the administration's wishes. The Dill-Rayburn bill abolished the FRC and terminated its current appointments. It also stripped the ICC of its control over telegraphs, cables, and telephones, and gave these powers, and those of the FRC, to a new Federal Communications Commission (FCC). Rather than include "too many controversial issues," which would delay the bill's passage, Dill told the press, the FCC was to be given extensive investigatory powers to report later on such hot political potatoes as the telephone monopoly, merging of international communication companies, and educational broadcasting.[23]

The Dill-Rayburn bill attracted little attention during the early stages of its progress through Congress. Dill reported his bill out of the Senate Interstate Commerce Committee, with only minor amendments, on April 17, 1934, and it met with a similarly easy reception in the House. David Sarnoff, no doubt relieved that the Roper committee and the two congressional committees had limited their recommendations to structural consolidation rather than policy reform, told the House committee that his company was "in hearty accord" with the main thrust of the bill.[24] Most of the House committee's attention focused upon telephone regulation, but one witness urged it to prevent a "conspiracy to suck [radio] into the vortex of commercialism and commercial expediency," by reserving channels for state and federal governmental broadcasting. Father John Harney of the Paulist Fathers also attacked the bill's failure to limit the power of commercial broadcasters or to safeguard those broadcasters who were more interested in selling education than soap.[25] The committee easily contained these reformist incursions, and it approved Rayburn's bill with little fuss.

The communications bill faced its severest test on the floor of the Senate. Although it had gone through the committees on the strength of its emphasis upon efficient administration and its restatement of existing law, the bill's shaky reformist credentials became the focus of the Senate debate. Dissatisfaction with the bill's limited scope crystallized around an amendment sponsored by Robert Wagner of New York and Henry Hatfield of West Virginia that reserved 25 percent of all broadcast channels for the use of nonprofit stations. Hatfield presented his amendment as a means by which the FRC's favoritism to the radio trust and other commercial broadcasters could be rectified before radio was entrusted to the new FCC. Under the amendment all broadcasting licenses would be declared null and void 90 days after the passage of the communications bill, and the FCC was directed to allot a quarter of them to "educational, religious, agricultural, labor, cooperative, and similar non-profit-making associations." Those stations would be permitted to sell advertising time to maintain their financial viability. Hatfield closed with a warning that "unless legislation of this type is soon enacted the few who might be injured by the amendment may find themselves bereft of the business they are now engaged in as the Congress will find it . . . necessary to take over all radio facilities and operate them for the common good."[26]

The Wagner-Hatfield amendment prompted the last major battle between commercial broadcasters and radio reformers in Congress before World War II. The industry, which had prepared itself well to defeat the amendment, lobbied fiercely against it. Opponents of the amendment, led by Clarence Dill, focused upon the amendment's authorization of nonprofit stations to sell advertising time. Crying crocodile tears, Dill argued that the last thing American radio needed was more advertising. Ignoring the argument that reservation of 25 percent of channels would reduce the total amount of advertising on the air, since nonprofit broadcasters would sell only enough advertising to sustain their stations, Dill won the day.[27] The Senate did, however, direct the FCC to report on the desirability of channel reservation. After desultory debate over the appropriate salaries for FCC staff, the Senate passed the bill on the voices on May 15, 1934. The whole process had occupied only five hours of debate.[28]

The House discussion on the communications bill was similarly short, but enlivened by Republican complaints about radio broadcasters' and regulators' bias toward the administration. Louis T. McFadden of Pennsylvania argued that radio was tainted by a corrupt bargain between the New Dealers and the national networks. Under this arrangement the networks provided air time on demand to the Democrats, while the FRC regulated radio in ways that were supportive of the networks. McFadden's Republican colleague Harold McGugin of Kansas added his own complaint that "radio broadcasters currying the favor of [the FRC] have given unlimited facilities to new-deal propaganda and have unwarrantedly denied the right of the air to those who would rise to criticize any part of the New Deal program." He then undermined his own point by conceding, "it is my understanding that a Republican Member of Congress can get on the air whenever he wants," before concluding lamely that "the ordinary citizen who is a Republican cannot get on the air."[29] Disposing of such objections was an easy task for a legislator of Rayburn's experience, and the House bill passed without a roll call on June 2, 1934. The conference process worked quickly, and President Roosevelt signed the Communications Act of 1934 into law on June 19, 1934.

The Communications Act of 1934

The new act, as it related to radio broadcasting, made only minor changes to the Radio Act of 1927. Under section 4 the new FCC had seven commissioners, instead of the FRC's five. FCC commissioners, like those of the FRC, were prohibited from financial interest in communications industries, and only four could be members of the same political party. The commission was empowered to appoint a secretary, general counsel, and other senior staff without complying with civil service laws, thus protecting the position of political appointees such as Herbert Pettey. In its original form the FCC was divided into three sections, covering radio, telephones, and telegraphs. Two commissioners were assigned to each section, with the chairman overseeing all three. This system was abandoned in 1937, and the seven commissioners then served at large across all sections. In other ways the procedure and organization of the new commission was almost identical to the FRC's.

Title 3 of the new act covered radio regulation. The "public convenience, interest, or necessity" criteria, still undefined, were transferred to the FCC, as was the statutory maximum license period of three years. The Communications Act also repeated the Davis amendment's requirement of zonal equality of broadcast power.[30] Section 307(c), requiring the FCC to "study the proposal that Congress by statute allocate fixed percentages of radio broadcasting facilities to particular types or kinds of non-profit programs," and to report its findings to Congress before February 1, 1935, was the smoldering wreck of the Wagner-Hatfield amendment.

The new act did nothing to further the use of radio in political debate, limiting itself to the repetition of the old requirement of equal time for political candidates in section 315. Dill's Senate version of the communications bill had included a significant broadening of section 18, expanding the equal time requirement to include not only candidates but also their supporters and opponents, and prohibiting any increased charges for political advertising over normal advertising rates. Dill's provision also included "public question[s] upon which the people are to vote" under the equal time rule. Lobbying by broadcasters, who vehemently opposed any expansion of section 18, succeeded in removing Dill's version from the act during the conference process.[31]

In his testimony to the Senate Interstate Commerce Committee hearings on the communications bill, Henry Bellows of CBS argued that any broadening of section 18 would impose intolerable burdens on broadcasters. Bellows was particularly concerned about a Nebraska Supreme Court decision in 1932, which had held a broadcaster liable for any slander or libel uttered by political candidates.[32] The new bill, Bellows argued, should protect broadcasters from such liability. Bellows also rejected the proposed expansion of section 18 to cover discussions of public issues, arguing that stations would refuse to cover any issues or candidates for fear of losing more and more of their time to political broadcasting. The result would be a diminution of radio time currently devoted to political and civic affairs. He won his argument about the expansion of section 18, but did not persuade the lawmakers to provide specific protection to broadcasters against liability for libel.[33]

The Communications Act incorporated few concessions to critics of the radio trust and network monopoly. The FCC inherited the FRC's dormant power to make special regulations concerning chain broadcasting, and the new act's sections 311 and 313 merely reiterated the old power to deny licenses to applicants who had been judged guilty of unfair competition. Taken as a whole, the broadcasting industry had won an almost complete victory over its critics; in the Communications Act as it applied to radio the New Deal had labored and brought forth a mouse.

Radio broadcasters won one more significant victory in June 1934, when their NRA code came up for hearings. For reasons that are unclear, the code process was slow to catch up with broadcasters. This, the *Literary Digest* reported, had made some in the radio world nervous, for a ratified code brought protection against antitrust actions. Some broadcasters were even fearful that the absence of a code was part of a general administrative design to use the pending communications bill to wreak massive change upon the industry.[34] These fears turned out to be groundless; not only did the Communications Act correspond almost exactly to the desires of the commercial broadcasters but the code making process, which culminated in late June 1934, was equally painless. The NRA broadcasting code followed both the NAB's submissions and the 1929 code of behavior for stations closely, although many local stations had to raise wages to satisfy the new minimum rate of $15 per week.[35] The events and maneuverings of 1934 had shown, according to the *Literary Digest*, that "radio, as a matter of survival, if for no other reason, has developed an amazing facility of placating its critics in high places."[36]

That assessment has been confirmed by most historians of American broadcasting during the 1930s. Philip Rosen argued that the whole idea of unified regulation served as a shield against the demands of radio reformers by giving the appearance of reform while providing nothing of substance that damaged the interests of commercial broadcasters. Robert McChesney has argued that the Communications Act cemented both the "dominant paradigm" of commercial control of radio and the collapse of radio reformers' dreams of creating a separate broadcasting system for educational programming. Never again would Congress seriously question the prevailing system of American broadcasting. "In the end," Susan Smulyan wrote of the 1934 act, "government regulation only strengthened the largest and commercialized broadcasting companies at the expense of the smaller and nonprofit broadcasters, and lessened competition, outcomes that mirrored most other interactions between the New Deal government and the economy."[37]

Yet the story of the Communications Act is not simply one of effective corporate lobbying. The broadcasters' seeming immunity from the New Deal pointed to their special position in American political culture. To protect their version of radio exceptionalism the broadcasters were forced not only to compromise their editorial independence to appease lawmakers and regulators but also to cloak themselves in the rhetoric of public service to blunt the attacks of those who saw radio as too important to be entrusted to profit-making corporations. The result was that the "American system" of broadcasting rested on an intricate web of legislative and informal understandings about the proper role of radio broadcasting in American civic life. Broadcasters, in fending off fundamental change to the legislative and regulatory system of 1927, had also perpetuated their anomalous position as wards of the state, dependent upon government regulation to give substance to their protestations of freedom.

6

The Federal Communications Commission and Radio, 1934–1940

"Whatever the cause," Charles Siepmann wrote in 1950, "the fact is irrefutable that, since its inception in 1934, the FCC has used its powers with a discretion that, except on rare occasions, has pleased the industry, as it has provoked the dismay and indignation of radio's more exacting critics." Others have been less polite. V. O. Key noted in 1961 that it "has often been staffed by a fairly contemptible set of men," while Robert MacNeil called it a "pathetic organization" in 1968. "Few have anything good to say about it," MacNeil went on, "except to offer excuses." John Whale concluded that the FCC had been made deliberately weak by the Communications Act of 1934, and that it had compounded this problem by behaving weakly, contenting itself mainly with pro forma license renewals, wavelength regulation, and "seeing that transmission towers were properly painted." In 1995 former NBC president Lawrence Grossman observed that "no one with any sense assumes the FCC is worth a damn."[1]

The FCC's regulatory activities and attitudes closely reflected the FRC's. Although only two FRC commissioners were appointed to the new body, its inheritance of its predecessor's staff, statutory powers, and regulations predisposed it to continue to acquiesce to network and commercial broadcast interests. This continuity was a product of the circumstances of the FCC's birth. Because the Communications Act passed Congress as a measure devoted to good governmental housekeeping rather than radio reform, there was little momentum for change. Consequently the FCC continued the FRC's pattern of controlling radio in accordance with the rhetoric of listener sovereignty and radio exceptionalism, while in reality steering a regulatory path of least resistance between the federal administration and the broadcasters. Hemmed in by these powerful forces, the FCC's history during the 1930s was a classic case of the dog that didn't bark.

The history of radio regulation between the wars, however, is not merely one of capture and acquiescence. The broadcasters, although they had little to fear from the FCC for most of the 1930s, remained wary of the potential power of their regulators and Congress. The benign regulatory structure that was initiated by Hoover, continued by the Radio Act of 1927, and cemented by the Communications Act of 1934 depended heavily upon self-regulation by the major broadcasters and bodies such as the NAB. The national broadcasters often behaved as if a major congressional hearing chaired by Robert Wagner, or a series of hostile license renewal hearings conducted by a rejuvenated FCC, were just around the corner.

The FCC Goes to Work

President Roosevelt's nominations to the FCC represented a careful balance of political interests, and had been vetted by patronage boss Jim Farley. FDR appointed Eugene Sykes, Chairman of the FRC, as the chair of the new commission. Sykes, a Democrat from Mississippi, embodied the corporate memory of federal radio regulation, having been a member of the FRC since its creation in 1927. The president also renewed the tenure of one other FRC member, Republican Thad Brown of Ohio. Three Democrats and two Republicans joined the FCC as new members. On the Democratic side, Roosevelt nominated an Oklahoman, Paul Walker, and two Texans, Irvin Stewart and Hampson Gary. Gary, who received a one-year term, was a seat warmer for Anning S. Prall, who joined the commission in 1935. Two other Republicans, Norman Case of Rhode Island and George Henry Payne of New York, completed the commission's bench.[2] Of these seven, Gary and Brown were assigned with Chairman Sykes to the FCC's radio division. Broadcasters expressed their support of the president's choices, and the seven nominees passed senatorial inspection with little opposition. The great majority of the FRC's technical and support staff, including Herbert Pettey, was transferred to the new commission.

The new commission's first major task was to study the channel reservation proposal embodied in the Wagner-Hatfield Amendment. The FCC held public hearings on this issue in October and November 1934, gathering 14,000 pages of testimony from 135 witnesses representing networks, educators, religious broadcasters, and others interested in nonprofit broadcasting.[3] The commercial broadcasters again expressed strong opposition to reserving channels for nonprofit operators. Rather than attacking the idea as against American traditions of free enterprise and private ownership, they stressed their current activities on behalf of educational, religious, and charitable institutions. Witness after witness attested that their stations devoted a large proportion, averaging 11 percent, of their total broadcast hours to good works. The broadcasters' case was strengthened by friendly testimony from a number of church and educational groups, who told the FCC that they enjoyed easy access to the networks' airwaves. Legislative reservation of channels, the commission heard, would damage this cooperation. Other groups testified that they would be embarrassed by passage of the Wagner-Hatfield Amendment because they did not have the resources to undertake their own broadcasting.[4]

The commercial interests did not have a monopoly over testimony to the inquiry. Groups such as the NCER argued in favor of reservation, as did a number of prominent individuals such as Lee de Forest. These contributions, however, seemed disjointed and amateurish compared to the broadcasters' slick orchestration of their case. By avoiding overtly selfish arguments revolving around the danger to their invested capital, the radio lobby captured the high ground by making their opponents seem ungrateful for the favors bestowed upon them. They were also assisted by an FCC that was extremely sympathetic to their cause. The commission took the broadcasters' testimony at face value, accepting their very wide definitions of "educational" programming. NBC even counted its enormously successful *Amos'n'Andy* program as part of its educational efforts.[5]

The FCC's report represented a complete victory for the commercial broadcasters, and a final defeat for the radio reform movement.[6] It flatly rejected any reservation of channels for nonprofit purposes, and accepted all of the commercial broadcasters' arguments. There was no "real demand" on the part of listeners for such a radical step, the commission found, and the more pressing need was to improve the coverage and variety of commercial stations rather than to add stations providing only "special services." The obligations imposed by the Davis Amendment, now section 307(b), the commission argued, were not compatible with channel reservation. Much to the delight of the commercial broadcasters, the FCC had turned an inquiry into channel reservation for nonprofit stations into a call for increased numbers and power of commercial stations. "It would seem a fundamental requirement," the FCC held, "that the general public throughout the whole country be provided with at least one radio service of general interest and dependable signal quality lest there be discrimination against areas not receiving any service." Under the old FRC assignment criteria, "general interest" and "dependable signal quality" were code for commercial broadcasts, and the FCC seemed happy to continue its predecessor's bent toward for-profit broadcasting.

The commissioners did throw a sop to nonprofit broadcasters by recommending a national conference to explore ways of increasing cooperation between commercial broadcasters and nonprofit organizations. The FCC also dedicated itself "actively to encourage the best minds among broadcasters and educators alike in order to develop a satisfactory technique for presenting educational programs in an attractive manner to the radio listener."[7] That conference in turn established the Federal Radio Education Committee (FREC), which operated throughout the 1930s chiefly as a means through which Congress and commercial broadcasters could avoid further action on nonprofit broadcasting. Erik Barnouw described the formation of the FREC as a skillful shunting of radio educationalists and other critics of commercial broadcasting into "busy work."[8] With the FREC hard at work, there was always another report or study to await before Congress could act.

The FCC's investigation reached the same conclusion as the FRC inquiry following the Couzens-Dill resolution in 1932, and it is hard to escape the conclusion that its findings were similarly preordained. Yet the section 307(c) investigation did add another element to the web of understandings and assumptions that characterized radio regulation between the wars. Just as the Couzens-Dill inquiry had led to the FRC's warning to broadcasters about advertising, so too did the 1934 hearings provide a warning about nonprofit programming. Taking the hint, the national networks and many local stations hired public service and educational liaison staff as evidence of a new era of cooperation between themselves and the vanquished educators.[9]

The FCC and Politics

Broadcasting policy under the FCC remained as politicized as it had been during the FRC years. The passage of the Communications Act and the creation of the FCC allowed Roosevelt to put his personal stamp on radio regulation, and relations between the new commission and the White House became closer after 1934. In January 1937, Postmaster General Farley recorded the following exchange in his diary:

Saw Anning Prall, Chairman of the Radio Commission, and went over several matters with him, among them the broadcasting station in which Stanley High, Sidney Weinberg, Judge Gerard and several others in our group are interested. The President said it was all right for me to tell Prall that we are anxious to have whatever consideration possible and proper extended to them, providing their financial set-up etc., meet with the requirements.[10]

Congressmen and senators also continued to lobby on behalf of constituents for license renewals and improvements in broadcast power and wavelengths. Until 1936 Herbert Pettey acted as the White House's chief liaison to the FCC, allowing the commissioners themselves to retain the appearance of nonpartisanship and impartiality. Pettey, who addressed FDR's chief political aide Louis Howe as "Boss," provided information about broadcast licensees, progress of license hearings, and sources of program funding. In February 1935, for example, he answered a query from Howe as to who was paying for a program on station WMAL that "is raising H—— with us." Pettey replied that, although the *Washington Post* supplied the material for the program, the station broadcast it as "a matter of public interest."[11]

Pettey resigned from the FCC at the end of 1936, and the administration was careful to replace him with someone equally sympathetic. Farley's diary at the end of December 1936 recorded that FDR had come under pressure to appoint Senator Couzens's former secretary. Farley, however, had his own candidate in mind, and persuaded the president to appoint Robert Berger. Like Pettey before him, Berger came to the job after running the Democrats' radio campaign, this time in the elections of 1936. "There are times when we have to talk confidentially to the person in that position," Farley advised the president, "and . . . Berger is thoroughly competent and we feel trustworthy."[12]

The FCC also came under pressure from the administration on policy issues. This was most striking in 1940 and 1941, when the commission announced an inquiry into newspaper ownership of radio stations. The president, tiring of what he saw as the newspaper owners' concerted opposition to the New Deal, had become alarmed at the prevalence of cross-ownership between the press and radio. Newspaper owners had been involved in radio since 1920, and by 1940 they owned or controlled almost a third of the nation's 730 AM stations, and a quarter of the construction permits for the new FM stations.[13] Roosevelt was particularly concerned about cases in which the only newspaper in a town also owned its only radio station. Proud of his ability to use radio as a means of circumventing newspaper opposition, the president feared that cross-ownership would deny him his most powerful political weapon. Accordingly he politely inquired in December 1940 of his new FCC chairman, James Lawrence Fly, when he proposed to have a hearing on newspaper ownership of radio stations.[14]

Fly, a former general counsel of the Tennessee Valley Authority (TVA) and a fervent New Dealer, was determined to propel the FCC into a more reformist role. His appointment represented a break in FCC history; his New Deal pedigree contrasted strongly to that of his predecessors Sykes, Prall, and Frank McNinch, who had run the FCC in the spirit of the technically oriented and pro-network FRC. In March 1941 the commission announced that it would conduct an investigation to determine whether new policies were required concerning radio-newspaper cross-ownership. These hearings, conducted amidst bitter complaints from the press that its First Amendment rights were at risk, dragged on from July 1941 until January 1942, and the commission did not complete its inquiry until the beginning of 1944. Although the FCC declined to promulgate any general rule on the issue, the hearings sent a message to publishers that their freedoms of action and criticism of the administration might not be absolute, at least as far as radio was concerned.

The FCC and Stations

"There is a belief that our predecessor . . . was dominated by the industry it was supposed to control," new FCC commissioner George Henry Payne declared in 1934. "I am very happy to say that such is not now the case."[15] Payne's announcement was premature. During its early years the FCC seemed to accord to radio regulation a low priority. The seven commissioners, responsible for the regulation of all electronic communications, had many more demands on their time than did their five predecessors on the FRC. Because the FRC had already done the hard work of reorganizing the broadcast band and applying the Davis Amendment, and because its procedures had received judicial approval between 1927 and 1934, the new commission saw little reason to disturb the status quo.

Although the Communications Act empowered it to grant broadcast licenses for a maximum period of three years, the FCC maintained the FRC's practice of issuing six monthly licenses. Involving nearly 600 broadcast stations and more than 700 experimental licenses in 1934, the renewal process was usually desultory. Acting on the basis of questionnaires about licensees' programs, equipment, and finances, the FCC routinely renewed licenses without hearings or delay. This process became more formal and extensive only when a station had been subject to an unusual number of listeners' complaints or to an unfavorable report by the FCC's engineering inspectors. The FCC also continued the FRC's refusal to define "public interest, convenience, and necessity," causing its procedure to remain mysterious to outsiders and riddled with discretion.[16] In an exchange with Democratic Senator William Dieterich of Illinois during his confirmation hearing in January 1935, Chairman-designate Eugene Sykes did little to clarify the mysterious ways of the FCC:

Senator Dieterich. What rule do you apply in determining who shall be permitted to use the wave lengths and to broadcast?

Commissioner Sykes. The law says that you base these grants on what is in the public interest, convenience, and necessity.

Senator Dieterich. I am asking you now what you consider public interest, convenience, and necessity are?

Commissioner Sykes. Primarily you want to see what kind of service they propose to render . . .

Senator Dieterich. I was going to ask you what rule you applied over two different institutions applying for a license to broadcast, before you assign a wavelength, and how you would determine the difference between them.

Commissioner Sykes. We would have a hearing. These people would come in and introduce testimony as to their financial ability, the nature and character of the programs they propose . . . and we would compare the two and decide which one of the two should have it.

Senator Dieterich. That is still so general that I do not understand what you take into consideration.

Commissioner Sykes. You take into consideration, of course, that they have got to have the financial ability to do it. They will go into the detail as to the nature and character of the programs that they propose to give to the people.

Senator Dieterich. Do you give preference to the stations who broadcast news, such as newspapers?

Commissioner Sykes. Oh, I think that is a very important item.

Senator Dieterich. And educational institutions?

Commissioner Sykes. Yes. Those things are gone into.[17]

The FCC also gave existing stations preference over new applications for licenses. Chairman Sykes claimed that court decisions had "practically" determined that if stations "are rendering a good service it gives them a preferential position. In other words, there is a sort of expectancy of renewal, provided their past conduct has been one of good service."[18] The courts, as we have seen, had in fact upheld the FRC's broad discretions without fettering the commission with such restraints. Over time the practical implications of these policies attracted increasing criticism from within and outside Congress.

The most immediate consequence of the FRC's reallocation of broadcast licenses was the escalation in the value of licenses. Fear of overcrowding and interference, coupled with FRC and FCC policies that favored existing stations, limited the supply of new broadcasting licenses at the same time that radio advertising revenues grew strongly. The result was that broadcast stations traded at prices many times the value of their physical assets. In 1936 CBS bought a station in California for $1.25 million, on a price-to-assets ratio of more than five. The most profitable stations commanded premiums of ten times the value of their assets. Radio stations were also leased for periods as long as 15 years, despite the fact that broadcasting licenses were valid for only six months at a time.[19]

Although the broadcasters and the FCC attributed these premiums to payments for goodwill, it was clear that the market had passed its own judgment on licensing renewal policies. The price premium represented the sale of the broadcasting license itself—which was specifically reserved to the people in perpetuity by the Radio Act of 1927 and the Communications Act of 1934. The FCC's critics accused it of abetting this trade in radio licenses through its preference to existing stations, which created strong expectations among potential purchasers that their investment was relatively safe, and through its announcement that it would not limit the amount of advertising and therefore the income-earning potential of a station. The result, as the *Nation* put it in 1937, was that the FCC had become "little more than a brokerage house or a trading post for the traffickers" of public property for private gain.[20]

Critics of the FCC during the 1930s also attacked it for continuing the FRC's bias toward the national networks. NBC, CBS, and then MBS all did very well out of the regulatory process during the FCC's first four years. Its emphasis upon high technical standards, continuous programming, and the financial standing of broadcasters worked in favor of the prosperous and well-equipped networks. Consequently the chains increased their control over the nation's broadcasting resources, from 32 percent of all stations in 1935 to 59 percent in 1940. When quizzed by senators in January 1935, Eugene Sykes admitted that the chains controlled 35 of the 40 cleared channels and the lion's share of total broadcast wattage. Pushed by Senator Burton K. Wheeler of Montana, who argued that the FCC had allowed the nation's airwaves to be controlled by the two major networks, and that it should limit their further expansion, Sykes replied, "We may have to do that some of these days."[21]

The FCC possessed four sanctions against licensees, of which three were used during the 1930s. The commission could revoke a broadcast license, but chose not to do so between 1934 and 1940. Instead it preferred to regulate stations through more subtle means, or, as Robert Landry put it in 1938, "to frighten rather than spank" errant licensees.[22] If it was dissatisfied with a station's programming or technical performance, the FCC could put it on probation by renewing its license for two months instead of six, or it could reassign the station to a less desirable wavelength or to limited broadcast hours. If the commissioners took exception to a specific program by a licensee, they generally responded with their fourth sanction: a stern letter advising a mending of ways before the next license renewal. Erik Barnouw described this as regulation through "the raised eyebrow."[23]

The most celebrated raising of the eyebrow occurred at the end of 1937. On December 12 NBC ran its regular Charlie McCarthy program, which featured a comedian and his ventriloquist's dummy. In this episode, however, guest star Mae West performed a routine about Adam and Eve, which was enlivened by grunts, sighs, and comments that many listeners found to be indecent. Letters of protest flooded in to stations, NBC, the FCC, and the NAB. FCC Chairman Frank McNinch told NBC that the skit fell "far below even the minimum standards which should control in the selection and production of broadcast material." He went on to repeat the familiar threat that the FCC would "take under consideration this incident along with all other evidence tending to show whether or not a particular licensee has conducted his station in the public interest." McNinch even threatened to hold affiliate stations, who were contractually obliged to take the program and who had no means of vetting it beforehand, responsible.[24] After a public apology from NBC, and the banishment of Mae West from its airwaves, the FCC's eyebrow subsided without further action.

McNinch also took exception to the expression "Oh, my God!" in a NBC broadcast of Eugene O'Neill's *Beyond the Horizon*. This, the chairman wrote, was profane, and illegal under section 326. This time NBC produced a Catholic clergyman's opinion that the expression was not profane but rather an anguished call for spiritual guidance, and it was excused. Stations running programs on birth control, astrology, and betting odds, or advertisements for patent medicines also received warnings and shortened licenses from the FCC during the 1930s.[25] That the FCC's eyebrow twitched only infrequently is testimony to the close relationship between broadcasters and regulators that had developed since 1927. Over time broadcasters learned the limits of the FRC's, and then the FCC's, tolerance regarding programming content, and practiced editorial control to avoid the commission's ire. At the end of 1936 the ACLU surveyed 25 cases in which licensees prevented various individuals and groups from using their facilities. "The restriction on free speech on the radio has been catholic," the ACLU concluded. "Radicals, liberals and even the Republican Party have suffered. Minority political parties, doctors seeking to warn the public of syphilis, trade unions and opponents of lynching have all felt the censor's hand." Licensees examined and cut scripts before broadcasts, cut off speakers in the middle of their programs, and hid controversial speakers in unpopular time slots.

Radio stations had good reasons to control the content of their programs. Controversial and unpopular material risked alienating listeners and reducing advertising revenues. Licensees also argued that, because they were not common carriers, their right to control programs was as absolute as that of a newspaper owner.[26] Because the FCC refused to define "public interest, convenience, or necessity," and because it operated retrospectively, licensees tended to err on the side of caution in selecting programs. This arrangement served to protect both broadcasters and the FCC at the expense of those whose views were deemed too controversial to be broadcast. The FCC could argue that it did not censor stations, and licensees could be confident that the commission would renew their licenses. Inherent in this arrangement was a consensus that stations served the public interest when they broadcast programs that supported rather than challenged majority cultural and political views, and that regulators and licensees shared the same conceptions of "good taste" and "public interest."

These understandings were created and consolidated through the close relationships that developed between the FCC and industry groups such as the NAB. Sometimes the NAB did the FCC's dirty work in disciplining and censoring stations. In 1940 the NAB Code Compliance Committee reported that Father Coughlin had been banished from the airwaves as a result of the "*voluntary* adherence to the NAB Code by the stations themselves." The committee noted with satisfaction that the silencing of Coughlin, who had long been a thorn in the sides of both the FCC and the Roosevelt administration, had occurred without publicity and without the FCC. The NAB did not explore the implications of its assumption of censorship powers that had been specifically denied to the public body entrusted with radio regulation, and doubtless the FCC was grateful that it had been relieved of the necessity to worry further about Coughlin's anti-Semitic and anti-Roosevelt broadcasts.[27]

The networks retained representatives in Washington to lobby the FCC, and the NAB kept its members informed about developments. Well aware that they earned their revenues from a free license of a public asset, the networks had strong reasons for keeping a close eye on the workings and personnel of the commission. On the other hand, local and unaffiliated stations far from Washington came into direct contact with the FCC only every six months through license renewals, and rarely appeared before the commission. The result was that the FCC tended to regulate networks and their stations through personal contact, and others outside the favored circle through sporadic letters and pro forma hearings.[28] Relations were also made closer through a revolving door between the commission and the major networks. This was particularly common in the legal sections of both commissions. By 1935 at least six senior former FCC attorneys represented networks and other broadcasters in commission proceedings. The Washington law firm of Littlepage and Littlepage, which specialized in FCC matters, was an eager recruiter of commission attorneys. One FCC lawyer moved from his position as assistant general counsel in the FRC to become a partner in Littlepage and Littlepage, and then returned as the commission's chief counsel two years later.[29]

This was neither illegal nor necessarily unethical, and to some extent it was the product of the specialized nature of radio law and the small number of its qualified and experienced practitioners. The same phenomenon had occurred during the early days of the federal income tax, and had been addressed by a rule preventing former Treasury attorneys from arguing cases in front of their old colleagues for a year after their resignations. Former FCC employees, however, escaped such restriction during the 1930s. Commissioner Sykes told his Senate confirmation hearing in 1935 that he saw no problem and much good sense in the practice. Senator Wheeler doubtless exaggerated the situation when he told him, "It is my recollection, although I may be wrong about it, that almost every time anybody ceased to occupy a position on or with the [FRC] he immediately turned up as the representative of some of the broadcasting companies, and that then those people would represent them a while and would be put back on the . . . Commission again." Yet Wheeler's comment reflected a general view among many critics of the FRC and FCC that they were too close to the broadcasters. The FCC's 1935 warning to its staff that they could not accept gifts or favors from broadcasters strengthened suspicions that this amity could lead to outright corruption.[30]

The FCC and Its Critics

By 1937 a broad coalition of interests had lost patience with the FCC. The result was that by 1940 the commission was besieged by its enemies and deserted by its friends. Rather than protecting the public interest, Paul Ward argued in 1937, "the commission has set itself up as the guardian angel . . . of those who are exploiting the last great resource in much the same fashion that our water, timber, land, oil, and mineral resources have been exploited and despoiled." The FCC, according to Ward, had become "one of the most corrupt federal agencies in history," showing favoritism to its pet law firms and the networks. Under its stewardship, which cost the public $1.5 million a year and the industry nothing, the networks had tightened their stranglehold over American broadcasting and profiteers had trafficked broadcast licenses for huge sums, secure in the knowledge that their investments were safe in the FCC's hands.[31]

Ward's criticisms reflected growing congressional sentiment that the FCC required urgent investigation. During 1937 a group of lawmakers, led by Senators Wheeler and Borah, and Congressmen William McFarlane of Texas and Lawrence Connery of Massachusetts, pressed for hearings into the FCC and its treatment of the networks. McFarlane and Connery sponsored a House resolution to this end in 1937, but administration pressure saw it languish in the House Rules Committee.[32] Rather than agree to an open-ended congressional investigation, FDR attempted to head off criticism of the FCC by changing its personnel. "Quite confidentially," the president's secretary Marvin McIntyre wrote to Wetmore Hodges in July 1937, "this commission is one of the sore spots." The recent death of Chairman Prall had worsened the situation, and "we have felt that a strong man to fill the existing vacancy would go far toward rectifying the whole situation."[33] FDR eventually got his strong man on the FCC, but it was not to be Hodges, who declined the invitation.

The FCC also came under fire over censorship. Acting on administration concerns about fascist propaganda from Europe, the commission in 1936 issued an order forbidding rebroadcast without FCC permission of foreign programs by American stations. This was the first time that the FCC had dropped its usual argument that it had no power to censor programs, and it represented a significant change in the commission's public position on freedom of the air. Civil libertarians were outraged; the *Nation* accused the FCC of using Hitlerian methods to combat a largely imaginary problem. Some German and Italian propaganda did reach American radios, but mainly through direct shortwave transmissions rather than rebroadcasting.[34]

The FCC even came under criticism from the broadcasters during the late 1930s. Many broadcasters became worried that the commission, and especially its new appointments, were disturbing the old understandings that had governed radio regulation since 1927. Most of all, the broadcasters were concerned that, finally, the New Deal might be catching up with radio. Sensing battles ahead, the NAB tripled its annual budget and installed a full-time secretariat in 1938 to argue its case more effectively to the FCC and Congress.[35] The industry's concerns were heightened by the FCC's reaction to the Mae West episode, because McNinch had appeared to disregard the facts of radio life by holding affiliate stations responsible for the content of network programming. Although the FCC's threats over the incident came to nothing, they represented the most public indication of tension between the industry and its regulators, and the beginning of a new era in FCC-station relations.[36]

Under attack from all sides, the FCC responded in a number of ways. It first attempted to pacify critics who accused it of improperly favoring commercial broadcasters and superpower stations. In 1938 the commission repudiated its earlier policy of refusing to reserve any channels for educational broadcasters, and provided 25 channels for school broadcasting. In the following year it also announced a new license allocation system to limit the number of cleared channels available to high-powered broadcasters. The commission then quietened industry protests about the frequency of license renewals by extending the normal license period from six months to a full year. The FCC also responded to criticism about the vagueness of its "raised eyebrow" by codifying objectionable forms of programming. In 1939 it announced that stations would be held accountable for 14 kinds of programming, including material that included religious and racial intolerance, fortune telling, favorable mention of hard liquor, torture, too much advertising, false information or quackery, and one-sided discussions of controversial issues. Obscenity, profanity, and defamation were also forbidden under the FCC's 14 commandments.[37]

The FCC also moved to limit network domination of the airwaves. In March 1938 the commission finally activated its power under section 303(i) to control chain broadcasting by announcing an inquiry into the desirability of rules to restrain the growth of networks. Four FCC commissioners began hearing submissions between November 1938 and May 1939, and in the process precipitated a breach between the commission and the major broadcasters that would last until the early 1950s. The FCC's *Report on Chain Broadcasting*, released in May 1941, represented a watershed in the commission's short history and a partial declaration of independence from the industry groups that had so effectively captured it.

President Roosevelt's appointment of James Fly to replace Frank McNinch as chairman of the FCC strained relations even further. In many ways Fly's appointment represented the long-delayed arrival of the New Deal to broadcast regulation. Appointed in February 1939, while the FCC was hearing testimony on chain broadcasting, Fly quickly asserted himself as a new type of chairman. Gone was the amiable associationalism of his predecessors. Instead, Fly was determined that the FCC would take its place within the New Deal governmental order as an instrument for the democratization of radio and for the trimming of excessive private corporate power. He was also quite prepared to operate in close cooperation with the White House and enjoyed the president's strong support.

It appears that FDR used Fly as a lightning rod, encouraging him to undertake the ill-fated newspaper ownership inquiry and to push the chain broadcasting investigation. By May 1941 the broadcasters and Fly were at each other's throats; the NAB described his policies as "punitive, capricious, biased and destructive," while the chairman famously returned the favor by describing the industry's leadership as akin to "a dead mackerel in the moonlight-it both shines and stinks."[38]

The immediate cause of the NAB's outrage was the *Report on Chain Broadcasting.* Compared to the FCC's previous investigations, the 1941 report was a radical document. All seven of its major recommendations involved attacks upon the networks and their privileges. The report represented a revival of the Brandeisian policies of the early New Deal, and aimed to allow affiliate stations to correspond more closely to what Erik Barnouw described as the idealized conception that "American broadcasting was a local responsibility exercised by individual station licensees."[39] The report recommended that affiliates could be bound to networks only on a nonexclusive basis and only for periods of one year. Networks could no longer control affiliates' time through options, and individual stations should be given the right to vet network programs to give them an opportunity to avoid a repetition of the Mae West incident. The most significant changes wrought by the report lay in its recommendation that a licensee be prohibited from owning more than one network and more than one station in a broadcast area.[40] The FCC agreed to the substance of all the report's major recommendations and proceeded to implement them in 1942.

The two oldest networks reacted with outrage, arguing that the whole "American system" of broadcasting was at risk. CBS declared that the FCC threatened to "cripple, if it does not paralyze, broadcasting as a national service at a time when radio should be encouraged to continue and enlarge its contribution to national unity and morale."[41] The networks had grown powerful because they had best implemented both listener sovereignty and radio exceptionalism, CBS complained, and now the New Dealers had ruined it all.

NBC responded even more strongly, for the FCC report was a direct attack upon its corporate structure. Under the commission's recommendations NBC stood to lose either its Red or Blue network, and so it rushed to court to challenge them. In 1943, however, the U.S. Supreme Court rejected the network's submissions and upheld the FCC's right to force divestiture in the interests of the "public interest, convenience, or necessity." That formula, Justice Felix Frankfurter held, was a "supple instrument for the exercise of discretion by the expert body which Congress has charged to carry out its legislative policy."[42] In October 1943 NBC complied by selling its less profitable network, the Blue, to Edward J. Noble and the American Broadcasting Company for $8 million.

Radio and the Interwar Regulatory Experience

In January 1941 James Fly contributed an article on radio regulation to the *Annals of the American Academy of Political and Social Science.* Belying his reputation as the nemesis of the American system, Fly's conception of the proper form and extent of radio regulation differed little from that put forward by the Hooverian associationalists and practiced by the FRC and FCC after 1927. His article showed the fundamental continuities in the radio regulatory experience spanning Harding's Normalcy, Hoover's New Era, and Franklin Roosevelt's New Deal. Although Fly's tenure as chairman of the FCC forced structural changes upon the networks, and particularly upon NBC, it did not fundamentally challenge the theory or practice of radio regulation that had been established by the Radio Act of 1927.

Fly discussed the possibility that the federal government might emulate the Australian and Canadian models by funding stations in competition with commercial operators. He rejected this idea because it rested on two faulty assumptions. The first was that private broadcasters and the federal government had "different opinions," and the second was that radio could only reflect diverse opinions through diversity in its ownership. If this were true, Fly argued, the problem of diversity "would not be resolved merely by having government and private stations; it would be necessary to have Republican, Democratic, prohibitionist, labor union, chamber of commerce, old age pension, and numerous other varieties." Inevitably, some groups or individuals would be left out because of the limitations of the broadcast band. Therefore, Fly argued in a Hooverian way, those stations fortunate enough to be licensed would become "special interest stations—engaged essentially in the service of private, not public, purposes."

It was pointless, Fly continued, for radio reformers to aspire to a freedom of the air that was equal to freedom of the press. Society championed freedom of the press because the ability to publish material was limited only by the supply of readers; "if printing presses were few and their output severely limited, a democratic society surely could not allow small groups of owners unlimited discretion as to what is and what is not printed." This was exactly the problem faced by radio broadcasters, their regulators, and their audiences. "A prospective radio speaker is not a publisher who can always find a printing press and run off a few extra pages; radio channels are limited and broadcast time cannot be stretched beyond twenty-four hours a day. . . . My own view is that a free market in ideas over the air can be attained without special interest stations and without the creation of a multitude of propaganda stations."[43]

Had the networks not been preoccupied with lobbying against the chain broadcasting inquiry, they might have taken comfort from this statement. Fly's message was both clear and familiar, repeating the same nostrums about special interests, public benefit, and the advantages of private ownership that the industry called the "American system" of broadcasting. Even the *Report on Chain Broadcasting*, despite its assault upon the contractual privileges of the networks, had not significantly undermined the dominance of network radio. The FCC report had loosened the bonds between affiliates and networks, and had caused a change in ownership of NBC's Blue chain, but it had not materially improved the competitive position of independent broadcasters. Despite its Brandeisian rhetoric, the report fell far short of transforming broadcasting into a vibrant collection of small, independent, and local stations. The New Deal as applied to broadcasting had not smashed the broadcast oligopoly but instead had simply expanded it. The FCC's refusal to take any steps to limit cross-ownership between newspapers and radio stations in 1944 only confirmed the suspicion that, regarding radio, the New Deal's bark was worse than its bite.

In 1946 Morris Ernst of the ACLU bemoaned these lost opportunities. The chain broadcasting and cross-ownership investigations had allowed the "two main streams of concentration" in broadcasting to flow without impediment:

> The first concentration leads to conscious and unconscious filtering of programs and news through the narrows of big business and big advertisers' requirements. The tightness of the bottleneck results in programs of low mental but high numerical appeal and in innocuous subject matter. The second concentration accounts for the predominance of Hollywood and New York attitudes, *mores* and taste in the programs of the nation. . . . In a real open market the present dominant influences might be pre-

ferred by the public, but it would then be a preference expressed in a competitive market place of listeners with critical judgment.[44]

Why did the theory and practice of radio regulation prove so durable after 1924? Clayton Koppes argued in 1969 that radio control was born an orphan in American political history, coming too late to be directly influenced by progressivism but too early to be a creature of the New Deal.[45] As we have seen, however, the broadcast industry came into being during the reaction against progressivism, and was nurtured by Hooverian associationalism between 1920 and 1927. Despite the efforts of those who advocated the public utility, or the British or the Australian regulatory models, broadcast regulation was largely frozen in its associationalist form by the Radio Act of 1927 and then by the Communications Act of 1934.

Although these statutes replaced the executive regulation of 1920–27 with supposedly independent commissions, they did little to change the structure of the industry. Convinced that the genius of American inventors, entrepreneurs, and competition would produce the best broadcasting industry for American conditions, Hoover's limited conception of his role as a radio traffic cop proved to be seductive. Broadcasters reveled in the autonomy that such regulatory restraint gave them, and they proceeded to transform what was a hobby in 1920 into a fully commercialized and highly profitable national industry by 1927. Once ceded, this autonomy became protected by increasingly powerful interest groups, which fended off major challenges to it until the early 1940s.

Commercial broadcasters, having created the "American system" and championed their versions of its two central elements of radio exceptionalism and listener sovereignty, suffered only two statutory defeats during the 1920s—the creation of the FRC and the passage of the Davis Amendment—of which only the latter proved to be damaging to their interests. The major broadcasters also showed themselves to be adept at avoiding the New Deal until the very end of the 1930s. When reform finally came knocking on the commercial broadcasters' door, it came not as a concerted attempt to install publicly owned broadcasting or to direct more firmly the content of radio programming, but rather as a crimped neo-Brandeisian program designed to modulate, but not replace, the balance of power between networks and affiliates. The recommendations of the *Report on Chain Broadcasting* were easily accommodated by the network structure; in 1940 networks and their affiliates accounted for 59 percent of all AM broadcasting stations, and by 1945 it was 95 percent.[46] The failure of the cross-ownership investigation only attested to the power of the major commercial broadcasters and their counterparts in the printed media to protect their interests, investments, and privileges.

Many factors contributed to the commercial broadcasters' success. As Robert McChesney has argued, broadcasters were often assisted by their opponents' failure to develop a coherent alternative vision for radio, and by their tendency to fragment into competing groups.[47] It is also clear that the radio reformers failed to excite a broad revolt against commercial radio and its programming. Most listeners seem to have been either supportive of or apathetic about the quality of their programming, and therefore were not receptive to any change that involved listener levies. The commercial broadcasters were also skillful in publicizing both the benefits and the indigenous quality of the "American system" of broadcasting, and in stigmatizing the reformers as statist, intrusive, culturally condescending, and un-American. The NBC listener who wrote to praise a program by wondering "why we don't have to pay for this" encapsulated the greatest advantage of the "American system." By funding itself through invisible costs and by regulating itself through state-sanctioned associationalism, the machine seemed to run itself, cloaked in the rhetoric of free speech and open access.

The commercial broadcasters also managed the political process far better than the reformers. Originally backed by some of the country's most powerful corporations, and speedily evolving their own resources and representative groups, the radio lobby emerged as a vocal and well-funded force in federal legislative and administrative forums. Commercial broadcasters were also blessed by the nature of their medium, which provided them with the opportunities both to reward their political friends and to punish their enemies. Radio offered politicians across the United States unprecedented opportunities for publicity and advertising, as well as the frightening possibility that its power might be denied them or, worse, granted to their rivals. Although they were dependent upon the state to save them from mutual interference and overcrowding, and from the demands of those who opposed commercial and networked broadcasting, the broadcasters were not merely hostages of the political process. Politicians of all persuasions quickly realized that they needed radio as much as it needed them.

Part II

Radio and the Business of Politics, 1920–1940

Give me control of the air that a man breathes, and he shall drop his opinion and adopt my opinion and he shall vote as I vote.

—HUDSON MAXIM, 1924

7

The Sellers

Stations, Networks, and Political Broadcasting

In October 1922 the *Wireless Age* announced that broadcasting, then only two years old, had created a new political era. Radio provided Americans with a new form of communication that would bypass the partisanship of newspapers to create a direct bond between voters, candidates, and office holders. Already broadcasting's potential had been made clear; had Woodrow Wilson been able to broadcast to Americans about the League of Nations he might well have been spared the stroke that incapacitated him. "Equally, Senators Lodge and Borah and other Republicans opposed to the league could have delivered their words directly into the ears of the same country-wide audience. And instead of partisan prejudice, as imperfectly reflected in the newspapers, the citizens . . . would have had the facts and opinions of each side direct from the mouths of the leaders." Henceforth "no vital issue can be decided fairly in this country . . . without the use of the radio telephone."[1]

Many politicians, political commentators, and social analysts agreed that radio offered a solution to a problem that had bothered political theorists and practitioners since the earliest days of the republic: that of informing citizens, and creating consensus among them, across geographic expanse, ethnic and cultural diversity, and partisan division. Soon, radio's boosters promised, all Americans would be able to hear their president and to join important national occasions such as inaugurations, congressional debates, and State of the Union addresses. As voters, they could also make more informed choices from broadcasts beamed into their homes at times best suited to relaxed and attentive listening. Examination of broadcasters' policies and practices regarding political programming and advertising reveals much about the ways in which stations and networks perceived their role in interwar political culture, as well as the tensions that accompanied their attempts to reconcile their rhetoric of public service with the reality of conducting commercial operations at a profit.

Early Political Broadcasting

Political programming caused problems for a number of early broadcasters. New York City's municipal station WNYC was dogged by controversy from its establishment in 1924. Suspicions that the station was a propaganda outlet for Mayor John F. Hylan engulfed the station in dispute and litigation. WNYC and the Hylan administration argued strenuously that the station would remain nonpartisan, but its professed neutrality came under increasing attack in 1925. *Radio Broadcast* argued that Hylan had used the station to further his own political fortunes and had placed improper restrictions upon his opponents' use of its facilities. "Evidently the taxpayer in New York has no redress; if he doesn't want to hear what a wonderful mayor the city has had for the last seven years and reasons for putting him back in office, his only recourse is to tune-in on other channels."[2] Government radio stations and political contests coexisted more harmoniously in Wisconsin, where state-owned WHA and WLBL broadcast all candidates free of charge with strict equality of time. Broadcast times were chosen by lot, and censorship was forbidden except for an agreement that discussion should be limited to state issues.[3]

Censorship of political material was not, however, unknown during the early days of broadcasting. In 1924 Hans Kaltenborn, the first radio news analyst, was taken off WEAF New York after Secretary of State Charles Evans Hughes objected to his opinion that the United States should recognize the Soviet Union. WEAF also refused in 1926 to broadcast Norman Thomas because of his opposition to compulsory military training. In 1927 the pacifist Mary Ford was cut off by WGL in the middle of her speech denouncing war, as was the socialist Victor Berger by WJZ. To such examples must also be added a much greater number of cases in which stations simply refused to broadcast some events and speakers. A Boston station, for example, denied airtime to an antiprohibition rally, because it thought that it was too controversial.[4]

Prior to the Radio Act of 1927 broadcasters had no legal guidance for their treatment of political broadcasting and advertising. The Radio Act of 1912, passed long before broadcasting began, was silent on the issue, and Herbert Hoover did not venture into such controversial territory between 1921 and 1927. Hoover's reticence did not, however, completely defuse the issue. After a brief flurry of Republican radio campaigning before the 1922 primaries, and strong Democratic protests at what they saw as politicization of governmental radio facilities, President Harding decided that no political speeches would be transmitted by federally owned stations.

Federal lawmakers addressed political broadcasting in 1927 with much trepidation. Debates over what eventually became section 18 of the Radio Act of 1927 were marked by concern over equality of access for all parties and candidates.[5] The legislators opted for a provision that gave minimal protection for political advertising; if a station chose to accept advertising from a candidate, it had to accept advertising from all his or her rivals, and it was forbidden to censor such material. Section 18, which was reiterated almost verbatim in section 315 of the Communications Act of 1934, did not require licensees to accept political advertising, nor did it oblige them to charge candidates the same rates as other advertisers.[6]

Sections 18 and 315 ensured equality of opportunity but not of outcome, and by failing to require broadcasters to provide free time for political advertising the legislators left the issue to be decided between buyers and sellers. No effort was made to ensure that poorer candidates or parties would be able to compete with better-off competitors, and no attempt was made to ensure uniformity across the nation. Sections 18 and 315 therefore did not disturb the balance of power within American political culture, whereby some parties and some candidates were more able to take advantage of radio advertising than others.[7]

In keeping with the limited scope of sections 18 and 315, both the FRC and the FCC were reluctant to promulgate regulations relating to political broadcasting. The FRC issued only one regulation concerning section 18, a warning to licensees that violation of the section would be sufficient grounds for license revocation. At the beginning of the 1932 political campaigns, FRC Acting Chairman Harold Lafount exhorted licensees to "be as liberal with their facilities as their government has been with them." Although Lafount acknowledged that stations were under no legal obligation to air political programming and advertising, he urged them to do so in the spirit of public service and good government.[8] The FCC issued three rules concerning section 315 between 1934 and 1940, defining a "legally qualified candidate," forbidding discrimination in the rates charged candidates, and requiring stations to maintain public records of requests for political advertising. It did not, however, direct stations to charge political and nonpolitical advertisers the same rates, and it did not require licensees to provide candidates with equally attractive broadcast times.[9]

In 1935 Democratic Congressman Byron Scott of California proposed amendments to section 315 to rectify what he saw as its major shortcomings. Noting that the section entrenched the power of wealth in American political life "to the prejudice of minority groups and individuals of small means," Scott argued that it had created "greater and greater confusion and disillusionment as to the value and use of radio as a means of public discussion." Section 315 was "fundamentally unsound in assuming that the public desires only the uncensored discussions on social, economic, and political issues of legally qualified candidates for office." In fact, Scott maintained, political discussion and advertising should not be restricted to short campaign seasons or to a small number of candidates.

Scott's amendments required licensees to schedule regular times for discussion of "social, political and economic problems." Stations were to divide this time equally among supporters and opponents of issues, and in return would be absolved of any liability arising from such discussions. Although Scott's proposal went further than Senator Dill's proposed amendments in 1934, it did not direct stations to devote time to political advertising. As it had done in 1934, however, the industry strenuously opposed any broadening of section 315, and Scott's amendments died in the House. Section 315 survived untouched until 1960, when Congress suspended its equal treatment provisions to allow broadcasters to exclude minor party candidates from the presidential debates of that year.[10]

Broadcasters' Policies on Political Programs and Advertising

Stations and networks were thus left largely to their own devices in determining their attitudes toward political material. For some licensees, wary of political programming and uninterested in its revenue, the decision was easy: they would broadcast no politics at all. For the vast majority of stations, however, political material offered opportunities not only to earn money but also to demonstrate their commitment to public service. In a survey of 23 local stations across the country in 1928, the *New York Times* found only two that refused political advertising altogether.[11] For the others, and for the national networks, political programming and advertisement policy was dictated by an often complex mixture of motives.

AT&T, in the process of setting up its national broadcasting system at the end of 1923, was a pioneer in political broadcasting policy. "When we considered the political situation we knew we were handling dynamite," William Harkness reminisced years later. "With a national election coming on in the near future, we knew we would be besieged with both local and national candidates desiring service which we realized could not be furnished without interfering with other commitments." Already sensitive about its image, AT&T wanted to avoid the perception that it was playing political favorites.[12] At the end of 1923 it decided to broadcast both major parties' nominating conventions for a fee, and then charge candidates for time after the conventions. In order to avoid an endless stream of requests from individual candidates, the company announced that it would deal only with the parties' national committees. The Democrats, short of funds, argued that broadcasters, and not the parties, should pay for the privilege of broadcasting conventions. The Republican National Committee (RNC) undermined its rival's argument by offering its convention to AT&T without charge, forcing the Democrats to follow suit.[13]

RCA and GEC also grappled with political broadcasting before the 1924 campaigns. They, too, were sensitive to the potential for bad publicity arising from any hint of political favoritism. When Republican Congressman James MacLafferty from California requested time on GEC's station KGO for "two or three" talks to his constituents, company officials politely declined. If they broadcast MacLafferty they would feel obliged to broadcast his opponents, and "eventually our broadcasting stations might become so popular as political arenas that our educational and musical programs would be crowded out."[14]

By the middle of June 1924 the major broadcasting companies had developed a common policy on political broadcasting. AT&T, RCA, Westinghouse, and GEC agreed that they would deal primarily with the two major parties, although requests from other parties would be dealt with on their merits. The companies also agreed that they would broadcast addresses only from "speakers of national prominence and dealing with policies and candidacies of more than local interest," and that speakers would be asked, but not required, to submit their scripts in advance. They also limited political programming to an hour per day, and to negotiate only with national party committees.[15] These policies, which privileged national issues, the two major parties, and candidates for federal office, became the basis for all political broadcasting during the interwar period.

These rules did not escape criticism. Those in more marginal political groups considered the radio group's agreement to be little more than a censorious cartel. Senator Robert LaFollette, who had accepted the 1924 presidential nomination from the Progressive Party, claimed throughout the campaign that he had been excluded from the airwaves by the "radio trust" fearful of his antimonopoly and progressive platform. RCA, for its part, denied that the Progressives had made any real attempt to request airtime, and pointed out that it had broadcast Mrs. LaFollette during the campaign "in order to have one Progressive at least on our programs." Although LaFollette died and his party collapsed soon after the 1924 election, the controversy confirmed the need for broadcasters to develop policies that were seen to be fair and impartial.[16]

Radio broadcasting during the 1924 political season, and especially that of the sensational Democratic convention in New York, demonstrated the effectiveness of these policies. RCA stations devoted more than 17 hours to the Republican convention and 110 hours to the prolonged Democratic meeting in New York, and stations owned by AT&T, Westinghouse, and GEC also brought almost complete coverage of the conventions to their listeners.[17] Charles Popenoe, who was in charge of RCA's political programs in 1924, found that he could not fill his hour per day, and so reduced political programming to four fifteen-minute periods per week, "with a special event thrown in occasionally for good luck." By the end of the campaign Popenoe had distributed 35 fifteen-minute slots almost equally between the DNC and RNC, with the Republicans receiving the 35th.[18]

Proof of the interest in radio politics came on election night, when nearly 400 stations broadcast the results. Only four years previously, solitary KDKA had begun the radio age in the same way. Many stations dedicated the whole night of November 4, 1924 to the election, interspersing updates with musical performances until the early hours of the morning. The 1924 radio campaign, and its frequent use of telephone hookups between stations, also hastened the creation of permanent networking. Propelled by increased demand for interconnection, AT&T widened its recently created National Broadcasting System by establishing permanent wire links between WEAF New York and stations in Providence, Buffalo, Pittsburgh, and Chicago.

The 1924 campaigns also helped stations to clarify their positions on censorship. Uncertain of their legal position, and anxious to maintain decorum in their programming, the major broadcasters asked for advance copies of radio addresses to ensure that their facilities would not be used to disseminate treasonous, obscene, or libelous material. In 1924, however, it appears that this rule was not strictly observed. RCA also threatened political speakers that they would be cut off if "unnecessary denunciation was indulged in," but this precaution did not prove to be necessary. Many local stations followed the same procedure. One Boston station announced in August 1924 that candidates using its facilities must speak politely, and that "a man may talk about what he stands for, what his party stands for, etc, but he may not revile or attack his political opponent or any other party."[19] It is not clear how these restrictions were enforced, if at all, and they tended to disappear as broadcasters grew more used to political programming.

Rumors that stations censored radio addresses were common, but usually originated in technical or weather problems that temporarily interrupted transmission. One listener accused WOR (Newark, New Jersey) of repeatedly cutting power during a speech by Congressman Hill of Alabama at the Democratic convention. "He was continuously cut off in the midst of words and sentences," Ralph Guinness of Allentown, Pennsylvania, complained. "When 'oil scandals' or 'predatory interests' were mentioned without reference to the Republican Party the sentence went over uncensored but when he said 'the Republican Party was dominated by the predatory ——,' he was cut off." Given the difficulties faced by radio technicians in transmitting speeches at all, it seems most unlikely that such deliberate editing actually occurred.[20] The only documented attempt at censorship at the 1924 conventions came from the Democrats themselves, who insisted on the right to switch off the microphones to avoid broadcasting politically damaging material. This right was not exercised during the convention, which was marked by almost continuous political embarrassment and divisiveness, and the right was not asserted at subsequent conventions.[21]

Networks and Political Programming

Although many of the rules for political broadcasting had been set during the 1924 campaign, three major developments caused broadcasters to rethink their policies after 1925. The triumph of commercial broadcasting meant that airtime became a valuable commodity to be apportioned between political and commercial advertisers. Because political organizations sought time only during particular periods of some years, their requirements caused great disruption to broadcasters who had sold blocks of time to commercial advertisers for periods as long as six months. The second great change was the advent of the national networks. The formation of NBC in 1926 and CBS in 1928 provided parties with highly attractive facilities, and the growing dominance of the networks over local and independent stations meant that the new chains had to deal with political programming very carefully. Finally, the passage of the Radio Act of 1927 forced stations and networks to modify their own policies to comply with section 18.

At first NBC was content to operate under the policies devised by RCA

Who's elected?

Surging crowds in the streets — the suspense of waiting — first one candidate in the lead, then the other — an outlying section upsets predictions — at last a message from the "choice of the people." The immediate thrill of it all, formerly confined to political headquarters, now goes into every home equipped with the foremost, reliable radio receiving set.

RCA

This symbol of quality is your protection

Radiola

TRADE MARK REG. U.S. PAT. OFF.

"*There's a* **Radiola** *for every purse*"

From $25 to $350. See your nearest RCA dealer today.

233 Broadway, New York

"Who's Elected?" Elections early in the radio age allowed manufacturers to push their products and to encourage the idea of a new radio citizenship. RCA advertisement, 1922. Reproduced from the Owen D. Young Collection, file 106, folder 230A, St. Lawrence University, Canton, New York.

and the other members of the radio group. As part of its commitment to public service, NBC committed itself to political programs and advertising. It also confirmed that it would cover nominating conventions without charge, but would at other times sell time at normal commercial rates to the national committees of both major parties. Merlin Aylesworth, president of the new network, announced in 1927 that his company would broadcast any candidate who had the money, except those whom he described as "the recluse, the intellectually superior person who voluntarily separates himself from the living, breathing, moving America. . . . The complete reactionary—those who oppose progress. The complete radical who is 'agin the government' no matter what it does."[22]

This policy had to be changed in 1928. NBC's attractiveness to commercial advertisers meant that the network's sponsored time was quickly tied up in long-term contracts. It thus became important to assure advertisers that their time would not be preempted by political speeches and advertisements. NBC decided that it would accept political advertising only between the end of the nominating conventions and election day during presidential election years, and that it would broadcast other political programming only as long as it could do so without prejudice to its commercial commitments.[23] The passage of the Radio Act and section 18 in 1927 forced NBC to include radical parties on its list of potential political advertisers, and to include their conventions in its free programming.

Juggling the interests of commercial and political advertisers between July and November of each quadrennium caused NBC and CBS a good deal of effort and sometimes embarrassment. Commercial and political advertisers all wanted the most attractive time slots, which were in the evening hours. Once the political parties had requested times to broadcast campaign speeches, the networks had to cajole commercial advertisers to make way. Companies were persuaded to give up their times in the name of public service, and in return for refunds or alternative time slots. These negotiations were time-consuming and frustrating for the networks, and often extremely irritating to advertisers, because the DNC and RNC frequently made last minute requests for large amounts of time. Network executives were also exasperated by politicians' failure to keep to their allotted time. Many speakers allowed their speeches to exceed their agreed length and to impinge upon yet more sponsored time. Although NBC at first hesitated to cut off long-winded speakers, it did go to considerable trouble to remind them to be punctual. They were not always successful, and prolix politicians caused angry sponsors, harried executives, and, often, furious listeners.[24]

NBC sent letters of thanks to all affected advertisers at the end of each campaign, noting with relief that life could now return to normal. Political broadcasting created "a very delicate situation," it told sponsors in 1932, which required the cooperation of commercial advertisers in the interests of good government and democracy. "Naturally we are not unmindful of the embarrassment of sudden cancellation of sponsored programs during this campaign but . . . the two great parties are of the opinion that Radio is so powerful as a means of communication to the American public that they evidently are determined to fight out the battle on the air."[25]

The free broadcast of the Republican and Democratic conventions also involved considerable financial sacrifice to NBC and CBS. In 1928 NBC broadcast 44 hours from both conventions, and in 1932 it devoted more than 46 hours to the Democratic convention alone, canceling 37 commercial programs and paying the relay costs from Chicago to 86 stations across the nation. Aylesworth and other NBC executives described these costs, which in 1932 they valued at $596,000, as their contribution to the nation's political education.[26] This sum, which represented the potential commercial value of the time devoted to convention broadcasts, was inflated. Much of the coverage came out of sustaining time, and many sponsors donated their slots without demanding refunds.

Those sponsors whose time periods were unaffected paid handsomely to reach the national radio convention audience; in 1928 NBC and CBS charged advertisers $11,500 and $4,000 per hour respectively during the conventions.[27] The networks' pecuniary loss was also offset by the goodwill that such service generated in the White House, on Capitol Hill, and among listeners. "We have received as a result of the broadcast of the conventions," a NBC memorandum noted in July 1932, "five times as much mail as we have ever received on any previous national sustaining program." The great majority of this mail was commendatory, although some listeners objected. One sent a telegram to NBC complaining that "as a regular listener of Amos'n'Andy I wish to enter a vigorous protest against further encroachment on their time by political blah."[28]

The networks also donated broadcasts of presidential nominees' notification ceremonies, election returns, and inaugurations. Broadcasts of inaugurations became progressively more extensive and sophisticated, as both networks tried to impress listeners with their technological prowess. CBS's coverage of FDR's second inauguration in January 1937, for example, involved a blimp, 26 broadcast points, two mobile transmitters, and a relay transmitter in the tip of the Washington Monument.[29] NBC and CBS also competed to deliver the most up-to-date figures on election night. For the election of 1932, NBC began its coverage at 8 A.M., and suspended its regular programming between 6 P.M. and 2 A.M. for continuous election news and commentary.[30]

Learning from each election, the networks provided increasingly detailed coverage of election results, and tailored their presentations to appeal to their audiences. There was no point providing "a mere hodgepodge of unintelligible figures" regarding voting figures and majorities, an NBC memo pointed out in October 1932. Instead, information should be presented in a radio-friendly way, expressed in relative terms and readily understandable ratios such as "Hoover is leading Roosevelt 3:2 in a third of the nation's precincts." The memo also suggested that NBC begin its election programming earlier than it had in 1928 and 1930 in order to "get the jump on the opposition." If information was slow to come in, the presenters could always fill in with "a feature story about the old lady in Maine who lost her teeth in the ballot box." In the event of a landslide, NBC decided to keep listeners interested by not declaring the result until the loser publicly conceded.[31]

The broadcasters' growing technical and programming sophistication created tensions in their relationship with the political parties. Network staff often complained about difficulties in dealing with publicity organizers. Broadcasting a campaign speech involved complex technical and logistic arrangements, and required close cooperation between political organizations and network staff. Telephone hookups to stations had to be arranged, tested, and operated within tight schedules and tolerances. When Herbert Hoover in May 1931 began a speech 90 seconds before its scheduled time, CBS decided literally at the last moment to cancel its broadcast and to substitute a musical program. The network did not want its listeners to be confused by a sudden and late entry into a presidential speech.[32] Network announcers, responsible for introducing speakers and ensuring smooth continuity with preceding and following programs, often found their work impeded by what they saw as incompetent party officials.

Although both major parties began to designate radio directors in 1924, they tended at first to appoint men who were experienced in the ways of print media but less familiar with radio's special requirements. Even those party employees who had some experience with radio often found that their expertise had been left behind by rapidly evolving technology and technique, and their efforts were often derided by the broadcasters' technical staff. This was most evident during the 1928 campaign, and the networks found both parties equally to blame. Norman Sweetser, who was in charge of NBC's political programs, complained about Republican radio director Paul Gascoigne after a broadcast of Hoover's speech in West Branch, Iowa, in August. Gascoigne "failed to observe our standby signal," Sweetser reported, "and Mr. Hoover made his appearance during my opening announcement. . . . During the closing announcement, the same conditions existed, so that I had to abandon any attempt to fill in the remaining moment." Gascoigne, Sweetser warned, "is utterly incapable of managing such a broadcast."[33]

The Democrats' radio director, Josef Israels, fared no better. Sweetser intimated that Israels's chief qualification for the job was that his mother, Belle Moskowitz, was Al Smith's closest adviser. "Mrs. Moskowitz should spank her son," Sweetser told Elwood after problems disrupted a Smith broadcast from Helena, Montana. "His batting average for stupidity is 1000."[34] The relationship between broadcast and political staff improved considerably after 1928, although tensions remained.[35] Some of the broadcasters' complaints may have been self-serving, but they also revealed a gap between the technical expertise of the networks and the parties' less developed understanding of the necessities of the radio age. Over time the RNC and DNC developed their own skills in radio programming and advertising, but the learning process was often slow and frustrated by both organizations' tendency to appoint new radio directors and staff for each presidential campaign.

Neutral Networks?

The networks worked hard to appear nonpartisan. In July 1936 all NBC station editors were reminded of company policy that "none of our news broadcasts, commercial or sustaining, must in any way reflect political opinions or take partisan views on any issue."[36] Sometimes this policy was taken to extremes. In September 1940 Bob Hope's writers suggested a joke in his opening monologue that thanked Roosevelt and Willkie for "giving up this time to make this broadcast possible." After a flurry of consultations, involving executive vice-president Niles Trammell, NBC forced Hope to change his script to "all of the political candidates."[37]

Franklin Roosevelt's election presented NBC and CBS with new challenges in political programming. The sense of national emergency arising from the banking crisis of 1932–1933 and the Depression in general, as we have seen, provided the rationale for many requests for airtime, and for the networks' willingness to grant them. At first the Republicans seemed to acquiesce in this flood of Democratic publicity. By 1935, however, the GOP had sufficiently recovered its composure to demand equal time to answer admin-

“Another Report to His Board of Directors.” Larry Keys’s cartoon was typical of the widespread perception that radio had become a vital informer and educator during the first Hundred Days of the New Deal. *Columbus (Ohio) Citizen*, May 8, 1933. Reproduced from the Basil O’Connor Collection, box 7, folder: “May 1–14, 1933,” Franklin D. Roosevelt Library, Hyde Park, New York.

istration speeches. NBC and CBS, and many local stations, took the view that the president and members of Congress should be given access to the airwaves without charge during nonelection periods. Their policy was to treat such broadcasts as educational programming rather than partisan campaigning. Members of the cabinet were also allowed easy and free use of network microphones. The networks resisted Republican demands for equal time to rebut presidential or cabinet addresses, although they did make efforts to ensure that Republican members of Congress and other party leaders were made to feel welcome in their studios.

This generosity was not wholly altruistic. Well aware of the benefits of pleasing legislators, and of their potentially vulnerable position as licensees of a lucrative public resource, both networks saw the value of donating time to politicians. "We have never refused our facilities to a single member of Congress," Frank Russell of NBC wrote his colleagues in a 1935 memo. "It is my feeling that this policy is absolutely sound and has operated in the best interest of radio from its very inception." Sometimes, however, openness had its costs. Although few of the more than 500 senators and representatives requested airtime, those that did often caused scheduling difficulties and embarrassment. In 1934 and 1935 NBC's broadcasts of Senator Huey Long caused a number of complaints from its affiliated stations, as well as resentment from the White House. Although it refused Long's request to buy time on NBC to air a series of talks, the network felt obliged to honor his occasional requests to be fitted in to the network's schedule.[38]

The effect of these policies was to allow the administration's voices to predominate between election periods. From the Republican perspective it appeared that this was a disguised subsidy to incumbent Democrats. Thomas Sabin, the RNC's radio director, complained in September 1935 to NBC about its refusal to sell political time to any party before the conventions:

> So far the policy is fair, but the Democratic National Committee has no reason for asking you for time in view of the fact that their candidate already occupies the White House. Therefore, only the Republican Party must take their hat in hand and wait on your doorstep. In other words, this policy gives you the right to put the President . . . on the air in a campaign speech and deny the right of answer to the Republican Party, and this we protest.[39]

Roosevelt's fireside chats, especially those near campaign seasons or those that seemed to take overtly partisan positions, elicited Republican demands for opportunities to rebut. Both networks felt pressured on this point after 1938, as rumors strengthened that FDR would seek a third term, and they eventually sought refuge in a collective solution. In August 1940 the NAB announced that equal time would be granted to rival candidates if the president used his radio speeches "as a vehicle for electioneering." The burden of proof, however, fell on the GOP, and the issue would be decided by each network.[40]

No fireside chat was ever deemed by the networks to be sufficiently partisan to merit rebuttal, although a few local stations refused to carry them. In September 1936, less than two months before election day, two NBC affiliates in Los Angeles, KFI and KECA, argued that fireside chats should be paid for by the DNC. The White House retaliated by publicly specifying to NBC that KFI and KECA were to be cut out of all Democratic paid advertising during the campaign. "The Boss concurs," presidential secretary Stephen Early scrawled on the memo to DNC publicity chief Charles Michelson.[41]

The networks invariably gave the president the benefit of the partisan doubt. In August 1936, for example, they broadcast without charge his speeches during a tour of drought-affected areas in the Midwest, despite GOP claims that the president was vote-harvesting in the middle of campaign season. Republicans were also upset when NBC and CBS provided free coverage of FDR's speech at a Chautauqua gathering in 1936 but charged GOP nominee Alf Landon for a speech to the same organization.[42] Radio and the networks had added a powerful new advantage to incumbency.

NBC reviewed its policies on political advertising and broadcasting at the beginning of 1936. Dealing first with political speeches, the company reaffirmed its policy to present "the various sides of political issues, and to have them presented fairly and adequately on a strictly non-partisan basis," and to accept political advertising from all national parties and candidates, at normal commercial rates, only between the close of the conventions and election day each presidential year. The network-owned-and-operated stations would sell time to all local and statewide candidates who could afford radio advertising. NBC declared that it would arbitrarily cancel sponsored network time only to accommodate broadcasts by presidential nominees. All other candidates and speakers would have to negotiate with existing advertisers for release of their time slots. These policies were reiterated without significant change in 1938.[43]

CBS's policies were essentially the same. A public exchange of letters between CBS and the RNC at the end of 1935 clarified and publicized the network's policies. These letters, eleven in all, were released by the RNC and later published by CBS in pamphlet form.[44] The RNC put three requests to CBS, all of which were denied. The Republicans first wrote to purchase a series of slots in which to broadcast "such vehicles as the Republican National

Committee may in its opinion deem to be proper for carrying the Republican message to the people." On December 27, 1935, CBS declined, repeating its policy not to sell time for political broadcasting until after the conventions."[45] If access to national radio was based solely on ability to pay, William Paley told RNC Chairman Henry Fletcher, "we have an absolute conviction that the air would be misused . . . [and] would very quickly build up an undemocratic and un-American situation in which the air belonged to those with money."[46]

The RNC wanted to use its time to broadcast dramatized political skits as a "modern radio technique to convey our message." "So long as these are truly represented . . . by the announcer as dramatic sketches, as is done in the presentations of commercial programs," Fletcher told Paley, "I fail to see any legitimate reason for your refusing them." This, too, contravened CBS policy, and the network insisted on its right to conduct radio campaigning in ways that it, and not the parties, thought fit. "Appeals to the electorate should be intellectual and not based on emotion, passion or prejudice," CBS First Vice-president Edward Klauber replied, and "we are convinced that dramatizations would throw the radio campaign almost wholly over to the emotional side. . . . [W]e do not believe [voters] could discriminate fairly among dramatizations, so that the turn of national issues might well depend on the skill of warring dramatists rather than on the merits of the issues debated."[47]

The RNC's third request was for equal time to respond to President Roosevelt's speech to Congress on the evening of January 3, 1936. Noting that the president was to be a candidate for reelection later that year, and that his decision to speak at night was designed to maximize his radio audience, Fletcher argued that his speech was a thinly disguised campaign address. "If you grant my request it will demonstrate that you are in no way influenced by fear of the party in power." CBS again refused, citing its right "to distinguish between the office of President . . . on the one hand, and the political parties and their candidates on the other. . . . This company cannot accept the principle that all broadcast activities of the Government . . . are in the nature of political activities and are to be mathematically balanced by similar broadcasts . . . by a political party in opposition." CBS might allot time to the GOP to rebut the president's speech, but it would not do so in advance.[48]

CBS used this exchange to respond to the RNC's suggestion that its policies were designed to favor the administration by arguing that its policies regarding sale of airtime and dramatizations applied to both parties equally, and that it had taken great care to balance its political programming. Between October 1935 and January 1936, Paley pointed out, CBS had broadcast 16 speeches from Republicans and 13 by Democrats, and had also donated time to anti-administration groups such as the American Liberty League. Clearing the airwaves to cover the president's speech was not a gift to the Democratic Party but rather "a donation to the American people."[49]

NBC, which had received identical requests from the RNC, responded similarly. Aware of the sensitivity of these issues, NBC executives worked through at least five drafts of their response to Fletcher.[50] Denied use of the two major networks, the RNC broadcast its dramatizations through MBS affiliate WGN, Chicago, which was owned by the fiercely anti–New Deal *Chicago Tribune*. Announcing that the skits would be broadcast, the RNC took a final shot at CBS and NBC, accusing them of denying the Republicans "freedom of the air." "Whether or not they are doing this of their own free will, or . . . through fear of the administration," the RNC declared, "they have abandoned their function as servants of the people, surrendered their independence and joined the 'dictators of the New Deal.'"[51] The first and most famous of these programs featured a young couple who canceled their marriage at the altar because of their inability to shoulder their share of the national debt, inflated by reckless New Deal spending. "They've ruined our chance to be—happy!" the disappointed bride complained. "It's a low-down, mean trick," her erstwhile groom replied, "loading us down with all that debt without even asking us."[52]

The Republicans' charge of network partiality toward the Roosevelt administration would have been even more vociferous had they been aware of the steady stream of private notes between the broadcasters and the White House. Quite apart from the chatty letters between David Sarnoff of NBC and William Paley of CBS to the president, both broadcasters gave private favors to the White House.[53] Lenox Lohr of NBC received a confidential request from FDR at the beginning of 1936 that he "lend me the services" of Dr. Stanley High, an employee in the network's talks bureau, for the forthcoming Democratic campaign. Lohr complied, but on the condition that High officially resign from NBC. Vice-president Frank Russell sent advance copies of the CBS-RNC correspondence to presidential secretary Stephen Early with the annotation, "I know you will consider in confidence."[54] CBS Vice-president Harry Butcher wrote to Marvin McIntyre, FDR's secretary, on the day after the 1936 election to express his delight at Roosevelt's landslide victory. After describing the "big election party" at his house, at which the guests were "all for the President before and after," Butcher noted that "while 80–85% of the newspapers were against the President, and vitriolically so, radio short cut the press and enabled the President to get his message direct to the people. And how they did respond!"[55]

NBC executives also found it undesirable to remain too aloof in their neutrality. Near the end of 1937 Russell contacted Early to let him know that the network had taken steps to prevent General Hugh Johnson, by then a vitriolic critic of the New Deal, from using his sponsored commentaries as platforms for "discussion of controversial issues." Early immediately dived for cover, dictating a confidential file note stating, "I told Mr. Russell while I was glad to see him personally, that I was not accepting the information officially; that we could not have any knowledge of the affair between NBC and General Johnson. . . . Mr. Russell said he thoroughly understood; that he had spoken to me personally only, not officially."[56]

Issues concerning dramatizations and advertising standards continued to haunt CBS during the 1936 campaign. In October it aired an advertisement featuring Republican Senator Arthur Vandenberg "debating" with recordings of FDR's voice. The advertisement was originally banned because it violated network policy against the use of transcriptions of the president's voice. Through a breakdown in communication, however, the "debate" ran on 66 CBS stations, although it was cut off on many when the error was recognized. The Republicans demanded that CBS rebroadcast the program, but the network reiterated its policy and refunded its charges. CBS executives were furious; Edward Klauber branded the advertisement as a stunt that damaged CBS's and radio's credibility with voters. "We tried very hard to be thoroughly impartial in this campaign," Harry Butcher wrote to Marvin McIntyre after the election, "and I believed we succeeded, but I must say the Republicans chose to make it very difficult."[57]

While the two major networks devised and defended their policies on political programming, unaffiliated stations had to make their own decisions. The FRC and FCC kept no records of how many stations accepted political advertising during the 1930s, but it is likely that the majority did. Many local stations, already struggling to remain viable during the Depression and in competition with networks, would have been grateful for the revenue from the frequent political contests that punctuated local and state politics. Local stations offered cheap advertising time in small units to candidates who had neither the constituencies nor the funds to justify network advertising. In upstate New York, local stations in 1940 offered candidates one-minute spots for between $5 and $10 each when sold in a group of 70.[58]

In Wisconsin, U.S. Senator Robert LaFollette Jr. regularly received invitations from local stations to advertise on their frequencies. In 1940, for example, WCLO (Janesville), WTAQ (Green Bay), and WTMJ (Milwaukee) each wrote to LaFollette to solicit his business. WCLO offered the senator 30 minutes for $40, and five-minute periods for $12.50 each; WTAQ offered rates as low as $3 for a 40-word announcement. "The power of radio in a political campaign is universally accepted," WCLO told LaFollette, and he could get his message into homes for "LESS THAN ONE TWENTY-FIFTH OF A CENT FOR EACH FAMILY."[59] LaFollette, whose campaign expenditures were invariably low, made his first radio advertisements in 1934. By then candidates across the nation had long recognized radio advertising as a permanent part of their political landscape.

Red Radio

Stations and networks also faced awkward issues when candidates from minor, and particularly radical, parties applied for radio time. Prior to the passage of the Radio Act of 1927, the major broadcasters generally limited their political broadcasting to the two major parties, although RCA did broadcast a speech by the Socialist Party in 1924.[60] The networks found themselves in a difficult position arising from their free broadcast of the Democratic and Republican conventions. The Socialist and Communist Parties of America sought similar treatment, putting the networks' protestations of nonpartisanship to severe test. In June 1928 the Workers' Party of America demanded that NBC provide it the same gavel-to-gavel coverage that was to be given to the Democratic and Republican conventions. "After discussion," NBC President Merlin Aylesworth informed his board, "I finally offered them the facilities of WEAF at eleven o'clock at night, for the purpose of summing up their platform and the speech of acceptance by the candidate for President. I adopted the same policy for the Socialist Party."[61] When Jack Perilla of the New York State branch of the Communist Party of America (CPA) wrote to NBC in September 1930 to request time, network executives simply sat on his letter until it was too late. Nonpartisanship and civic duty had their limits.[62]

The coming of the Depression made the broadcast of radical political groups even more sensitive. Some stations, put off by the requirements of section 315, and fearing a backlash from their listeners over broadcasts from unpopular candidates, decided not to sell any time for political advertising. Station KXO in El Centro, California, for example, announced that it would carry no political advertising at all. This was the only way, the manager told the press, that he could keep a Communist Party candidate off the air. The station had already been attacked by an angry mob over a broadcast by a Communist, and its owners dared not risk the price of free speech again.[63]

After much soul-searching, CBS aired a speech by Earl Browder, General Secretary of the CPA, in March 1936. William Paley hailed this decision as a noble exercise of public service, but many affiliates refused to carry the program. CBS was picketed by the National Americanization League and accused of treason by some members of Congress, who were not appeased by the network's decision to invite Republican Congressman Hamilton Fish to give a vigorous rebuttal of communism a day after Browder's speech.[64] Although NBC agreed to broadcast the acceptance speeches of the CPA candidates for president and vice-president in 1936, it decided against airing any more programs from the party. "The temper of our country at the present time does not warrant our giving the Communists and others a toe-hold on our network for propaganda purposes," John F. Royal advised Lenox Lohr. NBC relented in August, allowing the CPA a 15-minute speech on the condition that Browder did not solicit funds during the broadcast. Browder complied, but one affiliate station in Milwaukee interrupted his speech to announce the election of a new chief of police.[65]

The networks faced the same thorny issue in 1940. At the end of May the NAB asked Congress to amend section 315 to remove any obligation on stations to carry broadcasts by the CPA. "In these troubled days," the NAB argued, Americans had to think hard before they gave succor to "those in our midst whose only use of our free institutions springs from a desire to destroy them and the liberties of the people."[66] CBS supported this position, and investigated the possibility of amending section 315. This proved impossible, and CBS eventually broadcast a short extract from the CPA convention. NBC concluded that it would be untenable to deny the CPA airtime. Although section 315 applied only to "legally qualified candidates" and not to parties, NBC could not justify covering the Democratic and Republican conventions while ignoring the CPA's entirely. This would only make martyrs out of the Communists, providing them with more publicity than a short broadcast.[67] NBC therefore joined CBS in giving the CPA a slot hidden away in the late evening. Fortunately for both networks, the Communists' and Socialists' campaign funds did not allow for frequent network advertising. In 1932 and 1936 NBC sold the Socialist Party $1,972 and $10,500 worth of airtime. The CPA bought time to the value of $34,500 in 1936, which represented 4 percent of NBC's total political sales that year.[68] Had they been able to afford more time, section 315 would have compelled both networks and all stations to air many more advertisements for both parties, doubtless to the outrage of many of their listeners and affiliates.

Debtors and Creditors

Nowhere was the tension between radio exceptionalism and commercial reality more apparent than in payment for political advertising. As the two major parties came to rely more on radio, their expenditures on it grew enormously. The details and implications of those expenditures for the parties will be examined in the next chapter, but they were also of great significance to the broadcasters. Political organizations tended to be perennial debtors of the networks after 1928, forcing broadcasters to decide what sort of creditors they would be. Overall, for a variety of reasons, NBC and CBS treated their political debtors far more leniently than their ordinary commercial ones.

The networks first addressed the issue after the 1928 campaign. That election, contested during the Indian summer of 1920s prosperity, witnessed widespread use of radio by both major parties. Between them Republicans and Democrats spent more than $1 million on radio, and both the RNC and DNC finished the campaign heavily in debt to CBS and NBC. Although the RNC hoped that the fruits of victory would help it pay its debts, the DNC had no such comfort. The coming of the Depression, however, plunged both parties and the networks into a new and uncomfortable financial environment, in which all sides scrabbled for funds. By the end of 1931 the DNC owed NBC $137,000 from 1928, and the RNC still owed more than $100,000.[69]

Neither network had formally extended any credit to the committees during 1928 other than the customary seven-day terms given to all major advertisers, and both CBS and NBC were anxious that the slate be cleared before the next round of national campaign advertising in 1932. In August 1932 Henry Allen, the RNC's director of publicity, contacted Benson Pratt of NBC about the radio campaign for 1932. Already the Republicans envisaged buying $500,000 of network time, Pratt reported to his vice-president John Elwood. In reply to Elwood's query as to the Republicans' ability to pay, Pratt assured him that his uncle-in-law was the RNC's auditor, and that "consequently, if I find that there is any danger of not being able to collect, I can let you know immediately."[70] Such arrangements were indicative of the special treatment accorded to both national committees by CBS and NBC; nonpolitical advertisers were never allowed such informal understandings about payment for network time.

The election of 1932 also saw heavy use of radio, although not on the same scale as in 1928. Nevertheless, the two major parties bought a total of $472,000 of air time from NBC alone.[71] During the campaign both national committees disregarded their seven-day terms and fell behind on their payments. By October 20, with the election still more than two weeks away and the last-minute blitz still to come, the DNC owed NBC nearly $19,000 and the RNC $86,000. "I am of the opinion," NBC's treasurer wrote to NBC Vice-president John Elwood, "that we must bring pressure to get these bills paid. I suggest that both Committees clear up all outstanding amounts immediately if they are to continue to broadcast."[72]

No such pressure was brought to bear, and both parties ended the 1932 campaign heavily in debt. In May 1933 the DNC's debts of $155,000 to CBS and NBC represented more than 30 percent of its total deficit from the campaign.[73] The Republicans, thrown out of power by a landslide, almost immediately sought to make a deal with the two companies. At the end of January 1933 RNC Treasurer J. R. Nutt conferred with NBC about the GOP's debt of $74,000 and warned that the committee had finished the election with a large deficit "and that he could not see how this amount could be raised." Nutt asked both NBC and CBS for a reduction, and offered both networks a promise, but not a guarantee, that the RNC would pay its debts by July 1933. NBC did reduce the debt by $8,000 because of some charging irregularities, but also insisted on immediate payment.[74]

Nearly a year later the RNC still owed NBC more than $63,000. "I do hope you can find a way to help us obtain the money," NBC President Merlin Aylesworth wrote to George Getz of the RNC in December 1933. "We have had a difficult struggle for the past year to break even financially and it does seem to me only fair that the Republican Party pay this debt."[75] The Republicans finally paid off their radio accounts in 1935, but the DNC was even tardier. At the end of 1935 it still owed NBC nearly $111,000 from its 1932 campaign, and the network was little mollified by its promise to begin paying off that debt within 60 days.[76]

Frustrated by their experience with political debtors since 1928, NBC executives attempted to tighten their policies on payment for political advertising before the 1936 campaign. In March 1936 network president Lenox Lohr circulated a series of propositions to his senior colleagues for their comment. Some of these policies were uncontroversial; all 12 executives agreed that NBC should continue to charge political parties at standard commercial rates, and that the rule that parties pay for all costs associated with canceled sponsored programs should also be maintained. They also ratified the practice of encouraging parties to book time through advertising agencies, which then guaranteed payment. NBC also decided to persist with its earlier practice of allowing its affiliates to sell time to local or state candidates at any time, subject to their network and individual commercial obligations. In a further privileging of national over local politics, NBC reaffirmed its rule that its local stations would broadcast only candidates who paid cash in advance.[77] These policies were almost identical to those of CBS, and had operated since 1928.

Lohr's other proposals received more cautious responses. Several executives objected to the idea that parties should first pay off all their debts arising from the 1932 campaign before they could buy time for 1936. Although this proposition received majority support, Edgar Kobak argued that it ran the risk of "incurring antagonism of candidates who will later be in a position of authority over the industry." Janet MacRorie, NBC's programming director, thought that such a policy would contravene section 315. If one party had satisfied its debts while the other had not, the network could not deny airtime to the defaulter as it sold time to the other party. Persuaded by these arguments, Lohr reaffirmed existing policy to maintain informal pressure upon political advertisers to pay their bills promptly. At the time of these discussions, the GOP had paid off its debts to NBC, while the DNC still owed $55,000 from 1932. Both parties had paid off all their obligations to CBS.

These discussions reaffirmed the less controversial aspects of NBC's political advertising policies and avoided changes that would further inconvenience or irritate the major parties. The decision not to insist on prior payment of outstanding debts, in particular, meant that there would be no impediment to incumbent Democrats from buying advertising time in 1936. The Democrats in fact finished the 1936 campaign still $11,000 in debt to NBC from 1932. The political ramifications of imposing a prior payment rule at a time when the incumbent party was delinquent and the opposition party was not were clearly unpalatable. Lohr was also persuaded that all three major national networks should maintain similar policies on political advertising, further limiting NBC's freedom of action.[78]

The result of NBC's inconclusive policy revamp was that 1936 witnessed the same pattern of network accommodation to the demands of the RNC and DNC during the campaign and then heavy party indebtedness at the end of it. NBC billed political parties a total of $975,000 in 1936, made up of $850,000 for station time, $65,000 for special wire facilities, $57,000 for talent charges, and $3,000 for recordings. The distribution of that time between the parties, and their indebtedness to NBC at the end of the campaign, is shown in tables 2 and 3.

Table 2. NBC Billings by Party, 1936 Campaign.

Party	Network Time ($)	Local Time ($)	Total ($)	% of Total
Democrats	215,000	45,000	260,000	31
Republicans	320,000	67,000	387,000	46
Jeffersonian Democrats	127,000	1,000	128,000	15
Socialist	8,500	2,000	10,500	1
CPA	31,500	3,000	34,500	4
Union Party	7,500	2,500	10,000	1
Miscellaneous independent organizations	16,000	4,000	20,000	2
TOTAL	725,500	124,500	850,000	

NBC tried to reformulate its policies before the 1940 campaign. This time the central proposal was to offer both major parties credit of up to $50,000, after which they would have to pay in advance for airtime. A. L. Ashby, NBC's chief counsel, noted that the law required broadcasters to treat all candidates for the same office equally; it was not possible to offer one candidate 30-day terms and another 60 days. The effect of this advice was chilling upon the $50,000 credit proposal, for it could not be legally offered only to the DNC and RNC. The CPA and the Socialists, too, could demand similar treatment should they nominate candidates for president, and NBC was not prepared to countenance that. Ashby also correctly pointed out that different terms could be offered to candidates for different offices; there was no legal obligation upon broadcasters to treat candidates for president in the same way as candidates for sheriff. Consequently NBC could and did persist in its much tougher policies regarding local and statewide offices.[79]

Section 315 and political expediency combined to make political advertisers different from commercial ones; the existing policy of allowing the two

Table 3. Party Account Balances with NBC, November 20, 1936.

Party	Amount Paid ($)	Amount Due ($)
Democrats, 1936	196,231.91	56,280.51
Democrats, 1932		11,401.88
Republicans	188,447.12	187,633.68
Jeffersonian Democrats	122,698.67	0
Socialist	0	11,441.12
CPA	31,869.88	671.59
Union Party	10,028.00	0
Miscellaneous independent organizations	20,934.99	0
TOTAL	570,210.57	267,428.78

SOURCE: Figures for tables 2 and 3 provided in David Rosenblum to A. H. Morton, internal NBC memorandum, Nov. 20, 1936, NBCR, box 49, folder 17, file: "Political Broadcasting; Statistics, 1936."

major parties informal credit, in the form of long-delayed repayment of debts without interest, was a commercial inconvenience but a political necessity. Politicians could be badgered but not forced into payment of debts, and they always had to be treated generously in order to maintain their regulatory good will. John Royal, who had overseen political broadcasting since the formation of NBC in 1926, encapsulated this approach in his response to the 1940 policy review. Royal denied that there was any inherent conflict between the gentle treatment of political broadcasting and commercial prudence. His description of the political facts of life, and of the small price of radio exceptionalism, brought to a close NBC's sporadic attempts to force the political parties into being better debtors during the interwar years:

> We must not lose sight of the fact that we have been very fortunate in radio in getting away with the selling of time for presidential candidates. We might awaken some morning and find that we are going to have to *give* time to national campaigns, instead of selling it. I think a Congressman might get quite a long way advocating that the radio networks who are making so many millions, *give* a certain amount of time every four years. The press might be likely to support such a campaign. Don't let's go too far with putting the screws on.[80]

Policy into Practice

In 1940 the Sales-Research Division of NBC compiled a list of political advertisers on all three national networks between 1933 and 1939. That list revealed 104 organizations across the whole political spectrum. Of that number, 70 advertised on NBC, 45 on CBS, and 10 on MBS, with 21 groups, chiefly the RNC, DNC, and well-funded state election committees, using more than one network.

The great majority of these groups used network facilities only rarely and briefly; the open market model of sections 18 and 315, combined with network policy requiring cash in advance for all but national committees, meant that the distribution of network advertising was extremely unequal. The Association for Tax Equality's single advertisement on NBC in October 1936, for example, was dwarfed by the DNC's multiple appearances on all three networks between July and November in 1932 and 1936. Nevertheless, NBC's presentation showed that political advertising of all kinds provided a steady stream of customers for the networks, albeit bunched between July and November of each year, and with clear peaks representing each quadrennial national campaign.[81]

NBC also went to great lengths to monitor its own performance in polit-

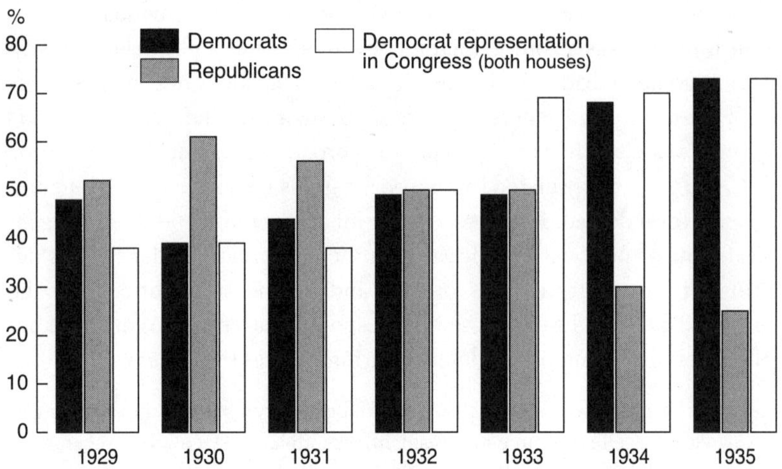

Figure 8. Democratic and Republican Legislators on NBC, 1929–1935: Percentage of Total Appearances.

Source: Graph constructed from data in NBC memorandum, "Analysis of Number of Appearances and Time Consumed by United States Senators and Representatives on NBC Red and Blue Networks, January 1, 1929–December 31, 1935," NBCR, box 49, file 17: "Political Broadcasts, Statistics 1936."

ical programming and advertising during the 1930s. Under pressure from Republicans, NBC carefully checked its political programming for balance between the two major parties. In January 1936 NBC compared its coverage of talks by President Hoover during the first three years of his term with that of FDR during his first three years. Much to their relief, the network's executives could assure the GOP that Hoover had received more airtime than Roosevelt. Between June 1928 and December 1931 Hoover had appeared 78 times on NBC, for a total of 53 hours. His successor, on the other hand, had appeared 79 times for a total of 45 hours between June 1932 and December 1935. NBC's coverage of Hoover had also cost the network much more in lost sponsored time, because FDR had often used sustaining time for his frequent but relatively short addresses to the nation.[82]

NBC also collated information on the distribution of time to Republican and Democratic legislators between 1929 and 1935. Its findings are represented in figure 8. It appears that NBC consistently favored the Congressional majority party in its broadcasts of lawmakers, although proportionately so. Taking both houses of Congress together, the Democrats were the minority party in 1929, 1930 and 1931, and enjoyed majority status from 1932 onward. In 1930, 1932, 1934, and 1935 NBC got the balance between Congressional preponderance and proportion of broadcasts almost exactly right; in 1929, 1931, and 1933 the imbalance favored the minority party. Considering that these figures covered more than 1300 appearances, NBC had reason to be proud of its even-handedness.

The average length of these political programs dropped markedly during the interwar period. In the early days of broadcasting, they usually took the form of a broadcast speech, often lasting 60 minutes. During the later 1920s and early 1930s, 30-minute speeches and talks became the norm, shrinking again to 15 minutes in the middle 1930s as network time grew more expensive. In 1935 NBC broadcast 239 legislators and government officials in 560 broadcasts, of which more than 96 percent were of 15 minutes' duration.[83]

By 1940 broadcasters had amassed 20 years' experience of political programming and advertising. Their efforts, and particularly those of the national networks, reflected tensions between radio exceptionalism and the demands of large-scale commercial enterprise. Radio, all agreed, was not simply a new form of communication analogous to the printing press, and thus could not inherit its traditions of partisanship and editorial freedom. Broadcasters were, instead, licensees of a public resource and guardians of a powerful means of informing, and perhaps influencing, voters and citizens. Accordingly broadcasters were afforded less freedom to favor particular political voices or to express their own political opinions than were newspaper owners. Licensees also remained extremely wary of their political advertisers. Political customers were either actual or potential regulatory masters, and their demands and debts were always seen in that context. How those customers saw political programming, and their relationship to its sellers, will be examined in the next chapter.

8

The Buyers

National Parties, Candidates, and Radio

At the end of March 1922 Republican Senator Harry S. New of Indiana was in a dilemma. While he was in Washington, deliberating over the Naval Disarmament Treaty, his opponents within the Indiana GOP were at work against him. New faced a formidable opponent, former Senator Albert Beveridge, in the forthcoming primary, and he desperately needed to be back home to shore up his support. With Congress still in session, and unlikely to recess until well into the summer, New had to be in two places at once.

Senator New resolved his dilemma on the night of March 30, 1922. He delivered a speech by radio from Washington to a group of Republican women in Indianapolis. Reading between the lines of the press coverage that New's broadcast received, his speech was not a masterpiece of oratory. The senator began his talk "in a prosaic . . . way, as a man would in talking over the phone. But the thing soon became so real that he grew emotional and departed at times from his written speech." Nevertheless, his radio campaigning attracted much interest; President Harding and his wife heard it on their set in the White House, and listeners from all over the Northeast and Midwest reported that the senator's voice had come through loud and clear. His audience in Indianapolis was also appreciative, and relayed "three cheers for our next Senator."[1] Despite its enthusiastic reception, his broadcast proved to be something of a false dawn. In early 1922 radio was still technically immature, and successful broadcasts over long distances tended to attract attention mainly for their novelty value. Harry New's experience of campaigning by radio also turned out to be bittersweet. Despite the favorable publicity from his broadcast, Beveridge defeated him in the primary.

Harry New was not the first politician in America to use radio for campaigning. That honor appears to belong to New York City Mayor John F. Hylan during his reelection campaign in 1921. Hylan reiterated his platform and record to listeners two days before the election, using a transmitter owned by a radio manufacturer. His opponent, Henry F. Curran, also delivered a radio speech on the following night. Curran's advance publicity was indicative of the primitive state of broadcasting at the time. "His campaign managers did not know last night the exact hour of the speech tonight," the press reported, "but it probably will be late in the evening. They said they did not know just where Mr. Curran would speak into the transmission apparatus, but that it would probably be at the home of some amateur operator." In fact Curran used the De Forest Company's equipment, but he too went on to defeat at the polls.[2]

Despite these unpromising beginnings, a growing number of broadcasters, and especially the major players such as GEC, Westinghouse, RCA, and AT&T, could offer politicians increasingly reliable service by the end of 1923. The ideological preconditions for radio campaigning also developed, as we have seen, through radio exceptionalism. This convinced broadcasters that their own self-interest and radio's destiny as a bringer of civic improvement required radio to be available to those engaged in, or aspiring to, political office. This confluence of technical development, radio exceptionalism, and broadcasters' self-preservation meant that radio was now ready to do political service.

"Radio will draw you close to the American fireside"

One sign of this readiness landed on President Calvin Coolidge's desk early in November 1923. Coolidge had been president for less than three months, propelled into the Oval Office by Harding's sudden death. Eugene McDonald, president of the newly formed NAB, wrote Coolidge a long letter which pointed out what radio could offer him. Harding's death, McDonald began, had reminded everyone of the physical demands of the presidency. The burdens of office had multiplied over the years, and shaking hands with thousands of people was a "veritable ordeal of physical endurance!" Speaking tours were even worse, as Harding's last days had shown. But now Coolidge could talk to an audience of 15 million Americans "with no more tax than the reading of a paper into the delicate microphone." If Coolidge made radio an integral part of his publicity program he could save not only his health but also transform the presidency itself:

> The President to most people is rather remote. They read of him as they do of the King of England or the Shah of Persia. A very small percentage of the population ever catch a glimpse of him and most of those who do, never cease talking about it. . . . Radio will draw you close to the American fireside for you will be speaking to your people as they sit in their living room. . . . Your voice and your personality will become familiar to them and in consequence . . . you will mean more to them than now.[3]

Coolidge made at least four broadcasts during the first six months of his presidency, but he was not the first president to speak on the radio. Woodrow Wilson had made an experimental broadcast in 1919, and Warren Harding had made several radio speeches in 1922 and 1923. Coolidge, however, was the first to use radio as a means of communication and political advancement. This is not to say that he used radio intensively during his tenure. Despite McDonald's enthusiasm, neither the industry nor radio political technique had developed sufficiently for the new medium to be used as a substitute for older publicity methods.

Contemporaries nevertheless viewed Coolidge as the first great political beneficiary of the radio age. As an accidental president inheriting a discredited administration, Coolidge needed to establish himself quickly, and his occasional broadcasts during the first six months of 1924 attracted much attention. His political friends and enemies all noted that the president adapted well to the microphone, which seemed to enlarge his retiring presence. "I am very fortunate that I came in with the radio," Coolidge admitted. "I can't make an engaging, rousing, or oratorical speech to a crowd . . . but I have a good radio voice, and now I can get my messages across to them without acquainting them with my lack of oratorical ability."[4]

Coolidge did not use radio to gain public support for particular measures, nor did he make speeches specifically to radio listeners. His broadcasts were always of speeches to live audiences, with radio acting as an electronic extension, rather than a replacement, of the meeting hall. Yet he was soon made aware of how effective that extension could be; one listener from Peekskill, New York wrote in March 1924, "Your real common sense addresses have been so well received that I am pleased to advise that several of my acquaintances of the so-called 'regular' democrat type who have heard you speak, have stated that . . . it is their intention to cast their votes for you." Some other Democrats ruefully agreed. In 1924 Charles Michelson noted that Coolidge "doesn't look as if he had the physique to stand the strain of an old fashioned campaign," and that the radio seemed to soften the "wire edge to his voice."

The invention of radio was thus yet another example of "Coolidge luck or destiny, or whatever it is that seems to make things come out right for him politically."[5]

Radio and the 1924 Campaign

The Democratic Party was less successful with early radio. Party leaders as diverse as William Jennings Bryan, Al Smith, Woodrow Wilson, and William McAdoo had at first welcomed broadcasting as a boon not only to American statecraft but also to Democrats. Bryan noted at the beginning of 1924 that the party had long suffered at the hands of an overwhelmingly Republican press, but now radio promised to even the scales. McAdoo was so impressed that he applied for a license to operate a station in Los Angeles to further his own ambitions for the 1924 presidential nomination.[6] The reality of early radio, however, proved far less rewarding. The nation's first scheduled broadcast in 1920 had delivered news of Democratic defeat in the elections of that year, and in 1924 the Democrats had the misfortune of staging the longest and most divided nominating convention since 1860 within easy hearing of millions of radio listeners.

Over the course of two weeks and 103 ballots, the party tore itself apart over the choice between Smith and McAdoo. Although the New York convention became a radio sensation and caused a significant jump in radio sales and listening audiences across the country, it also convinced many voters that the Democrats, being incapable of governing themselves, should not be allowed to run the country. Defeat came early to the Democrats in 1924, and it came through radio. In 1927 Meredith Nicholson remembered the New York convention in *Century Magazine* as "an exhibition of midsummer madness; and the radio, carrying to remote hamlets the clamor, the senseless demonstrations, conveyed the idea that a circus had become disorderly and unmanageable, with the performers and animals running wild."[7]

Although the 1924 campaign was the first to be conducted with the help of radio, it can scarcely be called a true radio election. Political organizations were too inexperienced with broadcasting, and too wedded to older media, to conduct campaigns based upon it. Notwithstanding that all presidential candidates and the two major parties broadcast some of their key speeches, and that radio coverage of the Democratic convention proved to be the programming sensation of the year, the 1924 campaign should be remembered as transitional for parties, broadcasters, and voters as they came to terms with the radio age. Instead of the million-dollar budget predicted at the beginning of the campaign, the Democrats and Republicans spent only $90,000 between them on radio.[8]

No complete records of the 1924 campaign expenditures by any party have survived. Those that remain tend to be Republican, and they confirm that traditional forms of publicity—speeches, pamphlets, press releases, newspaper plate, buttons, and posters—were the preferred means of selling Coolidge and other Republicans to the voters. A budget prepared by the RNC at the end of June 1924 called for a total expenditure of $90,000 for press publicity, comprised of publicists' wages, office costs, distribution of news matrices, and newspaper plate. Later budgets, which included costs for the Speakers Bureau, motion picture advertising, posters, and pamphlets, involved additional expenditure of nearly $700,000.[9] It seems clear that these estimates were very conservative; costs of buttons and campaign trains, for example, were not included. Louise Overacker, whose calculations of campaign expenditures are still the most authoritative, estimated that the GOP's state and national committees spent a total of $5.95 million in the 1924 campaign. If so, they spent only 0.8 percent of that sum on radio. The Democrats spent $40,000 on broadcasting, 2.5 percent of their total campaign budget of $1.6 million.[10]

The Republicans clearly won the radio campaign in 1924. Despite the efforts of RCA, GEC, and AT&T to divide radio time fairly between the parties, only the GOP was sufficiently organized to take full advantage of what was offered. In this campaign, the only presidential contest of the radio era to be fought without the benefit of sections 18 and 315, radio coverage was very unevenly distributed. John Q. Tilson, in charge of the RNC Speaker's Bureau, observed that the "Democrats and Progressives used the radio studios in only a few instances, although in a great many cases time was available had they asked for it. We had a very important advantage . . . in that we literally filled the air with Republican addresses from the various studios during the entire month of October."[11]

The Republicans also enjoyed a great advantage in the quality of their publicity advisers for the 1924 campaign. Bruce Barton, the most famous advertising expert of the 1920s, donated his time to the RNC campaign. Barton firmly believed in the power of radio to sell both goods and candidates, and he urged the party to take full advantage of it. Broadcasting, he thought, had forever changed the character and conduct of campaigns by enabling politicians to talk to voters without the formality of mass rallies. Because radio found its listeners at home, politicians could address them directly and warmly as individuals. A later and more imaginative president than Calvin Coolidge would take Barton's advice:

> It would be a great and impressive thing, if,—say every second Monday night, beginning October first,—the President of the United States would talk to his employers, the people, about the way in which their work has been handled. Let the subject be interestingly stated and announced in advance. Let the President tell me, a salaried man, why I am paying 25 percent less taxes this year. . . .
>
> In other words the radio has made possible an entirely new type of campaign. It enables the President to sit by every fireside and talk in terms of that home's interest and prosperity. LaFollette will roar and the Democrat will pound his stuffed shirt. But if the President will only talk to the folks (not address them) he will re-elect himself.[12]

While Coolidge and the Republicans took halting steps toward radio campaigning, their two main rivals in 1924 struggled to keep up. The Democrats, hamstrung by their internal divisions and limited funds, seemed unable to respond to the challenges to traditional methods of campaigning presented by radio. Although they used RCA and AT&T facilities to broadcast John Davis's major speeches, those in charge of the campaign exhibited no real vision as to how to conduct a radio campaign. This was in keeping with the whole tenor of Davis's campaign, which was universally criticized as underfunded, poorly led, and defeatist.[13]

Conditions within Robert LaFollette's campaign were even worse. His Progressive Party had been born out of protest against the two major parties' failure to control the power of business interests in American life. It survived on a hand-to-mouth basis, funding itself mainly from donations collected at rallies. By the middle of October the party had collected a total of $190,500, out of which nearly $76,000 had been devoted to buttons, pamphlets, and printing. Office costs and traveling expenses consumed another $91,000, leaving the party with little extra for such luxuries as radio hookups.[14] A report dated September 4, 1924, from the party's Chicago headquarters, which oversaw the western campaign, included a poignant entry under "Radio": "We need money for radio work. Very necessary."[15] None was forthcoming, and LaFollette's Progressives collapsed soon after winning 15 percent of the vote in November.

Bruce Barton again tried to interest Coolidge in a radio presidency after the Republican landslide of 1924. Rather than limit himself to broadcasts of public speeches, Barton suggested, the president should speak directly to the people from his White House study once a month to discuss the state of the union. Capitalizing upon his great victory, and upon his "acknowledged hit as a broadcaster," Coolidge could transform his popular mandate into policy through enlisting the listening millions in his cause. The president again declined, thinking that it was unnecessary to make dedicated radio addresses, which were expensive, when the press gave him daily and free coverage. Presidential fireside chats were thereby postponed until 1933.[16] Coolidge, nevertheless, appeared on the nation's radios much more frequently between 1925 and 1928 than he had previously; his Inaugural, State of the Union, and many lesser speeches were transmitted across the rapidly expanding broadcasting facilities of the nation.

You say radio, I say raddio: The 1928 Campaigns

Both major parties took giant strides in their use of radio in 1928. As the broadcasting industry matured rapidly after 1924, becoming commercialized, networked, and more formally regulated, political strategists and candidates had also developed ideas about how best to use it. This coincidence of industry development, statutory regulation, and campaign strategy made the Hoover-Smith contest of 1928 the first true radio campaign. The Republican candidate, Herbert Hoover, understood the industry well, having overseen it as secretary of commerce since 1921, and Al Smith had also made use of radio as governor of New York. The Democrats also found themselves unusually rich in 1928. After his nomination in June, Smith appointed John J. Raskob as chairman of the DNC. Raskob had made millions on the stock market and as a senior executive of the Du Pont Company and General Motors. He was determined that the Democrats would, for the first time in a generation, keep up with Republican spending. To that end he donated and lent more than $300,000 to the DNC, and attracted large donations from business associates such as Pierre du Pont, Irénée du Pont, and William H. Woodin. The 1928 campaign therefore witnessed a much more even balance between the two parties' financial and organizational resources than in 1924.[17]

Both the RNC and DNC needed large war chests to capitalize fully on radio broadcasting's potential. The triumph of commercialism and the formation of NBC and CBS significantly increased the cost of radio time between 1924 and 1928. When John Davis ran against Calvin Coolidge their campaigns had to pay only for technical costs; in 1928 the networks charged $10,000 per hour for their coast-to-coast facilities and airtime.[18] Although the radio audience was far larger in 1928 than in 1924, political parties had to find greater sums in order to reach it.

Indications of radio's new role in campaign strategy, and of its higher costs, were evident in the 1928 campaign budgets prepared by the RNC and DNC. The Republicans formulated a budget of $3.9 million toward the end of August. Nearly $650,000 was earmarked for administrative costs and $889,500 went to publicity, including postage, books, pamphlets, buttons, and foreign language publications. Another $517,500 went to Republican clubs and bureaus focusing on labor, farmers, African Americans, and others. The total allocation for radio was $350,000, a sum significantly greater than the $250,000 devoted to the Speakers' Bureau. In all, the RNC dedicated almost 9 percent of its total budget, and slightly over 17 percent of its total publicity expenditures, to broadcasting. These figures made the total GOP expenditure of $50,000 on radio in 1924 look paltry, and the disparity between the budgets for speakers and for radio indicated an important change in perceptions of the value of broadcast over stump speech. During the heat of the campaign the RNC increased its radio budget to $500,000, but then cut it to about $400,000 in the middle of October, when Hoover's victory seemed assured.[19]

The Democrats gave even greater importance to radio. The DNC originally budgeted for a total expenditure of more than $3.4 million, of which $600,000—or 17.5 percent—was set aside for radio. This appropriation was the single largest item of the campaign budget, slightly exceeding the entry of $540,000 for printed publicity and dwarfing those for candidates' travel ($100,000), administration ($276,000), and speakers ($75,000). Although subsequent budgets eased the radio appropriation back to $530,000, it remained as the single largest budgeted expense. When the RNC made its final tallies at the end of the 1928 campaign it, too, found that its actual expenditure of nearly $436,000 on radio was the single largest element of its total publicity expenditures of slightly more than $2 million.[20] Between them the RNC and DNC pumped $1 million into the networks' and independent broadcasters' coffers between July and November 1928.

Both sides organized their radio campaigns with far more sophistication than in 1924. Josef Israels, who oversaw the DNC's radio division, told the press in September 1928 that the Democrats planned an escalating radio campaign between September and November. Early in the campaign, CBS and NBC would air weekly broadcasts of speeches by Smith and his running mate Joseph Robinson. The Democrats planned to intensify their broadcasting during the last three weeks of the campaign, with speakers including Newton Baker, Franklin and Eleanor Roosevelt, and John Raskob, broadcasting every night on a variety of local and network stations. The Democrats promised to cover the whole of the nation with their radio campaign, although the

South—wrongly assumed to be safely Democratic—would receive only periodic attention.[21] The Republicans planned and executed a similar campaign of escalating intensity and a late October radio blitz.

The RNC and DNC also introduced innovations in selling their message and candidates on radio. The RNC organized "National Hoover Minute Men" to provide simultaneous programming on local stations across the eastern half of the country. Taking advantage of the cheaper rates and shorter advertising periods offered by local stations, the Minute Men provided five- or ten-minute addresses each night by more than 150 speakers on 100 stations in 28 states. Programming was closely coordinated so that the same issue was discussed on all stations on the same evening. This strategy subsequently became dogma for almost all campaign advisers for the rest of the century. The Minute Men began work on September 26 with broadcasts on prohibition, and they continued one issue at a time until election day.[22]

Campaign strategists in 1928 attempted to use radio not only to reach the whole electorate through broadcasts during peak listening times on the national networks but also to address targeted groups through what would later be termed "narrowcasting." Both the RNC and DNC booked large amounts of time during the morning to reach women at home. The Democrats, in particular, were worried about the weakness of Smith's support among female voters, which was attributed variously to his anti-prohibition views, his New York City manners and accent, and even to his wife's alleged lack of social graces. The Republicans, confident that Hoover stood to benefit greatly from disaffected female Democrats, also made heavy use of morning radio.[23]

Anxious to maximize audiences, both parties introduced other innovations to political advertising. In November Herbert Hoover made radio history by becoming the first presidential candidate to address listeners without the presence of a live audience. The Democrats presented 30-minute programs that mixed politics with entertainment, devoting ten minutes to speeches and the balance to performances by musicians, movie stars, and stage actors. A "serious study of the listeners' needs," Israels announced, "had led to the conclusion that the use of radio could be overdone and that every effort would be made to keep the programs to a minimum in number and time."[24] Only speeches by the presidential and vice-presidential candidates were allowed to take up entire programs, and only these occasions occupied one-hour segments. The 1928 campaign saw the birth of the "spot" advertisement, when both sides aired five-minute segments on local stations. The parties also broadcast radio plays to dramatize their candidates' lives and achievements, and presented weekly radio debates on issues such as prohibition and the tariff.[25]

An electronic revolution had overtaken politics by 1928, and few aspects of campaigning escaped it. The Democrats rescheduled keynote addresses at their convention so as to maximize their radio audiences; in Kansas City the Republican convention organizers muffled the sound of the chairman's gavel—the symbol of authority in live-audience politics—to avoid acoustic problems over the radio. Hoover hired the first radio speech consultant to join a national campaign. Professor Richard Borden of New York University attempted to bring more warmth and naturalness to Hoover's radio manner, although with marginal success. "Mr. Hoover," one radio expert wrote in 1941, "seems to have been wrapped at birth in a cobweb of awkwardness." Smith, on the other hand, had the opposite problem: he was too warm and natural. His strong New York City accent, and his propensity to pronounce the new technological wonder as "raddio," was widely noted as a major liability in areas west of the Hudson River. "His raucous voice, his intemperate language and that strange menacing voice," one Republican wrote to Senator William Borah of Idaho after the campaign, appealed only to "the milling crowds [who] applauded him in the half foreign and wet centers of population."[26]

Despite the high costs of radio politics, both parties expressed great satisfaction at its results. During the campaign Josef Israels wrote to an NBC executive about the Democrats' pleasant experience with radio fundraising. At the beginning of the campaign the party had spent $35,000 on an appeal in daily newspapers, and had received a total of $2,000 from readers. It had then spent $3,000 to broadcast an appeal for funds over NBC, and had been rewarded by more than $70,000. "I think there is no more conclusive proof," Israels concluded, "of radio's usefulness in getting right to the sensitive spot of the public, namely the pocket-book."[27]

Contemporaries shared Israels's enthusiasm. At first glance, the *New York Times* noted immediately after the campaign, the parties' combined expenditure on radio seemed extravagant. Yet the editors' belief was that "it is doubtful if any money spent in campaigns has done better service—alike to the parties and the country." Radio was cheaper than printed publicity in terms of number of voters reached per dollar, and the radio campaign had done much to educate the nation about the issues facing the country. Turnout had jumped to 56.9 percent from 48.9 percent in 1924, and the *Times* credited that to radio. It had also performed a vital national service by making voters better informed and more engaged in the political process.[28] Amidst the general celebration of the newfound power of radio, nobody seemed to notice that the losing party had spent more on radio than the winner.

The First Radio President

As befitted the winner of the first true radio election, Herbert Hoover was a frequent radio performer during his troubled presidency. His total of nearly 80 broadcasts between March 1929 and November 1932 represented a radio presidential record which more than doubled Coolidge's total and even compared favorably with FDR's early years in the White House.[29] Although Louis Liebovich and others have argued that Hoover was not a radio president, this is an ahistoric judgment, made by comparing Hoover's radio skills to those of his successor. In the context of his own presidency, and in comparison with Coolidge, Hoover made significant use of the new medium and eventually appreciated its role in assisting national economic recovery and his own political fortunes.[30]

Hoover's unprecedented use of radio did not, however, make him a broadcasting virtuoso. Media relations were not Hoover's forte, and he often treated reporters and broadcasters with a combination of contempt and ineptitude. He tended to equate quality of broadcasting with quantity of broadcasts, and continued and expanded Coolidge's habit of broadcasting live speeches instead of delivering addresses purely to radio audiences. This, in Liebovich's phrase, treated radio listeners as mere "eavesdroppers" rather than as participants in a public event.[31] Despite the work of his campaign radio consultants, Hoover retained his dull speaking style, packing his speeches with facts, figures, and complex arguments which simultaneously demanded and discouraged close listening and attention. During the 1932 campaign a supporter wrote to Hoover with some unsolicited advice for improving his radio style:

> In speaking over a national hookup, remember that 90 percent of the people out here in the Styx . . . are of high school education or less. Their vocabulary is not extensive. To them words like "regimentation," so plentifully sprinkled through your address . . . just don't exist. . . . Lay off the use of words not of the common everyday vocabulary of the man in the street.
>
> In radio talks be extremely careful of combinations of sibilancies. Tonight you used, for instance, "vast vistas." That's almost unpronounceable in any language. Certainly over the air it sounded as if you were trying out a new gargle.[32]

Advice also came from the broadcasting industry. At the end of 1929 William Paley of CBS suggested that Hoover deliver "exclusive radio talks to the whole Nation . . . from your study in the White House," at regular intervals on the two national networks. Paley combined tactful criticism of

Hoover's radio style with a vision of the potential power of effective broadcasting. Radio had now developed into a powerful medium of communication which ranked equal in importance to the press. It therefore demanded not only separate treatment but also a distinct strategy. The president would improve his standing, Paley suggested, by less frequent but more regular broadcasts. Hoover also needed to address listeners more directly, and more intimately, by changing the context in which he spoke to them. "Broadcasting alone from your study will . . . bring out your personality. . . . Radio's intimate relationship to the home provides for the President an opportunity to feel the Nation's pulse, based on the 'reactions' received in the White House mailbag."[33]

Paley's suggestions, which bore striking resemblance to Barton's advice to Coolidge in 1925, foreshadowed the fireside chat radio strategy that FDR employed so successfully after 1932. In its 1929 context, however, Paley's letter was both a disquisition on contemporary radio theory and an exercise in corporate self-interest. Hoover's frequent but unsystematic use of radio to broadcast speeches given to groups in various locations caused the networks a great deal of expense and inconvenience through its unpredictable disruptions to normal program schedules. Regular but scheduled presidential radio talks from the White House would be cheaper and more manageable for broadcasters and presidents alike.

In this and so many other things, Herbert Hoover was slow to heed good political advice. The idea of regular White House broadcasts did not appeal to him, and he politely deflected Paley's letter. Nearly a year later, in August 1930, NBC tried to interest the president in a series of educational broadcasts about the functions of government. The network planned a number of talks by members of the cabinet, the judiciary, and the Congress, and sought Hoover's participation. He again declined, citing pressure of work and his other broadcasting commitments.[34] Increasingly confined to the White House and preoccupied by the Depression, Hoover broadcast less and less frequently. During the first four months of 1931, at a time when his reputation for callous inactivity in the face of economic calamity was developing dangerous momentum, Hoover appeared on network radio just twice. Only in April 1931 did he recognize the value of the free publicity offered to him by the networks. When CBS offered to set aside 30 minutes each week for cabinet members to discuss their departments' work, the president practically ordered his secretaries to cooperate. Hoover himself, belatedly realizing that he was fighting for his political life, stepped up his radio activities in the last months of his administration in a doomed effort to turn back the Democratic tide.[35]

The GOP enjoyed superior access to radio facilities between 1928 and 1932 because of its preponderance in both houses of Congress and its occupancy of the White House. The Democrats received radio time through their congressional representation and their gubernatorial offices. The party also inaugurated a permanent publicity organization, funded largely by John Raskob and conducted by Charles Michelson. Michelson, a former journalist, used print media as his primary publicity vehicles in order to save money. Because the networks refused to sell time for political advertising outside the campaign season, Michelson's options for radio publicity were limited to the use of local stations and to the coordination of Democratic leaders' free broadcasts on NBC and CBS.[36]

Although the Depression crimped campaign budgets, the off-year elections in 1930 witnessed intensive radio political campaigns in key races. Joseph Ely spent more than 20 percent of his total expenditures of $64,000 on radio during his successful campaign for the governorship of Massachusetts, and Marcus Coolidge dedicated 35 percent of his budget to radio in his winning fight to represent that state in the United States Senate.[37] As election budgets shrank and donations declined during 1931 and 1932 the DNC and RNC had to make hard choices about their spending priorities for 1932. The increasing size and market power of the national networks added to these problems by greatly increasing the cost of airtime in 1932. The networks seemed immune to the deflation caused by the Depression. In 1928 the parties bought time on CBS at $4,000 per hour for its 19-station network; NBC charged $11,500 for its 49-station networks. In 1932 CBS, now offering 82 stations, charged $17,000 per hour during the evening, and NBC sold time on its full networks for $18,000 per hour.[38]

The major parties decided that radio, despite its high cost, was essential to modern campaigning. Although both the DNC and RNC cut back their campaign budgets significantly from those of 1928, they remained deeply committed to radio. The DNC, which spent a total of $2.2 million in 1932, again devoted about 18 percent of its resources to radio. The RNC dramatically increased its reliance upon radio, from 10 percent of the total budget in 1928 to 20 percent of total expenditures of $2.9 million in 1932. "We have just passed the million dollar mark in this campaign, as against three and one-half millions at the same time in 1928," Edgar Rickard of the RNC told Ambassador Hugh Gibson in Brussels in the middle of October 1932. "These radio speeches of the Chief's are an absolute essential, and they cost us all the way from twenty-five thousand to thirty-two thousand a crack!"[39]

Table 4. Network Political Campaign Broadcasts, 1932.

	Programs	Hours : Minutes
NBC Broadcasts		
Republican		
Major addresses	41	34:23
Republican Radio League	24	6:43
RNC daytime series	32	8:11
Pacific Coast broadcasts	10	2:45
Democratic		
Major addresses	41	30:32
Pacific Coast broadcasts	4	1:45
Socialist		
League for Industrial Democracy	1	0:15
TOTAL	153	84:34
CBS Broadcasts		
Republican	29	18:30
Democratic	26	17:15
Socialist	2	0:30
TOTAL	57	36:15
GRAND TOTAL: NBC + CBS	210	120:49

SOURCE: Figures provided in Roy V. Peel and Thomas C. Donnelly, *The 1932 Campaign*, p. 146. CBS total billing in 1932 quoted in *New York Times*, Nov. 13, 1932, sec. 8, p. 6.

Although both parties originally budgeted for a relatively modest total combined radio spending of $500,000, about half the 1928 outlays, they became embroiled in a broadcasting spending war as the campaign progressed. Both sides engaged in a last-minute radio blitz; the DNC ran up almost $100,000 of its total bill of nearly $206,000 to NBC during the last week of the campaign, and by election day the RNC and DNC had spent double their original radio budgets.[40] By November both committees had consumed $471,890 worth of time on NBC and more than $368,000 on CBS facilities. Table 4 shows the distribution of paid airtime between the parties.

Radio was again integral to both parties' campaigns. The Democrats and Republicans continued to schedule convention highlights in the evenings, when most listeners were home. In an attempt to avoid listener backlash, and to reduce talent cancellation costs, the parties also attempted to avoid preempting popular shows with their programming. The RNC and DNC expanded their campaigns to win women's votes in 1932 by airing regular daytime programs and speeches by prominent women.[41]

The Republicans, who outspent the DNC on radio, relied heavily on broadcasting to improve their thin chances of victory. "The 'miracle' that will re-elect you," Ward Gravatt wrote to Hoover in late September 1932, "lies in your own hands." Gravatt suggested that the president should "have a frank talk" with the voters via radio, so that they might better understand the pressures he was under.[42] There was, as well, a darker side. Radio could also insulate the unpopular president from an angry electorate. One self-professed well-wisher from California had this advice: "Dr Sir—I understand you are thinking of going out speaking over the country. don't do it—talk over the radio. there are some Bad Men who have lost all from various reasons they lay all their ills to you this is my Private Opinion Privately Expressed. Don't attend any large gatherings is my advice, a Friend."[43]

The Champ

It is a commonplace that Franklin Roosevelt was the first political star of the radio age.[44] As governor of New York between 1928 and 1932, Roosevelt followed his predecessor Al Smith's practice of using radio to argue for his measures, honing his radio skills in the process. The state Democratic organization booked an hour of radio time on a statewide hookup each month so that the governor could discuss his policies and circumvent the Republican lock on the state legislature. During his reelection campaign in 1930 Roosevelt and the Democrats spent nearly $25,000 on radio time, but not before carefully determining which stations to use. Prior to the campaign all Democratic county leaders outside New York City were sent questionnaires about the quality of reception of stations in their areas. Their responses were meticulously tabulated and used in planning the campaign. Alexander Robinton, Chairman of Herkimer County Democratic Committee, recommended WGY as having the best coverage of the central part of the state. "I investigated the matter, and find that about 9 of every 10 persons, Republicans as well as Democrats, tune in on the Governor when he is speaking over the radio. From my own experiences I am of the belief that the Governor's talks over the radio are one of the greatest aids in vote getting."[45]

The 1932 presidential campaign allowed FDR to demonstrate his radio skills on a national stage. Although the GOP outspent the Democrats on radio, only the most partisan Republican argued that Hoover outperformed his opponent behind the microphone. Once ensconced in the White House, FDR heeded the advice that Coolidge and Hoover before him had scorned, delivering his first fireside chat, on the banking crisis, eight days after his inauguration. In June 1933, after two fireside chats, the *New York Times* proclaimed the new president to be "a radio speaker of rare ability. . . . [H]is magnetic voice has vibrated in space to clarify for the people the meaning of bank

The Champ. This photograph was probably taken just before FDR's Fireside Chat on the Works Relief Program on April 28, 1935. Reproduced by the Franklin D. Roosevelt Library, Hyde Park, New York (NPx 48–49:311).

reform, inflation, legal beer, mortgage relief, taxation, and many knotty problems linked with international relations." By January 1934, FDR had given 24 radio speeches over NBC and CBS, including four fireside chats.[46]

Possessing a voice that transmitted across radio clearly and melodiously—Mark Sullivan once remarked that FDR could "recite the Polish alphabet and it would be accepted as an eloquent plea for disarmament"—Roosevelt took his broadcasting technique very seriously.[47] After working through many drafts of a script with his writers, and at least one rehearsal, he spoke slowly, at an average of 95 words a minute, and took care to use the simplest and clearest possible language. He customarily referred to himself as "I" and his listeners as "you" to create a sense of immediacy, and attempted to unite his audience by the use of familiar expressions—"I have no expectation of making a hit every time I come to bat"—and by identifying a small group, such as "chiselers," or the European dictators, against whom he and his listeners had to struggle.[48]

Well aware of the networks' strict scheduling, FDR often divided his scripts into five-minute sections so that he could time his speech precisely. He was also alive to the changing nature of the radio audience, and scheduled most of his fireside chats on Sunday, Monday, and Tuesday evenings, when audiences were largest and press coverage the following day most comprehensive. Roosevelt generally kept his radio speeches short, usually 15 minutes, and tried to interfere as little as possible with the networks' commercial commitments. He was also careful not to overexpose himself on radio, making only 16 fireside chats during the first two years of his presidency, and only 31 during his 12-year tenure. Despite, or perhaps because of, his reputation as a radio maestro, FDR spent less time on the airwaves during his first term than Herbert Hoover in his.

FDR also paid close attention to public reaction to his radio performances. He received digests of the avalanches of mail that his fireside chats elicited, and he kept a close eye on other indications of public reaction. Radio audience measurement techniques developed during the early 1930s, and by 1935 two competing ratings systems, devised by Archibald Crossley and by Claude Hooper, had emerged as industry standards. Both measurements rated FDR's radio speeches during the second half of the 1930s and into the 1940s. According to the Hooper ratings, FDR's audience varied from 10 percent of radio homes for a speech in June 1936 to a record breaking 79 percent for his fireside chat soon after Pearl Harbor. The president's Hooper ratings for five radio addresses between June 1936 and November 1938 averaged 18.4 percent of radio homes, a figure that rose to a commanding average of 53.8 percent over nine speeches between January 1940 and February 1942.[49]

Roosevelt's use of broadcasting reflected more than his proficiency with the mechanics and strategy of radio politics. The president's dislike of newspaper owners, editors, and columnists is well known. Although historians have discounted FDR's famous assessment that he was opposed by 85 percent of American newspapers, at least 60 percent did so after the crisis of the winter of 1932–33 and before the outbreak of World War II in 1939.[50] Radio appealed strongly to Roosevelt because it offered voters a chance to receive information unadulterated by newspaper proprietors' bias. The broadcasters' nonpartisan policies and avoidance of controversy also seemed both appropriate and useful to the president. In 1939 he announced a series of nationwide radio talks by members of his cabinet. "I like the idea of keeping the broadcasts entirely factual. . . . In some communities it is the unhappy fact that only through the radio is it possible to overtake loudly proclaimed untruths or greatly exaggerated half-truths." Given his views about the bias of the press, it was not surprising that the president was determined to prevent, or at least retard, the tendency of newspaper owners to buy and operate radio stations.[51]

Franklin Roosevelt also had more personal reasons for becoming a radio president. Radio offered the opportunity to perpetuate what Hugh Gallagher has called his "splendid deception" of the American people.[52] Radio allowed Roosevelt simultaneously to conceal his disability from the public and to negate its limits upon his movement. Through the microphone FDR could communicate his personality and policies to the nation without frequent speaking tours which would expose his paralysis to general view. Contemporaries, pointing to his mellifluous voice, often remarked that FDR was made for radio. The president himself, who had experienced the humiliation of toppling over on stages, and the rigors of holding himself upright by the strength of his upper body and the rigidity of the lectern, had good reason to value a medium that allowed him to do much of his public communication from a wheelchair in his study away from the public gaze.

"A mighty stream of material": The New Deal on Air

The new administration, led by its radio star in the White House, proved adept at publicity. By the end of Roosevelt's first year in office the Associated Press carried three times more news from Washington than it had done in 1930.[53] The New Deal proved to be intensely newsworthy because it combined astute news management with a dramatic escalation of the importance of the federal government in the lives of ordinary citizens. Americans received crash courses in banking, international finance, agricultural price support, the NRA, and securities regulation, as well as a flood of information about public works programs and other employment measures. Listeners also received much reassurance that FDR and the New Dealers were devoted to the improvement of conditions for all Americans.

The New Deal's publicity campaign consumed large amounts of taxpayers' money and governmental energy. By the middle of 1937 the number of publicity officers within federal departments had grown by nearly 500 percent since 1932, and in 1936 alone the federal government sent 670 million pieces of mail to its citizens. "From all these typewriters flows a mighty stream of material," columnist Lawrence Sullivan noted in 1937, and "all of it is prepared with a view to presenting the originating agency . . . in the best possible light."[54] Government radio programming took many forms, from crop reports by the Department of Agriculture to regular broadcasts of the armed services' bands. Table 5 shows the ways in which a Brookings Institution sur-

Table 5. Subject Content of Federal Agencies' Network Programs, January–April, 1937.

Type of Program	15 minutes	30 minutes	1 hour	Total by Type
Discussion of problems and policies	23	2	0	25
Discussion of work of the agency	12	3	0	15
Facts from research	9	0	0	9
Explaining agency's program	9	1	0	10
Feature stories or entertainment	5	4	4	13
Efforts to influence legislation/policy	3	1	0	4
Honoring or featuring personnel	1	0	1*	2
Ceremonial observances	3	1	0	4
Not classifiable	6	0	0	6
TOTAL	71	12	5	88

SOURCE: James L. McCamy, *Government Publicity: Its Practice in Federal Administration*, p. 96.
*Actual program time: 45 minutes.

vey classified 88 government broadcasts on network radio between January and April 1937.

In keeping with contemporary theories of effective radio technique, the great majority of federal agency programming was short. Just over 80 percent of the programs surveyed in the Brookings study were 15 minutes long, while only 5.7 percent occupied a full hour. Although 59 of the 88 programs were classified as educational, the 32 programs classified as "explaining agency's program," "feature stories," "efforts to influence legislation or policy," "honoring personnel," and "ceremonial observances" showed that the New Dealers were prepared to stretch their programming ambitions. These programs, which represented more than 36 percent of the survey's total, were also most likely to raise the ire of those who objected to governmental publicity as nothing more than advertisements for the administration.

One example of the mixed motives of governmental programming was the broadcast of the "W.P.A. Staff Meeting" on NBC's Red network on June 20, 1936. This program, featuring WPA chief Harry Hopkins, the governor of Pennsylvania, the mayor of San Francisco, an industrialist, an author, a representative of the American Farm Bureau Federation, and "several WPA workers," neatly combined educative, entertainment, and political functions. Despite its title, the program was in fact a dramatized and scripted question and answer session between Hopkins and the other participants. During the 15-minute program listeners learned that the WPA currently employed 2.5 million people, that it had already improved 125,000 miles of rural roads, that it paid decent wages, and that it was planning new projects to help the unemployed over the next year. One WPA worker, who had five children, asked whether he could remain on the WPA payroll. "While we in Washington do not decide who gets the job," WPA Assistant Administrator Thad Holt replied, "I am safe in saying that with a situation like yours, you will keep your job." This program, which was aired only weeks before the 1936 campaign season, was typical of much New Deal radio publicity. While NBC could claim it as an exercise in educational and civic programming, its political value in reassuring the unemployed that their welfare was in safe hands was clear.[55]

The administration's critics were quick to denounce the New Dealers' penchant for publicity as an insidious form of publicly funded electioneering. Although most New Deal publicity was directed through the print media, the press nevertheless argued that radio was especially vulnerable to being pressed into service as the administration's mouthpiece. *Editor and Publisher* explained in September 1933 why radio and movies had become the preferred means of government publicity:

> First because they can be commandeered at a moment's notice, without expense. . . . They question nothing, have no opinions, are removed from the great political controversies, and offer what is called direct contact with a considerable section of the sovereign voting population. Radio has to dance to Government tunes because it is under Government license. . . . Naturally both radio and motion pictures are effective instruments in a national crusade which depends in considerable part upon emotional appeal.[56]

Radio Campaigning, 1933–1936

FDR's first term was notable not only for the flood of New Deal publicity but also for the enormous popularity of two other radio speakers, Father Charles Coughlin of Detroit and Senator Huey Long of Louisiana, who emerged as FDR's only rivals as the nation's most effective radio politician.[57] Both men used network radio to extend their influence far beyond their own fiefdoms. Coughlin, who began his radio sermons in 1926 in an effort to swell his dwindling congregations, received more mail than any other American, including the president, in 1934. By then he had hired 100 clerks to process an average of 150,000 letters per week from his ten million listeners. After one broadcast in February 1932 Coughlin received 1.25 million letters, and in the first six months of 1936 his listeners sent in more than $324,000 in money orders. Coughlin's radio sermons became increasingly political after 1929, attacking Hoover, the banks, and industrialists for their inactivity in the face of the Depression. Under pressure from the Hoover administration, CBS banished Coughlin from its airwaves in 1931, forcing him to broadcast on a network of unaffiliated stations.[58]

The radio priest urged his listeners to vote for Roosevelt in 1932, but his honeymoon with the new administration was brief. He soon accused it of complicity with an international Jewish banking cabal and its plans for the deliberate impoverishment of workers. FDR, he told his listeners, was "the dumbest man ever to occupy the White House," and an "anti-God."[59] Coughlin's addresses were frequently cited by radio experts as models of propaganda technique. A 1939 study noted that his speeches invariably incorporated the "7 ABCs" of modern propaganda, including "Name Calling, Glittering Generality, Plain Folks, and Band Wagon." Coughlin's radio propaganda technique had clear parallels with Adolf Hitler's, whom Coughlin supported more and more explicitly in his increasingly anti-Semitic radio addresses during the second half of the 1930s.[60]

Huey Long also perfected his radio technique as he worked his way up through Louisiana's byzantine Democratic organization. Having served as governor for two years before winning election to the United States Senate in 1930, Long used radio to create his own personality cult and to publicize his "Share Our Wealth" plan.[61] Long's position as a U.S. Senator ensured him access to the national networks, and he used this exposure to portray his plans as viable alternatives to the New Deal. His radio style was clearly "Plain Folks," incorporating colloquialisms, homey expressions, and humor. He typically began his broadcasts by asking his listeners to telephone their friends and to tell them to listen. "About five or six a piece," the senator urged, "and tell them that I'm fixing to talk, get them on the phone."

After a musical interlude to give his listeners time to spread the word, Long began his rambling talks. In a 45-minute radio speech over WDSU, New Orleans, in February 1935, he told his listeners about Louisiana's debt moratorium scheme and his efforts to reduce utility charges, before turning to the failures of FDR and the New Deal. FDR, Long claimed, "is just two doses of Hoover. . . . Hoover was a headache, Roosevelt is two of them." He had ruined working people through the NRA and his support of the Wagner Act, and now the president proposed that poorer Americans should fund their own age pensions. Instead, Long claimed, the country should demand that its millionaires be shorn of all their income above $1 million per year. From those funds Long promised every American family a minimum annual income of $2,500, as well as a "household estate" of a car, a washing machine, and—not surprisingly—a radio.[62] Along the way, Long also told his audience stories of cotton pickers, greedy millionaires, his own experience battling utilities, and about his plans to teach "society" how to eat peas with a knife.[63]

Like the best of the New Deal publicists, Long was skilled at combining entertainment with political persuasion. Although Coughlin could not equal Long's humor and chose not to emulate his inclusive message, the combination of these two radio crusaders seemed for a time to threaten FDR's reelection plans. The administration, anxious to regain its dominance of radio politics, hit back at its most dangerous opponents. "You can laugh at Huey Long—you can snort at Father Coughlin—but this country was never under a greater menace," General Hugh Johnson told listeners during a free broadcast on NBC in March 1935. "Between the team of Huey Long and the priest we have the whole bag of crazy and crafty tricks . . . possessed by Peter the Hermit, Napoleon Bonaparte, Sitting Bull, William Hohenzollern, Hitler, Lenin . . . boiled down to two with the radio and the newsreel to make them effective."[64]

At the state and local levels radio made more modest headway in political campaigns between 1933 and 1936. During the New York City mayoralty race in 1933 NBC sold 16 time slots to the four main candidates for a total of $7,331.20.[65] For most local and state races radio remained as an occasional supplement to more traditional forms of campaigning. When Robert LaFollette Jr. sought reelection to the Senate from Wisconsin in 1934, he relied heavily upon speeches and personal appearances. During September and October LaFollette made only two paid broadcasts, which cost $56. His speaking schedule for the last week of the campaign called for 12 speeches and only one radio date.[66]

Radio did play a prominent role in the most celebrated state election campaign of the decade. When the novelist and socialist Upton Sinclair ran for governor of California on the Democratic ticket in 1934, he campaigned on a slogan and platform of End Poverty in California (EPIC). Sinclair promised a way out of the Depression by putting underemployed factories and farms to work under state supervision. The unemployed would be offered work in idle factories and ownership of what they produced. Farmers were promised higher crop prices through payment by state-funded vouchers, which would be good for payment of taxes. Sinclair also promised to create "land colonies" for the unemployed out of land held by speculators who "will be glad to rent the land to the state."

Sinclair's opponents, frightened by his initial popularity, undertook an intense and well-funded campaign against EPIC using movies, newsreels, billboards, newspapers, and radio. Faked newsreels, showing legions of hoboes about to invade California, were particularly effective. The radio campaign against Sinclair, conducted by the Lord and Thomas advertising agency, focused upon serials made specifically for the campaign. During the height of the battle 35 actors made a series of programs, including *The Bennetts*, which followed a middle-class family's discussions about the election and its eventual decision to vote against Sinclair in the interests of fiscal prudence and state pride. *Weary and Willie* portrayed two bums on their way to California to share the largesse promised by EPIC. Anti-Sinclair radio programs ran almost every day during the campaign; in the final week local stations ran spot advertisements as short as 35 words.[67] In its heavy and well-financed use of visual and radio campaigning, and in its relentless negativism, the successful campaign against Sinclair presaged many later electioneering techniques. In the context of the early 1930s, however, it was an aberration. Very few local and state candidates and political organizations during this period could afford the high cost of intensive newsreel and radio campaigning that sank Upton Sinclair.

The Election of 1936

"Talk will not be cheap this year," the *New York Times* warned federal politicians in May 1936. Once again CBS and NBC had raised their prices, and the parties could expect to pay more than $18,000 per hour for CBS's 96 stations and $16,000 for an hour on NBC's Red network. Neither side seemed put off by these costs, and plans for expanded coverage were well under way.[68] An early DNC campaign budget set aside $340,000 out of a total of $1.65 million for radio costs, a figure that was increased by FDR himself to $500,000 within a new total of nearly $2.3 million. The DNC's radio spending, which reached $540,000 by the end of the campaign, represented nearly a quarter of the total national Democratic expenditures in 1936. This dwarfed the budget of $183,000 for its New York headquarters, $382,000 for printed publicity, $32,000 for speakers, and $15,000 for motion pictures. The president himself cut the proposed expenditure of $88,000 for presidential trains down to $25,000; the radio maestro had recognized which medium was best suited to his strengths and disabilities.[69]

Once again the two parties choreographed their conventions to maximize their listening audiences. Nomination ceremonies for FDR and Republican candidate Alf Landon occurred during the evening, and the Republicans were careful to introduce their little-known candidate with carefully staged and timed applause.[70] Both sides shortened their programs to a maximum of 30 minutes, and the GOP began its radio campaign on August 1, nearly a month earlier than in 1932. The RNC and DNC made heavy use of spot advertisements on local stations, and the Republicans imitated the anti-EPIC tactic of frequent repetition of 35-word announcements. The women's divisions of both national committees undertook intensive radio programs during the morning hours, and the GOP targeted foreign-language voters through non-English broadcasting in ten industrial cities of the Northeast and Midwest.[71]

Both the RNC and the DNC attempted to introduce innovations into their 1936 radio campaigns. The Republicans urged sympathetic business advertisers to include two-minute segments prepared by the RNC into their existing programming. These messages bore no indication of their source and had the added attraction of being free advertising for the party. Although the GOP assured the companies that these segments were "strictly non-political, non-partisan, with no mention of personalities, or candidates," their emphasis upon the need for governmental economy and lower taxes had clear resonances with the political campaign against the New Deal. The Republicans had little success with this idea. When Fred Purnell of the RNC's Speaker's Bureau approached the Du Pont Company—whose senior executives were prominent opponents of the New Deal—to incorporate a segment on governmental economy into its programming, the company politely declined, saying, "We do not want to do anything which might be misinterpreted in any way, or which might subject us to demands that we contribute a similar amount of time to other announcements from political sources." The Democrats retaliated by mobilizing Democratic directors of major corporations to prevent any firm from cooperating in the scheme.[72]

Radio received full recognition for its role in Roosevelt's landslide victory. Charles Michelson conceded, "We had an even break on the radio, with the best radio voice in the world, which, added to the prestige of the Presidency, his gift of phrases, and the quality of his speeches, insured him audiences larger than the opposing candidate could hope for." Michelson did, however, regret that the radio budget was allowed to exceed its original allocation of $500,000, conceding that the extra money might have been better used elsewhere.[73] Michelson's mild regret must have paled beside the Republicans' dismay at the results from their radio expenditures of nearly $1 million. Landon won only 36.5 percent of the national vote in his uneven contest with FDR. For the third time in succession, the losing party had spent more on radio than the winner.

Radio and the 1940 Campaign

The last of the interwar presidential campaigns, and the fifth of the radio age, saw further expansion and refinement of radio campaigning techniques.

Although total campaign budgets for both the Democrats and the Republicans were less than in 1936, radio expenditures increased significantly. Erik Barnouw estimated that the two major parties' national and state organizations spent $2.25 million on broadcasting from their combined expenditures of $6.2 million.[74] This entrenched broadcasting as the single largest expense of modern campaigning. Both the RNC and DNC devoted a great deal of energy to integrating their radio campaigns with their other publicity efforts. Broadcasting, newspapers, speeches, billboards, and newsreel advertising were all coordinated so as to maximize their impact upon the electorate.[75]

Republicans and Democrats also worked hard to organize nominally independent organizations that were created to sell their candidates to specific groups. The RNC maintained close connections with a large number of groups who, for a variety of reasons, chose not to work under the aegis of the Republican Party. Organizations such as the Associated Clubs for Willkie, the No Third Term Democrats, and the Commercial Democratic Business Men for Willkie all bought radio time on their own accounts from the networks during 1940, while at the same time cooperating with the RNC's overall publicity strategy.[76] The DNC also coordinated a large number of "independent" groups such as the National Committee of Independent Voters for Roosevelt and Wallace and the Writers' Committee for Roosevelt. Women voters were again prime targets, and the Women's Division of the DNC, led by Dorothy McAllister, devised a series of one-minute advertisements for local stations. Each of the spots, about 130 words long, featured a woman representing a specific occupation and region, and was scripted in "the appropriate idiom of the individual represented." One advertisement featured a "secretary": "I am not a big business woman myself, but I happen to be in the Statistical Department of a big business house and every day my typewriter clicks off figures, in black not red. . . . The figures are extremely satisfying to my boss. The man who is responsible for my boss' satisfaction is the candidate who satisfies me, Franklin D. Roosevelt."[77]

The Women's Division of the DNC also coordinated a publicity program to mobilize women in contested political areas. Molly Dewson began work on a "Six-point Program for Democratic Women" during the 1936 campaign, and by 1940 her plan encompassed radio, the press, speakers, newsletters, and "donkey banks" to finance postage and transport costs. By 1940 her division ran more than 2,000 discussion groups and 30,000 members in one-third of the nation's counties. Local broadcasting was the domain of 1,000 state and county directors of radio, who publicized forthcoming programs in newspapers, through telephone committees, and by printed notices. To assist them

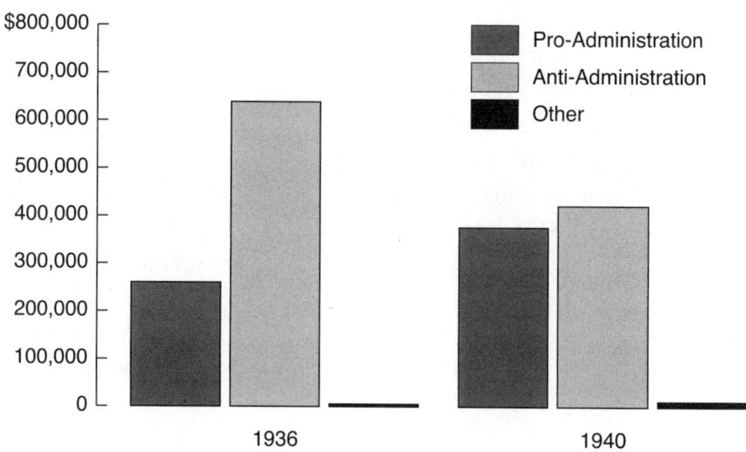

Figure 9. NBC Billings, 1936 and 1940 Campaigns.

Source: Graph constructed from data in NBC Research Division, "Political Campaign of 1940: An Analysis of Political Broadcasting over NBC Networks," Dec. 30, 1940, NBC MSS, file 337.

in this work, the Women's Division sent prepared radio scripts on issues such as "Unemployment Insurance," "The Federal Wage-Hour Bill," and "Next Steps in Social Security." Radio directors received advice on radio speaking, and they hosted "listening parties" to coincide with important Democratic broadcasts. Radio, Democratic women were told, "is God's gift to the Democratic party."[78]

Although Dewson's plan remained more an ambitious goal than a fully realized structure, it reflected both parties' increasing dependence upon radio advertising. At the end of the 1940 campaign NBC reported that it had sold time to 23 organizations, of which five represented Democratic interests and 16 supported the GOP. NBC also sold almost $9,000 worth of time, or slightly over 1 percent of its total political billings, to the Socialist Labor Party and to the CPA.[79] Because of smaller campaign budgets and the use of shorter programs on local stations, NBC devoted only 56 hours to political programming in 1940, a sharp drop from the 127 hours used in 1936. The network suffered a much smaller decline in its billings, from $904,021 in 1936 to $809,606 in 1940. As in 1928, 1932, and 1936, the losing party spent more on radio than the winners. Figure 9 shows the distribution of NBC billing between pro-administration and pro-Republican organizations in 1936 and 1940.

The gross mismatch between Republican spending on radio and their performance at the polls in 1936 was not repeated in 1940. Although the GOP still significantly outspent the Democrats on radio, Willkie's electoral performance was much more creditable than Landon's; he won 44.8 percent of the popular vote and 82 Electoral College votes. The Republicans had nevertheless failed yet again to translate large radio budgets into electoral majorities; the DNC, on the other hand, had proved to be highly skilled in using their more limited radio funds to maximum effect. During the 1930s Republicans tended to confuse radio quantity with quality, whereas the Democrats seemed better able to transform listeners into voters. By 1940 both major parties had learned that effective radio politics depended far more on careful targeting, good technique, and effective content than on mere volume.

9

The Product

Radio Politics and Campaigning

Charles Merriam of the University of Chicago was the foremost political scientist of the interwar period. He published 13 books, including updated editions of his classic work *The American Party System*, during the 1920s and 1930s. The 1922 edition of that book did not even mention radio, but within seven years Merriam had become a convert to the political power of radio. His second edition, published in 1929, elevated radio to the first rank of "agencies" of public education and political campaigning. The new invention, Merriam argued, had helped to restore an older form of campaigning that had enabled voters in a more rural, homogeneous America to receive firsthand knowledge of national candidates. Although old campaign techniques such as torchlight parades, stump speeches, and hand shaking marathons had largely disappeared, voters in 1930 could still draw their own conclusions about candidates and issues through their radios and in the comfort of their own homes. "In a sense," he concluded, "it may be said that in this respect the earlier conditions of campaigning have been restored, except that personal contact is of course minimized."[1]

Merriam's offhand remark that "personal contact is of course minimized" summed up the euphoric early response to radio in politics. Seduced at first by the new medium's potential to cover the nation, few analysts of the 1920s stopped to consider the consequences of this reduction in "personal contact." In their review of the 1932 campaign, Roy Peel and Thomas Donnelly were also prepared to overlook what they saw as political radio's drawbacks. The cost of broadcasting had made it "impossible for the minor parties to compete with the two major parties," and this they saw as "unfortunate." But they also argued that radio had greatly improved American political campaigning. "No longer can candidates protest that they had been misquoted in the press, and no longer can one song be sung in the West, while another is sung in the East. Radio has made political campaigning more honest, and it has also made government more interesting and popular."[2]

Enthusiasts of radio politics tended to equate information with education, and then education with engagement. Radio could blanket the country with reasoned debate over political issues; millions of listeners, many of whom had previously had little to do with political life, would then find politics more attractive and participate in it more actively. "The radio properly used will do more for popular government than have most of the wars for freedom and self government," *Collier's* magazine declared in 1928. "We fought for the privilege of managing our own affairs and then half of us decided that voting was troublesome and uninteresting. . . . The radio makes politics personal and interesting and therefore important."[3]

Contemporary observers of interwar politics predicted and then discerned the important changes that radio brought to both the style and substance of political life. During the 1920s commentators were overwhelmingly optimistic about these changes, but in the 1930s, as radio lost its initial luster and as Hitler, Long, and Coughlin demonstrated that it could also be used for demagoguery, more measured assessments appeared. By 1940 it appeared that radio had not revolutionized American politics, and that it had not replaced what Merriam had described as "personal contact" in political life. Radio, it now seemed, had only amplified, for both good and ill, the essentially personal nature of electoral politics; it was a powerful tool in the hands of both saints and sinners.

Radio and the Art of Political Oratory

Radio, Samuel Blythe declared in 1929, "has slain the political orator. He is out. The day of the spellbinder is over." Microphones, continental hookups, strict scheduling, and "rigid mechanical and other mysterious requirements," had turned orators into mere "talkers."[4] Old-fashioned oratory, in which speakers traversed the stage, waved their arms, and used emotional rhetoric to engage and entertain their audiences, was now extinct. Radio broadcasting required strict microphone discipline, forcing speakers to remain behind their lecterns to deliver consistent voice volume into the microphone. Many politicians, used to addressing large crowds, chafed under these restrictions. Al Smith was notorious for forgetting the microphones and wandering away

A TRAGEDY OF THE RADIO

[Copyright: 1924: By The Chicago Tribune.]

The Hon. Bunk broadcasts his widely advertised speech—

It is heard by countless multitudes throughout the land.

At the conclusion of his address he makes a few comments—

Which the sensitive instrument picks up and broadcasts to the multitudes.

And he loses the Radio vote and is snowed under in November.

"A Tragedy of the Radio." John McCutcheon's cautionary tale reflects the high hopes of the 1920s that radio could unmask demagogues and frauds. *Chicago Tribune*, July 6, 1924. Reproduced from the Cartoon Collection, box 3, file: "July 1924," Herbert Hoover Presidential Library, West Branch, Iowa.

from the lectern, and at times he would even move the microphone away—a cardinal sin to all radio technicians—in order to make direct eye contact with his audience. Smith's radio advisers during the 1928 presidential campaign resorted to fencing him into microphone range with a corral of chairs. "I'll promise to behave," Smith supposedly responded. "After this I'll remember. Only take those chairs away."[5]

Smith and other politicians also had to submit to the discipline of a script. Pre-radio oratory had favored those who could extemporize; speakers could move around the stage and respond more directly to the emotions of the audience. Radio, however, worked on tight scheduling, and politicians had to time their speeches carefully. Doing so without a script, and without careful rehearsal, proved too difficult for most. The *Saturday Evening Post* claimed that radio had come to the rescue of speakers too unimaginative or too nervous to depart from their scripts. For such a speaker radio was a "godsend . . . he needs no personal appeal or magnetism." Additionally, politicians speaking over networks used a script in order to avoid embarrassing or damaging misstatements. With the whole nation listening, candidates and leaders learned the necessity of choosing, and delivering, their words carefully.[6]

Old-time political oratory was also thought to be inconsistent with the domestic nature of the radio audience. Politicians were frequently reminded that radio listeners differed markedly from audiences at political meetings. Speakers could no longer assume that their audiences were partisan enthusiasts who had taken the trouble to leave their homes to hear their hero speak. Oratory under those circumstances was largely preaching to the converted, and its primary function was to mobilize supporters to go forth and do battle. The radio audience, on the other hand, was a heterogeneous body of people whose places of residence, occupations, and party affiliations were diverse. It included the converted, the unconvinced, the apathetic, and the hostile, and politicians had to adjust their technique accordingly.[7] A good political radio speaker, Orrin Dunlap wrote in 1936, "avoids controversy, attacks nobody, simply gives what is termed a heart-to-heart talk with the man sitting with his slippers on and his pipe in his mouth, reclining on his own armchair. . . . Appeals must be made to the listener's sympathies, his reason, his intelligence, but attempts to arouse sectional, class or religious prejudices are certain to fall flat."[8]

Dunlap's confidence that radio listeners were not susceptible to sectional or sectarian appeals stemmed from his faith in the insulating influence of the home. There, surrounded by family and possessions, radio voters were modern exemplars of the republican ideal, sovereign in their homes and deliberative in their political judgments. Despite the advent of female suffrage, the widespread belief that women made up the majority of radio listeners, and the feminine connotations of the domestic sphere, Dunlap portrayed the typical radio listener-voter in male terms. "Detached from the excitement of a mob the voter sits comfortably at home and eavesdrops on the appeals. He is swayed by cold facts and voice personality. He may be honestly persuaded but seldom swept off his feet. He cannot be commanded."[9]

These voters could also turn off a radio speaker who either bored or displeased them. "The individual is sovereign in deciding what he will listen to," Thomas Robinson declared in 1943. "With a flip of the hand he can turn off presidents, dictators, and kings." Political programming had to compete against other radio entertainment, and it was up to orators to hold their invisible audiences. Some speakers who had come of age before broadcasting found that thought unsettling. Owen Young, President of GEC and a prominent Democrat, told his old friend Newton Baker that his children, "as they nightly tour the radio field, are extremely disrespectful to public speakers, 'tuning them out' ruthlessly. For this reason when I have been speaking I have sometimes felt a depressing sense that out in the reaches of space hundreds and maybe thousands of people were 'tuning me out.'" After a while, Young thought, radio speakers would adjust to this idea and be as little disturbed by it as old orators were about "those who eat peanuts at a meeting."[10]

Politicians were bombarded with advice on radio technique from self-proclaimed experts during the second half of the 1920s and throughout the 1930s. In March 1928, as parties and candidates prepared for the forthcoming national campaign, the *New York Times* again reminded speakers that "brevity and appeal to reason" were essential to broadcasting success. Radio audiences, faced with many choices, would not listen to bores or demagogues; voters in their homes would accept only the very highest standard of political broadcasting. In return, however, they would reward candidates and parties who had best mastered good radio style.[11]

More detailed advice appeared during the 1930s. Orrin E. Dunlap published a list of 50 hints for broadcasters in 1936. Many of these had already become radio clichés. He urged speakers to be brief, conversational, and dignified on air, and to avoid rushing through their scripts. Dunlap recommended microphone discipline, careful voice modulation, simple words, short sentences, well-rehearsed and clearly typed scripts, and "a simple, direct, reasoned message." Most importantly, radio speeches should not be "crammed full of aims and cross aims." Because radio was "too swift a messenger," listeners frequently became confused when speakers tried to make multiple points in a single address. Dunlap recommended that radio orators limit their targets to "one dominant idea," and to concentrate their "bombardment on a major objective."[12]

Dunlap persisted with the 1920s notion of a sovereign and cerebral radio audience. Radio orators should pay close attention to their logic, he warned, for "the listener sits and thinks; you cannot glide over a weak spot with a verbal flourish or gesture." On radio "there is no place . . . for electromagnetic mud-slinging, high-sounding phraseology, hot air, meaningless platitudes and the bunkum of soap-box oratory." In 1936 such advice sat oddly with recent broadcasting experience, which showed that, in the hands of Long and Coughlin, radio could be an effective vehicle of demagoguery and propaganda. Dunlap did, however, recognize that the early dreams that broadcasting would remake campaigning were exaggerated. "Do not hide behind the microphone," he warned politicians. "It was a futuristic idea in 1924 that the candidate would sit at home and conduct an armchair campaign. The candidate who travels with the microphone is the winner."[13]

Newspapers and magazines frequently evaluated politicians' radio styles on the basis of these rules. During the 1928 campaign the *New York Times* described Al Smith's radio style as "novel." Despite his lack of microphone discipline, and his Lower East Side accent, the governor exuded both emotion and reason over the airwaves. "Smith's delivery is warm," CBS President Andrew White declared, "too dynamic perhaps for the placidity of the family circle—but studded here and there with a sparkling gem of humor or human interest anecdote." Herbert Hoover, on the other hand, "speaks as he would to an audience in a hall, rather than using the warm, friendly type of speech which is appropriate to the home." Four years later, at the end of the 1932 campaign, the *Times* again reviewed the radio performances of the nation's most important politicians. Once again Smith won praise for his humor and warmth, while Hoover's radio manner was described as "a little heavy in quality and reveals strain." Franklin Roosevelt won the highest praise of all; his voice was a "well trained instrument, capable of reflecting his moods and the color of his thoughts. . . . To have heard him . . . would be enough to convince the listener that he was sincere in utterance and good natured even in attack." FDR was a little too proficient for his own good; "it may be," one CBS expert believed, "that a personality a little too pleasant is disclosed in his speech."[14]

Radio and Amusement Guide polled its readers in June 1932 on the radio abilities of presidential hopefuls. The magazine did not reveal its methodology, but its survey showed that Newton D. Baker, and not FDR, was the radio champion. Arguing from the assumptions that the 1932 race was "a nose and

Table 6. *Radio and Amusement Guide* Ratings of Presidential Candidates' Air Personalities, 1932 (100 = perfect score).

Candidates	Men	Women	Urban	Rural	Average
Newton Baker	92	96	90	92	92.5
Franklin Roosevelt	92	83	80	81	84
Albert Ritchie	72	80	80	78	77.5
Alfred Smith	88	76	96	40	75
John Garner	85	75	44	94	74.5
Herbert Hoover	82	54	73	78	71.75

SOURCE: *Radio and Amusement Guide* 1 (June 1932): 1. Broadcast Pioneers Library, file: "Radio and Amusement Guide."

nose affair," and that Hoover was an indifferent radio performer, the *Guide* argued that the "air personality" of the eventual Democratic nominee would be crucial to the party's chances in November, and that therefore "radio will decide the election of the next President of the United States!"

Radio and the Art of Campaigning

Despite the hopes of its enthusiasts, radio did not usher in a radically different form of campaigning to interwar politics. Campaigns around the time of the Civil War relied upon massive parades, rallies, and picnics to create what Michael McGerr has called the "spectacular" style, which "encouraged the voter to see himself as a member of a well-defined community rather than as an unimportant figure lost in a sea of electors." The prominence of new issues in the 1880s such as civil service reform, tariff policy, and industry regulation brought forth a new educational style. Rather than devoting their resources to mobilizing the faithful, political parties concentrated on wooing independent voters through massive speech and pamphlet campaigns designed to "educate" them about issues. The coming of the educational campaign coincided with, and was influenced by, the decline in the partisan press during the later years of the nineteenth century.[15]

The McKinley-Bryan campaign of 1896 ushered in a new style that relied heavily upon advertising. This became the twentieth-century norm, transforming voters into consumers and policies and politicians into competing commodities. Campaigning became less concerned with enlightening voters and more interested in selling them the rational and irrational virtues of competing sets of propositions and images. Inherent in the advertising style is a heavy emphasis upon candidates rather than platforms or parties, and upon slogans rather than pamphleteering. As new technology such as photography, lithography, electric signs, phonographs, sound trucks, movies, radio, and television emerged, each was integrated into political campaigns and other national publicity efforts such as those surrounding intervention into both world wars.[16] Of these new media, radio and TV have had the greatest impact. Photography and lithography merely improved traditional forms of publicity such as pamphlets and posters, and electric signs only incrementally extended the visibility of banners and billboards.

Although some candidates used phonographic recordings as part of their campaign materials, these did not figure prominently in any campaigns during the twentieth century. Movies also failed to revolutionize campaigning. Although all national candidates after 1920 used newsreels to reach cinema audiences, few bothered with the time and expense involved in full-scale film production. With the prominent exception of the EPIC campaign in 1934, the movie industry itself was reluctant to become involved in political campaigning. Radio and TV, on the other hand, evolved new forms of political advertisements, provided candidates with quick production and distribution facilities, and, as we have seen, their operators were generally receptive to the needs of those candidates with the financial resources to employ them.[17]

Radio did not invent the advertising style, but it did provide a new means by which millions of voters could be sold candidates and platforms. The impact of broadcasting on political discourse and campaigning, however, highlights the dangers of categorizing campaign styles too rigidly and of overestimating radio's impact upon the ways that politicians and electors interacted. In practice the differences between the educational and advertising styles were often subtle; the advertising style still "educated" voters, albeit more about candidates than policies, and radio was seen as a vital new educative force in politics. Campaigns during the golden age of radio were still marked by massive pamphleteering and mailing campaigns designed to make voters aware of real and imagined differences in party platforms and policies.

There is no doubt that radio brought to many voters a more immediate and personal conception of candidates than they had received from older media. One listener wrote to Senator Thomas Walsh, who served as permanent chairman of the marathon Democratic convention in 1924, to express his admiration after "our six days listening." "Of course, I have known you nationally, by repute," Sidney Arthur told Walsh, "but I feel that I have almost come in contact with you 'on the air.' The deep resonance of your voice and the intensity of your sense of justice, have appealed to me immensely."[18] By bringing a form of personal campaigning into American homes, radio relieved voters from the obligation of attending meetings in order to get a personal impression of candidates. It also assisted those groups, such as women and the elderly, who had been marginalized or excluded by stump speeches, to form their own impressions of those who sought their votes. Radio did not, however, either immediately or single-handedly revolutionize American politics into wholly candidate-based advertising campaigns. Potential voters during the radio age still seemed to yearn for visual and physical contact with candidates.[19]

Radio broadcasting did not arrest the trend toward the more public candidacies that had characterized campaigns, especially for the presidency, since the end of the nineteenth century. Presidential candidates until the late 1880s were generally neither seen nor heard by voters; personal appeals for votes and national speaking tours were thought to be undignified for candidates and demeaning to the office. Bryan in 1896 ushered in a new era of modern presidential campaigning by his tireless speaking tours, but only underfunded or desperate candidates, such as Theodore Roosevelt in 1912, James Cox in 1920, and LaFollette in 1924, followed his example. Most presidential aspirants steered a middle course between reticence and barnstorming. Sitting presidents such as Taft in 1912, Wilson in 1916, and Coolidge in 1924 stayed close to the White House but engaged in set public appearances, while non-incumbents such as Hughes in 1912, Harding in 1920, and Hoover in 1928 undertook a few major speeches and numerous brief addresses either from their front porches or from the rear of their campaign trains.[20]

Candidates still felt the need to press the flesh. In 1928 Al Smith made 12 major campaign speeches, all of which were broadcast, but spent the rest of the campaign touring the country. Herbert Hoover, far better known and less confronting to provincial voters, still found it necessary to schedule large numbers of public appearances in front of live audiences from his campaign train.[21] Even Franklin Roosevelt, acknowledged as the radio master of the age and limited by his physical disability, made personal appearances in all four of his presidential campaigns. In 1936, for example, the president undertook a tour of western states by train, accompanied by 25 newspaper reporters, 8 photographers, 2 telegraph operators, and 5 radio announcers and technicians. Traditional campaign media subsided but did not disappear in the 1930s; in 1936 the RNC still sent out 18 million posters, 361,000 press releases, 42 million buttons, 15 million car stickers, and at least 400 million pamphlets to the electorate alongside its intensive radio campaign.[22]

The *Brooklyn Eagle* in 1924 described personal campaigning as "an implied compliment to the electorate . . . in the honest willingness to go to personal trouble and inconvenience to meet Mr. and Mrs. Voter in their home communities."[23] Despite the feasibility of a radio front porch campaign, politicians in the radio age still paid voters this compliment. Handshaking and baby kissing remain key features of modern political campaigns, as are speeches made to audiences outside radio or TV studios. Although these events are nowadays meticulously choreographed for TV, they are hardy survivors of an earlier, pre-technological era. Radio, the first of the electronic media, created a hybrid campaign style that combined education with advertising, and front porch oratory with mass exposure. Television furthered this hybridization by pushing candidates to the forefront and by returning to occasions such as nominating conventions and rallies the pomp and spectacle, albeit in a sanitized and highly controlled form, that they had manifested during the height of the spectacular style.

The mixed impact of radio upon political campaigning during the interwar years is best illustrated by comparing the hopes for a new political style in the 1920s and the more measured analyses of the 1930s. There were "epoch-making signs of the revolution," Helen Lowry observed in July 1924, which showed that radio had made politics "the possession, not of the few, but of the very general public. Politics has been Sovietized by the upheaval, even if private property hasn't." Radio had allowed millions of Americans to hear the political process at work, and "hundred per cent American institutions—fixed political methods, bosses and oratory—are going to have to be done over into a twentieth century mold to suit the exacting taste of Brooklyn newsboys, of college professors and of home-keeping females."[24]

Others shared these hopes for a radio revolution. "The character of political campaigns . . . was greatly changed by the telegraph and the telephone," the *Richmond Times-Dispatch* told its readers at the end of 1928, but "it was revolutionized by the radio. Men and women of the country went to the polls with a better understanding of the personalities of the candidates and of the issues involved." Radio deserved the credit for the increase in voter registration in 1928, for a jump in turnout over that of 1924, and for the greater interest and participation of women in the Smith-Hoover contest.[25] "Broadcasting is really a house-to-house canvasser," Andrew White of CBS told the press in 1928. "It accompanies the candidates into the home—direct to the family circle. The members of the family now form their own political opinions. . . . Today, mother may vote for Hoover and father for Smith, just because of impressions formed by listening in on the radio." The *Omaha World-Herald* argued that radio had put an end to what Michael Holt later described as Janus-faced campaigns, in which candidates could make different promises to various sections of the nation, and the paper even thought that the new medium would shorten national election seasons. A few radio speeches on national networks would spread more public knowledge about the issues of each campaign than old-fashioned campaigning could achieve in six months.[26]

The radio revolution would bring great changes. "As a row of houses goes down before a cyclone," Charles Willis declared in 1930, "the immemorial and apparently eternal institutions of campaigning are falling before the radio hurricane. No longer does the candidate kiss babies; no longer does he go to fairs and put himself on exhibition." After witnessing the two national parties' nominating conventions in 1928, the *Nation* remarked that radio had made the physical audience of delegates "relatively unimportant" compared to the broadcast audience, to whom proceedings were now primarily addressed. One writer declared in 1928 that radio had proved itself to be "the greatest debunking influence that has come into American public life since the Declaration of Independence." It had created a modern equivalent of the town meetings of colonial New England, the "only difference" being that modern listeners "cannot talk back."[27] The *New Republic* was even more ambitious in its historical analogies; in 1924 it argued that radio "does reproduce to some degree, for the first time in the United States, the conditions of the Athenian democracy where every voter, for himself, could hear and judge the candidates." Because radio made it easy and relaxing to listen to political debate, it promised to bring the "lazy, the illiterate, and the prejudiced, the mentally as well as the geographically remote" into the political nation. "Who can tell to what calamitous political excesses it may one day lead? See grandmother being converted to Socialism as she knits of an evening with her earphones on."[28]

Doubts about the Revolution

More skeptical evaluations of the radio revolution appeared during the 1930s. Even in the earliest years of broadcasting some commentators reserved judgment as to whether political life and campaigns would change either dramatically or for the better. "Fundamentally," the *El Paso Times* declared during the 1924 presidential campaign, "the sovereign voters are not much interested in what Presidents and would-be presidents have to say. What the sovereign voters do enjoy . . . is seeing how the great man's ears are shaped, how his nose wrinkles when he laughs . . . and in hearing fourth-hand what he said to Old Lady Robinson, who tackled him on the prohibition issue. The radio can't give them that, so where's the outdoor sport?"[29]

Robert and Helen Lynd, in their study of life and culture in Middletown, also questioned the idea that radio listening led to greater interest in political life. The inhabitants of Middletown seemed to use radio more for entertainment than for education, and the Lynds found no evidence of an upsurge in political interest or engagement in their community. Voter turnout had declined from 86 percent in 1892 to 53 percent in 1916, and in 1924, despite the influence of radio, only 46 percent of eligible voters bothered to vote. The late 1920s seemed to many to be a period of widespread political apathy, especially in comparison to the enthusiasm of the years before World War I. F. Scott Fitzgerald thought that "it was characteristic of the Jazz Age that it had no interest in politics at all," and Walter Lippmann recalled that in the 1920s "the opportunities to make money were so ample that it was a waste of time to think about politics."[30]

Radio could not alone reverse what in hindsight appears to be a slow but inexorable decline in public partisanship in the face of competing sources of identity and entertainment. Radio listening was a "fad," Bruce Bliven noted in June 1924. "In the long run, anybody who wouldn't sit through an hour's discussion of national or local issues in a lecture-hall will probably be equally impatient when tuning in on the oratory." Listening to the 1924 Democratic convention convinced many that "a political convention could be a grand show . . . and that a seat by the radio was as good as a ticket to the Garden," Frederick Lewis Allen remembered in *Only Yesterday*, his "informal history" of the 1920s. "Better, in fact; for at any moment you could turn a knob and get 'Barney Google' or 'It Ain't Gonna Rain No More' by way of respite."[31] Increasingly, it seemed to many radio sceptics, Americans sought respite rather than enlightenment from their radios.

Skepticism regarding the radio revolution grew stronger in the 1930s, despite the upsurge of partisanship during the Depression and the New Deal. Instead of pointing to radio's failure to excite the electorate into political engagement, as they had done in the 1920s, those who questioned the assumption that broadcasting would automatically improve political life looked with alarm at the success of Adolf Hitler, Huey Long, and Father Coughlin. Will Irwin typified this approach in his *Propaganda and the News*, published in 1936. Radio had replaced one form of spellbinding with another; successful radio oratory was "something akin to the pleasing conversation of the peddler dispensing brushes . . . [but] when at its most vicious, it is exactly as meretricious as the rolling periods of the old spellbinder." Within five years of the advent of commercial radio and national networks, Irwin noted, Long and Coughlin "were broadcasting effective fairytales to millions of wishful thinkers."[32]

Other critics observed that the old rules of politics seemed remarkably resistant to the cleansing effect of broadcasting.[33] In 1932, 12 years after radio broadcasting began, the two presidential candidates once again boarded campaign trains and made numerous speeches. Herbert Hoover made 22 speeches in 15 hours during his train journey from Washington to California in a performance that rivaled those of Bryan in 1896 and Cox in 1920. Such spectacles, the *New York Times* admitted during the campaign, "may indicate that we have been too hasty in assuming that the radio and talking pictures . . . have radically revolutionized our political campaigning. They have undoubtedly wrought a wondrous change in it, but have they destroyed the old human conviction that an actual personality is the most moving and vitalizing thing in the world—even in the world of politics?"[34]

Nearly four years later, as it anticipated the 1936 campaign, the *Times* returned to the incomplete radio revolution. Under a headline declaring that "radio campaigning demands a technique of its own, but it has not changed the basic rules of the game," the paper assessed the impact of radio upon political life as "uncertain." It had undoubtedly transformed Long and Coughlin into national figures, and it had perhaps increased public consciousness and knowledge of politics, although this latter claim was qualified by the fact that "the great political use of radio has coincided with a social crisis when the public, if ever, would be interested in its government." Yet the foundations of party politics—local organizations, patronage, money, and personal campaigning—had not crumbled before the microphone. "In national politics the radio has had less effect, despite all that has been said, than might be expected."[35]

Some critics of radio in politics argued that broadcasting had contributed to a dangerous inflation of campaign expenditures during the 1920s. Election funding had long been a contentious issue, fueled by concerns that democracy should not be for sale and by the historical tendency of the Republicans to raise and spend far more on election campaigns than the Democrats. The last presidential and congressional elections of the pre-radio age in 1920 cost about $10 million, divided almost four to one in favor of the GOP.[36] In 1928 the total rose to more than $17 million. In 1860, the *New York Times* pointed out, committees supporting Abraham Lincoln and Stephen Douglas spent about $150,000; now the DNC alone contemplated a budget of more than $7 million on behalf of Al Smith. With both national committees spending between $50,000 and $60,000 for each national radio hookup, broadcasting had added a significant new element to the costs of modern campaigning.[37]

These fears do not appear to have been well founded. Although figures for campaign expenditures are notoriously imprecise, it is clear that total campaign costs fluctuated through the 1920s, and for reasons other than radio. Total expenditures in 1924 were below those of 1920, mainly because of a collapse in Democratic fundraising in the wake of its disastrous convention. Campaign budgets in 1928 did rebound to historically high levels, but then subsided under the influence of the Depression. Expressed in terms of cost per vote, campaign costs were remarkably stable during the 1920s, despite the doubling of the potential electorate through female enfranchisement and new expenditures on radio. Louise Overacker calculated that the RNC and DNC spent an average of 19 cents per vote in 1912, 20 cents in 1920, 15 cents in 1924, and 20 cents in 1928. Given that prices in 1928 were 40 percent higher than in 1912, she concluded that the real cost per vote declined significantly during the first years of the radio age.[38]

Between enthusiasm and skepticism lay a body of opinion that radio's effects upon American political life were still uncertain. Radio "has not revolutionized politics," Samuel Blythe wrote in the *Saturday Evening Post* in 1929. "It hasn't changed politics one iota. But it has expanded politics, and, therefore, it is possible the revolution will come." Others remained unsure as to the long-term implications of the one-way nature of radio broadcasting for political debate and education. "The radio has furnished us a conversational meeting ground," Eunice Fuller Barnard wrote in 1924. "But it has not yet allowed us to any extent to converse. . . . How far it can directly accelerate political progress until there is more mutuality, more free interchange . . . is still in doubt." There was no doubt that radio could produce "an instantaneous national fixation of interest," but whether it could translate that phenomenon into a shared and active sense of citizenship remained to be seen.[39]

Other Lands, Other Ways

All sides did agree, however, that the United States offered and delivered superior opportunities compared to those provided elsewhere in the world for radio to prove itself as a political force. British broadcasting, which had long been a counterpoint for analyses of the American system, evolved very different and more restrictive ways of dealing with political debate and electioneering. Many in Britain held the same hopes for a radio-led political revolution as did American enthusiasts, hoping that the new medium would assist in integrating newly enfranchised women into the political system and lessen class divisions.[40] The BBC under Lord Reith, however, remained extremely nervous about allowing politicians and political material free rein on the airwaves during the interwar period.

As American broadcasters and their regulators moved toward a market-orientated regime for political advertising, the BBC developed a more restrictive system which doled out portions of free airtime to political parties during elections. At other times Reith and the BBC were sensitive to the danger of allowing the airwaves to be inundated with "controversy" and partisanship. Political advertising and programming revealed the ambiguities of the BBC's position as an independent but state-funded organization. In January 1924, for example, the cabinet decided that the BBC should not broadcast George V's speech opening Parliament, which was written by the government of the day, on the grounds that political speeches should not be broadcast. That rule was loosened for the national election later that year, but only a couple of campaign speeches were actually broadcast. Five years later, in the election of 1929, the BBC broadcast more speeches, divided between the Labour, Conservative, and Liberal parties in approximate proportion to their representation in the House of Commons. During the elections of 1931 and 1935 the BBC aired 9 and 12 campaign speeches respectively, on both occasions favoring the parliamentary majority.[41]

Perhaps as a result of their lack of practice, British politicians were frequently criticized for their poor radio technique. Of all the political leaders of the time, only Stanley Baldwin seemed at all interested in effective radio speaking. Neville Chamberlain refused even to prepare for his rare broadcasts, and in 1933 argued that "It would be very undesirable, especially in difficult and critical times like these, to make the Budget the subject of a controversial debate on the wireless before an audience which is uninstructed in all the complexities and problems of the financial position at home and abroad." British listeners evidently repaid these attitudes in kind; a *Daily Express* poll in 1935 revealed that only 40 percent of listeners tuned into political speakers, a sharp decline from the average of 60 to 65 percent for the BBC's nonpolitical programs.[42]

The BBC was even more cautious in its policy on political programming outside election campaigns. "It is obvious," the Ullswater Committee into broadcasting declared in 1935, "that a medium whereby expressions of political opinion can be brought into seven or eight million homes needs very careful safeguarding if it is not to be abused."[43] The BBC and Reith erred on the side of caution, forswearing all editorial comment and banning until 1928 "controversial material." Reith's definition of *controversial* tended to favor the incumbent government and the three established parties; insurgent and dissident groups, such as Scottish nationalists and Socialists, were denied airtime.

William Hard, who published a survey of political radio in Europe in 1932, noted that the socialist Norman Thomas, who represented a party without any congressional seats, would not be allowed near a British microphone. Different rules applied, however, to government ministers; in May 1926, during the General Strike, Reith permitted the BBC's facilities to be used for governmental broadcasts that were both partisan and controversial, but denied trade unionists' requests to put their case to the nation.[44] The result of these policies was to create, in Paddy Scannell and David Cardiff's phrase, "a hierarchy of political discourses" on British radio. In the most privileged position were statements by the government of the day, and in particular by the prime minister, on "issues of national importance." The BBC did not guarantee equal time for rebuttal of such addresses. The second tier of political debate, that between parties during elections, received limited but unequal resources. Lastly, the BBC maintained tight control over discussion of public issues and generally excluded subversive political voices.[45] Although the basic structure of this hierarchy differed little from those that had emerged in the United States during the interwar period, the publicly funded BBC proved far more reluctant to explore radio's potential to expand and improve political culture. The result was that American radio listeners were exposed to a far greater volume and variety of political programming than their English counterparts.

The situation in continental Europe was even more different. In 1924 the French cabinet issued a decree reserving use of radio stations to the government for official purposes, and even in 1932 cabinet approval was required before opposition parties could broadcast on publicly owned radio facilities. All discussions of public policy were also subject to tight governmental censorship. In Weimar Germany political programming was prohibited in 1924 so that radio might be "reserved for the higher things in life and unsullied by political strife."[46] This prohibition was loosened later in the decade, although only to the extent of allowing incumbents to broadcast. In the fateful presidential election of 1932 only President Hindenburg and his chancellor Heinrich Bruning were allowed access to the airwaves; rival candidates such as Adolf Hitler were not. If the German radio system were to prevail in the United States, the *New York Times* told its readers in September 1932, the current presidential contest between Herbert Hoover and Franklin Roosevelt would be very different. Radio's role would be limited to a speech by Hoover, two by his secretary of state Henry Stimson, and "a phonographic repetition of the speech by Mr. Hoover." Neither FDR nor Norman Thomas would be heard at all.[47]

Once ensconced in power, Hitler wasted no time in turning the restrictive German radio culture to his advantage. Josef Goebbels's Propaganda Ministry took over the German Broadcasting Company, which was then given a monopoly over all radio broadcasting. Hitler and Goebbels's faith in the power of radio to influence political thought was equal to that of any American radio enthusiast; during the 1930s German consumers were encouraged to buy cheap radio sets, and radio households jumped from 4.5 million in 1933 to 9.5 million in 1938. "We spell radio with three exclamation marks," the chief of Nazi radio declared in 1936, "because we are possessed in it of a miraculous power—the strongest weapon ever given to the spirit."[48]

Political broadcasting in the Australian and Canadian hybrid broadcasting systems also differed from the United States' experience, although less dramatically than in Germany or even Britain. Always aware of their enormous land areas and scattered populations, Australians and Canadians welcomed radio's unifying and educative potential as vital to the effectiveness of their statecraft and democracy. In Australia, radio was also hailed as a means through which women, customarily unwelcome at political meetings, could more fully participate in political life. Privately owned radio stations in Australia during the 1920s faced no significant restrictions upon their political broadcasting, and they quickly evolved a robust culture of political comment and advertising. The Australian Labor Party even established its own station, 2KY Sydney, in 1925, to ensure that "capitalist lies could be nailed daily" for the benefit of "workers sitting comfortably in their own homes."[49]

The creation of the ABC in 1929 introduced a new publicly funded element to Australian radio. Although the ABC was given great statutory discretion in its programming, the postmaster general reserved the right to prohibit particular broadcasts. The ABC proved to be more adventurous than the BBC in its political and "controversial" broadcasting, although it too trod cautiously around very contentious issues. The postmaster general exercised his powers of censorship on at least four occasions during the 1930s, and speakers were told early in the decade to avoid "live political issues."[50] Later, however, the ABC broadcast a steady stream of political programming, always with the objective of impartiality and nonpartisanship. By 1940 it had devised policies for allocation of free airtime to parties during elections. The ABC recognized only parties with parliamentary representation, but divided time equally between them. Each party leader was given an hour for opening addresses, 30 minutes during the campaign, and 30 minutes for closing appeals. Less generous arrangements were also made for state elections. Politicians of all parties were also free to buy as much time as they could afford on commercial stations.[51]

The Canadian experience mirrored Australia's. Local and commercial stations during the 1920s were free to accept or reject material and advertisements as they saw fit. National elections in 1925, 1926, and 1930 witnessed a steady increase in the amount of political advertisement and programming on radio, and a growing awareness by politicians of its usefulness. "Hitherto to most Canadians," Prime Minister Mackenzie King declared in the first national broadcast on July 1, 1929, "Ottawa has seemed far off, a mere name to hundreds of thousands of our people, but henceforth all Canadians will stand within . . . hearing of the speakers on Parliament Hill. May we not predict that as a result . . . there will be aroused a more general interest in public affairs, and an increased devotion of the individual citizen to the commonweal?"[52]

When the CRBC was transformed into the CBC in 1936, it was directed to allocate time as fairly as possible among parties and candidates who desired it. As was the case in Australia, parties received free time on CBC stations but were obliged to pay for airtime on privately owned facilities. As part of its mandate to use radio to build national unity, CBC gave time only to parties that had gained representation in the House of Commons, that fielded candidates in at least three provinces, and that put forward policies on "a wide range of national issues."[53] The CRBC and CBC displayed a similar reticence on "controversial" material as did the BBC and ABC. In deference to Canada's Catholic Francophone population in Quebec, and to the strong Methodist and Presbyterian tradition in rural Ontario, the CRBC denied its facilities to atheists, anarchists, and advocates of free love.[54]

Champions of the American broadcasting system during the 1920s and 1930s could therefore feel confident that their privately owned radio industry had delivered the most voluminous and diverse diet of political advertisements and programming in the world. Although it was true that American radio politics were significantly limited by the tyranny of the marketplace, and by dictates of taste, which made American airwaves as free of atheism, anarchy, and other subversion as any other nation's broadcasting, it was also true that the United States was the only major democracy in the interwar world in which radio listeners could hear, albeit occasionally, an election speech by a Communist. In the context of the challenges to, and failures of, democracy elsewhere in the world during the 1930s, this was no mean achievement.

Although the American system incorporated its own dynamics which powerfully sustained and reinforced the political status quo, these acted less oppressively than in other comparable democracies. The British, Canadian, and Australian tendency to limit free access to public radio facilities during election campaigns to parties with legislative representation, for example, was a greater systemic reinforcement of the political status quo than the American broadcasters' tendency to favor incumbent administrations and majority parties between elections. Although the Australian and Canadian systems provided easier access for radio politicians than the BBC, there remained real substance to William Hard's conclusion in 1932:

> American private broadcasting gives a more hospitable welcome to contending and contradictory schools of political and economic thought than any other broadcasting known at present to the world. . . . European broadcasting to-day still displays . . . a certain superiority in volume of programmes dealing with the academic *background* of citizenship. American broadcasting, on the other hand, continues to display to-day . . . a clear superiority in volume and vigor of programmes dealing with the instant *practice* of citizenship.[55]

10

The Consumers

Radio, Audiences, and Voters

"Outside the tight frame house, there's a northeast gale blowing," John Dos Passos wrote in 1934. The house was full of "dryness, warmth, and light," but was also "a lonely tangle of needs, worries, desires: how are we going to eat, get clothes to wear . . . raise our children, belong to something, have something belong to us?" After dinner the family sits in the parlor, "listening drowsily to disconnected voices, stale scraps of last year's jazz, unfinished litanies advertising unnamed products that dribble senselessly from the radio." Then the president of the United States begins to speak:

> He is leaning cordially towards youandme, across his desk there in Washington, telling in carefully chosen words how the machinations of chisellers are to be foiled for youandme, and how the manycylindered motor of recovery is being primed with billions for youandme . . . we are going to have good jobs, good pay, protected bank deposits, we edge our chairs closer to the radio, we are flattered and pleased, we feel we are right with the White House.

After FDR's "cordial explaining voice stops, we want to say: Thank you, Frank." But the president's fireside chat is less comforting the next morning, when the family discovers "the wagecut, the bank foreclosing just the same, prices going up on groceries . . . and that it's still raining."[1]

Dos Passos's conception of radio's ephemeral impact upon Americans' lives and politics was ahead of its time. Before the development of audience measurement techniques in the 1930s, and before social scientists had undertaken studies of radio and political behavior, the scope and impact of the new medium upon political life remained unclear.[2] As radio skeptics reexamined the impact of broadcasting upon political life they also began to question the assumption that radio had materially increased political education, interest, and engagement. By the middle of the 1940s, through the work of Paul Lazarsfeld and his colleagues, a much clearer understanding of the role—and limits—of radio in voter behavior had emerged. By then audience measurement techniques had also improved, allowing politicians and broadcasters to gauge more accurately the size and composition of their audiences.

The result of both these developments was to reinforce the skeptics' arguments that radio had not revolutionized American political culture. After twenty years of broadcasting, American voters had come to see radio as an information medium that assisted, but did not form, their political thinking and choices. This utilitarian view was also colored by a wary understanding of the false impressions that broadcasting could propagate. By the early 1940s many political analysts had come to agree with Dos Passos, and with an unnamed farmer who told a radio researcher in 1941, "I don't listen to political speeches for Roosevelt because they rile me up. I know all their arguments and tricks and they ain't no good. Sometimes when I listen [to FDR] I even get to thinking he's right and all the time I know he's wrong."[3]

Counting the Mail: Early Audience Measurement

Early audience measurement techniques tended to be crude and inaccurate. Commercial broadcasters and advertisers came by the late 1920s to rely heavily on the volume and tone of listeners' mail. By 1930 this had reached avalanche proportions, often prompted by offers of free products. NBC received 550,000 letters from listeners in 1927, and nearly 5 million in 1932.[4] Listener mail was a problematic indicator of audience size and composition. Although many listeners in the early days of radio wrote to distant stations to tell them about the quality of their signal, this form of listener response died out as networking eroded the excitement of DXing. Broadcasters noted a decline in the number of unsolicited listeners' letters over time, and both networks reported a sharp drop in the number of letters following the two parties' nominating conventions in 1936 compared to the response four years earlier.[5] Broadcasters never knew what proportion of their listeners bothered to write or telephone with their reactions to programs, and many suspected that those who did were unrepresentative of the audience at large. Stations received only a portion of listeners' letters; others went to individual announcers, to networks, and to sponsors. Some struggling or ambitious performers and broadcasters were not above generating their own fan mail through fake letters in order to win another engagement or higher fees.[6]

Although popular singers and performers could expect large amounts of fan mail after each program, not all politicians were so lucky. This was particularly the case when political broadcasts interfered with scheduled programming. In 1938 Thomas Dewey bought time on WJZ Manhattan to assist his New York gubernatorial campaign. His 30-minute slot came from an hour ordinarily devoted to a popular program, *Information Please*. Even though WJZ cut Dewey off promptly after 30 minutes, 920 listeners wrote to complain about the loss of half of "Information Please," while only nine objected to the sudden abbreviation of Dewey's speech.[7]

Some politicians and public figures, however, received a great deal of mail in response to their radio addresses. This was the case particularly for those speakers lucky or rich enough to have access to the national networks, or those with a truly national following. Father Coughlin received 150,000 letters per week in 1934, and Herbert Hoover and Franklin Roosevelt also received large amounts of mail. One listener from Long Beach, California, told Hoover early in his presidency that "to be rudely awakened at seven-thirty in the morning by the excited shouting of an eleven year old daughter that Mr. Hoover was speaking is interesting but to discover later that the child had recognised the voice of the President is of considerable significance. And she is but one of millions of children who know your voice, thanks to the radio."[8]

During the 1932 campaign Hoover received thousands of letters after each radio address; listener responses after one speech broadcast from Des Moines in October filled six archive boxes.[9] These letters came from all over the nation, many from writers who felt a new sense of connection to the political nation through radio. "Somehow I felt that the 'man' Herbert Hoover was talking directly to me," Oscar Brill of New York wrote. "You stepped forth from the radio and entered the family circle and spoke directly as if you were there in person."[10]

President Roosevelt's radio mail was even more voluminous. Each fireside chat between 1933 and 1935 elicited an avalanche of mail from listeners. The president's mail in 1933 and 1934 was almost uniformly favorable, and usually rapturous. "We hope you will continue these radio talks," Charles Barrell of New York City told the president after his first fireside chat on March 11, 1933. "They engender a spirit of confidence that is hard to describe. . . . I guess it's the real, genuine human touch that everybody has waited for so long." Many listeners complimented FDR on his radio style, and credited him with fully realizing radio's potential to educate the people in statecraft. Most of all, the president's correspondents congratulated him on his ability to reach out into their homes and to make them feel as if he cared about their individual conditions. "You called us 'friends' over the air and I hope you will not consider me presumptuous when I sign myself, Your friend, Archie Anderson."[11]

The first fireside chat, according to Roy Crawford of Evanston, Illinois, "was like a dear friend dropped in to our home for a few minutes chat. . . . There is no 'Gabriel' over the White House. There is a human in it! Thank Providence." Some writers took the opportunity to confess their earlier skepticism about the new president, but now proclaimed their conversion through radio. "In your pre-election speeches, I was almost at the point of hatred towards you," one New Yorker wrote. "But I can assure you that your Sunday evening talk, has won me over and I am 100 percent for you hereafter." "For the country's sake for God's sake for your sake and my sake somehow continue to make those Sunday evening radio addresses," wrote a listener from Indianapolis.[12]

Even FDR's radio fan mail abated over time. So too did the almost unanimous support that his early fireside chats had won from listeners who bothered to write. In April 1938, when the president addressed the nation on economic affairs, the White House received 38 folders of mail, 34 of which contained positive reactions. This was a far cry from the hundreds of folders needed to contain 1933's radio mail. When the president spoke to the nation after the outbreak of World War II, he received only six folders of mail in return.[13] By then radio from the White House had become an accepted, and unremarkable, phenomenon, and FDR had become embroiled in increasingly bitter disputes over domestic and foreign policy.

Eleanor Roosevelt was also a frequent radio speaker throughout the 1930s and received large amounts of listener mail. During her White House years she became a well-paid radio celebrity, requiring the services of a radio agent and speaking on her own regular sponsored programs. She donated her radio earnings, $72,000 in 1935, to a variety of charities.[14] In 1937 Mrs. Roosevelt delivered a weekly radio talk sponsored by Sweetheart Soap, and received six boxes of letters. Almost all the letters were favorable, handwritten, and most came from "shut-ins": women at home, the elderly, the unemployed, and invalids. Most complimented Eleanor for her diction, radio style, and warmth, and many writers assured the first lady that they now used Sweetheart Soap. Some also took the opportunity to tell her of their troubles and to ask for help.

Mrs. Eugene Burrell found Mrs. Roosevelt's description of life in the White House almost too vivid to bear:

> I heard your last broadcast . . . and the minues of which you spoke of Really made me hungry. . . . I never have anything good and nurishing for my body because my husband only Earns $27.50 every two and three weeks. . . . Mrs. Roosevelt God will Bless you if you will loan me $500 or $250. . . . I havent But ½ a loaf of Bread in my House and wish I had just a crum of one of those hams I heard you talk about hanging in your pantry.

Not all Mrs Roosevelt's mail was complimentary or beseeching. One writer, "Not-So-Smart-But-Smart-Enough," wrote in 1940 to congratulate her on her "heart-rending appeals over the radio to save all the rich kids in England." You "are not basically interested in poor people. . . . Well don't ever get it into your head that the Roosevelts are fooling anybody. We bet that F.D.R. is up there this week-end playing with his little model battleships."[15]

Broadcasters, too, received a steady but diminishing stream of letters from listeners of their political programming. Much of this mail, especially in the 1930s, tended to be critical and—from the stations' perspective—unfair. In 1936, for example, NBC received many listeners' letters criticizing it for selling time to the CPA during the presidential campaign. Emily Johnson considered it "unprincipled" for the network to broadcast the Communists and their "lies and impossible promises." Miss Johnson was particularly concerned for "lonely and married people in lonely places," who might be taken in by such dangerous propaganda. The Reverend Matthew Kelly of Baldwin, New York, found it impossible to understand how NBC, the beneficiary of a public resource, could be so greedy as to sell time to the CPA. "The harm you permit to be done is irreparable and your broad-minded policy is a violation of the place of confidence and trust imposed in you by all true Americans."[16] NBC pointed out to all these correspondents that it was legally obliged to provide time to all qualified candidates regardless of party affiliation. Its attempts to educate listeners about section 315 did little to change public opinion about the acceptable limits of free speech on the radio; an AIPO poll during the 1940 campaign revealed that 71 percent of respondents objected to the idea of equal access to radio for CPA candidates.[17]

Some listeners were also quick to think the worst of the networks when broadcast difficulties prevented clear transmission of political speeches. During the 1936 campaign a Roosevelt supporter sent a telegram to NBC stating, "We . . . would appreciate when the president . . . is gracious enough to permit you to broadcast his speeches that you [*sic*] engineers give to him at least approximately the same freedom from muddiness and fading reception that pertains when the yokel from Kansas yaps his howls. We hope that when President Roosevelt enters his second term that he will take cognizance of what appears to be a bias." NBC's protestations that atmospheric disturbances could undo even the most carefully transmitted broadcasts also fell upon deaf Republican ears. John Hynds of Buffalo, Wyoming, accused it of sabotaging a Landon broadcast by "that continual buzzing which only the NBC knows how to put on. . . . Any time Roosevelt with his 'my frans' comes on . . . the radio is always clear but any Republican celebrity may do his best and you might hear about one third of his speech. . . . You are in this town the object of public disgust."[18]

NBC reviewed its listener mail after the 1940 campaign, and found that it had received only 300 letters during the last five weeks of the campaign. This total was much smaller than during previous elections. More than half were requests for copies of talks, and 19 percent were critical of the network. Only 5 percent of the letters were complimentary. The complaints covered scheduling delays, poor reception, and last-minute cancellations. Some complainants accused NBC of bias against either FDR or Wendell Willkie, and some revealed that they still did not understand section 315 or NBC's policy to sell time only after the conventions. Overall, however, NBC executives were pleased by the public response to their political programming during the last election of the interwar era. They were also pleasantly surprised that, in contrast to 1936, "Socialist and Communist mail received by the Information Division was practically nil!"[19]

The Development of Modern Audience Measurement

Large stations and networks began to take a more active role in measuring their audiences in the middle years of the 1920s. At the beginning of 1926 WJZ sent 10,000 questionnaires to its listeners, of whom 4,000 responded to questions about quality of transmission, program content, and their program preferences. Respondents generally favored classical music over jazz, baseball over hockey, and travelogues over political talks. WJZ also reported a strong endorsement of its own policies of using only male announcers and for its acceptance of goodwill advertising and program sponsorship.[20]

In 1933 the *Literary Digest* employed its own polling techniques to ascertain listener programming preferences. Seeking a "cross-section of American opinion," the *Digest* included a coupon in its November 4, 1933, issue asking listeners to list nine of their personal "dislikes" and "likes" in radio programs. By the middle of December, 16,400 readers had cut the coupon, filled in their lists, and mailed them back. Although this response represented a tiny proportion of the total American radio audience, the *Digest* claimed that it represented a national "symposium" on radio from "every section of the country and every stratum of society." The responses rejected the emerging popular culture of the airwaves, and strongly endorsed highbrow broadcasting culture. Respondents expressed strong disapproval of jazz, "excessive, too long, cheap, superfluous advertising," "trashy, coy, cute, patronising, wisecracking announcers," and "political speeches and propaganda." Overall, however, "likes" outnumbered "dislikes" by a large margin, and included symphony orchestras, news commentaries, educational programming, religious services, and operas. Although some critics pointed to the open-ended nature of the survey and to the class bias of the *Digest*'s readership, the magazine trumpeted its survey as the most representative yet undertaken.[21]

Some more imaginative techniques for measuring audiences were also tried. In 1936 utility companies in New York noticed that popular radio speakers caused electric consumption to increase. When Al Smith began a radio speech at 10 P.M. on January 25, 1936, the New York Edison Company reported an increase in load of 35,000 kW. Power usage returned to normal very quickly after Smith stopped speaking at 11 P.M., leading the company to conclude that 350,000 radio sets had been switched on for his speech. FDR's Jackson Day speech on January 8, 1936, had also resulted in an increased load of 50,000 kW, or 500,000 sets. Both men, however, were defeated by the boxing match between Joe Louis and Max Baer in June 1935, which enriched New York Edison by the increase of 130,000 kW, through 1.3 million extra radio sets.[22] This method of audience measurement was scarcely ideal; it completely ignored listeners who still relied on battery-powered radios, as well as the possibility that some listeners were tuned to another program.

More scientific ways of measuring radio audiences began to emerge in the late 1920s. Both NBC and CBS undertook large-scale audience surveys in order to attract advertisers. In 1927 NBC commissioned Daniel Starch to quantify radio listening habits in 24 states east of the Rockies. Starch and his staff conducted 17,000 interviews to measure program preferences and listening in cities, towns, and farming areas. CBS preferred to survey its audience through listener mail response to offers of free goods. Incoming mail was then sorted by county and its volume was compared to total population figures.[23] Neither of these early efforts, however, could provide advertisers with the precision that they demanded about the attractiveness of particular programs and performers.

Pushed by its advertisers, CBS devoted enormous effort to improving its measurement techniques. In 1935 it experimented with a "program analyzer," developed by Frank Stanton and Paul Lazarsfeld, which provided instant reaction from listeners in New York and Los Angeles. Small groups of people were asked to listen to programs and to register their approval or disapproval of particular parts of shows by pressing one of two buttons connected to a recording device. The program analyzer, however, proved to be inaccurate because of the small size of its test audiences and its inability to gauge simultaneous audience response across the whole country. CBS persisted with it during the 1940s, but placed much more emphasis upon listening diaries filled out by groups of listeners.[24]

Radio audience measurement outside the networks took a significant step forward in 1929, when Archibald Crossley began to implement his "recall" method. Crossley, formerly director of research at the *Literary Digest*, began polling audiences by telephone about programs they had listened to the previous day. His results gave advertisers the sort of information they needed, and prompted the Association of National Advertisers and the American Association of Advertising Agencies (AAAA) to establish the Cooperative Analysis of Broadcasting (CAB) as a clearing house for his research. Well-funded by the CAB, Crossley continued to perfect his techniques by moving to same-day polling in 1934, and by dividing his respondents into four income groups. By the mid-1930s CAB researchers called their chosen radio homes four times a day so as to reach listeners while their memories were fresh. A typical CAB poll by 1940 involved 750 phone calls, divided proportionately into income groups, in a selection of 33 major cities. Each poll resulted in a "Crossley Rating," which told advertisers the percentage of radio homes that had listened to a particular program.[25]

Crossley's success spurred a number of rivals to develop different, and allegedly more accurate, methods. Claude Hooper and Lloyd Clark, who had first worked with Daniel Starch, formed Clark-Hooper Incorporated in 1934. Their company offered clients a "coincidental" telephone interview system, which polled listeners during programs. By 1935 Clark-Hooper's typical survey involved about 100,000 calls to 21 cities over a two-month period. Clark-Hooper became CAB's chief competitor throughout the rest of the decade, proclaiming its independence from both advertisers and networks and developing a strong reputation for accuracy and impartiality. CAB, increasingly hamstrung by its sponsorship from advertisers, was eventually disbanded in 1946. Arthur C. Neilson provided a third force in radio audience measurement in the late 1930s. He originally trained as an electrical engineer but established himself as an industrial market researcher during the 1920s. In 1935 he combined his two interests by creating a radio audience meter, which automatically recorded the frequencies and hours of operation of radio sets to which it was connected. By the end of 1940 Neilson had invested $600,000 in his invention, and by 1944 had installed it in 800 homes across the nation.[26]

Crossley, Hooper, and Neilson were fiercely competitive, and their struggles spurred considerable debate as to the relative virtues of their techniques. Hooper argued that his coincidental method was superior to Crossley's retrospective technique because it eliminated the need to rely on listeners' memories. This argument gained strength from research conducted by Herman Hettinger of the University of Pennsylvania and Frederick Lumley of Ohio State University in the early 1930s. Lumley found that listeners routinely "forgot" to mention to interviewers between half and two-thirds of the programs they had actually listened to, and that many found it difficult to distinguish between the real names of programs and those made up by interviewers.[27]

Crossley countered by claiming that coincidental phone calls produced uncooperative respondents, who resented interruptions during their favorite programs. Neilson argued that both methods were fatally flawed by their reliance upon telephone calls and personal interviews. His method could register the preferences of those listeners who did not own telephones, generate continuous data, and produce results without the mediation of memory or interview. Neilson's rivals pointed out that the higher cost of his device meant that it could not cover a sufficiently large number of radios to produce representative results. Networks and advertisers, impatient with the complexities of this debate, tended to use a combination of the Hooper system, listener diaries, and Neilson's meters.[28]

Audience surveys showed listeners to be only moderately supportive of political programming. In April 1936 nearly 54 percent of respondents to a *Fortune Magazine* survey reported that they would like more or the same amount of political broadcasting on radio, while nearly 28 percent wanted less. Nearly one in five respondents, however, wanted no political broadcasting at all. In June 1938, 63 percent of people surveyed by AIPO agreed that broadcasters were generally fair in the way in which they handled political material, while only 11 percent disagreed. When it came to listening to political programming, however, Americans seemed less approving. A survey conducted after the 1936 conventions revealed that the Republican and Democratic keynote speakers captured 21 percent and 23 percent respectively of radio homes, while only 10 percent and 5 percent of set owners listened to the GOP's and

Democrats' opening ceremonies. In 1939 an AIPO survey revealed that only 24 percent of listeners "usually" listened to FDR's fireside chats, nearly 39 percent did so "sometimes," and just over 37 percent "never."[29]

The networks and the ratings organizations periodically informed the White House about the president's ratings. In January 1940, CBS Vice-president Harry Butcher passed on the Crossley ratings to Stephen Early for FDR's recent Jackson Day Dinner speech. It won a rating of 25, signifying that a quarter of radio sets had been tuned to the program. This meant that the president had an audience of between 22.5 million and 33.75 million people. Butcher went on to break this audience into Crossley's socioeconomic groupings: 22 percent of "definitely upper middle class" listeners, and 31 percent of the "upper middle class," had listened to the speech, while 26 percent of the "lower middle class," and 24 percent of the "definitely lower class"—who made up 53 percent of the total radio audience—had also heard the president.[30]

Social Scientists, Radio, and Voter Behavior

Inherent in radio exceptionalism was the assumption that broadcasting would improve American political citizenship and participation. This included the belief that radio could form and change individuals' opinions and voting decisions. As commercial broadcasters explored ways to measure accurately the size, nature, and preferences of their audiences, a variety of scholars began to undertake research into the power of radio.

In keeping with the generally positivist nature of political science between the wars, voters were presumed to act rationally after sifting through information put to them through reasoned debate. "In the ideal democracy," James Bryce declared, "every citizen is intelligent, patriotic, disinterested. His sole wish is to discover the right side in each contested issue, and to fix upon the best man among competing candidates." Although Graham Wallas attacked this presumption in 1908 as a fantasy, few scholars at the time agreed with him that human nature and psychology were so important in voter choice as to make the essence of political participation essentially irrational.[31] Edward Bernays, who spent his career as a prominent advertising consultant analyzing consumer behavior, was also skeptical of the intellectualist assumption in voter choice. In *Crystallizing Public Opinion* he argued in 1923 that voting was not a particularly rational process, and that many voters tended to resist education or even information when making their decisions. Millions of voters chose the GOP, Bernays argued in a warning to political scientists and radio

"Just a minute, dearie, until I shut off Herbert Hoover." Even by 1928 the novelty of presidential broadcasting had worn off, at least for this listener. Alan Dunn, *New Yorker*, 1928. Reproduced from Thomas Craven, ed., *Cartoon Cavalcade* (New York: Simon and Schuster, 1943), p. 183.

exceptionalists, because they had voted Republican in previous elections, or because something in the Republican message "awakens profound emotional response" in them, or simply because "our neighbor whom we do not like happens to be a Democrat."[32]

Wallas's and Bernays's caution, however, did not register with most social scientists until the very end of the interwar period. Mass media research between the wars tended to develop in three directions, all of which aimed to ascertain effects of the media, and in particular radio, upon audiences. While audience measurers developed their techniques, a second group of researchers, including Herman Hettinger, Richard Mead, and Alfred and Elizabeth Lee, began to compile content analyses of radio programming. By far the most influential of the academic researchers, however, concentrated upon the ways in which radio influenced individual choice in commercial and political matters.[33]

The most celebrated researcher into the effect of radio upon voter choice during the 1930s and 1940s was Paul Lazarsfeld. Born in Austria in 1901, Lazarsfeld took a doctorate in applied mathematics at the University of Vienna, and taught psychology and statistics. In 1935, deeply concerned by Nazism and anti-Semitism, he emigrated to the United States and to the University of Newark. In 1937 he moved to Princeton University to establish the Office of Radio Research with a Rockefeller Foundation grant. Two years later Lazarsfeld moved permanently to Columbia University, which established the Bureau of Applied Social Research to house him. By 1940 Lazarsfeld had established himself and his bureau as the preeminent radio researchers in the world.

Although Lazarsfeld's research interests were varied during the 1930s, his work focused in the 1940s and 1950s upon the role of radio in voter behavior. In 1939 he published a study of the ways in which listeners had reacted to Hugo Black's elevation to the U.S. Supreme Court in 1937. Black had been a member of the Ku Klux Klan, and his nomination aroused a storm of controversy. Lazarsfeld used Crossley ratings to determine who had listened to Black's radio address to the nation, and found that upper and upper-middle income groups had listened in greater proportions than had the less well off. Black's audience was also much older than the national average, but evenly divided between men and women. Given that Black's audience was disproportionately well off, it seemed that radio, in this case at least, was limited in its ability to form mass opinion. Lazarsfeld reinforced this point in a 1940 study of the correlation between reading and radio listening. Those most interested in politics, he found, were in the upper half of the national income scale and were also the most active readers and radio listeners on issues of political importance.[34]

Lazarsfeld also conducted interviews with selected groups from all income levels before and after Black's speech, and measured changes in their opinions. He found that 61 percent of his respondents had not changed their view of Black or of the wisdom of his elevation to the Supreme Court; 21 percent had formed an opinion on the issue; and only 18 percent had changed their opinion, as a result of Black's radio talk. These findings presaged Lazarsfeld's later research on the role of radio as a political opinion-former. Those least likely to listen, he found, were those who had no opinion. Those who had listened to Black's speech were less likely to change their opinion than those who had not, and Black's audience was also more likely to take sides on the issue than were nonlisteners. Radio, Lazarsfeld implied, was most effective when it preached to the converted.[35]

This early research evolved into a much more ambitious study of the effect of radio upon the presidential and congressional elections of 1940. Lazarsfeld first published this study, *The People's Choice*, in 1944, and it has since become a classic work of voting behavior analysis. He and his assistants undertook a detailed survey of 2,400 voters in Erie County, Ohio between May and November 1940. Lazarsfeld first determined the sociocultural characteristics of his sample, and found that higher income, Protestantism, and age over 45 were strong indicators of Republican loyalty. Lazarsfeld then divided his subjects into categories according to voting intention. He found that half his survey group had already decided in May which party they would support, and that another quarter had made up their minds by the end of the two national conventions. The remaining 25 percent were either "waverers" or "unactivated."

The conclusions of *The People's Choice* brought down the curtain for radio exceptionalism and its few remaining adherents. Although Lazarsfeld credited radio advertising with a significant activating effect among those voters unengaged in the contest until August, he found that it had little effect on voter behavior. Campaigning did convert some people, he argued, but they "were few indeed." Lazarsfeld again relegated radio and other advertising to the role of reinforcement rather than conversion. The effect of both parties' campaigns, he concluded, could be apportioned 53 percent for reinforcement, 14 percent for activation, 8 percent for conversion, and 16 percent to "no effect."[36] Overall, more than 70 percent of total voting decisions corresponded to the sociocultural factors identified by the researchers well before the first radio advertisement had aired. Lazarsfeld could offer radio exceptionalists only the comfort that, "to the extent that the formal media exerted any influence at all on voter intention or actual vote, radio proved more effective than the newspaper." When asked to identify their most important source of political information, 38 percent of Erie County voters listed the radio, while only 23 percent relied more on newspapers.[37]

Lazarsfeld refined the implications of this study throughout the following twenty years. In 1942 he argued that radio had three potential effects upon public opinion. It was effective in arousing interest in political contests and issues, and it provided a valuable source of information for people interested enough to seek out political discussion. Lazarsfeld did concede that radio might be able to "determine the opinions of the population" in totalitarian societies, but in democratic societies radio would remain important as a reinforcer of opinion rather than as a significant means of political conversion. "In the political field," he concluded, radio would "probably make people more class conscious." If listeners generally listened only to programs with which they agreed, and if radio brought more information to their attention, "then the effect should be to make their own political decisions more consistent with their class situation and less dependent upon incidental local issues."[38]

In 1949 Lazarsfeld and Elihu Katz published *Personal Influence: The Part Played by People in the Flow of Mass Communications*, which further developed this conception of the media's role in opinion formation. Katz and Lazarsfeld argued that radio operated most effectively upon public opinion through the mediation of "opinion formers." Radio, and other media, were part of a two-step process in which they first affected opinion leaders, who then influenced the opinions of less engaged members of the population. Family members, neighbors, friends, and fellow workers, Katz and Lazarsfeld found, were the most important opinion formers among wavering voters in Decatur, Illinois, during the 1952 campaign. Of those who changed their opinions of the candidates, 40 percent could pinpoint a specific conversation with another person as crucial to their decision, and nearly two-thirds of those conversations were with family members.[39]

Lazarsfeld's research and conclusions were profoundly influential upon a whole generation of media analysts. In 1937 Kenneth Goode published findings garnered from commercial audience surveys that suggested that many "listeners" of radio programs paid almost no attention to programs. One survey found that 19,000 out of 36,000 telephone respondents could not identify the program to which they were listening at the time of the call, and that "three to six out of every ten radio programs broadcast day by day make so little impression on anybody that they are never recalled . . . even in response to an interviewer's prolonged questioning." In 1946 Robert Merton published a study of the radio War Bond drive of September 21, 1943, in which Kate Smith performed for 18 hours and raised $39 million. Merton devoted almost no discussion to radio's persuasive abilities, preferring instead to emphasize Smith's charisma and the receptive wartime national psyche as factors in the program's success.[40]

Fifteen years later V. O. Key argued that the consensus of research was that "the flow of messages of the mass media is rather like dropping a handful of confetti from the rim of the Grand Canyon with the object of striking a man astride a burro on the canyon floor." American radio and TV broadcasters, "lineal descendants of operators of music halls and peep shows as they are," had neither the ability nor the desire to change political opinions, but instead wished to affirm the status quo in order to maximize their audiences. Radio and TV had in fact contributed to a decline in political interest by providing the population with large amounts of free, accessible, and uncontroversial entertainment. Even in 1990 F. Leslie Smith repeated the Lazarsfeld view of media effect and the two-step process without cavil in a review of research on media opinion formation.[41]

Lazarsfeld's theory of media effects has not, however, gone uncontested. Some critics pointed to inherent problems in his methodology, and especially to its lack of a control group, as indications that his findings rested ultimately upon surmise rather than proof.[42] Some contemporary and later critics also attacked Lazarsfeld's assumptions about the modern media. The Frankfurt School of European cultural theorists, led by Theodor Adorno and Max Horkheimer, attacked the behavioralism and the simplistic stimulus-response model that underpinned Lazarsfeld's approach. As Daniel Czitrom has argued, Horkheimer and Adorno objected to Lazarsfeld's reliance upon "who says what to whom with what effect," at the expense of a critical examination of the content and the historical, political, moral, and social context of that message. The Frankfurt School instead focused upon the media as a vehicle for political and economic domination by groups wishing to entrench their hegemony. Radio thus became not an innocuous and neutral medium of entertainment and information, but rather the means by which art was debased and individual consciousness repressed, and, perhaps, fascism established.[43]

Others attacked what they saw as Lazarsfeld's uncritical acceptance of the commercial imperatives of American broadcasting. Some critics feared that he remained too close to the commercial broadcasters for analytical comfort. Unconvinced by their comforting conclusions about the impact of mass media, Denis McQuail argued that the Columbia behavioralists had been influenced more than they admitted by "the operating needs of the new media; the special interests of governments, advertisers and would-be propagandists; the natural public curiosity abut the new media and the more narcissistic interests of those operating the mass media."[44] Lazarsfeld's methodology, which positioned media effect firmly within the realm of personal choice and behavioral effect, also dissatisfied modern critics who sought a more encompassing view of politics and a more nuanced conception of political choice. Lazarsfeld's research, Robert Westbrook argued in 1983, represented "the interaction of the prophecy of positivistic social science and the social performance of managers," which differentiated little between a consumer's choice of soap and a voter's choice of party and candidate. In searching for his "Holy Grail of positivism, a predictive science of human behavior," Lazarsfeld had simplified the meanings of politics and political debate, and had thereby underestimated the potential role of media such as radio within them.[45]

"The general direction in which mass media research is moving," Colin Seymour-Ure noted in 1974, "is towards a greater awareness of the social context in which communication takes place." Simply because a particular electorate had not significantly changed its views after a "hypodermic" experience of a brief but intense episode of media exposure did not mean that the media had no effect on political choice. Such a conclusion "leaves us with a thoroughly incomplete and misleading picture of how media effects operate and how politics works."[46] Modern media theory has instead stressed the propensity of TV viewers and radio listeners to respond more selectively, and less dramatically, to both subliminal and overt media messages. In order to avoid the crude stimulus-response approach of earlier studies, Denis McQuail argued in 1990, media theorists now had to "pay more attention to people in their social context, look at what people know (in the widest sense) rather than at their attitudes and opinions . . . [and] look at structures of belief and opinion and social behaviour rather than individual cases."[47] In order to achieve this broader view of interwar political culture, and of radio's impact upon it, we must therefore broaden the focus from elections, candidates, and political parties to examine the ways in which radio both confronted and reinforced prevailing views and definitions of political and social citizenship.

Part III

Radio and Citizenship, 1920–1940

Radio takes its place alongside of the development of the printing press, and the establishment of the public school. Whoever controls radio broadcasting in the years to come, will control the nation. For good or ill . . . radio has become the unrivaled Master of human destiny.

—JOHN FITZPATRICK,
President of the Chicago
Federation of Labor, 1929

11

Radio and the Problem of Citizenship

Brave pronouncements of a new age of citizenship accompanied the spread of radio broadcasting after 1920. Radio might form new connections between the individual and the community to strengthen those dangerously stretched by urbanization, industrialization, cultural diversity, and regionalism. Workers might better understand their employers through radio; the drift away from the churches might be arrested through broadcast of religious services; women and immigrants might be better integrated into society; and rural life might be revived by providing entertainment and education to isolated and culturally marginalized listeners. Radio might also produce a new and more elevated popular culture that would combine entertainment, education, and information to unify a disparate population into a single electronic community.

Others were less optimistic. World War I had left many with a more skeptical conception of public opinion and its malleability. Instead of creating fortified individuals, radio broadcasting seemed to some skeptics to produce standardized attitudes and "crowd mentality." This debate was not unique either to radio or to the interwar years. The invention of the telegraph in the 1840s elicited the same sort of enthusiasm, especially for its capacity to unify a far-flung and increasingly fractious republic. Later the telephone was championed as a means by which new and closer communities could be formed in an increasingly urbanized and atomized industrial society. Lynn Spigel has shown that television also seemed to be a harbinger of closer community and shared values in post–World War II America. This form of technological utopianism—a tendency to freight technological advance with hopes for a better citizenry and a stronger republic—has been frequently noted by observers of the United States since the days of Ben Franklin, Thomas Jefferson, and Alexis de Tocqueville.[1]

It is also clear that the idea of radio as a social unifier revealed many of the cultural anxieties of the early 1920s. Concerns about ethnic, class, regional, and cultural divisions all molded the debate over radio and its impact. The broadcasters themselves—and in particular the new national networks—used these concerns to cement their dominance over American radio. By stressing the civic benefits of broadcasting, NBC and CBS portrayed themselves as much more than business enterprises. As self-proclaimed agents of the new citizenship, the networks hoped to escape both government regulation and public opprobrium. In this their tactics were similar to many other large corporations during the 1920s which portrayed themselves as "welfare capitalists" to diffuse public criticism and effective regulation.[2]

Conceptions of a new radio citizenship were also bedeviled by an inherent contradiction. Those who championed radio as a means of diminishing crowd mentality also welcomed it as a unifier of an expansive and heterogeneous republic. It soon became clear, however, that radio could not achieve the impossible. Broadcasting could not simultaneously revive individual sovereignty and promote sociocultural unity. Americans who had hoped that radio would achieve this miracle were sadly disappointed by the early 1930s.

The Problem of the Modern Citizen

"The private citizen today," Walter Lippmann observed in 1925, "has come to feel rather like a deaf spectator in the back row, who ought to keep his mind on the mystery off there, but cannot quite manage to keep awake." To Lippmann and others the divergence of democratic theory from modern practice was painfully obvious. "The vast scale upon which affairs go on once seemed enough to make men despair of the possibility of their orderly control," John Dewey wrote soon after the end of World War I. "Men felt dwarfed, shrivelled in the face of the vastness of economic and political conditions." Two generations of rapid immigration, industrialization, urbanization, and technological advance had left Jeffersonian and Jacksonian conceptions of society in tatters. Instead, a new America and a new society had developed, dominated by teeming cities and huge industrial combinations, and variegated by a myriad of ethnic groups.[3]

Lippmann and others argued that American society had become too big, too complex, and too interdependent to be understood by individuals who had no training or expertise in citizenship. Declining voter turnout and increasing apathy were inevitable results of this sense of powerlessness. Presidential election turnout had steadily declined since 1896, when 79 percent of voters went to the polls. By 1920 that figure had dropped to 49 percent, sparking widespread concern about low voting rates and the consequences for modern democracy.[4] Lippmann's sympathies, he declared, were with the non-voter, "for I believe that he has been saddled with an impossible task and that he is asked to practice an unattainable ideal." Lippmann's celebrated argument in 1922 was that public opinion was composed of the "pictures inside the heads" of individuals, and that those pictures had ceased to reflect the realities of a complex world. The accuracy of citizens' worldviews had been diminished by censorship and distortion in the news media, the inability of most people to devote sufficient time to the study of public affairs, and the sheer complexity of modern statecraft. What was needed was "an independent, expert organization" to "make intelligible" the facts around which enlightened public opinion could develop.[5]

Three years later, in *The Phantom Public*, Lippmann was even less optimistic about the ability of "the average man" to comprehend events around him and to perform a meaningful role in modern governance. As Michael Kirkhorn has pointed out, Lippmann's growing enthusiasm for a disinterested elite to interpret the news led him to a greater skepticism about the value of popular thought. Lippmann followed this reasoning to its logical conclusion of questioning the whole rationale of democracy and popular sovereignty. Good government, he thought, should be conducted by experts who would "initiate, administer, settle" important issues of state, with "the least possible interference from ignorant and meddlesome outsiders," including the public. "The force of public opinion is partisan, spasmodic, simple-minded and external. It needs for its direction . . . a new intellectual method which shall provide it with its own usable canons of judgment."[6]

Although Lippmann wrote mainly about the printed media, he did consider the role of radio in the formation and education of public opinion. He was not convinced that it could achieve the education necessary for public opinion to regain its place as the most important decision-making forum in a democracy. Even if every aspect of government were broadcast, he wondered, how many people would listen to the proceedings of the Sinking Fund Commission or the Geological Survey? "Life is too short for the pursuit of omniscience."[7]

Seba Eldridge agreed with Lippmann's observations, but came to even more extreme conclusions. "The American citizen appears to be in a somewhat parlous condition," he wrote in 1929. "Evidences multiply that he has failed grievously to practice the self-determination imputed to him by the accepted theory of democracy; and grave doubts are raised that he can ever approximate, in practice, the attainment of that ideal." Voter turnout had declined; the people continued to make bad choices at the polls, and party machines prospered in the absence of public condemnation. "To put it briefly," Eldridge concluded, "we are attempting to control a machine-made civilization by a handicraft citizenship." Radio broadcasting was of only marginal use as long as listeners continued to demand light entertainment rather than serious programming. It was better for citizenship and voting rights to be determined by an intelligence test which might exclude half of currently eligible voters.[8]

John Dewey came to more optimistic conclusions. At the end of 1918, in his essay "The New Paternalism," he predicted that the most lasting legacy of World War I would be its "remarkable demonstration of the possibilities of guidance of the news upon which the formation of public opinion depends." He did not, however, abandon his faith in the ability of citizens eventually to understand, and therefore influence, public affairs. Through freedom of expression and "full publicity," it was possible to resuscitate individual thought and participation.[9] What was needed, he argued in *Individualism Old and New* in 1930, were new conceptions of individualism and community which better corresponded to the corporate, interdependent, and cosmopolitan realities of modern America. New media such as the movies and radio could contribute to this process through their creation of a new "common and aggregate mental life."

Dewey argued for a continual process of public education so that individuals could be empowered to participate in the modern world. Communities could exist only when they shared aims, beliefs, aspirations, and knowledge, and therefore they required effective communication between individuals. Such communication could not be read out of the democratic equation, he warned, nor could it be entrusted to experts whose relationship to public aspirations and participation was tenuous. Dewey therefore objected to Lippmann's and Eldridge's relegation of the citizen to the role of a mere spectator of public affairs. He argued that the challenge before modern statecraft was instead to encourage enlightened public participation through education and communication.[10]

Lippmann and Dewey were members of a generation of American social theorists who were deeply influenced by Ferdinand Tonnies's 1871 thesis that industrialization involved a wrenching social transformation from "community"—*gemeinschaft*—to "society," or *gesellschaft*. Old bonds of family, kinship, and neighborhood gave way to more impersonal relationships based on contract and on constructed, rather than personal, social interaction. Edward A.

Ross, who did much to popularize Tonnies's ideas, described this process in 1901 as one in which "powerful forces are more and more . . . replacing living tissue with structures held together by rivets and screws."[11]

Thomas Bender has argued that Tonnies's thesis struck deep chords within American fears for their community. Americans had worried about their social cohesion since the earliest days of white settlement, and republican thought in the eighteenth century had emphasized the need for a virtuous and united community. Coinciding with the advent of mass industrialization, urbanization, and immigration, Tonnies's *gemeinschaft-gesellschaft* model was unduly dichotomized by Americans who had long subscribed to a worldview of community "decay and dissolution," and who still longed for their idealized rural simplicity and cohesion. The possibility that *gemeinschaft* and *gesellschaft* could be placed on a continuum of social change, rather than opposed as a Manichean choice, Bender argues, was not contemplated by American social theorists until well after World War II.[12]

Interwar attitudes to radio challenge this view. Many considered that radio broadcasting, seen at the time as one of the miracles of the new technological age, would also act as a powerful force toward a new sense of community. In this way radio might re-create *gemeinschaft* within a society that had outwardly surrendered to *gesellschaft.* Although this belief was most evident in the context of political culture, radio's champions also extended its unifying effects to other facets of American life.

Early-twentieth-century social thought also focused upon what was called the "crowd mind." This concern was not new, but it was also more than a restatement of worries about the "mob" that had pervaded social theory for centuries. Whereas the mob had been portrayed as working-class and disaffected, the "crowd mind" envisaged by social theorists in the late nineteenth century assumed a distinctly middle-class hue, and its prime characteristic became not anger but apathy. Modern crowds were increasingly portrayed as flocks of bewildered sheep rather than as herds of stampeding bulls.[13] Their chief attribute was a desire to conform to the majority view. Individuals, powerless and ignorant, were increasingly susceptible to the temptation to let others do their thinking for them. Mass production and increasing specialization of knowledge only increased this tendency, Abram Lipsky argued in 1925, because it was now "possible for the average man to be expert only in the small field of his regular occupation. . . . Except in rare instances, an individual does not feel sufficient confidence in his own opinion to pit it against that of a multitude." Instead "crowd-mindedness" had replaced independent thought for most American citizens.[14]

Observers of the interwar period stressed different consequences of this crowd mentality, but all agreed that it was a grave social pathology. Ortega y Gasset, in *The Revolt of the Masses*, blamed the cheapening of culture upon the "triumphs of hyperdemocracy." The problem was not that "mass-man" was a fool; in fact he was better educated than ever before. Yet the temptations of crowd thinking had led him to accept "the stock of commonplaces, prejudices, fag-ends of ideas or simply empty words which chance has piled up within his mind, and with a boldness only explicable by his ingenuousness, [he] is prepared to impose them everywhere."[15] Jay Nash argued in 1938 that Americans had fallen victim to the disease of "spectatoritis." It was easier to listen to the radio than to read a book; it was more convenient to watch a movie than to practice a hobby. Consequently the machine age had "multiplied the mechanisms for the carrying of symbols," but spectator-citizens had lost their ability to discriminate between them. Purveyors of those symbols on the nation's radio stations, movie screens, and newsstands therefore gained untrammeled power to manipulate the public mind. American democracy and republicanism, which depended upon the independence of citizens, could not survive in such a culture.[16]

A distinct minority of sociologists and political scientists, and a great majority of radio broadcasters, saw a much more optimistic future for community, individuals, and democracy in an age of mass communication. Well before the radio age, Charles Horton Cooley foresaw a revival of democracy and public opinion through improved communication. The post office, railroads, telegraph, and telephones had all made it possible for "society to be organized more and more on the higher faculties of man," Cooley thought, and "we may expect the facility of intercourse to be the starting-point of an era of moral progress." Faster communication would also make possible the formation of a new, enlightened public opinion, which would ensure the continued vitality of democracy.[17]

William Donovan argued in 1936 that, although the coming of *gesellschaft* had lessened the importance of the individual, the great development of the twentieth century would be to reverse that process into a form of industrial *gemeinschaft*. Democracy was first conceived as a means of government for city-states that were small enough for all citizens to be in range of "a herald's voice." Now, Donovan argued, "strangely enough the radio is bringing back a certain approximation to ancient circumstances. . . . There can be no greater value through this medium of education than this development of the individual in the midst of the closer integration of human society."[18]

Others saw in radio a powerful unifying force which had arrived at a crucial period in American history. Rapid growth and increasing diversity were not completely positive developments, for they brought with them the possibility that the republic might become increasingly fragmented. Stephen Kern and Menahem Blondheim have shown that traditional concerns about the political and social ramifications of the size of the United States—both in space and population—continued through the nineteenth century and into the first half of the twentieth century. These concerns contributed to the speed with which new technologies such as the telegraph and the telephone were accepted by those who worried about the cohesiveness of the post–Civil War republic.[19]

Radio, through its freedom from wires and code, promised far greater unification. "Radio is a magic fluid that finds its way into every crevice of human life," Samuel Rothafel and Raymond Yates declared in 1925. It could unite the poor family "wintering in the dreary North River at Hoboken" with those "lounging in the luxury of a Fifth Avenue mansion" and the "lonely trapper of the silent Yukon." Alfred Goldsmith and Austin Lescarboura were more explicit about radio's ability to ameliorate class tension and to foster social unity. Broadcasting would prove to be an emancipator from ignorance and a leavener of public opinion, allowing the worker to learn "that the man in the office is not a Simon Legree," and this would allow the nation to be governed by an informed people. The republic could then prosper, for "the strength of our government depends more than that of any other government upon the intelligent interest of the voters in the affairs of the nation."[20]

Radio and Education

All sides of the debate over the problem of the modern citizen agreed that the future depended upon educating citizens to understand and participate in the modern world. "The devotion of democracy to education is a familiar fact," John Dewey argued in 1916, because only education could provide the informed citizens that democracy required. But twenty years later William J. Donovan was still concerned that more than 80 percent of American adults over 21 had not completed high school, and barely 3 percent had college training. Good citizenship and good democracy therefore demanded not only better education for young people but also lifelong education for adults.[21]

Robert McChesney and Elaine Prostak have analyzed the rise and fall of educational broadcasting between the wars, and their studies describe the extinguishing after 1925 of the early promise of educational radio by the growing power of commercial broadcasters, divisions within the educational broadcasters themselves, and listener apathy. Earlier chapters of this book have also shown the travails of educational radio stations at the hands of Congress, the FRC, and the FCC.[22] What remains to be examined are the ways in which early hopes about radio's role in civic education were translated into reality during the 1920s and 1930s.

The enthusiasm for radio education during the early days of broadcasting was palpable. Many universities set up broadcast stations as part of their extension programs and in order to provide their engineering and journalism students with experience in radio. By 1925 there were 128 educational stations across the country, mostly run by tertiary institutions.[23] Radio educators created organizations such as NCER and the National Advisory Council on Radio in Education (NACRE), and argued that the new medium would make lifelong education possible for millions of Americans. Anning Prall, Chairman of the FCC, encapsulated this optimism in a speech in 1935. Prall began by pointing out that the American republican experiment had always depended upon an educated citizenry. For too long, he warned, Americans had limited education to schools and scholars, and to the "printed symbol." But this approach had "overlooked the many who are not scholastic. We have left almost entirely out of the picture that large multitude of men and women beyond the compulsory school years, who must find their learning in the everyday experience of life." Radio, Prall believed, would make education attractive to children, accessible to adults, and beneficial to the republic.[24]

These hopes went unfulfilled during the interwar period. Although about 30 percent of the nation's schools were equipped with radio by 1930, there was very little material to listen to. Beset by regulatory requirements and hampered by funding problems, many educational stations disappeared from the airwaves after 1925. By 1931 only 49 remained, most of which were low-powered and unable to provide sustained programming. In 1930 only eight states had established radio education programs. The most sophisticated of these was the *Ohio School of the Air*, which provided an hour of educational programming every school day. Programs directed at rural schools in the Dakotas and Iowa were also broadcast during the early 1930s.[25]

As the ranks of educational stations thinned, few commercial stations devoted time during school hours to educational programs. These time slots were increasingly filled with material directed at adult female audiences, which were more attractive to sponsors. Between 1927 and 1930 the two major national networks devoted only 1 percent of their schedules to children's educational broadcasting. NBC also allowed its adult educational programming to decrease by more than half, from 9.7 percent of its schedule in

1927 to 4.2 percent in 1930.[26] NBC declared that it was prepared to devote more airtime to "responsible educators," but only after they could develop a coherent scheme for effective radio education for both adults and children. As Robert McChesney has argued, however, this policy should be seen in the context—well known to NBC—of profound divisions between the two most prominent bodies associated with radio education as to the best way to proceed. The NCER pushed hard for reservation of channels for educational broadcasting, and for compulsory allocation of commercial radio time for educational programs, while NACRE devoted itself to working with commercial broadcasters to encourage but not force them into radio education. Not surprisingly, both networks found the NACRE approach more attractive, and they gave it strong support.[27]

Divisions between radio educators assumed their most public form in 1931 over a bill written by Joy Elmer Morgan of NCER and sponsored by Republican Senator Simeon Fess of Ohio. The Fess bill required the FRC to allocate 15 percent of the nation's radio channels for the exclusive use of educational broadcasting. NCER gave strong support to the bill, while NACRE, NBC, CBS, and the NAB opposed it vociferously. They argued that it threatened the vitality and quality of the "American system" of broadcasting, and that it was unnecessary because broadcasters would be happy to air more educational material if only the educators could agree on how to present it. The Fess bill did not even reach committee hearings in 1931, and its defeat presaged the broadcasters' victory over the Wagner-Hatfield Amendment in 1934.[28]

Educators were also divided over the proper content of radio adult education. Broadcaster-friendly organizations such as NACRE pushed for programs that did not overburden listeners with intellectually demanding material. It was better, they thought, that learning be popularized so as to attract larger audiences and greater support from broadcasters. NCER, on the other hand, favored more systematic and ambitious radio education aimed at providing listeners with formal and detailed courses on high culture, science, and government. Education sugar coated as quiz shows was inadequate to solve the educational problem of the modern citizen. This vision of radio education involved strong elements of cultural and intellectual uplift, but it was also vulnerable to accusations of cultural elitism.[29]

In the absence of consensus over radio education, private broadcasters were able to define it in ways that best suited their own commercial priorities. William Paley argued that most American listeners would not tolerate programs that were overtly didactic. Instead, he thought, American democratic culture and listeners' preferences favored applied knowledge; a good concert was more educational than a program on the history of music. Broadcasters had an obligation to serve "an almost universal audience," rather than specific sections of the population. To that end majority interests had to come first, and the majority of Americans were not interested in classrooms of the air. "We indeed consider," Paley declared in 1934, "the criterion of success in . . . educational programs [is] a presentation so dramatic that the listener could distinguish it from pure entertainment only with difficulty." Paley did not mention that his reading of American democratic culture also did least damage to his network's commercial need to broadcast popular entertainment programs that would attract large advertising revenue.[30]

Judith Waller, NBC's director of public service programming in Chicago, agreed with Paley that radio would never replace the school or the university. She preferred that radio present "public service" programs rather than educational material, because listeners wanted to make their own choices about their education. Even those listeners who clamored for educational programs, Waller found, secretly preferred to listen to comedians such as Jack Benny. These "intellectually dishonest" people "want to appear very highbrow before their friends . . . but down inside, and within the confines of their own homes, they are, frankly, bored if forced to listen to the majority of educational programs." Frank Arnold, an expert in radio advertising, put the case against adult educational programming even more succinctly in 1933. The whole debate over radio education was a modern example of the "homely expression that you can lead a horse to water but you cannot make him drink." Listeners chose entertainment over education every time.[31]

NBC and CBS did succeed in developing a number of programs that successfully combined educational value with commercial viability. NBC's Walter Damrosch Music Appreciation Hour offered a combination of music and background commentary. The program, part of the network's sustaining time, reached perhaps seven million students in 70,000 schools and between three and four million adult listeners in 1937. In that year NBC strengthened its credentials in "serious" musical education by creating the NBC Symphony Orchestra to lure Arturo Toscanini out of retirement. Toscanini's first broadcast concert was a radio sensation, and prompted Lee de Forest to write to NBC that it was "the capstone to the structure of broadcasting, the realized perfection of my life's dream."[32]

CBS started *The American School of the Air* in 1931, and in 1933 began presenting the Swift Premium Ham shows, hosted by Emeritus Professor William Lyon Phelps of Yale and dedicated to the appreciation of books and music. By the end of 1934 Phelps had captured 16 percent of the national radio audience, providing his sponsors with value for money and his network with considerable educational prestige. In 1930 CBS contracted Professor William Chandler Bagby of Columbia to collaborate with his colleagues in a series of talks on history, literature, music, and art. Both networks also presented regular talks by professors, politicians, experts, and publicists on a huge variety of issues ranging from international diplomacy to veterinary care.[33]

The most famous civic education program of the 1930s was NBC's *America's Town Meeting of the Air.* Run by the League for Political Education, the program aired debates over social issues conducted before live audiences. It soon evolved into a self-conscious attempt to re-create the traditions of self-government and civic education supposedly lost as a result of urbanization. Later in the 1930s the program became symbolic of the ways in which democracy might fight back against totalitarianism. Harry and Bonaro Overstreet, of the League of Political Education, argued in 1938 that the "psychological gaps" between individuals had become too wide, and that radio allowed an opportunity to create a "simultaneous process of thinking" across a far-flung and disparate nation. In so doing it might disprove the Fascist and Bolshevik view that it was "impossible for a highly complicated, industrialized, citified civilization to conduct its affairs by those modes of common discussion and mutual understanding that were successful in a village society."[34]

The success of these programs challenged the broadcasters' assertions that educational material was unpopular. NCER and NACRE argued that networks and stations tended to understate listeners' demand for such material in order to maximize their offerings of more profitable sponsored shows.[35] Educational programming, they thought, would create its own demand if only it were given a chance. In 1929 one survey conducted by the Commonwealth Club of San Francisco of 7,000 listeners revealed that 71 percent of respondents wanted more educational radio programs.[36] Audience research by Paul Lazarsfeld in 1940, however, produced more ambiguous results. In *Radio and the Printed Page* Lazarsfeld examined how listening habits and preferences varied with levels of education and income. He found that listeners of both sexes without college education listened more than those with degrees, and that the difference was most marked between women (see fig. 10).

Lazarsfeld's other findings, however, did little to advance the radio educationalists' cause. After classifying listeners into five categories according to their interest in reading, he found that listeners who read least, or who read only "popular" fiction, showed strong preferences for entertainment over educational programs. Those listeners who read "better fiction" were most likely to listen to educational programming. As figure 11 shows, however, both

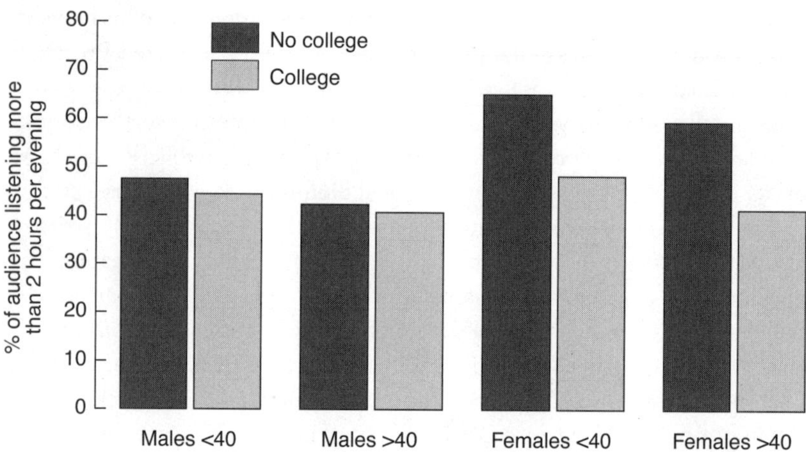

Figure 10. Radio Listening by Sex, Age, and Education, 1940.
Source: Graph constructed from data in Paul F. Lazarsfeld, *Radio and the Printed Page*, p. 19.

groups placed educational programs quite low on their orders of program preference. "The programs . . . which are definitely preferred by people lower in the cultural scale," Lazarsfeld concluded, "are those which can be characterized as of definitely bad taste." There was no point trying to enforce "serious" or educational programming upon uninterested listeners, he thought; the challenge was to improve the educational quality of those programs that ill-educated listeners did want to listen to.[37] Although riddled with unexplored assumptions about cultural hierarchy and the linkages between educational standards, wealth, and cultural interests, Lazarsfeld's findings were clear: those listeners who needed educational programs most listened to them least.

By 1940 it was clear that radio had disappointed the radio educationalists' hopes. Hamstrung by perceptions of elitism, undermined by their own divisions, and overwhelmed by the lobbying power of commercial broadcasters, radio educators were unable to influence the new medium's programming in a significant way. Instead of assisting supposedly bewildered citizens to understand better an increasingly complex world, interwar broadcasters preferred to entertain rather than educate them.

Radio and the News

Although broadcasters chose not to emphasize education in their programming, they showed more willingness to inform listeners about current events. Instantaneous communication offered enormous advantages to radio in the dissemination of news, and created great opportunities for it to establish itself at the heart of modern statecraft. Radio could bring news to listeners all over the nation without waiting for reporters to prepare copy, editors to improve it, machines to print it, and newsboys to distribute it. Citizens could keep up-to-date with local, national, and international news merely by turning on their radios, which could provide them with information in accessible and condensed form without the effort and concentration required to buy and read newspapers. In an increasingly busy world, radio news might prove to be an important antidote to the problem of the modern citizen.

Broadcasters moved quickly into news broadcasting. AT&T's WBAY appears to have broadcast the first scheduled radio news program in September 1922. Its "Radio Digest" provided listeners with an hour of news each afternoon.[38] Early radio news programs relied heavily on wire press services and were amateurish in their presentation; many small stations were content merely to read out sections of newspapers. The national networks provided five-minute bulletins at least three times a day, and NBC's Blue network pioneered a daily 15-minute newscast in 1930. Research conducted for NBC in 1936 revealed that many listeners tuned in specifically to hear the news; audience size grew by as much as 18 percent during bulletins. AIPO surveys in April 1937 and March 1939 also revealed that 70 percent of respondents depended on radio for some of their "daily news," and 60 percent of listeners

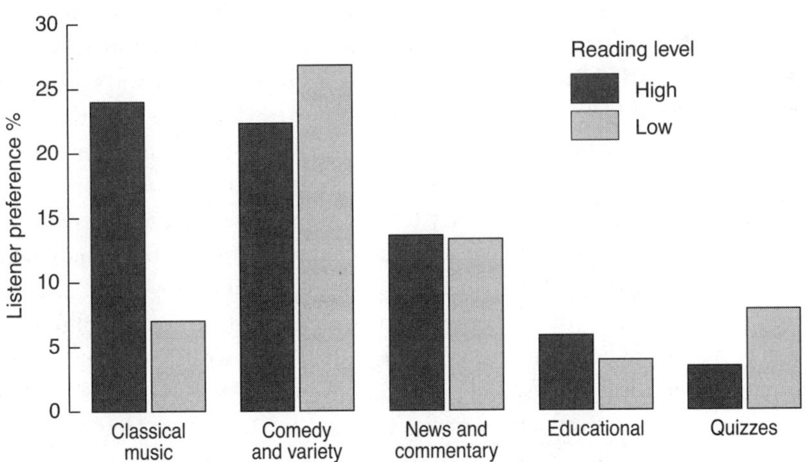

Figure 11. Radio Program Preferences According to Reading Levels, 1940.
Source: Graph constructed from data in Paul F. Lazarsfeld, *Radio and the Printed Page*, p. 41.

regularly listened to news programs. Such findings made news more attractive to sponsors, and thus encouraged broadcasters to air more of it.[39]

Radio news also benefited from its coverage of sensational events. When news broke in 1932 that Charles Lindbergh's baby was missing, CBS rushed broadcasters and technicians to the family's home and changed its schedule to provide blanket coverage of the search. At first NBC stayed aloof, but it soon covered the story with equal intensity. In September 1938, as Neville Chamberlain and Adolf Hitler negotiated the fate of Czechoslovakia at Munich, NBC broadcast 443 programs and updates of the crisis in ten days, devoting an average of three hours per day to the story. Such was the hold of the Munich crisis upon American radio listeners that James Rorty called it a turning point in political and diplomatic history because "for the first time history has been made in the hearing of its pawns."[40]

In less sensational times, however, broadcasters devoted relatively small amounts of time to news. The newspapers, as we shall see, objected to radio stations' use of wire services, and independent news gathering was an expensive exercise. Consequently most broadcasters tended to provide very short news programs of unremarkable quality. In 1932 news occupied 2 percent of NBC's total broadcast time. The onset of the Depression and the newsworthiness of the New Deal gradually forced stations to put more effort into news broadcasts. At the beginning of 1938 NBC devoted 3.4 percent of its time to news and commentary, compared to 58 percent to music, and 17.8 percent to drama.[41] With the worsening crisis in Europe, however, news broadcasts became more common. In the winter of 1938–39, 10 percent of all the networks' program time was devoted to news and commentary, and this figure rose steadily during World War II as listeners demanded detailed reports on the war's progress. NBC, CBS, and MBS devoted 15.5 percent of their time to news in the summer of 1942, and 18 percent in the winter of 1943–44. By that time over 60 percent of Americans nominated radio as their most important source of news.[42]

Apart from bringing immediacy to events and crises, major broadcasters also worked hard to tailor news to the characteristics of their audience. Whereas metropolitan newspapers could target specific geographic and socioeconomic groups, the networks sent programming to all sections of the nation and to an audience almost infinitely varied in its wealth, education, occupations, political beliefs, and prejudices. Audience research revealed that radio news was most influential among younger, less well off and less educated listeners. A majority of all listeners, however, viewed radio news as fairer and more trustworthy than newspapers. They seemingly agreed with their president that the newspapers had lost a great deal of their credibility through their virulent partisanship and anti-FDR sentiment during the 1930s. In a *Fortune* survey in 1939, which asked respondents which medium they trusted most, 40 percent of replies nominated the radio while only 27 percent gave newspapers their vote.[43]

The result was that networks and stations attempted to appeal to the lowest common denominator of listener education and interest without surrendering to what they saw as the sensationalism of the tabloid press. Although the experience of radio between the wars broadly supports Herbert Gans's conception of the news as assertive of the values and aspirations of the white, male upper middle class, it was not specifically directed at that group. Paul Lazarsfeld noted in 1942 that radio news tended to shy away from detailed information, which appealed most to "a small, well-educated minority," and to stress instead "the barest essentials of current news designed for the larger masses of people."[44]

A combination of radio exceptionalism and self-interest also created a more elevated tone to radio news than that of many newspapers. Always conscious of their role as purveyors of information and entertainment to the whole family, and of the danger that their licenses might be revoked by regulators responding to public or political pressure, broadcasters were very careful about the sorts of news that they broadcast. Radio news tended to avoid emphasis upon gory or sexual crime; many stations even refused to use the word *rape*. Because radio audiences were more geographically dispersed than newspaper readers, radio news tended also to avoid stories of purely local interest. Radio audiences, perhaps conditioned by the new medium's annihilation of distance, seemed to respond more positively to international news than did newspaper readers. Radio news also tended to be much more cautious in its political coverage than were newspapers; clearly the broadcaster's dependence upon regulatory goodwill, and the knowledge that their listeners covered all political persuasions, made them nervous of partisanship. In one comparison of press and radio news in Cincinnati in 1939, newspapers devoted 133 percent more space to crime, 120 percent more to natural disasters, and 57 percent more to political news than did the city's radio stations. Cincinnati's broadcasters, however, devoted nearly twice the attention to foreign news and comment than did its newspapers.[45]

The Rise of the Radio News Commentator

News commentary proved to be one of the most significant aspects of radio news. The radio commentator performed a mediating function similar to newspaper editors' and columnists', interpreting news to provide listeners and readers with what Lippmann had described as "pictures in their heads." As Michael Schudson has argued, interwar interpretative journalism in print and on radio was part of a broader movement away from the late-nineteenth-century form of descriptive and "objective" journalism. It was also a product of concerns that citizens were no longer able to assimilate on their own the flood of information created by the complexity of the modern world.[46]

Hans Kaltenborn is generally considered to have been the first radio news commentator. A former reporter, Kaltenborn began commenting on the news on AT&T's New York station WEAF toward the end of 1923. Although Kaltenborn was joined by a handful of commentators on other stations during the 1920s, it was not until the 1930s, with the Depression and then the worsening international situation, that news commentary became a programming staple. In 1930 there were six commentators at work, but in 1939 there were more than 20, including such household names as Boake Carter, Lowell Thomas, Elmer Davis, Raymond Gram Swing, Walter Winchell, and the durable Kaltenborn. These commentators became highly paid celebrities; in the depth of the Depression Kaltenborn earned $800 per week.[47]

During the interwar years the most successful commentators became as widely trusted and discussed as their peers in print. An American Independent Press Organization (AIPO) survey in 1939 revealed that 70 percent of respondents listened regularly to news commentary, and that 68 percent of that group expressed confidence in commentators' honesty and fairness. Radio commentators tended to appeal more strongly to less educated and less affluent listeners than did columnists and editorial writers. In 1939 Hadley Cantril surveyed a group of regular listeners of Boake Carter's commentaries and found that 74 percent of wealthier listeners thought that he was less informative than newspaper columnists, while 70 percent of poorer listeners took the opposite view.[48]

Although news commentary was seen as a significant contribution to civic education and debate, it was frequently problematic for broadcasters. The most popular, and therefore the most commercially valuable, commentators were also the most controversial, and broadcasters often found themselves caught between satisfying advertisers' desires for ratings and their own need to avoid offense to their political and regulatory masters. Sponsors, too, put pressure on broadcasters when they considered that commentators' views tainted their products among sections of their audience. The result of these tensions was that radio news commentary, like so many of broadcasting's other activities, never quite achieved all the civic benefits that were promised of it.

Hans Kaltenborn learned early about the perils of radio commentary. In 1924 he criticized Secretary of State Charles Evans Hughes for rejecting an overture from the Soviet Union for diplomatic recognition. Hughes heard the broadcast and complained strongly to WEAF and AT&T. Kaltenborn refused to retract his views, claiming the same freedom of speech as that accorded to writers of newspaper editorials. Always nervous about its standing with regulators, AT&T publicly reasserted its "fundamental policy of constant and complete cooperation with every government institution that was concerned with communications." Kaltenborn's contract was not renewed, but he continued his commentaries on WOR. That station, too, came under pressure after Kaltenborn's criticisms of New York City Mayor Jimmy Walker. WOR did not buckle, however, and allowed Kaltenborn his editorial freedom.[49]

Kaltenborn's commentaries also made his sponsors nervous. At the end of 1938 he signed a lucrative deal with General Mills for 13 weekly talks. Although Kaltenborn agreed to submit his scripts in advance to General Mills, the company declared that it would not censor him. In fact both sides broke their agreements: Kaltenborn refused to provide his scripts, and within two weeks of his first commentary he had been called in to discuss matters with the chairman of the board. The problem was Kaltenborn's outspoken anti-Fascism, and in particular his virulent attacks upon General Franco and Adolf Hitler. General Mills had been threatened with a boycott of its Gold Medal flour by a group of German American bakers, and prominent Catholics warned the company that it risked a backlash from their congregations, who perceived Kaltenborn's attacks upon Franco as anti-Catholic. One priest wrote to General Mills "in a friendly spirit" about the damage Kaltenborn was doing it:

> Your organization will regret it for a long time . . . if . . . your millions of Catholic customers get the idea that General Mills is ever so faintly associated with any activity supporting the Loyalist cause and what it represents in Catholic eyes. . . . You are manufacturing articles which go into the intimacy of Catholic homes where little children cluster around the breakfast tables. Articles admitted into these sacred surroundings . . . must come there free from even the slightest taint of suspicion.

General Mills' chief public relations officer at the time was Henry Bellows, who had been a member of the FRC and then a vice-president of CBS. Well aware of the regulatory and commercial sensitivities of controversy on radio, Bellows appealed to Kaltenborn to moderate his views, and General Mills dropped Kaltenborn a month later. Pure Oil took him over, and loyally supported him. David G. Clark concluded his study of Kaltenborn's relationship with sponsors by pointing to the limits of radio commentary as a form of public debate. "Successful airing of controversial issues," Clark maintained, "depends not so much on commentator or network willingness to speak out, as on sponsor willingness to stand the gaff."[50]

Much also depended upon the network's attitudes to news commentators. CBS remained nervous of them after its experience with Father Coughlin, whose broadcasts strained the network's relationship with both the FCC and the White House. CBS also suffered periodic embarrassment from its long-running Ford program. William J. Cameron, a Ford Motor Company executive, used commercial intermissions to rail against the New Deal and its socialism. Later in the decade CBS watched with growing concern as its star commentator, Boake Carter, became more extreme in his anti-FDR views. Carter's talks, laced with conspiracy theories and rumors, threatened to return the network to its old problems with Coughlin, but they also rated extremely well. After much hesitation, CBS finally placed political expediency over commercial convenience and dropped Carter.[51]

Nor was NBC immune to problems with commentators. Walter Winchell, a virulent anti-Nazi, delivered increasingly anti-German talks after 1937. During 1939 and 1940 he began referring to German political leaders as "Ratzis," Hitler as a "madman," and Joachim von Ribbentrop, Hitler's chief diplomat, as "von Ribbentripe." "Since we are neutral," one listener wrote to NBC after a particularly vitriolic Winchell talk in March 1940, "it was very poor taste and is one of the little things that might stir up resentment [and] may bring us into war. Is this in your estimation Mr. Winchell's endeavor and what is Mr. Winchell's racial background?" NBC Vice-president John Royal recognized in May 1939 that "we are faced with a serious problem on Winchell. He has been gradually getting off the deep end. . . . His editorials are caustic and vitriolic, and I don't think they should be permitted." Little, however, was done. Despite pressure from NBC, Winchell refused to submit his scripts in advance, and his ratings remained high. Nearly a year later, in March 1940, Royal noted with resignation, "I assume . . . that Winchell's importance on the Blue, and his rating, are such that we do the best we can and if he doesn't wish to live up to our policies, we should just let it go."[52] Winchell may also have had protection even more powerful than high ratings; he was widely recognized as FDR's favorite commentator, and was in frequent contact with the White House.[53] With powerful friends and high ratings, Winchell continued his broadcasts without significant interference. Buffeted between sponsors' sensitivities, network expediency, political pressure, and commentators' prickly independence, however, radio news commentary never achieved the level of calm and enlightened news mediation once envisaged by Lippmann and the radio exceptionalists.

The Press-Radio War

Broadcasting's ability to engender a new age of civic education through detailed news coverage was also hampered by the growing hostility of the print media. Alarmed by radio's ability to bring news to the nation instantaneously and arrestingly, and concerned over its growing attractiveness to advertisers, the press refused it access to news gathering agencies and ceased to print radio schedules free of charge. Behind these issues lay a deeper contest for pre-eminence in informing and guiding public opinion. Although broadcasters eventually won their struggle over access to news and free publication, their victory was won through a partial surrender of their earlier vision of radio as the solution to the problems of twentieth-century citizenship. Broadcasters, concerned most of all to maintain their commercial viability and to ward off further regulation, took care to be gracious winners by attenuating their earlier rhetoric of a new age of enlightenment that would owe little to the print media for its dynamism.

Competitive tensions between newspapers and radio began to emerge after the formation of NBC and CBS in 1926 and 1928. The new national networks sharpened competition between print and ether for advertisers' dollars, and broadcasting's share of total advertising revenues grew steadily during the last years of the 1920s.[54] It is important, however, not to attribute the press-radio war simply to a struggle for advertising dollars. Bruce Barton reassured newspaper owners in June 1931 that print media would remain supreme because "people are four-fifths eye-minded and only one-fifth ear-minded." During the late 1920s, furthermore, there seemed to be enough revenue for everyone; despite large increases in radio advertising, newspapers across the nation enjoyed an increase of over 10 percent in circulation and advertising sales between 1926 and 1929.[55]

As figure 12 shows, radio advertising never approached the newspapers' total during the 1920s and 1930s, although it certainly narrowed the gap during the early years of the Depression. Although every advertising dollar became precious after 1930, it is unlikely that newspaper proprietors seriously considered that radio would overtake their place as the nation's principal advertising medium. Nevertheless, many were concerned by evidence that some of their largest advertisers had shifted their advertising campaigns to radio

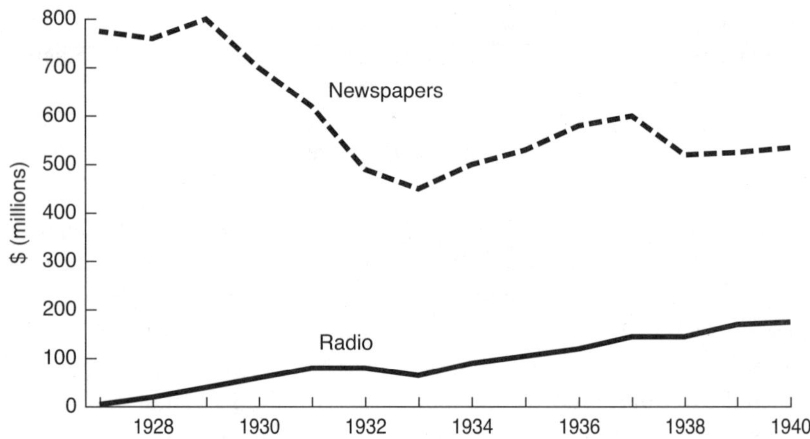

Figure 12. Advertising Expenditures in Newspapers and on Radio, 1927–1940.
Source: Graph constructed from data in Mitchell V. Charnley, *News by Radio,* p. 10.

during the worst days of the Depression.[56] After 1933, however, both print and radio advertising began to recover strongly.

Although unhappy with broadcasters' inroads into their advertising revenues, newspaper publishers were also concerned by their encroachment upon news analysis and commentary. This struck at the heart of the press's traditional role as the pre-eminent forum for narrating, discussing, and analyzing public affairs. If radio were to usurp this, publishers feared, their circulation, and thus their advertising revenues, would further decline. To add insult to injury, it was well known that radio commentators invariably lifted their material from newspapers or from agencies such as United Press (UP) and transformed it into popular radio programs.[57] This dovetailed with newspapers' concerns about radio's increasing ability to scoop them on news stories. The press had invested millions of dollars in news-gathering and distribution organizations, and radio's tendency to appropriate news represented a frontal attack upon that investment. The growing sophistication of radio technology also enabled it to bring events live to audiences, further eroding the newspapers' ability to break news. Robbed of its immediacy, the press increasingly emphasized its interpretative functions, and thus resented the growth of radio news commentary.[58]

As pressure to cut costs increased after 1929, newspaper interests began to retaliate against radio. Despite the fact that the two major networks offered only very short news bulletins, the American Newspaper Publishers Association (ANPA) resolved in 1931 to regulate more tightly broadcasters' access to newswire services and to charge for publication of radio schedules. Two years later, after radio's intensive coverage of the Lindbergh kidnapping and the early New Deal, the newspapers tightened the screws still more. UP canceled its contract to supply news to CBS in October 1932, and Associated Press (AP) followed suit in April 1933. The press-radio war had begun.[59]

CBS responded by creating the Columbia News Service (CNS) in the early summer of 1933. CNS was directed by Paul White, formerly of UP, and paid for by sponsorship from General Mills. Within three months CNS was a fully functional news gathering service, with bureaus in New York, Chicago, and Los Angeles and freelance journalists in most American and major international cities. Now flush with material, CBS expanded its news programming to three bulletins totaling 25 minutes each day.[60] NBC was less provocative in its response. Merlin Aylesworth told the ANPA that newspapers, magazines, and radio were "complementary" in their ability to disseminate news, because each had its own special characteristics. Radio had the advantage of speed, but it could not match newspapers in their ability to provide detail and context. "While the public no doubt seeks the news flashes and glorified headlines over the radio," Aylesworth reassured the ANPA, "it also seeks the amplified news to be found in favorite newspapers."[61]

Despite Aylesworth's and NBC's conciliatory tone, however, they too were denied the services of AP and UP. The network therefore hired a journalist, Abel A. Schechter, to gather its news. Schechter's one-man operation was rudimentary compared to CBS's efforts; without bureaus, reporters, or freelancers, Schechter used only his telephone to gather enough news for a short daily bulletin.[62] NBC's reluctance to follow CBS into full-scale news collection stemmed from a number of considerations. The older network had enjoyed close relations with newspaper interests since its inception; by the end of 1933 about 30 of NBC's affiliates were owned by publishing concerns, while CBS had fewer press-owned affiliates.[63]

NBC was also deeply worried by the publishers' rhetoric. Apart from its complaints about radio advertising and radio's parasitic news gathering methods, the ANPA also attacked radio at its most vulnerable point. Even in 1931, before full-scale hostilities broke out, the ANPA called for tighter regulation of broadcasters to prevent them from abusing the airwaves to earn inflated profits. Many publishers complained that they had to earn their living in an unregulated and fiercely competitive market, while radio stations and networks could hide behind their licenses and the pliant FRC. It seemed only fair, therefore, that the government step in to limit broadcasters' abilities to advertise so as to negate their competitive advantage over print. Other newspaper representatives also wondered aloud whether radio broadcasters, beholden to the federal government for periodic renewal of their licenses, could be trusted to present impartial and fearless reporting.[64] Always sensitive to antimonopoly arguments, and deeply concerned about the political power of an enraged press, NBC was in no mood for a protracted battle. It sued for peace with the ANPA and organized a conference with them at the Biltmore Hotel in New York City in December 1933.

The Biltmore agreement, publicly revealed in March 1934, represented a triumph for NBC and the press and a puzzling back down by CBS. The networks agreed to disband their own news services and to obtain their news free from what would be the Press-Radio Bureau, which was to be controlled by the newspapers and their agencies. The networks agreed to limit their news bulletins, with the exception of coverage of events deemed to be of "transcendental importance," to two five-minute bulletins per day, timed after the release of morning and evening papers. The networks also agreed to pay the costs of the Press-Radio Bureau, to restrict individual news items to 30 words each, to limit their commentators to providing "background information" rather than "spot news," and to refrain from seeking sponsorship for news bulletins. NBC expressed great satisfaction with the agreement. In March 1935 Vice-president Frank Mason observed that for less than $15,000 per year the network received "the cream of the news . . . from four press associations day and night." A metropolitan newspaper, Mason noted, typically paid $100,000 per year for a single press service.[65]

NBC and the press had good reason to be pleased with the Biltmore agreement, but CBS's acceptance of it was more surprising. It had recently invested heavily in CNS, and had developed a competitive advantage in news gathering over NBC. The Biltmore agreement swept away that investment and that strategy. Although Paley later described the agreement as a "big mistake," good reasons at the time propelled CBS to sign it. It was as vulnerable as NBC to the newspapers' refusal to publish program schedules, and it was equally nervous about the prospect of tighter regulation. Because NBC refused to support its aggressive response to the press, CBS faced the prospect of maintaining CNS, and suffering sanctions from newspapers, while NBC reaped the benefits of cheap news through cooperation with the press. The need to cut costs, especially those not payable by its chief rival, also weighed upon CBS executives.[66]

The newspapers did not have long to savor their triumph at the Biltmore. CBS refused to live up to the spirit of its capitulation, and pressed hard at the definitional edges of "transcendental importance" so as to continue covering events, such as the kidnapping trial of Bruno Hauptmann in 1935, free of restriction. The deteriorating situation in Europe after 1936 and the arrival of Edward R. Murrow provided CBS with both the events and the talent to expand its coverage of international news without the mediation of the Press-Radio Bureau. NBC, on the other hand, abided by the spirit of the agreement much more closely. It even advised its listeners at the end of each bulletin to read their local newspapers for more detailed news.[67] While CBS eroded the Biltmore agreement from within, unaffiliated and local stations attacked it frontally. Although NBC and CBS could only commit their own stations to the Biltmore rules, they assumed that their affiliates would also be subject to them. This struck affiliated and independent broadcasters—many of whom had made their own arrangements with local newspapers for provision of news—as the height of arrogance and as an abuse of market power. In the wake of the agreement NBC and CBS received thousands of letters from aggrieved listeners protesting against the proposed reduction in their news bulletins.[68]

A group of independent broadcasters set up the Trans-Radio Press Service to provide news to stations unwilling to accept the Press-Radio Bureau's restrictions. Run by veterans of CNS, and buttressed by patronage from the Yankee Network, Trans-Radio provided news to 250 stations by the beginning of 1936.[69] Its success forced the Press-Radio Bureau to drop most of its restrictions. In 1935 two of the major news agencies, UP and William Randolph Hearst's International Service, broke ranks with the Biltmore cartel by announcing that they would henceforth sell news to all comers. By the end of 1935 independent and affiliated stations could contract for as much news as they wanted, and could schedule as many bulletins each day as they felt appropriate. Only NBC-owned stations remained true to the Press-Radio Bureau and to the Biltmore rule of two five-minute bulletins per day. By then the press-radio war was effectively over, though the bureau struggled on until its unlamented demise in 1940.[70]

Relations between the print media and broadcasters continued to improve after 1935. Competitive pressures over advertising revenue lost their sting as sales grew in both print and radio; between 1935 and 1937 newspaper revenue jumped by more than 14 percent, while radio advertising climbed 46 percent from its much lower base. Many publishers, weary of fighting radio, joined it instead; by the middle of 1936 nearly a quarter of the nation's stations were owned or controlled by newspapers.[71] For their part, CBS and NBC sent signals to publishers that their aspirations in news, commentary, and civic information were limited and not fundamentally antagonistic to those of the press. Both networks made it clear that entertainment, and not news or analysis, was their central concern.[72]

Broadcasters were encouraged by the FCC in 1941 to retreat further from the traditional editorial and commentary functions and freedoms of the press. In the context of FDR's concerns about cross-ownership, and in the midst of calls for radio to exercise its power responsibly during the war, the FCC declared that broadcasters should forgo editorializing on political issues. Although the FCC clarified its rule, known as the Mayflower doctrine, to allow stations to air balanced accounts of controversy, most broadcasters welcomed the excuse offered by the Mayflower doctrine to avoid controversy altogether.[73] Broadcasters, despite the rhetoric of radio exceptionalism and radio citizenship, were generally happy to leave the politically risky work of news gathering and editorializing to the print media.

The end of the press-radio war and the effective collapse of the Biltmore agreement demonstrated the folly of attempts to restrain the flow of news within a political culture deeply imbued with freedom of speech and antimonopoly principles. Yet the outcome of the press-radio war was also made possible by the major broadcasters' calculated withdrawal from their earlier aspirations to be pre-eminent purveyors of information and formers of public opinion. Frightened by the power of the press, and hemmed in by their position as licensees, it seemed wiser, and commercially more attractive, for radio's major organizations to retreat from independent news gathering and editorializing and to concentrate instead upon entertainment interspersed with occasional news bulletins and coverage of specific events. In so doing the young industry not only contradicted its rhetoric of radio exceptionalism but also allowed the press to continue its dominance over the public sphere until well after World War II.

Propaganda and the Duped Radio Citizen

"Propaganda," as Frederick Bartlett defined it in 1940, "is an attempt to influence opinion and conduct . . . in such a manner that the persons who adopt the opinions and behavior indicated do so without themselves making any definite search for reasons."[74] Memories of the propaganda campaigns of World War I had sensitized many sociologists of the 1920s and 1930s to opinion-forming techniques and to the possibility that radio might become the most effective propaganda vehicle yet devised. Broadcasters and advertisers, who argued that the dangers of propaganda were grossly exaggerated, countered these concerns. During the 1930s, however, the balance of argument had swung strongly against these pollyannas; the rise of totalitarianism abroad, demagoguery at home, and events such as the *War of the Worlds* dramatization in 1938 convinced many that radio's impact on listeners was not always to the good. These fears reinforced concerns about the standardizing and anaesthetizing effects of broadcasting and cast more doubt upon earlier hopes for a new age of civic education. Radio, it appeared by 1940, could be as easily used to fool citizens as to enlighten them.

Concerns about radio and propaganda surfaced almost as quickly as broadcasting itself. In March 1922, only 15 months after KDKA's first program, an article appeared in the *New York Times* about the potential danger of communists setting up a powerful station in New York City to "spread their gospel along the upper reaches of the ether clear to San Francisco." In January 1929 Congressman Clay Briggs, a Democrat from Texas, asked FRC Chairman Orestes Caldwell what could be done to prevent broadcasters from giving a "one-sided presentation of something, and build[ing] propaganda for it." Caldwell acknowledged the danger, but assured Briggs, "My belief is that the public will quickly find out any abuse, and the public always has control of the situation by turning a little dial."[75]

Caldwell's optimism about the power of the sovereign listener was a distinctly 1920s phenomenon. In that decade, while enthusiasm for broadcasting and hopes for radio citizenship were still high, broadcasters and advertisers tried to persuade Americans that their distrust of propaganda was unfounded. In 1928 Kimball Young argued, "We must look upon propaganda as a positive rather than a negative device in the control of opinion and conduct." Whereas censorship was essentially repressive, he argued, propaganda, responsibly conducted, enabled citizens to understand their world more clearly.[76] Edward L. Bernays went even further in *Propaganda*, also published in 1928. "The conscious and intelligent manipulation of the organized habits and opinions of the masses is an important element in democratic society," the master advertiser believed. There was no point pretending that citizens could any longer make up their own minds on important issues, but "fortunately the sincere and gifted politician is able, by the instrument of propaganda, to mold and form the will of the people."[77]

For most observers, however, the lessons of World War I were far more worrying. Whereas Bernays and others stressed the beneficial aspects of wartime propaganda for national unity and public education, others worried that it had ushered in a new age of manipulation which would leave citizens increasingly vulnerable to exploitation from unscrupulous advertisers on the one hand and manipulative politicians on the other.[78] In his classic study in 1927 of World War I propaganda, Harold Lasswell noted that the modern science of "controlling public opinion testifies to the collapse of the traditional species of democratic romanticism and to the rise of a dictatorial habit of mind. . . . To illuminate the mechanisms of propaganda is to reveal the secret springs of social action, and to expose to the most searching criticism our prevailing dogmas of sovereignty, of democracy, of honesty, and of the sanctity of individual opinion."[79]

Those who searched for Lasswell's "secret springs of social action" during the 1930s broadened their definitions of propaganda and focused upon radio as the most important device for its dissemination. In 1933, as Hitler claimed power in Germany and FDR unveiled the New Deal, Frederick Lumley predicted in *The Propaganda Menace* that a new age of propaganda was at hand. Both international relations and domestic politics would be conducted through propaganda, leaving citizens with the illusion of information but with the reality of "suppression, distortion, [and] diversion." The only protection against this lay in educating people to "think straight." Lumley was unclear, though, as to how this could be done in a society already awash with advertising, public opinion consultants, and propaganda.[80]

In 1925 Lumley had argued that both political propaganda and commercial advertising were forms of social control because they created needs and opinions to create ostensibly voluntary, but in reality manufactured, behavior toward preordained ends. Leonard Doob noted in 1935 that the essential ingredients of successful propaganda—repetition, cultural congruence, and flattery—were equally important to effective advertising. "Advertising 'pays' because business men have the resources which enable them to carry on propaganda continually." Six years later Clyde Miller argued that the connection between propaganda and modern business practices had grown even closer. "Propaganda has popularized and made acceptable assembly-line production with its regimentation of workers. . . . The trend is speeded up by radio propaganda programs, commercial and political."[81]

Miller's focus upon radio propaganda had become a familiar refrain by 1941. O. W. Riegel saw both foreign and domestic propaganda all about him in 1934, and thought that broadcasting was most to blame. "The mechanical perfection of radio broadcasting may not itself have stimulated the acceleration of the welding of mass populations into self-conscious and militant 'nations,' but at least it can be said that modern nationalism has perceived and appropriated this potent instrument of mass control." Will Irwin ended his 1936 study of the degeneration of news into propaganda by arguing that radio had given more than any other medium to those who wished to mold public opinion instead of merely informing it. Radio, Irwin claimed, "through the magic inherent in the human voice, has means of appealing to the lower nerve centers and of creating emotions which the hearer mistakes for thoughts."[82]

The assumption that the spoken word over radio was more effective in influencing opinion than written text held sway over those who worried about radio propaganda. This proved to be very resistant to Paul Lazarsfeld's debunking research, and it reflected both the strong hold of radio exceptionalism upon popular thought and a growing sense of the passivity of the radio audience. "The wireless listener bobs like a cork on the waves," Rudolf Arnheim observed in 1936. "[He] hears . . . an endless succession of totally unconnected things, and so entirely without a breathing space that he does not manage subsequently to ponder and consider what he has heard."[83] Concerns about radio propaganda also fed directly into the broader debate about the fate of the modern citizen. The "crowd mind" seemed to be particularly susceptible to political and commercial propagandists. Arnheim, Doob, Irwin, and Lumley were convinced of the vulnerability of the modern individual both within and outside the crowd to manipulation, and they had little faith in the broadcasters' and advertisers' conception of a new and fortified sovereign radio citizen. Instead of creating discriminating and skeptical listener-citizens, radio had delivered to the propagandist a huge and passive audience ripe for mass indoctrination.

Those who feared the combination of radio and propaganda found much evidence to support their case during the 1930s. The rise of Nazism, in particular, seemed to show the power of radio to seduce normally civilized people into barbarity. Opportunities to hear German radio propaganda were frequent for American radio listeners during the 1930s. In January 1934, NBC rebroadcast Hitler's address to the Reichstag. Goebbels' office provided a summary of the speech in English after the address, and NBC engineers noted that the chancellor could be heard "as clearly as if he had been in one of the New York studios."[84] Such network broadcasts were rare, however, because they were invariably in German and because neither CBS nor NBC wished to appear to be spreading Hitler's gospel. Much more prevalent were shortwave broadcasts emanating directly from Europe. By the beginning of 1937 there were at least two million shortwave receiving sets in the United States, and their owners could listen to a steady stream of German, Italian, Spanish, and Soviet broadcasts. Germany's four shortwave stations, all of which were easily audible at night across the United States, presented a mixture of German and English programs eight hours a day and seven days a week. Mussolini's Italian propagandists were equally active; by the end of 1936 listeners around the world could hear "news" from Rome in 12 languages.[85]

The most memorable lesson of the interwar period on the power of radio to dupe citizens, however, came neither from propagandists nor foreigners. Between 8 P.M. and 9 P.M. on October 30, 1938, Orson Welles presented a dramatized version of *War of the Worlds* on CBS. Although Welles's script used established conventions of radio news, including news flashes, "live" reporting, and eyewitness interviews, he was careful to insert four reminders that his program was fictional. At the end of the play he reassured his listeners that the performance was nothing more than a Halloween offering, a "radio version of dressing up in a sheet and jumping out of a bush and saying Boo!"[86]

By then it was too late; on the following day newspapers across the country reported that hysteria had gripped large numbers of listeners who had been convinced that the apocalypse had come. "We had tuned in to listen to Orson Welles but when the flashes came I thought it was true," one listener recalled. "I felt why can the children not be with us, if we are going to die[?] Then I called in to my husband: Dan, why don't you get dressed? You don't want to die in your working clothes."[87] The reaction was particularly strong in New Jersey, where Welles had set his drama. Thousands of listeners attempted to flee the state, and many more jammed police phone lines seeking information about the invasion. New York City police received 2,000 calls within 15 minutes of the broadcast, and even in far off Oklahoma, California, and Alabama anxious inquiries flooded in to police and broadcasters. "Like the concentric rings that sweep out when a rock is dropped into a placid pool," the *New York Daily News* reported, "fear and near-hysteria billowed across the country."[88]

CBS, deeply embarrassed, promised never again to present dramatizations in the form of "news." Welles expressed his deep regret and surprise that so many listeners had missed his disclaimers of authenticity. In private, however, he was unrepentant. "The radio was believed in America," he recalled later. "That was a voice from heaven, you see. And I wanted to destroy that as dramatically as possible." The *New York Post* blamed the panic on listeners who had tuned into the play late after listening to *The Charlie McCarthy Show* on NBC. Those latecomers would have missed the first two warnings that the program was a dramatization.[89]

Public reaction to the panic reflected a mixture of ruefulness and disbelief. One listener from South Bound Brook, New Jersey, blamed it on the recent Munich crisis and the increasing danger of war. "We have all been living, day and night, tuned in for bad news and the word that might mean life or death to millions." Other listeners drew broader inferences from the incident. The nation had become so used to radio propaganda from FDR and the New Deal, "Mrs. A.K.J." of Fleetwood, New York, wrote to the *New York Herald Tribune*, that it would now believe anything. "I can still hear a convincing radio voice persuading twenty-six million of us that there were 'men from Mars' called 'economic royalists' who had been dealing death rays to us unhampered for twelve long years."[90]

Sociologists and others interested in radio and propaganda rushed to analyze the *War of the Worlds* phenomenon. Hadley Cantril, a member of Lazarsfeld's Office of Radio Research, published a detailed examination of the broadcast in 1947. He calculated that about six million listeners had tuned in to at least part of the program, and that the audience was spread evenly across gender, age, and wealth categories. Cantril concluded that about 28 percent of the audience, or 1.7 million people, mistook the dramatization for actual news, and that about 70 percent, or 1.2 million, of that group were "frightened or disturbed" by it. Those listeners who were "closest to the borderline of economic disaster" were the most likely to have misunderstood the program. These listeners had been most impressed by the dramatic quality of Welles's production, and they were also the most trusting of radio as an information medium. Welles's use of "news bulletins" and fictional but prestigious scientists and military figures further increased the verisimilitude of the program to listeners whose frames of reference were limited by economic insecurity, little education, and an increasingly bewildered view of a world on the verge of war.[91]

The *War of the Worlds* panic demonstrated not only the power of radio to captivate the interwar imagination but also the hollowness of claims for an enlightened and discriminating radio citizenship. If, after 18 years of broadcasting, it was still possible for so many listeners to be so easily fooled, it seemed clear that broadcasters had failed to achieve their self-proclaimed mission to rid citizens of their supposed bewilderment and ignorance. The limits of interwar radio citizenship become even clearer when we turn to those who were denied full membership in the radio community.

12

Radio at the Margins

Broadcasting and the Limits of Citizenship

Early in the 1920s Maurice Bradford thanked Harry P. Davis, Vice-president of Westinghouse, for some radio components. "Ye Gods! A Wonderful, wonderful present! I'll be radio frequencying all night for the next three months!" Although he was "shut off from everything" and isolated from his family, Bradford could now go to baseball games, listen to Woodrow Wilson, and hear dance music. Radio had banished his old feeling that there was "absolutely nothing worth living for. . . . Why, you really *are* someone again! These people that you listen to every night . . . go right on talking to you as if you were 'one of them' once more, and for the time being you are!"[1]

As a prisoner serving a life sentence in a New Hampshire jail, Bradford was the most extreme example of those who were described between the wars as "shut-ins." This term encompassed not only prisoners but also the elderly, chronically ill, and others whose personal circumstances isolated them from the world. In a society that valued personal mobility and civic participation highly, shut-ins were the most pitiable examples of the isolated modern citizen. To these shut-ins we can also add the "shut-outs," those who, although not confined to prisons, hospitals, asylums, or homes, were nevertheless excluded from full citizenship in interwar society. Women, labor activists, African Americans, and rural dwellers were all shut out, to varying degrees, from modern American political and economic culture. Some were simultaneously shut in and shut out; many women of both races were shut out from large areas of commerce, politics, and culture, and also shut into their homes as daughters, mothers, and wives. Radio's enthusiasts promised some of these groups the possibility of greater cultural and political integration. Through its annihilation of distance, its ability to communicate with the illiterate, and its ubiquity, broadcasting could bring the margin dwellers closer to the communal hearth.[2]

Like the radio exceptionalists' hopes for a new age of education and civic enlightenment, however, these hopes were only partially fulfilled. Although broadcasters frequently paid lip service to radio's capacity to reach out to America's shut-ins, they focused only upon those groups who offered them the greatest commercial opportunity and who posed least threat to the interwar gendered, racial, cultural, and economic status quo.

Some marginal groups, such as recent or first-generation immigrants, received little or no direct attention from major broadcasters or sponsors but were nevertheless invited to join the broader radio community. In her study of Chicago's ethnic workers during the 1920s and 1930s, Lizabeth Cohen credits radio with a strong normative influence in integrating immigrants into a national commercial culture that helped them transcend the bonds of their tightly segregated ethnic neighborhoods. While early Chicago radio helped to strengthen ethnic ties through local stations broadcasting foreign-language programs, the triumph of network and commercial radio at the end of the 1920s gave the city's myriad ethnic groups new and shared cultural links. Increasingly exposed to the same mass culture, Cohen suggests, workers previously divided by language, culture, and history could now find common ground in discussing the latest antics of *Amos'n'Andy* and by sampling the products of the sponsors who brought programs to them.[3]

Radio may also have assisted other American workers to feel a closer identity with their worlds of work and culture during the interwar years. By the late 1930s radios were ubiquitous in white urban working-class neighborhoods, and the greater willingness of poorer and less well educated listeners to listen to, and to trust, radio programs and advertising was well known to audience researchers. The urban working class thus became a prized market for broadcasters, and it was granted great influence over radio programming. Stations played to what they saw as workers' tastes, and advertisers focused upon staple household goods that featured prominently in the consumption patters of white urban workers.

There were, however, clearly defined limits to radio's contribution to ethnic assimilation and to working-class identity. When the Office of Education of the Department of Interior proposed in 1938 a series of programs highlighting the contributions to American life of various immigrant groups, NBC declined on the basis that it might cause social division and ethnic tension. CBS did produce the series, *Americans All, Immigrants All*, but not before inverting its original title so as to accentuate its inclusive patriotic purpose. The series ran for 26 weeks, to great acclaim. The programs stressed each group's contribution to American development and minimized nativism and racism.[4] Networks and national advertisers had no interest in foreign-language broadcasts, and their assimilative efforts were confined to increasing the number of consumers. The networks considered radio to be a modern form of melting pot, which would work to eradicate ethnic differences and tensions through broadening the hegemony of Anglo-American values and culture. Those who sought programs that addressed specific ethnic groups in their own languages and on their own terms were forced to listen to a handful of local stations clustered in large cities. In an industry increasingly dominated by networks and commercialism, the future of those stations became precarious as they struggled against unsympathetic regulators and increasing commercial competition.

Radio was similarly selective in its treatment of working-class listeners. Workers were welcomed into the broadcasting fold as consumers, but not as dissidents or activists. We have already seen the travails of WCFL and WEVD at the hands of regulators, and the refusal of the networks to open their studios to speakers whom they considered subversive.[5] This was particularly true during the 1930s, when labor activism was at its height and the New Deal had convinced many business groups that class war was at hand. News journalists at two stations in Cincinnati owned by the Crosley Corporation were told in May 1935, "Our news broadcasts . . . will not include mention of any strikes. This also includes students' strikes and school walkouts." Even in 1943 Mark Woods, a former NBC executive, told the FCC that while NBC was happy to broadcast symphony music sponsored by General Motors, it would not accept a similar program from the AFL.[6]

Labor groups were also kept from the air by industry nervousness, later enshrined in the NAB Code, about "controversial issues." The 1939 code banned stations from broadcasting one-sided discussions or solicitations for membership by any group. Networks and stations routinely characterized talks by labor leaders as "controversial" and programs from trade unions as solicitations, and banished them from the air.[7] On the other hand, programs and advertisements by organizations such as the National Association of Manufacturers or quasi-political commentary sponsored by corporations were common on network schedules. The result, according to radio critic Charles Siepmann in 1946, was that "discrimination against labor is probably the most flagrant example of abuse by radio stations of their privileged position."[8]

Broadcasters' limited and limiting conceptions of radio citizenship were even more apparent in their treatment of three other marginal groups in interwar society. White farmers and white women, like urban workers, were specifically targeted by broadcasters, the better to deliver their purchasing power to advertisers. Beyond that, however, the broadcasters chose not to go. Radio did not attack, or even question, the values and institutions that had placed women and provincials into positions of cultural, political, and economic subordination. To the shut-outs—and in particular to African Americans—radio offered even less. The result was that the radio age left the limits of citizenship in 1940 much as it had found them in 1920.

"The backwoods . . . will undoubtedly dwindle": Radio and the Hinterland

The advent of broadcasting coincided with widespread concern that American society had split along an urban-rural divide. The Democratic Party was ripped apart at its 1924 convention as rural forces loyal to William McAdoo refused to compromise with urban supporters of Governor Al Smith of New York; the nation saw rural anti-evolution and fundamentalist thought at its most extreme during the Scopes trial of 1925, and declining rural incomes widened the economic gap between factory and farm. The result was a bitter struggle between cosmopolitanism and provincialism for control over the cultural and political direction of the nation. As the most conspicuous medium of mass communication and cultural dissemination, radio inevitably became part of that contest.[9]

Congressional hearings in January 1929 over renewal of the FRC revealed the degree to which urban-rural tensions had infiltrated perceptions of radio and culture. During Merlin Aylesworth's testimony, discussion suddenly turned to "sectionalism." When asked how NBC could contribute to the bridging of the "thought barrier" between city and country, he replied that radio would prove to be even more important than the automobile. Congressman Robert H. Clancy of Michigan responded that "ruralites" had for many years regarded cars as "a sort of blowgun sent out by the city people to kill their chickens," and he hoped they would be more enlightened about radio. The hearings then degenerated into bickering over the relative moral worth of urban and rural life, and Aylesworth was subjected to detailed questioning from Ewin Davis of Tennessee as to how many of his senior executives had been born on farms. Strong intervention from the chair was required before the committee could focus again on the matter in hand.[10]

Radio enthusiasts held high hopes that radio would help to diminish such tensions by improving communication between urbanites and ruralites. But their vision of this communication was essentially one-way: radio could help integrate the nation by reaching out to rural America with the sounds and culture of the city. Elihu Root, New York's elder statesman and a member of NBC's advisory council, remarked that prior to radio the insane asylums were disproportionately populated by farmers' wives "because of the lack of social stimulus and the loneliness of life amidst constant drudgery verging close onto penal servitude." Programming for rural audiences, Root thought, should be designed as much to provide relief *from* farming as to provide information *about* it. Two years later the *New York Times* agreed that "the 'shut-ins,' to whom more than to any other class radio has come as a real boon, are not alone the prisoners of illness, misfortune or old age. The healthy, normal shut-ins of rural life are the more numerous beneficiaries."[11]

As representatives of an industry increasingly dominated by networks centered in New York, and as propagators of modern consumer culture, radio exceptionalists thus described the urban-rural conflict in ways that portrayed rural America as the problem and urban culture as the solution. Provincial America was in decline because of its isolation and backwardness, and its residents' capacity for good citizenship was consequently impaired. The result was that while urban America moved forward with confidence into modernity, rural America remained mired in ignorance, bigotry, and backwardness. Its salvation therefore depended upon its successful integration into the modern "national culture," which was defined in urban terms. In an article on the promise of radio published in 1924, Bruce Bliven predicted that, because of radio, "the 'backwoods,' and all that the word connotes, will undoubtedly dwindle if it does not entirely disappear as an element in our civilization."[12]

The broadcasters also wanted to diminish the backwoods, but for their own reasons. Although nearly 49 percent of the American population in 1920, and almost 44 percent in 1930, lived in non-urban areas, the rural radio market remained underexploited during the 1920s and 1930s. This was mainly because rural radio ownership tended to lag behind urban areas. Although farmers and other non-metropolitan residents of the Midwest had very high rates of radio ownership, equal to those of their urban cousins, those in the mountain, southern, and plains states were well behind. In 1938 only 35 percent of American rural families had radios in their homes, compared to 72 percent for urban dwellers. The differences were even greater between regions of rural America; in the South Atlantic and South Central states—which contained half of the nation's farmers—only 5 percent of farm families had radios in 1938.[13]

Map 5.

Source: Radio Today, Jan. 1936. George H. Clark Papers, series 14, box 196.

There were many reasons for this gap. National farm income dropped throughout the 1920s as crop prices suffered from dislocations of world trade and overproduction. Disposable farm income dropped from $4.5 billion in 1929 to $2.5 billion in 1933, leaving many farmers without the means to buy or maintain radio sets. Rural listeners were also discouraged by their primitive infrastructure. Only 10 percent of farmers enjoyed access to the AC power grid in 1930, leaving the rest to rely on battery-powered sets that required frequent recharging. Despite the work of the Rural Electrical Administration (REA) during the New Deal, 60 percent of farmers still remained off the grid in 1940. Those on more isolated farms also suffered from interference and weak signal strength. The particularly low rate of radio ownership in the South was directly attributable to its large number of desperately poor black farmers who were both financially and culturally excluded from radio listening.[14] Map 5, produced by *Radio Today* in 1936, shows the disproportionate "size" of the metropolitan Northeast and Midwest within the radio market.

The national networks therefore put farm programming quite low on their priorities. The most successful farm program was NBC's *National Farm and Home Hour*, which began in 1929 on 32 affiliate stations. It continued throughout the 1930s, and became an unofficial publicity agent for the United States Department of Agriculture and its farm relief policies. CBS also programmed directly to farmers via its provincial affiliates, and both networks developed crop price and weather-reporting schedules. Nevertheless, the limits of these services were highlighted by NBC in 1937, when Phillips Carlin, the head of its Blue Network, directed that there should be no mention of "droughts, past and present." Farmers, he thought, needed weather reports but not reminders of such calamities.[15]

The networks were generally content to integrate farm and provincial listeners into their urban-based programming. This was in keeping with their broader assumption that farmers were cultural mendicants, eager for whatever uplift radio might provide. Only rarely did the networks reflect rural culture to urban listeners. During the hillbilly craze of the late 1920s and early 1930s, both networks aired shows featuring quasi-parodic performances and skits on rural life and customs. As Susan Smulyan has argued, hillbilly programs entertained urban listeners by confirming their preconceptions of backwoods culture as quaint and simple-minded.[16]

These attitudes pervaded networks' and advertisers' approaches to the rural market. Advertising consultants tended to portray farm listeners in ways that suggested not only cultural difference but also backwardness. Charles Morrow Wilson, in a pamphlet published by NBC in 1937, described farmers' buying decisions as "meditative and comparatively slow-motioned." They reacted badly to high-pressure salesmanship and resented "smart patter and quick-fire wisecracks." Most of all, farmers objected to jazz and the decadence and urban brashness that it represented to them. The way to their hearts and pockets was through "relaxed, kindly 'human interest'" entertainment that avoided condescension in favor of "an informal 'your-world-and-mine attitude.'"[17] Both networks, however, continued to play to their more lucrative urban markets and to devolve the costs and effort of rural programming to their affiliates.

Some rural listeners repaid the networks' indifference with hostility of their own. To many, especially in the plains and mountain states, networks represented the same predatory influences as the chain stores and trusts that had already eroded their local economic autonomy. In 1928, 16 Nebraska farmers wrote to George Norris, their United States Senator, to complain about the growing influence of network radio. The "chain stations" had so monopolized the air that it was almost impossible to hear local stations. Instead of listening to programs that appealed to them, farmers were forced to listen to what the networks, based in New York, told them to hear: "Now Senater we believe that the farmer has just as much right too the air as these eastern mabobs, as we farmer's till the soil and work from daylight to dark have no other time, but in the evening and then are compelled to listen to a lot of Italian singing & playing that we do not want nor understand."[18]

Not all stations were so condemned. Stations that focused upon rural and provincial listeners were of varying power and range, but many performed important roles within their local communities and their wider listening radii. Pamela Grundy's study of North Carolina piedmont mill culture during the interwar years positioned radio stations—and especially WBT in Charlotte and its commercial hillbilly programs—as mediators between mill workers, whose mind-set still bore the marks of their agricultural origins, and the new industrial culture of layoffs, pay cuts, and stretch outs. Local radio, Grundy concluded, helped to legitimate agrarian culture to its listeners, and thus fortified a sense of community in the face of their economic difficulties.[19] Local stations in regions that were more focused upon agriculture similarly reinforced rural culture by providing not only weather, crop, and livestock information, but also programming and advertising that tended to reinforce the importance of farming and farmers.

Some farmers' stations were powerful and well organized. WLS operated from Crete, Illinois, with a transmitting power of 5kW and an effective nighttime listening area covering most of the Mississippi Valley. Owned by the publishers of the *Prairie Farmer*, and affiliated with NBC, WLS marketed itself explicitly as a farmer's station. Its programming included daily market reports, farm news, hillbilly music, and shows sponsored by companies such as Sears, Roebuck and International Harvester. Listeners could also tune in to *Johnny Muskrat Fur Talk*, *The Prairie President*, and the *National Farm and Home Hour*. In keeping with its regional focus, and perhaps also with its audience's programming preferences, WLS took only two hours per day of NBC New York's programming in 1929.[20]

Beyond their frequent assertions that radio exercised a powerful integrative effect upon the backwoods, social scientists and audience analysts paid little attention to the rural radio audience between the wars. In 1933 Malcolm Willey and Stuart Rice ventured a "hypothesis" that radio was a cultural leveler between country and city, but they also presented a counterargument that "agencies of mass impression," such as regional radio stations, intensified localism and "local patterns of attitude, habit and behavior." Network radio, the movies, national advertising, and increased travel may well have resulted in previously isolated provincials now wearing "the garments of Hollywood," they thought, but this "*overt standardization* may be accompanied by retention of *inward differences.*" Available data was insufficient to determine the question with any certainty.[21]

Similarly inconclusive results emerged from the Lazarsfeld group's only major research into radio's impact on a farming community. In 1941 William S. Robinson published a study of Pike County, Illinois. In 1930 only 31 percent of the county's farming families owned a radio, but that figure rose dramatically after the REA electrified it in 1937. Robinson surveyed a sample of farmers who had bought a radio after 1937, and quizzed them on whether it had made them more interested in national and international affairs. Only 48 percent of his male respondents and 42 percent of his female sample group answered affirmatively. Of his 99 male subjects, only 27 admitted to forming at least one new opinion as a result of a radio program, and most of them specified the *National Farm and Home Hour* as the source. Those new opinions were overwhelmingly pro–New Deal.[22]

Despite this evidence of the success of the New Deal's agricultural publicity, however, Robinson's research did little to confirm the radio exceptionalists' hopes that broadcasting would unshackle farmers from isolation and backwardness. If in 1941 less than half of a group of Illinois farmers were prepared to concede that they had changed a single opinion because of radio, it is very likely that the backwoods elsewhere in the United States remained proudly resistant to the metropolitan culture propagated by the national broadcasters.

Ethereal Sisters

"The radio telephone, it seems to me," Christine Frederick wrote in September 1922, "is primarily an invention for the benefit of woman. Its greatest achievement is banishing isolation. Isolation! Who better than a woman can thoroughly understand the full meaning of this dreaded word?" Whether on farms, or housebound in cities, women were the most numerous of America's shut-ins. Frederick predicted that they would soon become avid radio fans, and that their days would be enlivened by programs on physical education, child care, housekeeping tips, fashion, and etiquette.[23] Her enthusiasm was prescient, but in 1922 radio was still a strongly gendered technology. In the years before scheduled broadcasting, when radio was the preserve of the armed forces and a growing band of amateurs, men and boys dominated the new technology. Usually channeled away from scientific studies in high schools, and grossly underrepresented in technical trades, women were ill-equipped to join the radio craze.

Women were also removed from early radio by the conventions of domestic architecture; with their wires, leaky batteries, and long antennae, amateurs' radio sets belonged more in the male domains of the shed and den than in the female-orientated living areas of houses.[24] Over the following decade, however, radio became progressively more domesticated. As the amateurs' home-constructed sets were replaced by commercially produced valve receivers, radios became easier to operate and more presentable as domestic appliances. Instead of the exposed wires, bread-board bases, and earphones of the amateurs' creations, sets now came in neat and sometimes ornate wooden cabinets styled to mimic bureaus and cocktail cabinets. These new sets were marketed as much to women as to men, as manufacturers aimed to shift radio listening into living rooms and kitchens, and from small groups of predominantly male DXers to mass audiences of men, women, and children.[25]

After radio receivers left the shed and infiltrated the living room, but before car radios became prevalent, radio listening was tied closely to home life. Radio manufacturers and broadcasters argued that radio would provide a focus of entertainment for the whole family within the home. Visions of domestic harmony through radio struck responsive chords in a society deeply divided along gender, cultural, and generational lines. Social problems such as the growing rebelliousness of the young, the growth of speakeasies, the prevalence of jazz, and the potentially immoral allure of movies and cars might soon be solved by radio and its ability to restore homes to their old primacy in social life. Alfred Goldsmith and Austin Lescarboura predicted in 1930 that radio might even increase the birthrate. Too many young women were put off family life by its "obscurity and drudgery." Now housework and motherhood would become more attractive to women, for radio would make housekeeping "a fascinating endeavor." Pierre du Pont, speaking against Prohibition in 1933, argued that improvements in working people's homes through electricity, gas, phonographs, and radio meant that men would never again be lured away to saloons for relaxation and comfort. The new "working man's club" was in his home, alongside his wife and family and in front of the radio.[26]

Commercial broadcasters contributed to the domestication of radio through their recognition of the value of the female audience. Increasingly

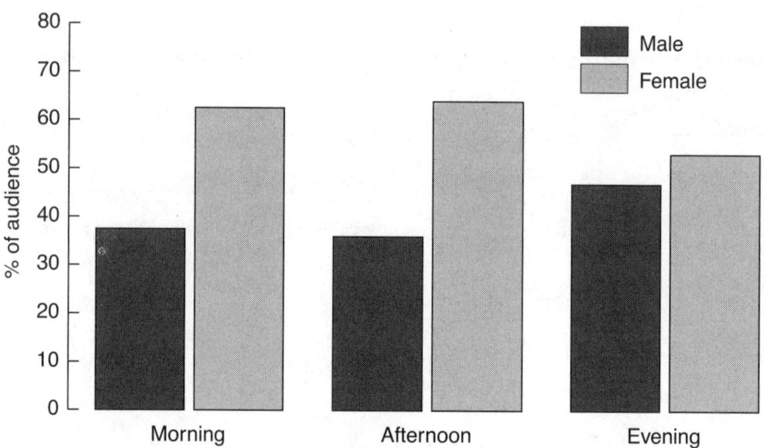

Figure 13. Radio Listening by Sex, 1936 Winter Audiences.
Source: Graph constructed from data in CBS, *Radio in 1936*, p. 14.

concerned with maximizing their advertising revenues, stations began to develop their daytime schedules by promising advertisers access to large numbers of women at home. Of the 30 million women over 21 in the United States, NBC told its advertisers in 1927, 70 percent did not have paid employment. Those women were the purchasing agents of the nation, responsible for the vast majority of household expenditure.[27] Companies that sold food, household goods, and clothes could therefore reach their most important customers through daytime radio. Surveys by CBS in 1936 found that women listened to the radio more often and for longer periods than did men. CBS also confirmed that the daytime radio audience was overwhelmingly female, and that nighttime listeners were more evenly divided by sex (see fig. 14).[28] Nevertheless, opinions varied over the listening behavior of women. Francis Ollry and Elias Smith concluded in 1939 that women were "better" listeners than men because they were more responsive to programs and scored higher in "radio mindedness." Ernest Robinson, on the other hand, was unwilling to concede full agency to female listeners. Although he agreed that women were immune to "the almost entirely masculine diversion of ether searching, or knob twiddling," they were also particularly prone to "hearing without listening." Housewives, he believed, used radio more as an "occasionally apprehended background of noise" than as a medium of information.[29]

"Radio mindedness" also became equated with femininity through the application of gendered stereotypes. In his 1933 textbook on radio advertising Frank Arnold portrayed the female listener and purchasing agent in passive terms that confirmed traditional power relations within families:

Let us suppose the product being advertised is . . . coffee. What actually occurs at the conclusion of the program is something like this:

The man of the house, who has been listening with appreciation to the musical treat, turns to his wife and says, "Mary, what kind of coffee are we using?' She replies, giving the trade-mark name. . . . Addressing his wife he says, "My dear, tomorrow morning . . . I wish you would order a pound of that coffee for me," and then he adds, "If it is as good as the program, it must be some coffee."

The next morning 100,000 or more housewives buy their first pound of this particular commodity.[30]

Women were acknowledged and encouraged by radio programming and advertising to consider themselves a vital part of the nation's economic life, but within the confines of their domestic sphere. Broadcasters consciously defined and limited their women's programs to matters related to, and confirmatory of, traditional female roles within the home and family. CBS's daily *Radio Homemakers Club* program, for example, included in 1929 segments entitled "Sewing Circle," "The Home Decorating Studio," "The Beauty Boudoir," and "Children's Corner." Only one segment, "What's New in Washington," dealt with the world outside the home.[31] Although Judith Waller described in 1950 the subject matter of women's programming as "infinite," her examples focused upon domestic concerns:

Food, handicrafts, household hints, party plans, quilts, home sewing, style, beauty, health, problems of child care, human-interest stories, book reviews, interviews with interesting people, news, interior decoration, pets, the romance of common things around the house, plans for a postwar world, home canning, ways of meeting contemporary shortages and curtailment, juvenile delinquency—anything that's pertinent to the home and community life of the American woman or which can help her to be a more interesting dinner-table companion for her family.[32]

The archetypal women's program of the interwar period, and the most explicit form of gendered radio culture, was the daytime soap opera. Lineal descendants of nineteenth-century romance novels, and close relations of popular women's magazines, soap operas embodied the nexus of commercialism and domesticity that molded all women's programming. "It is the hope of every advertiser," James Thurber noted in his mocking analysis of "Soapland" in 1948, "to habituate the housewife to an engrossing narrative whose optimum length is forever and at the same time to saturate all levels of her consciousness with the miracles of a given product, so that she will . . . mutter its name in her sleep."[33] Even their name reflected the commodity most associated with their sponsorship. In 1931 only four soaps appeared on network radio, but in 1939 there were 61. By the end of 1935 Procter and Gamble, the most enthusiastic sponsor of soap operas, was the single largest user of network radio in the world and NBC's most valuable client. It occupied 778 hours of NBC's annual schedule, of which 664 were soaps.[34]

Soap opera audiences received numerous variations upon a single theme. Most of the dramas were set in small towns, and their central characters were almost always middle-class. Because of their small budgets and hurried production, few special effects were used and plots revolved around a small number of characters.[35] The soaps legitimated and reinforced traditionally feminine and domestic values. Robert Allen argues that the soaps' orientation toward female listeners and what were construed to be women's issues represented "the articulation of whole sets of concerns denigrated by or totally excluded from mainstream fictional discourse: home life, everyday social relations, family matters, the effect of external factors upon the home, and strategies for dealing with the multiple roles women were expected to adopt." As such, they occupied a distinctly feminine niche in a culture that was overwhelmingly patriarchal.[36] This is not to say, however, that soaps were subversive of that patriarchy. They tended to legitimate domesticity, and the subordination of female shut-ins, by romanticizing the limited cultural and civic horizons afforded to women at home.

A variety of factors contributed to the broadcasters' decision that women and their programming belonged in the home. As purveyors of respectable middle-class culture, stations and networks were careful to avoid any challenge to idealized conceptions of family, femininity, and home. Chief among these was the image of contented housewives interested only in their family's moral and physical welfare. As we have seen, broadcasters were under great pressure from regulators and advertisers to ensure that their programs were acceptable to all members of the family. Inherent in that responsibility was an acceptance of the middle-class ideal of nonworking women as the moral and cultural guardians of the home. When NBC broadcast the Adam and Eve sketch by Mae West and Don Ameche in 1937, it was widely condemned for betraying the sanctity of American homes. "The home is our last bulwark against the modern overemphasis on sensuality," one newspaper declared, "and we cannot see why Miss West and others of her ilk should be permitted to pollute its sacred precincts with shady stories, foul obscenity, smutty suggestiveness, and horrible blasphemy."[37]

Broadcasters were also encouraged by their advertisers to focus women's programming upon domesticity. White women at home represented the most valuable segment of the female radio audience, for they possessed the greatest purchasing power. There was little point in targeting working women, who tended to be poorer and often out of earshot of daytime radio. Advertisers therefore focused upon women as homemakers, and they insisted that radio programming do the same. Soap operas were also attractive vehicles for advertisers, because they could be produced more cheaply than programs involving famous actors or large musical groups.[38] Broadcasters and advertisers also argued that women preferred programs about domestic life. Orrin Dunlap claimed in 1925 that female listeners favored "educational advertising" about home management and child rearing over "the same string trio morning after morning." Even in 1950 Judith Waller argued that the average woman listener was not interested in news bulletins or programs about economic or political affairs. These were "still very much a man's world," and they often presupposed geographic, economic, and political knowledge that most women did not have. Wise broadcasters and advertisers, she thought, played to women's real interests in their homes and families.[39]

Audience research into women's program preferences told a more ambiguous story. Paul Lazarsfeld was convinced that women and men had fundamentally different interests. He believed, in a revealing comparison, that "the average American woman, just like the average American youth, is not interested in current affairs."[40] Hadley Cantril and Gordon Allport, however, found that women placed domestic topics such as health, fashion, and cooking quite low on their programming preferences, and that there was little difference between men and women in their desire to hear news programs. A survey of rural women in 1940 found that although half of the respondents listened to soap operas, only a quarter of them enjoyed them.[41]

America's most famous female radio listener and broadcaster, Eleanor Roosevelt, criticized NBC in 1935 for its assumptions about women's radio tastes. She suggested that the network hire a female news commentator who could enliven daytime broadcasting with discussions of "public questions past and present." Although she acknowledged that many women avoided discussing public policy, Mrs. Roosevelt put that down to insufficient information and opportunity. Women wanted information about politics, economics, and world affairs, she thought, but broadcasters seemed determined to deny it to them.[42]

Women were also denied the chance to join the new profession of radio announcing. Although some early broadcasters used female announcers, very few women could be heard by the mid-1920s. "Why aren't there more women radio announcers?" one listener asked in 1926. "Why cannot women be employed as 'teachers of the public' before the microphone as well as in the school room?" Broadcasters replied by pointing to technical reasons and audience preferences; early loudspeaker technology and the tonal characteristics of AM radio supposedly made higher-pitched female voices sound shrill and dissonant. In England the BBC even argued that women were "temperamentally less suitable than men" to radio work and that "the physical strain imposed upon the announcer is greater than could be borne by the average woman."[43]

Audience surveys in the mid-1920s purported to buttress the broadcasters' argument. One survey, conducted by WJZ in 1926, found that listeners of both sexes preferred male announcers by a margin of 100 to 1. WJZ offered a number of contradictory reasons for this. While noting that female voices tended to sound shrill on many home radio sets, WJZ conceded that soprano voices reproduced perfectly over the air. The station also argued that women's voices tended to have too much "personality" on air, and that the "woman announcer is said to have difficulty in repressing her enthusiasm and in maintaining the necessary reserve and objectivity." Nine years later, when Hadley Cantril and Gordon Allport found that 95 percent of their subjects preferred male voices over radio, women had been virtually banished from the airwaves.[44]

By then, however, no one seriously argued that cellos broadcast better than violins, or that loudspeakers of the 1930s were incapable of reproducing female voices. Cantril and Allport claimed instead that "prejudice" was to blame; listeners reacted negatively to female broadcasters because they transgressed gendered boundaries of power and presumptions of female domesticity. As John Potts has argued, radio announcing rapidly became a "public voice" of "authority, judgement and knowledge," and thus belonged to the male sphere. This was particularly so in newsreading, news commentary, and other programs on public policy and business. If women would only limit their announcing to "material that is poetic or reflective in nature," Cantril and Allport concluded, they might "be entitled to a larger share of the work of announcers than is at present given them."[45]

Prejudice against female broadcasters continued a long tradition of male resistance to female public speech. Vocal women, as Kathleen Hall Jamieson has pointed out, had since the days of ancient Greece been associated with infertility, prostitution, and witchcraft as female subversions of good government and patriarchy. Connections between shrillness, madness, and public speech by women also predated broadcasting by many centuries. Women had long been denied access to the public sphere by legal restriction and customary prohibition, and so it is not surprising that their supposed inability to use radio should have been discovered so soon after its invention. First ladies, for example, were barred by custom throughout the nineteenth century from delivering formal speeches, and listeners had to wait until 1929 before they heard a president's wife speak on radio.[46]

Women were further discouraged from radio careers by a lack of role models; listeners might never hear a female announcer, and even women speakers were infrequent. Elsie Janis, NBC's first woman announcer, began work in 1934 but was relegated to weather announcing and variety shows. CBS's and unaffiliated stations' efforts to hire women were equally desultory until well after World War II. When WQXR New York hired Lisa Sergio as a news commentator in the late 1930s it attracted considerable publicity and cemented its reputation as an avant garde broadcaster.[47] Women had to wait until the advent of television, and the middle years of the 1970s, before their assumed attributes of warmth, empathy, and attractiveness made them desirable as announcers and newsreaders.[48]

Women were almost equally unwelcome in other areas of broadcasting. Although they had no trouble in securing work as receptionists, typists, and secretaries, very few managed to infiltrate radio's executive ranks. Although Michele Hilmes and Catherine Heinz have shown that women were represented in stations' and networks' senior administrative structures throughout the 1920s and 1930s, they also showed that most female executives followed far more difficult and halting career paths than those of their male peers.[49] The tribulations of American women in broadcasting were similar to aspiring female radio executives in Britain, Canada, and Australia. Lord Reith hired a handful of women to run the BBC's talks and education programs, but he also insisted that female employees resign upon marriage. His most senior female executive, Hilda Matheson, was forced out of the BBC in 1932 amid allegations that she was too leftist in her political views.[50]

Those women who did succeed within broadcasting were generally employed in "female" areas of programming such as education, soap operas, and home management. Of NBC's three most senior female employees during the interwar years, Judith Waller, Janet MacRorie, and Bertha Brainard, only Brainard—the network's director of commercial programming—worked outside radio's feminine sphere. Waller became NBC's director of educational programming, and MacRorie vetted soap operas and other scripts to ensure that they did not offend family audiences.

Peggy Stone was one of the very few prominent women at CBS in the 1930s, and her career was indicative of the difficulties faced by all women in the industry. Stone joined CBS in 1930 as a secretary in the affiliate relations department. Her boss, Sam Pickard, recognized her talents and promoted her to be his deputy. In 1936, when Pickard was fired, Stone took over the department. Without her patron, however, she was unable to operate effectively within CBS's overwhelmingly male hierarchy, and she was forced out in 1938. By then Stone had learned that CBS's corporate culture was comfortable with women as loyal lieutenants but not as captains.[51] Broadcasters were happiest of all when they could conceive of women as shut into their homes as listeners and consumers, eagerly awaiting the next installment of their favorite soap opera and making careful note of the name and product of its sponsor.

African Americans and Interwar Radio

No group was more shut out from interwar radio, and the new citizenship it propagated, than African Americans. Farmers and women found it difficult to receive adequate or sympathetic cultural and occupational recognition from radio, but their numbers and importance as consumers nevertheless guaranteed them significant attention. For a variety of reasons both internal and external to the industry, however, radio offered African Americans almost nothing. They remained over the cultural, social, and commercial horizons of radio throughout the 1920s and 1930s, and their absence from the nation's airwaves provide a stark reminder of the limits of interwar radio citizenship.

Lawrence Levine reported a joke of the 1930s that summed up many African Americans' skepticism that radio might help them communicate better with whites. A black Mississippi sharecropper went to inspect a radio station and was asked to tell listeners about the contentment of blacks in the Deep South:

> Now there's the microphone, Sam. Jes' talk into it.
> This the microphone, boss?
> That's right, Sam.
> And when I talk into it, the whole world can hear me?
> That's right, Sam.
> Outside of Mississippi? All over the world?
> Sure enough, Sam. Jes' you go ahead and tell 'em.

So Sam walked over to the microphone, grabbed on to it with both hands and hollered:
HE-E-E-E-ELP![52]

African Americans made up about 10 percent of the total interwar population, but they were still predominantly southern and rural. Of the nation's 12.5 million black citizens in 1930, 75 percent lived in the old Confederacy, and more than half lived in rural areas. Although their migration from farm to city and from South to North had significantly increased after World War I, blacks represented less than 4 percent of the population of the Northeastern and North Central states in 1930.[53] These states were the hub of the radio wheel, but their relatively small African American populations were unable to exert pressure upon broadcasters to cater to their tastes and market.

African Americans' power as radio listeners was further limited by their position as the poorest and most isolated of Americans. As figure 14 shows, black rates of radio ownership in both urban and rural areas were dramatically lower than those for both native-born and immigrant whites. Whereas total rates of radio ownership differed little between immigrant and native-born whites, African American families' aggregate radio ownership rate of 7.5 percent lagged far behind the national figure of 40 percent. The difference was greatest in rural areas, where 25 percent of whites owned radios compared to only 0.3 percent of black farming families.[54] Even in the more prosperous 1940s, more than 20 years into the radio age, only 50 percent of one group of black sharecroppers in the Mississippi Delta owned radios.[55] These differentials can be partly explained by the much lower family incomes of African Americans. The huge gap between black and white radio ownership in rural areas, in particular, suggests that black farmers enjoyed almost no discretionary income to spend upon such comparative luxuries as radio. Other factors, intimately connected to segregation, racism, and isolation, contributed to depress African American radio ownership. Black farms were the least electrified in the nation, and their preponderance in the South meant that African American farmers had fewer stations to listen to than did northern and western farmers. The absence of stations directed specifically to black audiences or concerns, and a general white southern unease with black cultural expression, education, and "uppityness," may also have discouraged even better off African Americans from purchasing radios.

Most radio stations, and all the national networks, repaid African Americans' low rates of radio ownership and meager disposable income with an almost complete lack of programming and cultural recognition throughout the

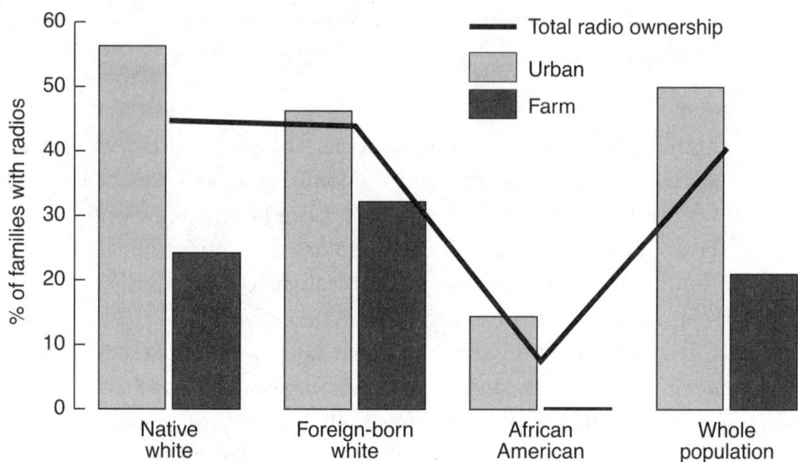

Figure 14. Color, Residence, and Ethnicity of Radio Families, 1930.
Source: Graph constructed from data in Herman S. Hettinger, *A Decade of Radio Advertising*, p. 49.

interwar period. Although radio exceptionalists such as Malcolm Willey and Stuart Rice predicted that radio promised much in the way of "social leveling," it quickly became clear that this would not be an exchange but instead an extension of white cultural and racial hegemony. Of all media, Willey and Rice went on to say, radio was the "most free from racial or class discriminations. The negro who cannot enter the white man's church, college or theatre can hear on his radio the white man's sermons, lectures and entertainment with complete equality."[56] Nevertheless, African Americans who wanted to hear their own cultural, social, and political activities acknowledged and legitimated on radio listened largely in vain.

Exclusion of African Americans from interwar radio took many forms. Their attempts during the 1930s to purchase or establish stations all came to nothing. In 1930 the Harlem Broadcasting Corporation tried and failed to buy a station in New York City. Seven years later the Gold Star Radio and TV Corporation was equally unsuccessful in creating a network of African American stations in New York, Philadelphia, Chicago, New Orleans, and Los Angeles. The reasons for these failures are unclear, but the result was that none of the nation's 778 radio stations in 1939 were owned or operated by African Americans.[57]

The fate of African American programming was almost as disheartening. With the exception of an annual NBC broadcast during the 1930s on African

American education as part of American Education Week, the networks were extremely reluctant to program directly to black audiences or to hire African American performers.[58] The entire industry operated under an unofficial color bar, which relegated most black employees to their traditional sphere of janitorial tasks and denied them opportunities to train for more prestigious and better paid technical occupations. Some famous programs explicitly excluded African Americans; when Arturo Toscanini came to NBC in 1937 he insisted that the NBC Symphony Orchestra be all white. African Americans did contribute to many radio bands and orchestras, and some also received small amounts of air time as gospel singers and comedians, in segments derisively described as "coon acts." Most of these performers did their work anonymously, because broadcasters saw little point and much danger in drawing the attention of their predominantly white—and significantly southern—audience to them.[59]

Across the nation only a handful of pioneers in unaffiliated stations ventured into African American programming. Probably the earliest of these was Jack L. Cooper, who in 1929 began *The All-Negro Hour* on WSBC Chicago. WSBC was one of four stations to broadcast to Chicago's numerous ethnic groups in the late 1920s, and Cooper's hour-long variety show, featuring African American performers, took its place within that multicultural context.[60] Black listeners outside WSBC's limited range, however, found almost nothing directed to their interests. In his survey of African American radio programming between the wars, J. Fred MacDonald could find only scattered offerings from a few local stations across the country during the second half of the 1930s. Of these, WJTL Atlanta's broadcast from 1935 of a daily 15-minute news bulletin on African American affairs was particularly significant because it was the first systematized attempt to use radio as a medium of civic information and education for black listeners.[61]

African Americans were most often portrayed in radio dramas and minstrel programs by white actors in a continuation of the blackface theatrical tradition. The most famous of these shows was *Amos'n'Andy*, by far the most popular radio program of the interwar period. The show's writers and actors, Charles Correll and Freeman Gosden, were whites who had learned their trade on the vaudeville circuit. They began their routine featuring the fortunes and misfortunes of two African Americans who had migrated from Georgia to Chicago as *Sam'n'Henry* on WGN Chicago in 1926. After a contractual dispute with WGN, Correll and Gosden moved in 1928 to WMAQ and renamed their show *Amos'n'Andy.*

By that time, thanks to its distribution of prerecorded episodes to stations around the country, their program had become a national fad, with an unprecedented 60 percent of the radio audience. Tiring of the difficulties of prerecording up to 36 shows in advance, Correll and Gosden joined NBC and simultaneous networked radio in 1929. Sponsored by Pepsodent, *Amos'n'Andy* instantly became NBC's star program until it was poached in 1939 by CBS. At the height of its popularity between 1928 and 1933, movie theaters scheduled their screenings around *Amos'n'Andy*'s broadcast time of 7 P.M., and many employers allowed their workers to end their shifts in time to be home for it.[62]

Amos'n'Andy portrayed African Americans in ways that confirmed the stereotypes and prejudices of its overwhelmingly white audience. Although Amos and Andy were sympathetically portrayed, both displayed laziness, ignorance, and obtuseness. The show's humor arose from their mispronunciation of words, Andy's grandiose self-delusion, and Amos's stupidity. Both characters spoke in an exaggerated minstrel dialect, and their predilection for scams, gambling, and idleness above honest work confirmed African Americans' stereotypical image in the interwar white mind. *Amos'n'Andy*, Melvin Ely argues, played to whites' curiosity about blacks while simultaneously confirming their prejudices about them. It also skirted around white southern racial sensitivities, presenting African Americans as fundamentally content in a segregated world. Andy's business schemes always victimized blacks rather than whites, and Correll and Gosden's scripts avoided any hint of racial tension. When Andy became involved in a fistfight, listeners were told that his opponent was also black, and when the original program's Sam admired women at the beach, the audience was reassured that all the bathers were African American. Overall, Ely concludes, *Amos'n'Andy* never threatened the "racial fantasy land in which most white Americans lived" during the interwar years, and it confirmed the prevailing white conception of African Americans as "an appendage to American society rather than part of its essence."[63]

Correll and Gosden were also careful to avoid political controversy and partisanship. Although they ensured that their scripts were politically evenhanded during the 1932 election, they did occasionally include morale boosting comments during the Depression, and support for FDR during the Hundred Days. They did not, however, allow their characters to advocate improved civil rights for African Americans. No criticism of segregation, lynching, or disfranchisement passed their lips, and when they voted or engaged in politics the results were invariably farcical and sometimes corrupt. Even their endorsements of the New Deal confirmed white images of black simple-mindedness. "Socialism" became "social risk" in Amos's tortured syntax, and his support of FDR's bank holiday was as derogatory of his own intellect as it was supportive of the president: "De president of de United States is fightin' fo' more dan just 'mergency banking relief—he is workin' out a plan to have a system in de banks dat will not only he'p 'em fo' all time to come, an' dis banker says dat dat's zackly whut's goin' happen an' Mr. Roosevelt means bizness, an' he's gittin' action, so yo'see, dis bank holiday is really a great thing fo' de country."[64]

Many of *Amos'n'Andy*'s African American listeners recognized that the program confirmed the limits of black citizenship. In 1931 Robert Vann, editor of the *Pittsburgh Courier*, organized a petition against the demeaning portrayal of blacks in *Amos'n'Andy*. Vann collected 740,000 signatures from his African American readership, but NBC completely disregarded his petition. The National Association for the Advancement of Colored People (NAACP) also refused to support Vann's call for the program to be taken off the air, arguing that its portrayal of blacks was essentially harmless. Only in the early 1950s, when *Amos'n'Andy* began its last and least successful incarnation as a syndicated TV show, did the civil rights movement protest strongly against it.[65]

Broadcasters between the wars also paid little attention to other complaints from their African American listeners. In April 1924 the National Race Congress of America wrote to a Washington station about its propensity to play songs including the word *nigger*. The station, however, appears not to have responded.[66] By the end of the 1930s black listeners and organizations had become more assertive against derogatory descriptions of African Americans. At the beginning of 1936 the Chicago branch of the NAACP wrote to NBC to complain about the use of *darky* in a show about the Civil War. NBC never broadcast terms such as *kike* and *dago*, branch president A. C. MacNeal wrote, leading "to the inescapable conclusion in the minds of all Americans who happen to be colored that [NBC has] deliberately set out to insult over twelve million Americans apparently feeling that such an insult cannot be successfully resented."[67]

Although NBC replied to MacNeal with expressions of regret, it continued to broadcast language that offended many of its black listeners. When one wrote in 1937 to protest against the use of *nigger*, the network responded without apology that the actual word used was most likely *negra*. Two years later, after an interview with Arkansas Governor Carl E. Bailey in which he described his family as including "five sons, one daughter, one daughter-in-law, three niggers, one dog, two horses and a wife," NBC received 32 phone calls and many more letters of protest. The network blamed the governor, but more privately reminded its broadcasters and advertising agencies to avoid using such language.[68] It declined, however, a suggestion that it desist from broadcasting any songs including *nigger*, *darky*, or *coon* as being too arbitrary and difficult. Such objections did not, as we have seen, apply to *strike* or *drought*, because the sensitivities of employers and white farmers were more important to NBC than those of black listeners. The problem of derogatory language was deeply rooted in NBC's corporate culture; in 1931 its vice-president John Royal tried unsuccessfully to interest GEC in sponsoring 13 shows featuring Paul Robeson. The singer would be "a great hit with the niggers," Royal told GEC, "and it is true that darkies buy General Electric articles as well as anyone else."[69]

Although they reveled in the commercial success of blackface comedy such as *Amos'n'Andy*, networks and sponsors ventured only rarely into broadcasting African Americans themselves. When the advertising agency J. Walter Thompson produced an *All Colored Program* in 1937 for Fleischmann's Yeast, it lasted only six weeks even though it starred Louis Armstrong. That same year also saw the debut of Eddie Anderson, the most famous black radio actor of the interwar period. Anderson played Jack Benny's butler Rochester, in a role that confirmed many white stereotypes of blacks as lazy, licentious, and almost illiterate. Both Anderson and Armstrong were encouraged to speak in minstrel dialect to distinguish themselves from white characters and to reinforce their personas as simple-minded entertainers.[70]

J. Fred MacDonald has argued that portrayals of blacks on radio between the wars conformed to three stereotypes. There were "coons," or minstrel-like clowns, "toms," or passive and virtuous retainers, and "mammies," which encompassed almost all of the few radio depictions of black women. That these three stereotypes corresponded closely to those of "Sambo" and the black mammy during slavery spoke volumes about the failure of interwar radio to challenge long-standing white perceptions of African Americans.[71] They were consequently denied access to the airwaves to make contributions to community solidarity or to its public policy. One listener wrote to NBC in 1931 to complain that she had heard no black performers on any of the programs by the Emergency Unemployment Relief Committee. "The Depression struck all colors," Lillian Green reminded NBC, and "I am sure every colored citizen will voice my sentiment when I say please let us hear some of our colored artist on [the] program."[72]

"Respectable" radio stations and the major networks also worked against cultural miscegenation in their disapproval of jazz during the 1920s. Correctly perceived as an African American cultural expression, jazz brought with it many associations with blackness, uninhibited sexuality, and primitivism.[73] NBC and CBS loudly proclaimed their refusal to allow jazz on their airwaves, until its popularity forced them to reconsider. The furor over jazz, however, remained symbolic of the white cultural and social establishment's resistance to all forms of African American culture and expression over radio. Radio's role in popularizing jazz—and thereby in helping to legitimate African American cultural expression—was significant but largely involuntary. Jazz infiltrated programming more through listener demand than broadcasters' enthusiasm or cosmopolitanism. Many stations, especially those in the South, were much more comfortable in broadcasting white hillbilly music and white crooners such as Rudy Vallee and Bing Crosby.[74]

Because radio did not afford the opportunity for listeners to see blackness, Michele Hilmes has argued, it was forced to create it by "saying, in effect, *Here* is blackness on radio: marked by minstrel dialect, second-class citizen traits, cultural incompetence."[75] Through their propensity to deny African Americans any significant place on the nation's airwaves, and by their tendency to portray them in subservient and demeaning roles, broadcasters willingly continued the historical denial of full African American cultural, political, and social citizenship.

Despite their promises of a more inclusive community united and educated by radio, interwar broadcasters consistently refused to challenge the marginalization of those considered to be problem or unimportant groups within American society. Preferring instead to view immigrants, farmers, women, and African Americans through an economic prism, which valued audiences only in terms of their attractiveness to advertisers, broadcasters chose not to question this hierarchy of wealth and cultural agency. They thus paid far more attention to farmers and women, who commanded significant purchasing power, than to African Americans, recent immigrants, or labor activists. By accepting the class, ethnic, regional, gendered, and racial limits of interwar citizenship, however, the major broadcasters consciously limited the scope of its new radio community so as to privilege already empowered groups and values within it.

13

Radio and the Politics of Good Taste

Broadcasters during the 1920s and 1930s were convinced that they would play a central role in the interaction between the nation and its citizens. But such aspirations were neither socially nor politically neutral. The broadcasters used their influence to guide citizenship in directions that buttressed the existing balance of power within American society; those who strayed too far from the Democrat-Republican axis, or from private enterprise, or from other ideals encompassed in "Americanism"—defined in racial, gendered, and class terms—found little space on the nation's airwaves. In their broader cultural work, too, the broadcasters exercised a strongly prescriptive influence by disseminating a self-conscious form of popular culture that, in the name of "good taste," excluded those who threatened either the commercial imperatives of radio or the cultural hegemony of those who ran it.

The Cultural Work of Interwar Radio

"There is a new kind of culture in the world, and particularly in America," George Gershwin declared in 1930. "A culture of abundance, of many quick movements—ball games, prize-fights, jazz, preaching, science, symphonies, the sharing of adventure with men like Byrd and Lindbergh. And the voice, the instrument, the supreme interpreter of this new culture is the radio."[1] Historians of interwar America have generally agreed, seeing in the period a contest between Victorian or producer-capitalist values and a new consumer culture. The interwar years witnessed the triumph of consumerist values, which were later given substance with the return of peace and prosperity after 1945.[2]

The concomitant rise of new mass media and modern advertising after

1850 was vital to both the onset and outcome of this struggle. Syndicated newsprint, the telegraph, the telephone, photographs, phonographs, movies, and radio helped create a more unified culture across the nation that propagated new consumerist values. Motion pictures established this pattern by creating what Warren Susman described as a new "culture of sight and sound," which produced powerful new vehicles for the propagation of symbols, myths, and rhetoric, and which "made us more susceptible than ever to those who would mold culture and thought."[3]

The movies' contribution to the culture of abundance occurred in the public sphere. Millions of Americans left their homes each week to engage in a shared ritual within a shared cultural space. At the same time the movies also served to cement a new and increasingly sharp cultural hierarchy. Whereas opera and Shakespearian drama attracted huge audiences across socioeconomic boundaries in the middle of the nineteenth century, during the 1920s and 1930s Americans received their culture in different, and increasingly class-based, spaces. Those who sought "entertainment" patronized movie "palaces," while those who desired cultural uplift attended "temples" dedicated to "serious" music or "legitimate" theater. This segregation of cultural facilities fed directly into a growing division between "high" and "low" culture, with the new media of phonographs and movies increasingly identified with the latter.[4]

Radio's contributions after 1920 to the new culture of sight and sound were profound. While the movies created a new shared *public* culture, broadcasting brought that new culture into the *domestic* sphere. Radio brought to its audiences largely uniform programming from the outside world, but listeners received and translated that material within and through the infinitely varied private spaces of their homes. Radio audiences thus became more culturally mobile but also more segmented and private in their responses to programs.[5] It was therefore appropriate that broadcasters paid rhetorical homage to the sovereign listener as the most powerful arbiter of the new culture of abundance. That power was privately exercised, and all the more powerful for that. The moviegoer and the theater patron, by contrast, found that their sovereignty had to be expressed, and most likely moderated, through public statements of dissatisfaction. Received privately and "free," radio, in John Erskine's phrase, "is the easiest of all the arts to walk out on."[6]

The rhetoric of listener sovereignty and the reality of radio's domestic setting allowed broadcasters to present themselves as mediators of the growing gulf between the high culture of "serious theater" and the mass culture of

Hollywood melodrama. They also distinguished the American tradition of democratic culture from what they saw as more elitist Old World traditions. The BBC, American broadcasters frequently argued, was dedicated to a policy of involuntary cultural uplift. American broadcasting, on the other hand, was "democratically controlled . . . by the listening majority," Herman Hettinger argued in 1935.[7] This application of American exceptionalism to broadcasting served not only to legitimate the networks' service to the republic but also to entrench their commercial and ratings-driven programming within American notions of democracy and freedom of choice.

This role also proved useful in the broadcasters' fight to maintain their privileges as licensees without charge of a public asset. The networks defended their market dominance by pointing to their commitment to provide entertainment and public service. NBC and CBS were careful to include an element of "democratic" cultural uplift into their definition of public service. "There is an extreme to which so called 'good' programs can be forced on the listener," NBC executive Phillips Carlin wrote to his colleague John F. Royal in 1939. "Our responsibility is to keep a good taste level always slightly ahead of the masses thereby striving to bring the mass interest up in its standards." NBC therefore broadcast boxing title fights and Arturo Toscanini within its schedules, and CBS broadcast orchestral music with dance tunes. Along the way the broadcasters contributed significantly to a middlebrow culture that combined appeal to mass audiences with attempts to popularize elements of high culture in the name of gentility and good taste.[8]

Those who thought well of middlebrow culture argued that radio had done much to improve the cultural standards of the nation. Radio was credited with reviving popular interest in classical music and for the growth in the number of symphony orchestras and piano sales between the wars. Others thought that the new medium had publicized previously marginal musical forms such as folk, hillbilly, and jazz. In 1941 Sherwood Gates argued that radio had also increased American literacy rates and improved the nation's reading habits by awakening interest in self-education and the world of ideas.[9]

Others were less charitable. Even in 1924, after reviewing the "outrageous rubbish, verbal and musical," on the nation's airwaves, Bruce Bliven concluded, "Radio serves to remind us of the painful fact that high standards of intelligence and discrimination are not the inevitable by-products of an age of wonderful mechanical invention." Seventeen years later Senator Burton K. Wheeler took William Paley to task for allowing CBS to broadcast dime novels, gangster plays, and other "trash." Radio should provide cultural and moral uplift to all its listeners, Wheeler lectured Paley during Senate hearings in

1941, and "you should make an effort to present programs that appeal to the higher and better things of life." From Britain C. F. Atkinson told American broadcasters in 1935 that their programming bore some resemblance to ancient Rome's bread and circuses, by which the powerful provided spectacular entertainment to the masses in return for their political quiescence. "It is a dangerous road that art travels in the chariot of business," Atkinson warned; "a gradual and imperceptible change of direction, and we reach the Colosseum."[10]

The broadcaster's rhetorical obeisance to sovereign listeners concealed not only their commercial interest in maximizing audiences but also deeper issues of cultural and political authority. Broadcasters and networks, as we have seen, imposed their own sociopolitical agendas upon political programming and upon their portrayal of marginal and dissident groups. The same process occurred within their decisions about programming. These were made amidst a rhetoric of cultural worth, good taste, and audience preferences, but they also incorporated a process first described by Antonio Gramsci as cultural hegemony.

Cultural hegemony, the means by which elites use culture to entrench their power by noncoercive means, has become the dominant paradigm for critiques of popular culture and the organizations that propagate it. It was particularly attractive to those who objected to the Frankfurt School's dismissal of popular culture and its portrayal of audiences as passive and unthinking. Gramsci argued that controllers of the mass media disseminated "entertainment" designed to deaden or channel independent thought by audiences, and to conceal inequalities of power and wealth. Effective cultural hegemony requires both flexibility and subtlety; in seeking to legitimate cultural expression that buttresses elite power, it fosters popular culture, tolerates audience resistance, and even provides "choice" between a range of nonsubversive cultural forms. Lulled by this modern equivalent of bread and circuses, ordinary citizens become willing collaborators in their own repression.[11]

It is clear that the major broadcasters between the wars exercised a form of cultural hegemony. American radio listeners were presented with cultural choices, and their preferences were often reflected in programming by broadcasters anxious to maximize ratings. But broadcasters limited the range of those choices to exclude voices and views that they considered to be destabilizing of the socioeconomic and cultural values underpinning the "American system." As we have seen, the networks took care to exclude political radicals from the air, and their nervousness about labor unrest and other controversies was palpable. In addition, some of the nation's most popular radio stars sent clear messages to their audiences that radicalism was an inappropriate response to the economic crisis. Will Rogers laced his programs with homilies about the need to return to old values of individual self-reliance and thrift, while *Amos'n'Andy* combined distracting humor about the Depression with reminders of its potential benefits. "Times like dese does a lot o' good," Amos believed, 'cause when dis is over, which is bound to be, an' good times come back again, people like us dat is livin' today is goin' learn a lesson an' dey goin' know whut a rainy day means."[12]

Margaret T. McFadden came to similar conclusions in her examination of the cultural work done by Jack Benny's show. The national economic collapse caused a crisis in masculinity for millions of American men, who suddenly found themselves unable to provide for their families. Americans of both sexes also found themselves at odds with the modern economy and the consumerist values that buttressed it. *The Jack Benny Show*, according to McFadden, provided "temporary ideological resolutions" to these anxieties. By laughing at Jack's miserliness, his distrust of banks, and at his black butler Rochester's propensity to gamble, white male audiences could assert their own agency and racial superiority. If Jack, with all his neuroses and effeminacy, could still control his family, then there was hope for all white American men brought low by the Depression.[13] Along the way audiences were also enlisted into the general moderation of 1930s mass culture and New Deal politics that left the nation's structure of power and wealth largely untouched.

As cultural arbiters and defenders of middlebrow culture, and as guardians of public calm during the Depression, the networks made clear distinctions between good and bad taste that flowed easily into sociopolitical judgments as to the limits of acceptable discourse. Radio executives joined movie moguls and newspaper proprietors as defenders of middle-class values and the institutions that sustained them. The result, as Michelle Hilmes has argued, was that radio programming between the wars revealed the operation of "a set of basic, class-bound assumptions about who should be allowed to exert cultural authority on the ether."[14]

Cultural Authority and Industry Self-Regulation

The early broadcasters were painfully aware that their rhetoric of radio exceptionalism, and their status as licensees of a public asset, made them vulnerable to charges both of cultural monopoly and crass commercialism. If radio really was so powerful, why shouldn't it be more tightly regulated in the public interest? As we have seen, the broadcasters fended off more rigorous control by a combination of arguments concerning free speech, private enterprise, and their own ability to manage the ether in an enlightened and fair-minded way. Each broadcaster was under a statutory obligation to operate in the public interest, but the industry as whole, through the NAB, also promulgated codes of behavior designed to establish radio as a guardian of good taste and social responsibility.

These attempts at self-regulation were strongly influenced by the motion picture industry's experiences in the early 1920s. After a series of sex and drug scandals, and amidst concerns about the immoral influence of movies upon the young, the major Hollywood studios created the Motion Pictures Producers and Distributors Association (MPPDA) in January 1922. The MPPDA served as a lobbying and public relations agency, but its most famous activity was to censor movies. It hired Will Hays, a former chairman of the RNC, as a "movie czar" to keep movies clean and producers out of trouble with morals groups and regulators. Hays's informal censorship style was formalized in 1930 by the Lord-Quigley Code, which forbade nudity, sexual innuendo, excessive violence, illegal drugs, miscegenation, and profanity. It also enjoined studios to uphold marriage, the sanctity of the home, the fairness of government, and the value of religious belief. The industry's acceptance of the code indicated a general view that a little self-censorship was far preferable to either outside regulation or public opprobrium.[15]

The radio industry borrowed heavily from Hollywood's self-regulation and self-censorship model, but diverged from its practice. The diffusion of the radio industry, with over 600 broadcasters by 1930, made it impracticable to vet each broadcast before it was transmitted. The NAB in 1929 opted instead for a code of ethics that was nonbinding upon stations, but which was trumpeted as proof of broadcasters' social responsibility. Although it prohibited any material "which would commonly be regarded as offensive," the NAB made no attempt to define offensiveness. It made similarly vague declarations that stations should ensure that "no dishonest, fraudulent, or dangerous person, firm, or organization may gain access to the radio audience," and against false advertising. The bulk of the 1929 document, however, was taken up with suggestions about the proper conduct of advertisement policies, agencies, salesmen, and copyright issues.[16]

The NAB issued revised codes in 1931, 1935, and 1939, but none added much substance to the 1929 document. The 1939 code was the most prescriptive in its categorization of acceptable programming, and was the most explicit about how radio's cultural authority should be exerted. All the codes demonstrated the limits of self-regulation; despite their increasingly firm language, their only sanction was an implied expulsion from the NAB, and the limits placed upon stations' freedom were expressed as much in the language of commercial self-interest as in the rhetoric of social responsibility. The NAB proved incapable of providing the tight and uniform regulation achieved by the MPPDA, preferring instead to produce manifestos that created the illusion of consensus through resort to vagueness.[17]

The 1939 code addressed issues that had created problems for the major broadcasters over the preceding ten years. In the wake of Father Coughlin's broadcasts, the NAB declared that radio should not be used to create religious division, but rather to "administer broadly to the varied religious needs of the community." Children's programs, which had been criticized by educationalists for their propensity for horror and sensationalism, were now to promote respect for parents, authority, "clean living, high morals, fair play and honorable behavior." The code paid most attention to policies concerning "controversial public issues." Promulgated at the end of a highly politicized decade, it discouraged stations from becoming mouthpieces of demagogues or subversives. If broadcasters chose to air controversy at all, the code declared, they should do so in their sustaining time and in an even-handed way. News bulletins should not editorialize but should present information "free of bias."

The 1939 code concluded with a list of "Accepted Standards of Good Taste," which banned advertisement of spiritous liquor, patent medicines, astrology, dating agencies, gambling, and of content "which describes, repellently, any functions or symptomatic results of disturbances, or relief granted such disturbances through use of any product."[18] The last prohibition, directed against advertisement of laxatives, was symptomatic of the vacuity of all the NAB codes, which left the task of translating principle into practice to stations and networks.

The NBC Advisory Council and Program Policy

As the nation's first radio network, NBC saw itself as a role model for radio broadcasting generally and for networked radio in particular. It created internal structures and policies to monitor programs to ensure that they upheld its corporate image, its ideas of cultural legitimacy, and its commercial viability. These policies remained under constant, but ad hoc, review by senior executives, who professed great confidence in their abilities to define and implement "good taste" on the radio.

NBC's commitment to monitoring program content in the public interest did not rely completely on internal decision makers. When James Harbord announced the company's creation in 1926, he declared that NBC would be guided by an advisory council of 20 eminent Americans. This idea was probably borrowed from the BBC, which had established three advisory committees between 1923 and 1926.[19] Harbord promised that NBC's committee would be "representative of various shades of public opinion," and that it would assist it to produce the best programs. The council would also act as a court of appeal for any complaints from listeners. "We believe," Owen D. Young wrote in his letter of invitation to council members, that "while a Democracy is learning how to handle an instrument of such power, it is most important that the decisions of [NBC's] executives should be subject to review and correction." In addition, he thought, the existence of an advisory council would quieten critics of network radio and advocates of government control and censorship.[20]

The NBC Advisory Council was indeed an august body. Its original members included Edwin A. Alderman, President of the University of Virginia, Dwight Morrow, Charles Evans Hughes, John W. Davis, William F. Green of the AFL, Elihu Root, Walter Damrosch, and Mrs. John Sherman as its only female member. Young took the chair, and new members, including Alfred E. Smith and Newton D. Baker, joined as the membership was thinned by deaths and resignations during the 1930s. The council was also notable for its empty chairs; women, although a majority of the radio audience, were grossly underrepresented, and those at the lower end of the socioeconomic scale had only the conservative William Green to represent the interests of "labor." Other culturally or socially marginal groups, such as African Americans, Socialists, and other "radicals," were not represented at all. The council thus leaned heavily toward those groups and values that occupied the highest ground of the interwar political, economic, and social landscape, and its bona fides as the guardian of middlebrow culture and commercial broadcasting were cemented by the absence of any publicly identified critics of NBC, networking, or commercial radio.[21]

During congressional hearings in early 1934, Democratic Congressman William Sirovich of New York pressed NBC president Aylesworth on the representativeness of the advisory council. It was made up of "distinguished personages," Sirovich conceded, but was there not room for some representatives of the "common masses" who listened to the radio? He went on to suggest that Jane Addams and other "women and men who have dedicated their lives upon the altar of their fellow men" and who "serve the other side of the economic fence" might have been included. Aylesworth responded in three ways. He pointed out that "the plain, common masses . . . are represented by complaints which come before us," and by the 15 million letters that NBC received each year. He then argued that William Green represented the laboring masses, that Damrosch was "very much interested in mass music," and finally conceded the point by complaining that if "every group" was represented the council would end up with 100 members and become ineffective.[22]

By then, however, the advisory council had proved itself to be nothing more than, in Owen Young's phrase, "a decorative body of names." It met only once a year between 1927 and 1939, and it was given little real work to do. Young's early suggestion that the council be given a permanent secretariat and a formalized role in NBC's affairs was never implemented; very few listeners ever complained to it; and NBC management ignored it almost completely. Its meetings quickly assumed a comfortable and uncritical routine, with committees on labor, education, and religion presenting papers that invariably endorsed current policy and congratulated NBC for its good work. At the council's sixth meeting in February 1932, for example, William Green thanked NBC for its annual Labor Day picnic broadcasts and for its courtesy to AFL leaders who wished to speak on the radio. He made no mention of NBC's policies concerning the coverage of strikes, or of its tendency to provide far more air time to employer groups than to labor organizations. All in all, Green concluded, NBC provided "splendid service" to American workers.[23] The advisory council's uneventful life and unlamented demise in 1945 had made it clear that it was NBC management that ran network programming policy and set the cultural tone of its offerings.

CBS did not establish an advisory council. Established two years after NBC, it was generally less apologetic about networking and less sensitive to fears of a radio trust. Although active in congressional lobbying and industry self-regulation, CBS was generally content to allow NBC to take the lead in stressing the public service obligations of network radio. In 1936, however, amidst fears that the New Deal might institute more rigorous controls upon broadcasters, CBS did assemble its own group of luminaries to discuss radio regulation. It broadcast interviews with its eight advisers—who included Postmaster General James Farley, FCC member George Payne, Norman Thomas of the Socialist Party of America, and the ubiquitous William Green—under the title of *Broadcasting and the American Public.*

CBS's advisers, like those assembled by NBC, gave strong endorsement to the "American system" of broadcasting in general and of CBS's program policies in particular. Each of the eight were asked to respond to a series of leading questions—"What do you think of . . . our American system of open competitive enterprise—as against the European systems of strict governmental monopoly control?"—and each responded with measured praise for the status quo. Even Norman Thomas, who had little to thank the networks for, gave his grudging support to the "American system." Every member of the panel rejected the idea of more broadcasting regulation, and all expressed satisfaction with the quality of CBS programs. James Francis Cooke, a prominent writer and composer, noted "conservative estimates" that between 40 and 50 percent of the networks' schedules was devoted to matters "that are quite definitely cultural, educational and inspirational. . . . I really do not think," he concluded, "that the public . . . could digest very much more without academic dyspepsia."[24]

Network Management and Cultural Authority

Although untroubled by zealous regulation, prescriptive industry rules, or active advisory councils, network and station executives did not have completely free hands in devising program policies. Radio managers were constrained by a commercial imperative to maximize their market and by their desire to avoid greater regulation. They were also hemmed in by their own rhetoric of listener sovereignty, radio exceptionalism, and public service. Overarching all these considerations were the sociocultural backgrounds and motivations of those who ran stations and networks. Overwhelmingly drawn from urban, white, male, middle-class, and corporate backgrounds, they consciously and unconsciously set policy and standards to reflect their own views of culture, good taste, and American values.

Although the rhetoric of listener sovereignty was buttressed by the need to maximize market size, listener preferences were always mediated by other factors in determining network program policies. By the end of the 1930s, as we have seen, networks and major advertisers had developed increasingly sophisticated audience measurement techniques to determine which programs were most popular with listeners. But the ratings only worked retrospectively; they could not measure audience preferences about what it *wanted* to hear, but only what it *did* hear. This reduced the rhetorically sovereign listeners to consuming rather than participatory roles in program creation. Networks devoted little effort to gauging audience preferences independently of their existing program schedules.

Much more detailed research explored listener program preference by income level. This was important information for commercial broadcasters in their quest to strike the middle point of both cultural taste and the consumer market. Having discovered that radio listening—and the propensity to be influenced by advertising—was highest among listeners with middle and low incomes, broadcasters were careful to mold their programming around those listeners' preferences. Commercial radio felt little compunction in dancing with the listeners who listened to it most. "If the cultured minority refuses to vote for the type of program they want," the NAB declared in 1933, "it is largely their own responsibility when they fail to get it."[25]

In 1931 Herman Hettinger and Richard Mead found that low- and middle-income listeners in Philadelphia greatly preferred music over news and religious programs over educational features. Preference for classical music, news, and educational programs declined with income, whereas interest in children's, women's, and comedy programs went up. The popularity of sport, dance music, and religion, however, was relatively stable across income levels. Research later in the decade confirmed that Jack Benny, Rudy Vallee, *Amos'n'Andy*, and the *National Barn Dance* were disproportionately popular among listeners in the bottom half of income categories. Educational programs, on the other hand, drew more heavily from high- and medium-income listeners.[26]

Network programming throughout the 1930s, with some important exceptions, followed these patterns closely. Between 1931 and 1934, NBC and CBS devoted an average of 61 percent of their broadcast hours to music, of which slightly over two-thirds was nonclassical. Both networks devoted the rest of their time to a variety of program types, in proportions that mirrored their middle- and low-income listeners' preferences. Only in news, educational, and public affairs programming—those areas usually associated with radio's public service obligations—did the networks deviate significantly from the wishes of the majority of their listeners. In 1937 NBC broadcast a total of 19,800 hours of programs, 60 percent of which were devoted to music and 17 percent to drama. NBC categorized 8 percent as educational and 3.5 percent as news. This pattern remained stable until World War II forced networks to reorientate their schedules toward news and information programs at the expense of their musical offerings. Even in 1944, however, music and drama still occupied 54 percent of NBC and CBS schedules, while news and information occupied 19 percent.[27]

Comparisons between programming on networks in the United States and in other nations during the early 1930s show that CBS and NBC devoted more of their time to music, and to popular music, than did the BBC, Germany's Reichs-Rundfunk, and Australia's ABC. In 1930 BBC listeners received a radio diet of 59 percent music, of which about 40 percent was classical. The BBC also devoted about 18 percent of its time to news and "talks," which included all kinds of spoken programs. The Reichs-Rundfunk broadcast almost the same proportion of music as did the BBC, but devoted more than 27 percent of its schedule to news and talks. The ABC's programs in 1935 were also dominated by music—49 percent—but with a much higher share of popular music (30%) than was the case in Germany or Britain. The ABC also emphasized news and talks (25%), but also sport (11%). American listeners, however, received more religious broadcasting than did Britons, Germans, or Australians.[28]

Part of the networks' conception of entertaining the public was to avoid offending or shocking it. Pressured by criticism of the amount and tone of radio advertising, and by fears of greater federal interference, the major broadcasters formulated their program policies to maintain "good taste" on the radio and to assert their credentials as responsible corporate citizens. "Radio broadcasting is being condemned by too many people primarily because of distasteful or bad advertising," NBC's chief salesman wrote to his staff during debate over the Communications Act of 1934. "If we do not protect our listeners there will be no advertising in a very short time."[29]

Network program and advertisement policies were also designed to reassert broadcaster control over programming, which had increasingly devolved to advertising agencies and sponsors. In August 1934 NBC created its Department of Continuity Acceptance, led by Janet MacRorie, to enforce standards of "program quality, good taste and integrity" upon all scripts and advertisements. Advertising agencies were required to submit material two days before broadcast, and decisions of the continuity department were final. Programs and advertisements could not offend any religious belief, and they must not contain "obscene and off-color songs or jokes" or any other "language of doubtful propriety." Advertisements were not to contain false statements, fictitious testimonials, or references to competitors.[30]

By 1939 these rules had expanded significantly. Programs were forbidden to deal with suicide or to describe murders in any detail. Drinking was not to be romanticized in any way, and ridicule of public figures was also banned. Children's programs on NBC had to satisfy the NAB's rules concerning respect for parents and authority, as well as NBC's own requirements to avoid horror, torture, profanity, vulgarity, kidnapping, or "morbid suspense or hysteria." Advertisers of therapeutic or personal hygiene products came under special scrutiny. NBC reserved the right to censor any advertisement that promised cures for ailments or which described bodily functions in explicit terms. The network refused to air advertisements for deodorants, laxatives, hair restorers or removers.[31] Programs that dealt with capital punishment, euthanasia, descriptions of surgical procedures, syphilis, or any form of sexual activity also fell foul of MacRorie's department. So complete was NBC's censorship code by the end of the 1930s that advertisers were not even allowed to mention it, or its restrictions, on air.[32]

CBS devised very similar rules. It also justified its policies by a combination of public service and self-interest; basic standards of decency were required in order to maintain popular trust in radio and to ensure that the radio audience continued to grow. CBS also announced that it would limit advertising to a maximum of 10 percent of broadcast hours during the evening and 15 percent of the daytime schedule. This differential reflected the nature of daytime radio, which was predominantly "educative in both cultural and practical fields" for its female audience. Because daytime commercials often provided "valuable help in solving household economic problems," more of them could be aired. NBC quickly followed suit, creating almost perfect uniformity in the program and advertising policies of the two major networks for the rest of the decade.[33]

Good Taste in Practice

Anxious to avoid offense to any significant section of their audience, and to avoid adverse publicity, NBC and CBS scrutinized their scripts with great, and sometimes petty, vigilance. In so doing they fell hostage to the complaints of pressure groups who objected to particular programming. The networks became guardians of a reactionary form of middlebrow culture, bounded by the imagined values and sensitivities of an idealized American home on the one hand and the complaints of irate listeners on the other. They consequently stood aside from some of the most significant cultural changes of the interwar period.

We have already seen that the networks avoided jazz and its African American cultural overtones. Crooners, too, were frowned upon by network censors, who responded to complaints from some listeners about the unmusical, vulgar, and immoral nature of this new style of popular singing. Despite the enormous popularity of Rudy Vallee and then Bing Crosby, NBC in particular was slow to give them significant airtime. It was much more responsive to critics such as Cardinal O'Connell, who in 1932 warned his Catholic congregation in Boston about the crooners' "bleating and whining, with disgusting words, the meaning of which is a low-down source of sexual influence."[34]

Concerned about their family audiences, the networks were careful to avoid sexual innuendo of any type. Although public attitudes to sex and divorce had relaxed somewhat during the 1920s and 1930s, the networks remained prudish about any discussion of these topics. CBS banned any mention of venereal disease until 1937, and even the most innocuous jokes were carefully scrutinized for double meanings. When Al Jolson told his audience in 1934, "My father was a great baseball player but I was his first error," questions were asked of Janet MacRorie. She admitted to having given "careful consideration" to cutting the joke, but had finally decided that it could be broadcast because "it was intended as a play on words rather than salacious comment." Four years later MacRorie and Don Gilman of NBC's Hollywood office exchanged memos as to whether the word *screwy* should be used on air, before deciding that it was an acceptable slang word for *unbalanced* and that it "has no other secondary or suggestive meaning unless used in that connection."[35]

Somehow the infamous Mae West "Adam and Eve" sketch escaped MacRorie's blue pencil in 1937, but the outcry against it chastened both networks into even greater vigilance. NBC declared in 1939 that its programs would mention divorce only when it was portrayed in an unattractive way, and in 1940 it attempted to stamp out depictions of "effeminate gentlemen" in its dramatic and comedy programs.[36] MacRorie was concerned that "effeminate or sex-perverted characters" had become prevalent in many of NBC's most popular shows, including Jack Benny, Burns and Allen, and Bob Hope. She was also worried by dramatizations of the work of novelists such as John Steinbeck, "who frequently introduces perverted characters." Although recognizing the popularity of homoerotic humor—Philips Carlin of NBC detected "a certain note in the laughter accompanying the use of these characters which indicates that the audience is conscious of the fact"—network executives were insistent that it should not be allowed. "Female gentlemen" were too culturally challenging to be tolerated on a network that aspired to enter every American home.[37]

NBC's reluctance to encourage or even acknowledge changing views on sex and sexuality was typified by an incident involving a conference on birth control in November 1929. The network refused to broadcast any proceedings of the conference on the grounds that contraception was "the kind of subject which was not yet ripe for introduction . . . to the homes of America." NBC also argued that its millions of Catholic listeners would object. Professor Harry Ward, Chairman of the ACLU, argued that NBC had abrogated its public service obligations by avoiding this controversy. "Cultural progress," he told network vice-president John Elwood, "is largely a process of transferring matters of opinion to the domain of knowledge. Obviously, then, controversial subjects are those upon which the greatest possible amount of information is necessary." If the American public was to resolve its divisions over birth control, Ward thought, radio had to play its part in furthering education and debate on it.[38]

Owen Young referred the matter to the NBC Advisory Council, who deliberated on it in January 1930. Charles Evans Hughes, soon to depart for the U.S. Supreme Court, told the council that NBC was under no duty to broadcast controversial material; in fact its prime obligation was to maximize its commercial viability by "keeping in mind the needs and desires of its audience." Any discussion of contraception, he thought, was "unpalatable and even offensive to vast numbers" of listeners, and was therefore unsuitable for broadcast. Hughes's colleagues agreed, and unanimously endorsed the network's policy.[39]

Both networks were presented with similar difficulties in dealing with national Prohibition and its repeal. Prohibition and birth control, Harry Ward warned NBC in 1929, created the same problems for broadcasters because "many people 'believe' one thing and practice another and seek to protect their 'beliefs' by a complete intolerance toward those who openly disagree with them in both opinion and practice." While Prohibition was in force, CBS and NBC banned jokes about it. Although the Eighteenth Amendment was repealed by large majorities in 1933, the networks continued to treat issues relating to drinking very carefully. Even in 1937 NBC still considered comedy and drama involving drunken characters to be unsuitable, and it especially forbade any scene involving a drunk woman.[40]

Repeal also forced the networks to clarify their positions on advertisement of alcoholic beverages. Although repeal had legalized beer, wine, and spirits alike, both CBS and NBC decided to allow only beer and wine advertisements. In announcing its policy at the end of 1933, CBS justified this distinction in familiar language. Although it was reluctant to discriminate against any legal product, Columbia felt that advertisement of "hard liquor" would be offensive to many American households. But this concern did not extend to beer and wine, which CBS unilaterally defined as acceptable. Citing the "common knowledge" that "wine-drinking countries are temperate countries," the network argued that beer and wine advertisements enabled listeners "to be informed about the milder beverages." After some debate between its senior executives, NBC followed suit. The networks' decision did not, however, bind either their affiliated or independent stations, most of which enthusiastically accepted liquor accounts.[41]

NBC tightened its policies still further in 1939 as a result of pressure from FCC Chairman Frank McNinch. In a speech to the NAB in 1938, McNinch suggested that broadcasters ask themselves the same question that the FCC might ultimately have to decide: was advertisement of any intoxicants "in the public interest, convenience, or necessity"? Although a large majority of Americans had voted for repeal in 1933, McNinch declared, "the minority on this subject . . . has, I believe, a right to have its homes protected against that which is offensive." Quick to take the hint, NBC announced in March 1939 that it would no longer accept advertisements for beer or wine. But CBS and MBS continued to do so, leaving NBC in a commercially exposed and politically ineffective position. McNinch and the FCC did nothing more to discourage such advertising, most of NBC's affiliates continued to take beer and wine accounts, and the network failed to reap any political or commercial reward for its high-mindedness. Trapped by its own rhetoric of public service and by its solicitousness for commercially significant cultural minorities, NBC did not accept wine or beer accounts until 1949.[42]

Network Radio and Religion

Religious broadcasting presented the networks with particularly acute problems in reconciling competing demands of public service, audience maximization, and "good taste." Both CBS and NBC found that religious programs could quickly create bad publicity unless they were carefully controlled. By the early 1930s they had developed almost identical policies that, in the name of antisectarianism, buttressed established denominations and faiths at the expense of marginal or dissident religious groups.

The networks' caution over religious broadcasting in some ways reflected division and ambivalence within American churches themselves about the implications of radio for religious life and institutions. The advent of broadcasting coincided with deep concerns about a decline of religiosity. Churches across the country seemed to be losing their congregations to other forms of leisure and community involvement made possible by the automobile, the movies, rising disposable incomes, and shortened working hours. As the newest form of mass communication, radio offered both promise and threat to organized religion. Its promise lay in its ubiquity, which enabled it to reach those who were either unable or unwilling to join communal forms of worship. These spiritual shut-ins might once again join the fold, albeit at a distance. The excitement of the new medium might also give new relevance to religious observance to those who felt physically or psychologically disconnected from their religious communities.[43]

Some clergy were more ambivalent about radio's promise. Broadcasting, fundamentalist Roger Babson warned at the beginning of 1923, was "the greatest single force for good or evil that is known today," and American churches should move quickly to control it "in the interests of righteousness." Otherwise the new medium would go the way of motion pictures, which had been appropriated by commercial forces of dubious morality.[44] By the end of 1923 churches operated at least 12 stations across the country, and by 1925 there were 71 stations in the hands of religious groups. Evangelical denominations, eager to spread the word beyond their physical congregations, led the charge. "I hope that our radio system will prove so efficient," Baptist minister John Roach Straton declared, "that when I twist the Devil's tail in New York, his squawk will be heard across the continent." Baptists and Pentecostals soon gained a reputation for being the most enthusiastic radio broadcasters, while liturgical Presbyterians, Lutherans, and Catholics lagged well behind.[45]

In a survey of opinion on the impact of radio upon the churches in 1924, the *New York Times* noted that the Catholic Church continued to insist that its parishioners physically attend mass each week, and that very few rabbis had ventured on to the airwaves. Many Protestant ministers also emphasized the threat of radio above its promise. By removing the need for a physical community of worshipers, warned Presbyterian Edward Young in 1923, radio removed the "sense of fellowship in worship, the inspiration of human faces, and the offering of united prayer" that was essential to true spiritual experience. Audience research published by Hadley Cantril and Gordon Allport in 1935 lent some credibility to these views. In a comparison of responses by radio listeners and the live audience to an evangelical meeting in Boston, Cantril and Allport found that those outside the hall were more resistant to the fervor of the meeting, and less willing either to announce their conversion or to donate funds. Others feared for the future of rural and isolated churches if radio sermons became prevalent. How could small, underfunded churches hold on to their congregations in the face of radio competition from the great metropolitan cathedrals, with their superb organs, trained choirs, and silver-tongued orators? If local churches were to lose their role as social and spiritual centers, rural communities would lose still more people to the cities and to urban values.[46]

Fears that religious broadcasting would replace the congregation were partly mollified by the difficulties faced by religious broadcasters after 1925. Most of the 71 religious stations operational in that year were low-powered and part-time. Nearly all of them were reassigned to shared frequencies as the FRC rationalized the radio spectrum, and many fell short of its technical standards. By the end of 1928 the number of religious broadcasters had dropped by more than a third to 50, and that decline continued into the 1930s. The FRC also made life difficult for religious broadcasters by its declaration in 1929 that it would not grant or renew licenses to "propaganda stations." As a general rule, the commission declared, "particular doctrines, creeds and beliefs must find their way into the market of ideas by the existing public service stations." Most religious broadcasters either lost or surrendered their licenses, and instead bought or received time from commercial broadcasters.[47]

NBC moved quickly to undertake religious programming, but it also learned an early lesson about its pitfalls. In July 1927 network president Merlin Aylesworth agreed to a request for airtime from Judge Joseph Rutherford of the Jehovah's Witnesses. Claiming that a conspiracy existed between the Catholic Church, newspaper interests, and broadcasters to silence his organization, Rutherford challenged NBC to broadcast his sermon. Anxious to show good faith, Aylesworth arranged for a hookup to transmit Rutherford's address. The judge repaid Aylesworth's generosity by launching a stinging attack upon the Protestant churches and the Catholic clergy, whom he described as apostles of the devil. Deeply embarrassed, NBC banned Rutherford from its stations and asked its advisory council in March 1928 to establish policies for orderly religious programming.[48]

The advisory council created a "Committee on Religion," composed of Protestant, Catholic, and Jewish representatives. It devised a package of policies to prevent any repetition of the Rutherford incident by establishing firm network control over religious programs. These policies, promptly accepted by NBC management, limited access to the network's facilities to "recognized outstanding leaders" from the three "great religious faiths" of Protestantism, Catholicism, and Judaism. NBC also declared that its religious programming would be "nonsectarian and non-denominational," and that churches could not use their airtime to evangelize, to solicit funds, or to attack any other denomination or faith. Religious broadcasters were required to conform to the network's conception of good taste, which in this context meant presenting religion "at its highest and best" without doctrinal conflict or offense to any listeners. The network also announced that it would not broadcast religious programs on Sunday mornings, in order to avoid competition with church services. Finally it declared that it would not sell time to any religious group. Churches would either be granted free time, on NBC's terms, or not be heard at all.[49]

Although barred from NBC's studios, the Jehovah's Witnesses continued to make life difficult for the network. At the end of 1933 their congressional friends sponsored an amendment to the Radio Act of 1927 to outlaw any discrimination in religious broadcasting. If a station accepted programming from one religious group, it would be obliged to accept material from all. During hearings on the bill in March 1934, Judge Rutherford's attorney complained that, by allowing Protestants, Catholics, and Jews to use all available time for religious programming, the networks had imposed a religious test that discriminated against "independent schools of Christian thought." Although he conceded that the Witnesses attacked Catholicism as "not in accordance with the word of God," Rutherford's attorney argued that they did so in the spirit of religious education rather than sectarianism. The networks' action, he concluded, represented an abuse of power and an attack upon American traditions of freedom of religion.[50]

NBC, CBS, and organizations such as the National Council of Catholic Men successfully opposed the bill and justified exclusion of the Jehovah's Witnesses in the interests of religious harmony. Before the advent of network radio and the creation of NBC's policies, Aylesworth told the hearings, he had despaired that America could ever achieve a "community church," in which Jews, Catholics, and Protestants could join in worship. "But I do say to you, in my humble opinion, the way we have handled the religious broadcasts, we have come nearer to getting a community church than it will ever be possible to get in any other way."[51]

While NBC battled the Jehovah's Witnesses, CBS encountered its own difficulties from Father Coughlin's increasingly anti-Semitic and politicized sermons.[52] Under intense pressure from the Hoover administration and the FRC, CBS dropped Coughlin's popular broadcasts in 1931 and promulgated policies that echoed NBC's rules. It created a committee of religious leaders, drawn from the major Protestant denominations, Christian Scientists, the Catholic Church, and from the Jewish community, to advise it. CBS, too, refused to sell time to any religious group, and banned any hint of sectarianism from its religious programs. Like NBC, CBS pointed to these policies as evidence of its sense of social responsibility, which in Columbia's case came at considerable cost. Coughlin's broadcasts, Vice-president Henry Bellows told congressmen in 1934, had been very popular. In their place CBS had broadcast in sustaining time a weekly *Church of the Air*, featuring services by representatives of denominations and faiths selected by the network's religious advisers. All participants were required to observe CBS's belief that "there is essentially a religious unity in all forms of faith," and that religious conviction in all its forms should be respected. "To the Roman Catholics," Bellows reported, "I have said 'Remember that you are going to have Unitarians, Jews, Atheists, people of all kinds, listening to you. I want them to get out of your program something they find good.'"[53]

The networks' attempts to create a "community church" reflected their more general concern to foster a culture of good taste that would be acceptable to the overwhelming majority of their national audiences. This majoritarian notion of good taste predisposed NBC and CBS to abhor any hint of controversy in their cultural or religious programming in order to maximize their audience and to minimize irritation to legislators, regulators, and advertisers. But in removing controversy from their offerings the networks also drained their cultural and religious programming of its potential to acknowledge or encourage social and cultural dispute and change. By banishing advocates of birth control, evangelism, and other controversial issues and beliefs from their facilities, the networks acted consciously to keep the cultural and religious peace in the face of increasingly strident incursions from dissident groups within interwar society. Network radio thus threw its enormous weight behind the hegemony of the political culture that spawned and sustained it.

Conclusion

In retrospect it is clear that 1940 marked the end of an era in radio history. World War II closed twenty years of peacetime development of the broadcasting industry, and imposed new responsibilities and restrictions upon it.[1] In 1941 a reinvigorated FCC disrupted the cosy regulatory atmosphere of the interwar years by forcing NBC to sell one of its two networks. NBC reluctantly complied by selling its Blue network to the American Broadcasting Company.[2] Soon after the war, television—long delayed by technical difficulties and then the demands of war production—created a new age of mass communication. Shunted into the shadow of their new and more glamorous rival, radio broadcasters suffered precipitous falls in their ratings, advertising revenues, and prestige. In 1950 about 7 percent of American homes had TV; five years later nearly 70 percent had joined the television age. By 1956 Americans had reduced their average daily radio listening time from 4.4 hours in 1948 to 2.2 hours. By then the golden age of radio was long gone.[3]

During its first 20 years radio broadcasting had left indelible marks upon American life. By providing readily accessible and "free" programming directly to listeners' homes, it blurred the distinction between public and private culture and entertainment. Listeners could now participate in public events such as sporting contests, concerts, and speeches without leaving home. Radio's rapid spread during the 1920s and 1930s allowed listeners across the United States to hear the same programs and the same news bulletins. Its role as an advertising medium furthered the development of the consumer economy and a truly national market, familiarizing millions of listeners with the brand names and slogans of nationally available household goods. In the process they received a steady diet of middlebrow culture, which, although disappointing to those who hoped for a higher level of cultural refinement, nevertheless provided millions of Americans with greater and more accessible cultural variety than they had previously enjoyed.

Radio's effects on public policy and political debate were also significant. Its regulatory challenges created new institutions, and caused legislators, judges, and broadcasters to think hard about the new medium's future in relation to national defense, the First Amendment, the telegraph, and the telephone. As broadcasting developed into a highly capitalized industry dominated by three networks, it evolved a complex and subtle triangular web of understandings between broadcasters, politicians, and regulators which buttressed the networks' position and protected the primacy of advertising, entertainment, and private ownership within it. These institutions and understandings not only nurtured radio's development but also provided, with minimal adaptation, the regulatory framework for television after 1945.

Radio's connections to interwar political culture became more important, and more subtle, through its rapid application to election campaigning, political advertising, and government publicity. Most broadcasters, mindful of the need to maintain regulatory and legislative goodwill, and propelled by their own rhetoric of public service and radio exceptionalism, donated and sold airtime to candidates and parties throughout the interwar years. The growing interdependence of politicians and radio also blurred regulatory and legislative boundaries; lawmakers became the broadcasters' regulators, customers, and debtors. Each of these roles brought benefits and tensions, forcing both groups to engage in a sometimes complicated ballet of mutual support. Politicians soon found that they needed broadcasters' goodwill as much as radio required legislative and political protection.

This interdependence positioned radio broadcasting at the center of interwar political culture. During its golden age radio was assumed to be the most influential of the new mass media, and its ubiquity made it far more important to the political process than either the telegraph or the telephone. Radio exercised very strong influence upon the ways in which candidates and parties addressed their electorates, and upon campaign strategy and execution. The high cost of network broadcasting and its rigorous scheduling and technical demands also ushered in a more professional approach to campaign organization. By 1940 both major parties, and most broadcasters, had developed experience and expertise in radio politics that proved to be easily transferable to television after World War II.

Although radio's influence on interwar political culture was powerful and long lasting, it was not profoundly disruptive. Its greatest impact was upon the ways in which politicians competed for votes and upon the ways in which organs and functionaries of the state communicated with the wider population. Yet its communicative capacity was not allowed to develop in ways that threatened the prevailing distribution of power within interwar society.[4] The new medium's rapid development and quick adoption ensured that its influence was focused upon buttressing rather than eroding the political and economic system that had nurtured it. Radio's political, cultural, and social work was thus disproportionately beneficial to the two-party system, to the existing racial, gendered, and ideological boundaries of interwar citizenship, to the consumer economy, and to the most powerful of the nation's corporations. The major broadcasters were also successful in ensuring that listeners remained passive consumers rather than active participants in the programming process. Controlled by its commercial need to focus upon the most attractive consumer markets, hemmed in by regulators anxious to avoid controversy, and overseen by a political establishment keen to maintain its predominance, radio powerfully served the interests of the interwar sociopolitical status quo.

Radio's development into an agency of political and social reinforcement was neither preordained nor inevitable. It occurred amidst prolonged debate over the new medium's social destiny, and through the policies of the nation's most powerful political and business organizations. In its rapid journey from unregulated hobby to oligopolistic industry, radio attracted enormous attention and concern from those convinced that it held the promise of a new beginning for American citizenship, governance, and community. These ideas—described here as radio exceptionalism—saw radio as a cleansing influence upon political culture rather than as its handmaiden. In many ways the story of interwar radio and political culture is a story of the skillful co-option of radio exceptionalism by broadcasters, politicians, and regulators to serve their own ends.

The radio exceptionalist argument that radio was unique in its potential to recast American social and political life was not original. Many earlier technological advances had been championed as beneficial to the political and social health of the republic. The post office, canals, railroads, the telegraph, the telephone, and even electric light had all been incorporated into a form of technological utopianism that envisaged a new, more unified, better informed, and more inclusive national community. Those connections were often made very early in each invention's development: the telegraph was first put to use during the Whig national convention in 1844; some early telephone companies allowed their subscribers to listen to political speeches; on election nights some electric light companies flashed progress results on to the night sky with powerful searchlights.[5]

It was therefore appropriate that radio should begin its golden age by transmitting results from the 1920 presidential election. Although radio exceptionalists' hopes were greatly attenuated after 1920, their inherited tradition of technological utopianism persisted and soon attached itself to television. As he announced the development of TV for domestic use in 1939, RCA president David Sarnoff promised Americans a new age of civic education, enlightenment, and engagement in almost identical terms to his earlier pronouncements about radio. TV would bring new interest in political life, education by television would capture children's imaginations, the nation's "cultural level" would rise, and televised sermons would finally arrest the modern decline in church membership. "Thus the ultimate contribution of television will be its service towards unification of the life of the nation, and at the same time the greater development of the life of the individual." Through it, Sarnoff promised, "America will rise to new heights as a nation of free people and high ideals."[6]

Sarnoff's rhetoric has recently been repeated by a host of enthusiasts for the networked computer and its potential for "teledemocracy." "Today's telecommunications technology," former NBC president Lawrence Grossman argued in 1995, "may make it possible for our political system to return to the roots of Western democracy as it was first practiced in the city-states of ancient Greece. Tomorrow's telecommunications technology almost certainly will." Promises of a new age of direct democracy, in which "netizens" will control public policy through electronic town hall meetings and Internet referenda, have become familiar features of the computer age. They have so far drowned out skeptics' arguments that the Internet revolution, like those of its predecessors, may only further entrench the power of existing sociopolitical elites.[7]

Notwithstanding the persistence of technological utopianism, Americans have shown a remarkable ability to integrate technological "revolutions" into their lives. Only two and a half years after the first radio broadcast, the *New York Times* argued that radio had "already ceased to astonish anybody, has no miraculous quality for anybody, and is treated by everybody as a matter of course."[8] The volume of radio exceptionalism during the 1920s and 1930s indicates that the *Times* was too quick and too sweeping in its dismissal of a radio revolution, yet the interwar experience ultimately vindicated its skepticism. Radio was indeed subsumed into the political culture and everyday lives of interwar Americans, influencing but not revolutionizing them. The radio age began amidst bold promises of listener sovereignty and a new age of citizenship. As Americans in their millions gathered around their radios in December 1941 to hear their president lead them into war, however, they did so not as radio exceptionalists, but as listeners and consumers. Radio's ability to entertain, inform, educate, and persuade its listeners had been enlisted to serve, but not to disrupt, its broader culture and those who were powerful within it.

Notes

Abbreviations

ACLU	American Civil Liberties Union
Annals	*Annals of the American Academy of Political and Social Science*
CMMF	Committee on the Merchant Marine and Fisheries, United States House of Representatives
CMMRF	Committee on the Merchant Marine, Radio and Fisheries, United States House of Representatives
DNC	Democratic National Committee
FCC	Federal Communications Commission
FDRP	Franklin D. Roosevelt Papers, Hyde Park, New York
FRC	Federal Radio Commission
HCHP	Herbert Clark Hoover Papers (HIA)
HHPL	Herbert Hoover Presidential Library, West Branch, Iowa
HIA	Hoover Institution Archives, Stanford, California
H.R.	House of Representatives
HRCIFC	Committee on Interstate and Foreign Trade, United States House of Representatives
HSUS	*Historical Statistics of the United States*
NAB	National Association of Broadcasters
NAM	National Association of Manufacturers
NARA	National Archives and Records Administration
NBC MSS	National Broadcasting Company Manuscript Collection, Library of Congress, Washington, D.C.
NBCR	National Broadcasting Company Records, State Historical Society of Wisconsin, Madison, Wisconsin
OF	Official File (FDRP)
PF	Presidential Files (HIA)
PPF	President's Personal File
PPSF	Presidential Papers, Subject File (HHPL)
PSF	President's Secretary's File (FDRP)
RG	Record Group
RNC	Republican National Committee

RST Report of the President's Research Committee on Social Trends, *Recent Social Trends in the United States*
SICC Interstate Commerce Committee, United States Senate

Introduction

1. Unnamed speaker quoted in Potts, *Radio in Australia*, p. 103.

2. See "The President's Voice," *New York Times*, Nov. 12, 1921, p. 12; Koppes, "The Social Destiny of Radio," pp. 365–68. Ickes quoted in Tyson, ed., *Radio and Education 1934*, p. 70.

3. *RST*, pp. 153–56, 215; Cantril and Allport, *The Psychology of Radio*, p. 31.

4. Lazarsfeld, "The Effect of Radio on Public Opinion," in Waples, ed., *Print, Radio, and Film in a Democracy*, pp. 66–70.

5. For pioneering works on the role of TV in political life, see Lang and Lang, *Politics and Television;* MacNeil, *The People Machine;* Siepmann, *Radio, Television, and Society;* Campbell, "Has Television Reshaped Politics?"; Donovan and Scherer, *Unsilent Revolution.*

6. McLuhan, *Understanding Media*, p. 300; McDonald, *Don't Touch that Dial!* p. 2. See McChesney, *Telecommunications, Mass Media, and Democracy*, p. 4, and Smulyan, *Selling Radio*, p. 4 for discussions of determinism and triumphalism in radio historiography.

7. Hilmes, *Radio Voices*, p. xvii; McChesney, *Telecommunications, Mass Media, and Democracy;* Rosen, *The Modern Stentors;* Smulyan, *Selling Radio.*

8. McChesney, *Telecommunications, Mass Media, and Democracy*, p. 251. See also Pool, *Technologies of Freedom*, p. 149.

9. Thompson, *Media and Modernity*, pp. 11, 244; Meyrowitz, *No Sense of Place*, pp. 6, 145, 308. See also Kern, *The Culture of Time and Space.*

10. Ely, *The Adventures of Amos'n'Andy;* Grundy, "'We Always Tried to Be Good People'"; McFadden, "America's Boyfriend Who Can't Get a Date." See also Higgins and Moss, *Sounds Real.*

11. See Becker, "Presidential Power," p. 16; Henderson, *On the Air*, p. 184; Wolfe, "Some Reactions to the Advent of Campaigning by Radio."

12. For content analyses of interwar political broadcasting see Buhite and Levy, *FDR's Fireside Chats;* Black, *Democratic Party Publicity in the 1940 Campaign;* Bormann, "This Is Huey P. Long Talking"; Braden and Bradenburg, "Roosevelt's Fireside Chats" and "Franklin D. Roosevelt's Voice and Pronunciation"; Janowitz, "The Techniques of Propaganda for Reaction."

13. Farber, "Political Culture and the Therapeutic Ideal," pp. 681. See also McGerr, *The Decline of Popular Politics*, p. 10.

14. See Savage, *Broadcasting Freedom*, for recent research on radio during World War II.

15. See, for example, Henderson, *On the Air*, p. 184.

1 | *The Radio Age*

1. Rorty, *Our Master's Voice*, p. 265.

2. Aitken, *The Continuous Wave*, pp. 40–86; Davis, *The Empire of the Air*, p. 10.

3. For the development of the audion valve and the patent battles it caused, see Aitken, *The Continuous Wave*, pp. 162–250; Davis, *The Empire of the Air*, pp. 14–18; Morgan, *Pageant of Electricity*, pp. 280–316; Hijiya, *Lee de Forest and the Fatherhood of Radio*, pp. 70–75.

4. Schiffer, *The Portable Radio in American Life*, p. 42; Douglas, *Inventing American Broadcasting*, p. 205.

5. U.S. Naval Service, "Memorandum for the Secretary of the Navy," Jan. 4 and Feb. 13, 1915, Daniels Papers, box 508, file: "Communications Service." For descriptions of the development of naval radio see Aitken, *The Continuous Wave*, pp. 253–301, 495; *Inventing American Broadcasting*, pp. 102–43.

6. Captain David W. Todd, Director of Naval Communications Service, "Memorandum to the Secretary of the Navy," Jan. 23, 1917, and U.S. Naval Radio Service, "Memorandum for the Secretary of the Navy," Jan. 4, 1915, Daniels Papers, box 508, file: "Communications Service"; U.S. Naval Radio Service, "Memorandum for the Secretary of the Navy," Feb. 13, 1915; Douglas, *Inventing American Broadcasting*, pp. 272–73.

7. Captain David W. Todd, "Memorandum to the Secretary of the Navy," Jan. 23, 1917, Daniels Papers, box 508, file: "Communications Service."

8. CMMF, Hearings on Government Control of Radio Communications (H210-1), Dec. 12, 1918, pp. 5–8, 49, and Daniels to the Speaker of the House of Representatives, July 19, 1919, Daniels Papers, box 509, file: "Communications Service—General, 1919 Jun.–Dec."

9. CMMF, Hearings on Government Control of Radio Communications (H210-1), Dec. 19, 1918, p. 314; Young, "Proposed Draft of a letter to the Chairman of the Committee on Naval Affairs, U.S. Senate," undated, Young Papers, 11-14-1.

10. See Daniels to the President of the United States Senate and Speaker of the House of Representatives, July 28, 1919, Sullivan Papers, box 6, file: "Daniels, Josephus." See also Young, proposed draft letter to chairman of the Committee on Naval Affairs, U.S. Senate, undated, 1919, Young Papers, 11-14-1.

11. Young to Miles Poindexter, Nov. 11, 1919, and Young to Glenn D. Frank, May 21, 1930, Young Papers, 11-14-1; GEC internal memorandum, July 15, 1919, Young Papers, 11-14-1; Stanford Hooper, "Memorandum for Chief of Bureau of Steam Engineering," May 22, 1919, Hooper Papers, box 2, file: "Correspondence May–Aug., 1919." See also undated memorandum, General Electric Internal Correspondence, undated, Young Papers, 11-14-1, file: "Wireless—Government."

12. Banning, *Commercial Broadcasting Pioneer*, pp. 32–40; Lewis, *Empire of the Air*,

p. 151. For a more jaundiced view of the creation of RCA see Davis, *The Empire of the Air*, pp. 23–31.

13. David Sarnoff to Owen D. Young, Jan. 31, 1920, Young Papers, file 89, box 223C.

14. For a discussion of the competing claims to priority in broadcasting see Archer, *History of Radio*, pp. 207–8, and R. Franklin Smith, "Oldest Station in the Nation?" in Lichty and Topping, eds., *American Broadcasting*, pp. 114–25.

15. *New York Times*, Mar. 2, 1922, p. 20.

16. Jome, *Economics of the Radio Industry*, p. 70; *HSUS*, 2:796; Sterling and Kitross, *Stay Tuned*, p. 62.

17. Page, "The Nature of the Broadcast Receiver and Its Market in the United States from 1922 to 1927"; *New York Times*, Mar. 2, 1924, sec. 9, p. 17, Jan. 3, 1926, sec. 8, p. 13:5, and Jan. 13, 1929, sec. 2, p. 12:4; *Literary Digest* 82 (July 19, 1924): 22–23.

18. Schiffer, *The Portable Radio in American Life*, p. 55.

19. *New York Times*, Jan. 9, 1927, sec. 8, p. 11:2. For details of the automobile radio market see Victor M. Ratner to Owen D. Young, Apr. 30, 1936, Young Papers, 11-14-50, folder 21.

20. Advertisement quoted in Lears, *Fables of Abundance*, p. 194; diffusion figures: Sterling and Kitross, *Stay Tuned*, p. 533.

21. *HSUS*, 2:796; Roosevelt Papers, PPF 853.

22. In 1930 the ten richest states in per capita income were (in descending order) New York, Delaware, California, Connecticut, Illinois, New Jersey, Massachusetts, Nevada, Rhode Island, and Michigan. The top ten radio states were (in descending order) New Jersey, New York, Massachusetts, Rhode Island, Illinois, Connecticut, California, Wisconsin, Michigan, and Iowa. Of these only Delaware and Nevada do not appear in the list of top ten radio states. Delaware was ranked 16th and Nevada 32d. In 1930 the ten poorest states were (in descending order) Kentucky, New Mexico, Tennessee, North Dakota, Georgia, North Carolina, Alabama, Arkansas, Mississippi, South Carolina. The bottom ten radio states were (in descending order) Florida, Tennessee, New Mexico, Louisiana, North Carolina, Georgia, Alabama, Arkansas, South Carolina, and Mississippi. Of these only Kentucky and North Dakota do not appear in the list of the bottom ten radio states. Kentucky was ranked 37th and North Dakota was 25th. In the Deep South I count South Carolina, Georgia, Florida, Alabama, Mississippi, Arkansas, and Louisiana. These figures and rankings derived from data in Willey and Rice, *Communication Agencies and Social Life*, pp. 188–89, and *HSUS*, 1:243–45; *New York Times*, Apr. 3, 1932, sec. 5, p. 4.

23. Figures calculated from CBS, "Radio in 1936," p. 8, Young Papers, file 87.2.132, folder 267T.

24. Hettinger and Neff, *Practical Radio Advertising*, p. 41.

25. Mail and telegraph figures: Willey and Rice, *Communication Agencies and Social Life*, pp. 112, 127, 130; telephone figures: p. 138.

26. Lynd and Lynd, *Middletown,* pp. 269, 263, 173.

27. DeFleur, *Theories of Mass Communication,* p. 40; Hettinger and Neff, *Practical Radio Advertising,* p. 113.

28. *HSUS,* 2:796, 1:224.

2 | *Radio Advertising and Networks*

1. Mills quoted in *New York Times,* Feb. 3, 1924, sec. 7, p. 9.

2. Banning, *Commercial Broadcasting Pioneer,* pp. 90, 154.

3. See Starch, *Principles of Advertising,* p. 866; Quiett and Casey, *Principles of Publicity;* WEAF booklet, "The Scope of the National Broadcasting System," July 17, 1924, NBC MSS, file 480.

4. *New York Times,* Jan. 10, 1925, p. 12.

5. Ibid., Mar. 22, 1924, p. 14, Mar. 11, 1925, p. 10, and Mar. 12, 1925, p. 18.

6. Ibid., Apr. 24, 1924, p. 30; *Radio Broadcast* quoted in Archer, *History of Radio,* p. 253; Sarnoff to Rice, June 17, 1922, Young Papers, 11-14-50, box 2.

7. *Literary Digest,* June 14, 1924, p. 46; *New York Times,* Dec. 20, 1924, p. 20; Archer, *History of Radio,* p. 254.

8. Smulyan, *Selling Radio,* pp. 65–92; McChesney, *Telecommunications, Mass Media, and Democracy.*

9. *New York Times,* Sept. 13, 1925, sec. 11, p. 5. NBC listener quoted in Metz, *CBS,* p. xix.

10. *Printers' Ink,* Feb. 8, 1923, pp. 175–76; NARA RG 173, file 1600-C, box 134. Family circle comment quoted in Marchand, *Advertising the American Dream,* p. 89.

11. Lee, *Publicity;* Bernays, *Crystallizing Public Opinion,* p. 199; Phelps to S. W. Edwards, Aug. 27, 1924, NARA, RG 173, F 1600-C, box 134.

12. See H. K. McCann Company, *Radio Broadcast Advertising* (1928), NBC MSS, file 646; Felix, *Using Radio in Sales Promotion;* Arnold, *Broadcast Advertising;* Dunlap, *Advertising by Radio;* Elder, "Measuring Radio Advertising Sales Power"; Hettinger and Neff, *Practical Advertising;* Hettinger, *A Decade of Radio Advertising;* Arnold, *Broadcast Advertising,* pp. 58, 42.

13. See *New York Times,* June 2, 1929, sec. 9, p. 15; Hettinger, *A Decade of Radio Advertising,* pp. 39–40. See also McNair, *Radio Advertising in Australia,* pp. 208–10; Archer, *History of Radio,* p. 361. For other examples of the debate over radio advertising see *Cong. Rec.,* Senate, 70th Cong., 2nd sess., 1929, 70, pt. 4:3752, and Rorty, "The Impending Radio War," *Education by Radio* 1, no. 35 (Nov. 1931): 142.

14. NBC Interdepartment Correspondence, Jan. 28, 1936, Kobak Papers, box 2, file: "National Broadcasting Company, General, 1934–1960."

15. Bernays, *Biography of an Idea,* p. 432; Marchand, *Advertising the American Dream,* p. 94.

16. Sanger, *Rebel in Radio,* p. 31.

17. Quoted in Marchand, *Advertising the American Dream,* p. 94.

18. See Hettinger, *A Decade of Radio Advertising*, p. 123; "Broadcasting in the United States," *Annals* 177 (Jan. 1935): 10. For a full list of advertisers on NBC and CBS between 1927 and 1936 see "NBC and CBS Network Advertisers," NBC MSS, file 640, and NBC Interdepartment Correspondence, L. N. Wailes to Ellen Davis, May 22, 1936, NBC MSS, file 33.

19. Smulyan, *Selling Radio*, p. 102.

20. Bruce Barton to Lammot du Pont, President of E. I. Du Pont de Nemours and Company, May 18, 1935, E. I. Du Pont de Nemours and Company Records, box 3, file: "Advertising Department—July 1932–Dec. 1935."

21. Hettinger, *A Decade of Radio Advertising*, pp. 115, 113; J. E. Brown, Acting U.S. Supervisor of Radio, Detroit, to Director of Radio, Department of Commerce, Apr. 9, 1932, NARA, RG 173, entry 2, file BC-1, folder 8: "Broadcasting."

22. Marchand, *Advertising the American Dream*, p. 288.

23. See Arnold, *Broadcast Advertising*, pp. 166–71, for the script of this program.

24. Dygert, *Radio as an Advertising Medium*, p. 7; Peter, "The American Listener in 1940," p. 6.

25. Advertising expenditures 1928–37: Dygert, *Radio As an Advertising Medium*, p. 7; advertising expenditures 1938–39: Peter, "The American Listener in 1940," 6; shares of the national advertising dollar, 1930–33: internal NBC memo: E. P. H. James to Paul Winchell, May 1, 1934, NBCR, box 23, file 36: "American Newspaper Publishers Association, 1934"; shares of the national advertising dollar, 1936: Rose, *National Policy for Radio Broadcasting*, p. 97.

26. *New York Times*, May 17, 1931, sec. 9, p. 11, and June 28 1931, sec. 9, p. 9.

27. NBC pamphlet, "The First Ten Years: A Study of the Growth of the National Broadcasting Company, 1926–1936," NBC MSS, file 94. For a congressional critique of the amount—but not the fact—of radio advertising, see Ewin L. Davis of Tennessee, speech to AAAA, Apr. 15, 1932: *Cong. Rec.*, 72nd Cong., 1st sess., 1932, 75, pt. 8:8699–8701. Edna Henrichs to Milton J. Cross, Feb. 10, 1935, NBC MSS, file 374. See also E. A. Schaper to the FRC, Sept. 14, 1931, NARA, RG 173, entry 2, file BC-1-6.

28. Cantril, *Public Opinion, 1935–1946*, p. 713. See also Sayre, "Attitude toward Radio Advertising," in *Journal of Applied Psychology* 23 (Feb. 1939): 23–33, 28. Caldwell quoted in *New York Times*, Apr. 15, 1931, p. 26.

29. For Sarnoff on superpower see CMMF, Mar. 13, 1924 (H346-4), p. 159.

30. *New York Times*, July 27, 1924, sec. 8, p. 15; WEAF booklet, "The Scope of the National Broadcasting System," July 17, 1924, NBC MSS, file 480.

31. For the FTC investigation see Mauritz A. Hallgren, "The Patriotic Radio Trust," *Nation* 123 (July 20, 1927): 53–55, and Representative Ewin L. Davis, CMMF, Report to Accompany H.R. 9108, Feb. 27, 1926.

32. Sarnoff to Edgar W. Rice, June 17, 1922, Young Papers, 11-14-50, box 2.

33. See NBC to Harmond Petersen, Aug. 21, 1929, NBC MSS, file 94.

34. NBC to Harmond Petersen, Aug. 21, 1929, NBC MSS, file 94.

35. The *Eagle* quoted in the *Literary Digest* 91 (Dec. 4, 1926): 26–27. Aylesworth quoted in ibid. 91 (Oct. 2, 1926): 13.

36. See NBC to Harmond Petersen, Aug. 21, 1929, NBC MSS, file 94, pp. 2, 6.

37. Hettinger and Neff, *Practical Radio Advertising,* pp. 329–30.

38. See NBC Interdepartmental Correspondence, Ellen Davis to L. B. Wailes, May 22, 1936, NBC MSS, file 33, and "The First Ten Years: A Study of the Growth of the National Broadcasting Company, 1926–1936," May 15, 1936, NBC MSS, file 94.

39. Hearings before the CMMF on H.R. 1540 (H515-B), Jan. 24–31, 1929, p. 655.

40. Untitled NBC memorandum, NBCR, box 16, file 65, "Columbia Broadcasting System 1933." NBC's profits declined to $400,000 in 1933, but then jumped by more than 38 percent in the following year: *Education by Radio* 4 (1934): 13; *New York Times,* June 21, 1934, p. 35.

41. *New York Times,* Feb. 27, 1925, p. 26, and July 24, 1925, p. 19. See also hearings before the CMMF on H.R. 1540 (H515-B), Jan. 24–31, 1929, pp. 678–79; "Who Profits from Radio Broadcasting?" *Education by Radio* 4 (Apr. 1934): 13; E. F. Hutton and Co. report, "Radio Corporation of America," Feb. 29, 1928, in Young Papers, 11-14-77; "Radio Corp. of America," *Barron's: The National Financial Weekly,* Sept. 24, 1934, in Baker Papers, box 196, file: "Radio Corporation of America," 1934; Raskob Papers, file 1890.

42. For Paley's biography see Paper, *Empire,* pp. 3ff.; Metz, *CBS,* pp. 9–27.

43. NBC Interdepartmental Correspondence, Comptroller to President, Mar. 1, 1933, NBCR, box 16, file 65: "Columbia Broadcasting System 1933." NBC's gross sales in 1932 were $27,381,124.

44. Robinson, *Radio Networks and the Federal Government,* pp. 28–29.

45. Brindze, *Not to Be Broadcast,* pp. 26–28; Rose, *A National Policy for Radio Broadcasting,* p. 63.

46. Sarnoff, "Statement to the Stockholders of Radio Corporation of America," Nov. 21, 1932, and "Government Wins Radio Suit," *Knickerbocker Press,* Oct. 25, 1932, in Young Papers, file 185, folder 329A; Young to Glenn Frank, May 20 and 21, 1930, Young Papers, 11-14-1 (folder 12 of 41).

47. See NBCR, box 20, file 1, "NAB: General 1933," for NAB's activities regarding copyright. See also Mackey, "The Development of the NAB"; White, *American Radio,* pp. 68–100; McChesney, *Telecommunications, Mass Media, and Democracy,* p. 108.

3 | Regulatory Models and the Radio Act of 1927

1. See Francis St. Anstell to Wallace H. White, Dec. 4, 1926, White Papers, box 51, file: "Radio Miscellaneous, 69th Congress," and Dill's discussion of channel allocation and availability in *Cong. Rec.,* 69th Cong., 1st sess., 1926, 67, pt. 11:12335–38.

2. Mander, "The Public Debate about Broadcasting in the Twenties," p. 179. See also C. Wood Arthur of the Radio League of America to William E. Borah, Dec. 6, 1926, Borah Papers, box 237, file: "Radio Legislation, 1926–1927 (1)."

3. Radio League of America to William E. Borah, Oct. 1, 1926, Borah Papers, box 217, file: "1925–1926: Radio/ Re. Leg."

4. See *United States* v. *American Bond and Mortgage Co.*, 31 F.2d 448 (1926): "It does not seem to be open to question that radio transmission and reception . . . are interstate commerce." The U.S. Supreme Court had declared telegraph messages to be commerce in *Western Union Telegraph Company* v. *Pendleton*, 122 U.S. 347 (1887).

5. H. B. Thayer to Hoover, Jan. 23, 1922, NARA, RG 173, entry 1, file 1179-2, box 101. See also Simon Bitterman to Hoover, May 7, 1922, NARA, RG 173, file 1600-C, box 134.

6. Chief Radio Inspector (name illegible) to David B. Carson, Director of the Bureau of Navigation, Department of Commerce, Feb. 1, 1922, NARA, RG 173, entry 1, file 1179-2, box 101.

7. David Sarnoff, "Uncensored and Uncontrolled"; Grover A. Whalen, "Radio Control" and Hudson Maxim, "Radio—The Fulcrum," *Nation* 119 (July 23, 1924): 90–91.

8. Briggs, *The Birth of Broadcasting*, pp. 67, and 107ff.

9. *New York Times*, Feb. 11, 1925, p. 20.

10. "On the Air," *Nation*, Feb. 11, 1931, p. 146. See also Rorty, *Order on the Air!* p. 27, and Frost, *Is American Radio Democratic?* for other calls for nationalization of radio broadcasting during the 1930s.

11. McChesney, *Telecommunications, Mass Media, and Democracy*, p. 114.

12. Wallace H. White to R. F. Bickford, Jan. 9, 1924, White Papers, box 42, file: "Commerce—Radio 68th Congress"; NAB, *Broadcasting in the United States*, p. 53.

13. NAB, "Government Program Sponsorship," *Cong. Rec.*, Senate, 72 Cong., 1st sess., 1932, 75, pt. 5: 5432.

14. *New York Times*, Apr. 19, 1925, sec. 10, p. 15. Hard quoted in James H. Hanley, "Radio in the United States and England," Nov. 1933, Norris Papers, box 27, file: "Radio (1926–1931)".

15. NAB, *Broadcasting in the United States*, pp. 91, 48.

16. See Thompson, *Wiring a Continent*, pp. 12–13, 27–34, and 440; Morgan, *Pageant of Electricity*, pp. 72–89; Czitrom, *Media and the American Mind*, pp. 21ff.; Gabriel Kolko, *The Triumph of Conservatism: A Reinterpretation of American History, 1900–1916* (New York: Free Press, 1963), pp. 47–50, 179–180; and Fischer, *America Calling*, p. 74. For the debate over railroad control see Hines, *War History of the Railroads.*

17. For the development of the Australian system see Potts, *Radio in Australia*, pp. 16–20; Johnson, *The Unseen Voice*, pp. 12ff.; Counihan, "The Formation of the Broadcasting Audience," p. 201; Inglis, *This Is the ABC*, pp. 5–24; Jones, *Something in the Air;* and McNair, *Radio Advertising in Australia*, pp. 122–60.

18. Quoted in Johnson, *The Unseen Voice*, p. 57.

19. For the development of Canadian broadcasting see Siepmann, *Radio, Television, and Society*, pp. 154–67; Kerwin, *The Control of Radio*, pp. 13ff.; and McNeil and Wolfe, *Signing On*, pp. 196–252.

20. Quoted in Johnson, *The Unseen Voice*, p. 63.

21. See, for example, *New York Times*, Aug. 4, 1935, sec. 9, p.11, and Robert J. Landry, "Radio and Government," *Public Opinion*, Oct. 1938, pp. 557–69, 559, in Clark Papers, series 116, box 437. The Australian model received regular and approving mention in NCER's bulletin *Education by Radio* throughout the 1930s. See, for example, 4 (1934): 59, 64, and Eugene J. Coltrane, Special Representative of NCER, to William E. Borah, Jan. 30, 1933, p. 4, Borah Papers, box 470, file: "Radio 1932–33."

22. Jome, *Economics of the Radio Industry*, p. 249; Kerwin, *The Control of Radio*, p. 25. For a less optimistic view of the likelihood of adopting the Australian model see Rose, *National Policy for Radio Broadcasting*, pp. 260–64.

23. Herbert Hoover to Secretary of State, Apr. 24, 1922, HIA, Commerce Department Files, box 15, file: "Radio—Commerce Department." See Representative Ogden Mills of New York, *Cong. Rec.*, House, 67 Cong., 1st sess., 1921, 61, pt. 3:2923.

24. "Uncle Sam to Broadcast to Us All," *Literary Digest* 76 (Feb. 1923): 28. By 1937 nearly 25 percent of all radio frequencies were assigned to various departments of the federal government: McCamy, *Government Publicity*, p. 127. Congressional attempts to create a more ambitious governmental radio system continued throughout the interwar period, but all died in committee. See *New York Times*, Apr. 11, 1929, p. 22; Rosen, *The Modern Stentors*, p. 44; and Schmeckebier, *The Federal Radio Commission*, p. 45.

25. George W. Carey, "Herbert Hoover's Concept of Individualism Revisited," in Hawley, ed., *Herbert Hoover as Secretary of Commerce*, pp. 217–54.

26. Hoover broadcast after the Fourth National Radio Conference, Nov. 12, 1925, p. 5: HIA, Commerce Department Files, box 97, file 222A; Benjamin, "Radio Regulation in the 1920s," p. 426.

27. Rosen, *The Modern Stentors*, p. 62; Hoover to CMMF, HIA, Commerce Department Files, box 118, file 363-A.

28. Quoted in J. F. Dillon, Radio Inspector of San Francisco, to Broadcasting Stations, Sixth Radio District, July 7, 1922, NARA, RG 173, file 1600-7, box 133; see also D. B. Carson to Dillon, Aug. 16, 1922, ibid.

29. Hoover statement to the CMMF on H.R. 7357, Mar. 11, 1924, HIA, Commerce Department Files, box 118, file 363-A.

30. Hoover, Opening Address before the Third National Radio Conference, Oct. 6, 1924, p. 7, HIA, Commerce Department Files, box 15, file: "Radio—Commerce Department." See also Hoover reminiscences, Columbia University Oral History Project, pp. 16, 17.

31. Hawley, "Herbert Hoover and Economic Stabilization," in Hawley, ed., *Herbert Hoover as Secretary of Commerce*, pp. 52–60.

32. Hoover, Opening Address to the Third National Radio Conference, Washington, D.C., Oct. 6, 1924, p. 3, HIA, Commerce Department Files, box 15, file: "Radio—Commerce Department." See also *New York Times*, Mar. 10, 1929, sec. 11, p. 21.

33. For the first National Radio Conference recommendations see HIA, Commerce Department Files, box 115, file 210. See also Sarno, "The National Radio Conferences," pp. 191–93, and *New York Times*, Apr. 2, 1922, sec. 8, p. 2. Press Release,

Recommendations of the Second Radio Conference, Apr. 2, 1923, HIA, Commerce Department Files, box 117, file 302; Hoover, Opening Address to the Third National Radio Conference, Washington D.C., Oct. 6, 1924, HIA, Commerce Department Files, box 15, file: "Radio—Commerce Department."

34. See Hoover broadcast after the Fourth National Radio Conference, Nov. 12, 1925, p. 5, HIA, Commerce Department Files, box 97, file 222A.

35. A. N. Goldsmith memo to James G. Harbord, Aug. 10, 1925, "Present Status and Trend of Broadcasting," Young Papers, 11-14-50 (box 4 of 41).

36. *United States* v. *Zenith Radio Corporation* 12 F.2d 614 (1922); *Hoover* v. *Intercity Radio Company* 286 F. 1003 (1923).

37. Morris L. Ernst, "Radio Censorship and the Listening Millions," *Nation* 122 (Apr. 1926): 473.

38. Eugene McDonald Jr. to Wallace H. White, Apr. 20, 1926, White Papers, box 51, folder: "Radio—Miscellaneous 69th Congress." See also Rosen, *The Modern Stentors,* pp. 94–95.

39. Hoover, press release July 9, 1926, "Radio Situation Due to Uncompleted Legislation," HIA, Commerce Department Files, box 98, file 604; C. C. Dill, radio address, "Regulation of Radio," undated (but internal evidence suggests Sept. 1926), White Papers, box 51, file: "Radio Miscellaneous 69th Congress."

40. See *Cong. Rec.*, House, 67th Cong., 4th sess., 1923, 64, pt. 3:2328(1926) 55 and 2785; Garvey, "Secretary Hoover and the Quest for Broadcast Regulation"; McKerns, "Industry Skeptics and the Radio Act of 1927."

41. See Hoover quoted in Pool, *Technologies of Freedom,* p. 119, and Norman Thomas radio address, "Radios and Democracy," May 24, 1926, Borah Papers, box 217, file: "1925–1926: Radio/ Re. Leg." See generally Mander, "The Public Debate about Broadcasting in the Twenties," p. 184, and Rosen, *The Modern Stentors,* p. 4.

42. See Dill, *Radio Law,* p. 104; Rosen, *The Modern Stentors,* p. 4.

43. See A. L. Ashby quoted in Arnold, *Broadcast Advertising,* p. 134.

44. See C. C. Dill, "Regulation of Radio," p. 4, White Papers, box 51, file: "Radio—Miscellaneous 69th Congress."

45. *Cong. Rec.*, House, 69th Cong., 1st sess., 1926, 67, pt. 5:5479; White Papers, box 51, folder: "Radio—Miscellaneous 69th Congress."

46. White to Allen H. Babcock, Dec. 21, 1926, White Papers, box 50, file: "Radio—Miscellaneous 69th Congress."

47. See *New York Times,* Apr. 29, 1926, p. 9; "Politics in Radio Control," *Literary Digest,* May 22, 1926, p. 12; "Tangle in Radio Situation Worse," *Yakima (Wash.) Republic,* May 8 1926, in White Papers, box 73, "Scrapbook—Radio 1926."

48. White Papers, box 51, folder: "Radio—Miscellaneous 69th Congress," p. 8.

49. *Cong. Rec.*, 69th Cong., 1st sess., 1926, 5479; Orestes Caldwell, "Freedom of Speech and Radio Broadcasting," *Annals* 213 (1935): 187; the undated and untitled nine-page speech by White in White Papers, box 51, file: "Radio Miscellaneous, 67th Congress."

50. C. C. Dill, "Regulation of Radio," p. 3, White Papers, box 51, file: "Radio—Miscellaneous 69th Congress."

51. W. G. Cowles to Senator Hiram Bingham, May 12, 1926, quoted in *Cong. Rec.*, Senate, 69th Cong., 1st sess., 67, pt. 11:12499, 12358, 12501–3.

52. Robinson quoted in *New York Times*, Apr. 29, 1926, p. 9. See also Eugene McDonald to Wallace H. White, Apr. 20, 1926, White Papers, box 51, file: "Radio—Miscellaneous 69th Congress."

53. George W. Norris to Clarke G. Powell, Dec. 27, 1926, Norris Papers, box 27, file: "Radio 1926–1931"; "Politics in Radio Control," *Literary Digest*, May 22, 1926, p. 12; Godfrey, "Senator Dill and the 1927 Radio Act," p. 482. See also Rosen, *The Modern Stentors*, p. 96.

54. Walsh quoted in *Cong. Rec.*, Senate, 69 Cong., 2nd sess., 68, pt. 1:1034. For industry response see *Radio Retailing* 4, no. 5 (Nov. 1926); William Brown, Vice-president of RCA, to William Greene, Chairman of CMMF, Jan. 2, 1923, Young Papers, box 122, file 259K.

55. *Providence (R.I.) Journal*, May 14, 1926, White Papers, box 73, "Scrapbooks—Radio 1926."

56. *Bluefield Telegraph*, May 12, 1926, and *Joliet Herald News*, June 12, 1926, White Papers, box 73, file: "Scrapbook—Radio 1926."

57. McDonald to Borah, Apr. 30, 1926, Borah Papers, box 217, file: "1925–1926 Radio/ Re. Leg."

58. Norman Thomas, speech delivered over Station WRNY, May 24, 1926, Borah Papers, box 217, file: "1925–1926 Radio/ Re. Leg."

59. Davis: *Cong. Rec.*, House, 69th Cong., 1st sess., 1926, 67, pt. 5:5558, 5483. Blanton: *Cong. Rec.*, House, 69th Cong., 2nd sess., 1927, 67, pt. 5:5572, and 68, pt. 3:2567.

60. See Bingham's comments in *Cong. Rec.*, Senate, 69th Cong., 1st sess., 1926, 67, pt. 11:12498.

61. *Cong. Rec.*, Senate, 69th Cong., 1st sess., 1926, 67, pt. 11:12501–4. Dill quote on p. 12504.

62. See Dill, *Radio Law*, pp. 86ff.; Ford, "The Meaning of Public Interest, Convenience, or Necessity," p. 206.

63. The Radio Act is reproduced in Barnouw, *A Tower in Babel*, pp. 300–315.

64. Rosen, *The Modern Stentors*, p. 109; Pool, *Technologies of Freedom*, p. 119.

65. McKerns, "Industry Skeptics and the Radio Act of 1927," p. 130.

66. *Washington Post* quoted in the *Literary Digest* 92 (Mar. 1927): 1. See also the *Nation* 124 (Feb. 1927): 133, and 122 (Apr. 1926): 443–44, and "Radio Censorship and the Listening Millions," 122 (Apr. 1926): 473–75, for criticism of the Radio Act of 1927.

67. Kolko, *Triumph of Conservatism*, pp. 2, 179.

4 | *The Federal Radio Commission, 1927–1934*

1. *Cong. Rec.*, House, 69 Cong., 2nd sess., 1927, 68, pt. 3:2582.

2. FRC, *Second Annual Report*, 1928, p. 2.

3. See Wallace White, undated speech notes, Mar. 1929, White Papers, box 64, unfiled.

4. FRC Annual Reports to Congress, 1928–1933.

5. *Cong. Rec.*, Senate, 71st Cong., 2nd sess., 1929, 72, pt. 1:710ff.

6. Quoted in Schmeckebier, *The Federal Radio Commission*, pp. 55–58. See also Rev. W. A. Burke to Thomas J. Walsh, Feb. 3, 1929, Walsh Papers, box 124, file: "Radio."

7. Woods to Walter H. Newton, Nov. 12, 1930, HHPL, PPSF, box 148, file: "Federal Radio Commission—Correspondence—1931 May." See also Walter S. Goodland to George Vits, Feb. 2, 1931; Vits to Newton, Feb. 4, 1931; White House memo, signed "H," Feb. 8, 1931, all ibid., box 148, file: "Federal Radio Commission Correspondence 1931 Feb."

8. James G. Strong to Newton, Oct. 10, 1931, and Stimson to American Embassy, Mexico City, Oct. 17, 1931, ibid., box 149, file: "Federal Radio Commission Correspondence 1931, Oct.–Nov."

9. Pettey to Howe, Oct. 4, 1933, Howe Papers, box 90.

10. *Cong. Rec.*, House, 70 Cong., 1st sess., 1928, 69, pt. 4:3980–86.

11. Celler: *Cong. Rec.*, House, 70th Cong., 1st sess., 1928, 69, pt. 4:3875, 4497; Davis: Mar. 2, 1928, p. 3986.

12. See *Cong. Rec.*, Senate, 70th Cong., 1st sess, 1928, 69, pt. 5:5157 (McKellar), and 5164 (Bratton). See also William King of Utah's comment: ibid., 5288. Voting figures calculated from the House roll call recorded in ibid., House, 69, pt. 4: 4589.

13. See Rosen, *The Modern Stentors*, p. 130.

14. See FRC, Second Annual Report, 1928, p. 9; Schmeckebier, *The Federal Radio Commission*, p. 31; White, *The American Radio*, p. 139.

15. FRC, Fourth Annual Report, 1930, p. 25.

16. Quoted in FRC, First Annual Report, 1927, pp. 6–7.

17. FRC, *Practice and Procedure before the Federal Radio Commission*, 1930; FRC, *Federal Radio Commission Rules and Regulations* (1934), pp. 66–86.

18. See Rosen, *The Modern Stentors*, p. 136; Davis, *The Empire of the Air*, p. 66.

19. FRC, "Statement Relative to Public Interest, Convenience, or Necessity," Aug. 23, 1928: FRC Annual Report, 1928, pp. 166–70.

20. Quoted in Hampson Gary, "Regulation of Broadcasting in the United States," *Annals* 177 (Jan. 1935): 15–21, 19.

21. See Brindze, *Not to Be Broadcast*, p. 158; Rosen, *The Modern Stentors*, p. 133.

22. White, *The American Radio*, p. 101. For specific examples see Barnouw, *A Tower in Babel*, p. 260; Severin, "Commercial vs. Non-Commercial Broadcasting," pp. 498–502; Rosen, *The Modern Stentors*, pp. 168–69. For a detailed report on the state of ed-

ucational broadcasting in 1930 see *Report of the Advisory Committee on Education by Radio.*

23. Sterling and Kitross, *Stay Tuned,* pp. 92, 135, 197.

24. John Fitzpatrick, President of Chicago Federation of Labor to United States Senators, Jan. 5, 1929, HHPL, PPSF, box 151, file: "Federal Radio Commission—Public Opinion and Relations 1929 Jan.–Mar."

25. CMMF, Hearings on H.R.15430, Jan. 8–19, 1929 (H515-1-A), pp. 338–39.

26. Schmeckebier, *The Federal Radio Commission,* p. 52.

27. McChesney, *Telecommunications, Mass Media, and Democracy,* pp. 21, 23.

28. Clarence Dill, press release Oct. 6, 1931, Clark Papers, series 116, box 441.

29. See, for example, *Cong. Rec.,* Senate, 71st Cong., 3rd sess., 1931, 74, pt. 3: 2530–31.

30. Rosen, *The Modern Stentors,* pp. 165–68, and McChesney, *Telecommunications, Mass Media, and Democracy,* pp. 142–43.

31. *Cong. Rec.,* Senate, 72 Cong., 1st sess., 1932, 75, pt. 12:13121–26.

32. *New York Times,* Nov. 29, 1932, sec. 8, p. 6.

33. CMMF, Hearings on H.R. 15430, Jan. 8–19, 1929 (H515-1-A), pp. 338–39.

34. *New York Times,* Dec. 14, 1930, sec. 10, p. 17.

35. *Cong. Rec.,* House, 73rd Cong., 2nd sess., 1934, 78, pt. 3:2646–48.

36. Quoted in Pool, *Technologies of Freedom,* p. 123.

37. Rose, *National Policy for Radio Broadcasting,* pp. 218–22. For movie censorship see Black, *Hollywood Censored,* pp. 13ff., and *Mutual Film Corporation* v. *Industrial Commission of Ohio* 236 U.S. 230 (1915).

38. *Near* v. *Minnesota* 283 U.S. 697 (1931). See Louis G. Caldwell, "Freedom of Speech and Radio Broadcasting," *Annals* 177 (Jan. 1935): 179–207, 188.

39. See Rosen, *The Modern Stentors,* p. 138.

40. James H. Hanley, "One Year on the Federal Radio Commission," Apr. 14, 1934, Norris Papers, box 27, file: "Radio (1926–1931)."

41. Quoted in Chase, *Sound and Fury,* p. 71.

42. FRC, Fifth Annual Report, 1931, p. 67. See also Chase, *Sound and Fury,* pp. 60–79, and Branyan, "Medical Charlatanism."

43. Quoted in Barnouw, *A Tower in Babel,* p. 216.

44. WEVD and the House of David examples cited in Brindze, *Not to Be Broadcast,* pp. 153, 157.

45. See Orbison, "Fightin' Bob Shuler"; E. J. Shives to Hoover, Sept. 3, 1932; Frank Doherty to Harold A. Lafount, Sept. 1, 1932, all in HHPL, PPSF, box 256, file: "Republican National Committee, California, 1932, Sept. 1–20," and box 149, file: "Federal Radio Commission Correspondence, 193—Dec."

46. Smith Public Papers, file 200-517; Young Papers, file 11-14-50 (box 10 of 41); and *New York Times,* June 23, 1927, p. 22.

47. Louis G. Caldwell, "Freedom of Speech and Radio Broadcasting," *Annals* 177 (Jan. 1935): 179-207, 203.

48. For contemporary accounts of the development of radio law see Dill, *Radio Law*, and Davis, *The Law of Radio Communication.*

49. Le Duc and McCain, "The Federal Radio Commission in Federal Court," p. 393.

50. Ibid., pp. 407–10.

51. *FRC* v. *Nelson Brothers Bond and Mortgage Company*, 289 U.S. 266 (1933). See also *Technical Radio Laboratory* v. *FRC* 36 F.2d 111 (1929) on the FRC's licensing powers.

52. On exclusive federal jurisdiction: *City of New York* v. *FRC* 36 F.2d 115 (1929). On FRC's use of character and past record: *General Electric* v. *FRC* 36 F.2d 111 (1929). On rules of evidence: *Technical Radio Laboratory* v. *FRC* 36 F.2d 111 (1929). On FRC's fact-finding powers: *FRC* v. *Nelson Brothers Bond and Mortgage Company* 289 U.S. 266 (1933). On discretion to define "public convenience, interest, or necessity": *KFKB Broadcasting Association Inc.* v. *FRC* 47 F.2d 670 (1931), and *FRC* v. *Nelson Brothers Bond and Mortgage Company* 289 U.S. 266 (1933).

53. See Murphy, *The Meaning of Freedom of Speech*, pp. 4–5, 248; Benjamin, "Radio Regulation," pp. 86–104.

54. *Trinity Methodist Church* v. *FRC* 62 F.2d 850 (1932). See FRC, Seventh Annual Report, 1933, p. 11.

55. Le Duc and McCain, "The Federal Radio Commission in Federal Court," p. 403.

5 | *A New Deal for Radio?*

1. Coltrane to Borah, Jan. 30, 1933, Borah Papers, box 370, file: "Radio 1932–1933."

2. 1928: Owen D. Young, Memo, Aug. 27, 1928, Young Papers, file 11-14-126 (box 1 of 2). 1932: James G. Harbord, "Justice for Sale under Reign of Tammany," RNC, 1932, HIA, Hoover Papers, PF, box 17, file: "Campaign Material, Republican National Committee Pamphlets," and *New York Times*, Oct. 28, 1932. See also Robert J. Landry, "Radio and Government," *Public Opinion* , Oct. 1938, pp. 557–69, 560, in Clark Papers, series 116, box 437. For the Aylesworth rumor see *Cong. Rec.*, Senate, 73rd Cong., 2nd sess., 1934, 78, pt. 8:8834.

3. On Bellows and FDR see *New York Herald Tribune*, June 20, 1934, in Clark Papers, series 116, box 437; *Cong. Rec.*, Senate, 73rd Cong., 2nd sess., 1934, 78, pt. 8:8834. See Bellows to Early, Mar. 6, 13, and 14, 1933, FDRP, OF 130, box 5, file: "Radio Broadcasts 1933 Jan.–June." On CBS's liberal image see Brindze, *Not to Be Broadcast*, p. 54, and *Cong. Rec.*, Senate, 73rd Cong., 2nd sess., 1934, 78, pt. 8: 8834. On William Paley's politics see Paper, *Empire*, p. 51.

4. Quoted in *Cong. Rec.*, Senate, 73rd Cong., 2nd sess, 1934, 78, pt. 8:8834. For NBC's attitude see Frank M. Russell to Stephen Early, Mar. 13, 1933, Early Papers, box 16, file: "Russell, Frank M."

5. Steele, *Propaganda in an Open Society,* p. 24.

6. Quoted in *Cong. Rec.*, Senate, 73rd Cong, 2nd sess., 1934, 78, pt. 1:862–63.

7. Harold Lafount, press release, Aug. 14, 1933, FDRP, OF 136, box 1, file: "1936 Jan.–June."

8. Howe Papers, boxes 89 and 106. For Eleanor Roosevelt see McChesney, *Telecommunications, Mass Media, and Democracy,* p. 182.

9. *New York Herald Tribune,* June 19, 1934, in Clark Papers, series 116, box 437. NBC figures showed that Republicans received 13 percent of the Democrats' airtime: James G. Patterson Memo to James Harbord, June 14, 1934, Baker Papers, box 164, file: "National Broadcasting Company, 1934."

10. See Steele, *Propaganda in an Open Society,* pp. 33–45.

11. Mullen to Trammell, Oct. 14, 1933, NBCR, box 21, file 49, "David Sarnoff, Sept.–Dec. 1933."

12. *New York Times,* May 19, 1934, p. 4, and June 18, 1934, p. 38.

13. The *New York Herald Tribune,* June 20, 1934, in Clark Papers, series 116, box 437. See also Walter Lippmann, "Freedom of the Radio," *New York Herald Tribune,* June 22, 1934, ibid.

14. Rosen, *The Modern Stentors,* pp. 174, 162.

15. Quoted in *New York Times,* Dec. 13, 1929, p. 30. See also ibid., June 1, 1930, sec. 9, p. 8.

16. For a compilation of bills relating to the regulation of broadcasting between 1903 and 1931, see *Cong. Rec.*, Senate, 71st Cong. 3rd sess., 1931, 74, pt. 7:7055–60.

17. ACLU, "Radio Censorship: Proposal for a Federal Investigation," Mar. 1934, Young Papers, file 11-14-101, "American Civil Liberties Union."

18. McCosker to Farley, Apr. 13, 1933, and McCosker to FDR, Apr. 12, 1933, FDRP, OF 228, file: "National Broadcasting Company 1933–1934."

19. Rosen, *The Modern Stentors,* p. 175.

20. Daniels quoted in McChesney, *Telecommunications, Mass Media, and Democracy,* pp. 180–81. For a similar view from the Democratic rank and file see E. M. Elliot to FDR, Mar. 24, 1933, FDRP, OF 136, box 1, file: "1933."

21. McChesney, *Telecommunications, Mass Media, and Democracy,* p. 181.

22. Rosen, *The Modern Stentors,* p. 176.

23. *New York Herald Tribune,* Feb. 27, 1934, in Clark Papers, series 116, box 437.

24. See HRCIFC, Hearings on H.R. 8301 (H677-3), May 8, 1934, pp. 83, 292.

25. HRCIFC, Hearings on H.R. 8301 (H677-3), May 16, 1934, pp. 279–87.

26. See the *Cong. Rec.*, Senate, 73rd Cong., 2nd sess., 1934, 78, pt. 8:8828–29 for the full text of the amendment, and pp. 8832ff. for Hatfield's discussion of it.

27. See McChesney, *Telecommunications, Mass Media, and Democracy,* pp. 200ff.; Barnouw, *The Golden Web,* p. 25.

28. *Cong. Rec.*, Senate, 73rd Cong., 2nd sess., 1934, 78, pt. 8:8846–50, 8852–54.

29. *Cong. Rec.*, House, 73rd Cong., 2nd sess., 1934, 78, pt. 10:10306–309 (McFadden), and p. 10327 (McGugin).

30. Section 307(b) Communications Act of 1934.

31. See Senate Report No. 781, 73rd Cong., 2d sess., Apr. 17, 1934, White Papers, box 63, file: "Federal Radio Commission." For the industry's lobbying see *New York Herald Tribune*, June 21, 1934, in Clark Papers, series 116, box 437.

32. *Sorenson* v. *KFAB and Wood et al.* 243 N.W. 82 (1932). This decision never received approval from the federal courts, but broadcasters used it to demand indemnities from all political broadcasters and advertisers throughout the 1930s: NBCR, box 13, file 11: "Political Broadcasts—Indemnity by Speakers, 1932," and internal NBC memo, A. L. Ashby to M. H. Aylesworth, June 23, 1932, box 13, file 14: "Political Campaign Broadcasts 1932." For a discussion of the *Sorenson* decision see White, *The American Radio*, p. 174.

33. SICC, Hearings on S.2910, 73rd Cong., 2d sess., Mar. 9–15, 1934 (S434-3), pp. 63–69.

34. *Literary Digest* 118 (July 28, 1934): 9.

35. For NRA codes for radio manufacturing see *New York Times*, Aug. 6, 1933, sec. 10, p. 7, and for the broadcasters' code see Barnouw, *The Golden Web*, p. 31, and Sterling and Kitross, *Stay Tuned*, p. 192.

36. *Literary Digest* 118 (Aug. 11, 1934): 23.

37. Rosen, *The Modern Stentors*, p. 161; McChesney, *Telecommunications, Mass Media, and Democracy*, p. 226; Smulyan, *Selling Radio*, pp. 152–53.

6 | The Federal Communications Commission and Radio, 1934–1940

1. Siepmann, *Radio, Television, and Society*, p. 26; Key, *Public Opinion and American Democracy*, p. 388; MacNeil, *The People Machine*, p. 259; Whale, *The Half-Shut Eye*, p. 132; Grossman *The Electronic Republic*, p. 219.

2. *Chicago Daily News*, July 3, 1934, in Clark Papers, series 116, box 437. For brief biographies of these FCC commissioners see *Education by Radio* 4 (1943): 33–34.

3. *New York Times*, Oct. 14, 1934, sec. 10, p. 11.

4. FCC, "Report of the FCC to Congress Pursuant to Section 307(c) of the Communications Act of 1934," p. 4, FDRP, OF 1059, box 1, file "FCC 1935."

5. Barnouw, *The Golden Web*, p. 26.

6. See McChesney, *Telecommunications, Mass Media, and Democracy*, pp. 188–225.

7. FCC, "Report of the FCC to Congress Pursuant to Section 307(c) of the Communications Act of 1934," pp. 3–4, FDRP, OF 1059, box 1, file "FCC 1935."

8. Barnouw, *The Golden Web*, p. 27.

9. McCamy, *Government Publicity*, p. 127.

10. Farley Papers, Private File, reel 3, Jan. 8, 1937 (dictated Jan. 10, 1937).

11. Howe to Pettey, Feb. 19, 1935, and Pettey to Howe, Feb. 27, 1935, Howe Papers, box 91, file: "Radio—Sept. 1934–Nov. 1935."

12. Farley Papers, Private File, reel 3, Dec. 30, 1936.

13. Charnley, *News by Radio*, p. 32; Sterling and Kitross, *Stay Tuned*, p. 191.

14. Kang, "Franklin Roosevelt and James L. Fly," p. 29.

15. Quoted in Barnouw, *The Golden Web*, p. 28.

16. Tracy F. Tyle, "The Power of the FCC to Regulate Programs," *Education by Radio* 5 (1935): 49–50.

17. SICC, 74th Cong., 1st sess., Confirmation of the Members of the FCC (S474-4), Jan. 23–Feb. 2, 1935, p. 47.

18. Ibid.

19. Ibid., p. 48; *Nation* 144 (Apr. 1937): 455–56; Ernst, *The First Freedom*, p. 132.

20. *Nation*, 144 (Apr. 1937): 456.

21. SICC, 74th Cong, 1st sess., Confirmation of Members of the FCC (S474-4), Jan. 23–Feb. 2, 1935, p. 49.

22. Robert J. Landry, "Radio and Government," *Public Opinion* , Oct. 1938, p. 564, in Clark Papers, series 116, box 437.

23. Barnouw, *The Golden Web*, pp. 33, 28–30.

24. See Mark Ethridge, "The Government and Radio," *Annals* 213 (Jan. 1941): 115.

25. Barnouw, *The Golden Web*, p. 169; Kitross, *Stay Tuned*, p. 189.

26. ACLU, *Radio Is Censored!* pp. 9, 11–23.

27. Ed Kirby, NAB Code Compliance Committee, to NAB Board of Directors, Sept. 24, 1940 (the emphasis is Kirby's), Early Papers, box 2, file: "Coughlin, Father." For the NAB's attitudes toward self-regulation see Neville Miller, "Self-Regulation in American Radio," *Annals* 213 (Jan. 1941): 95–96, and for its actions against Coughlin see Brown, "Selling Airtime for Controversy," pp. 207–8.

28. Robert J. Landry, "Radio and Government," *Public Opinion* , Oct. 1938, pp. 557–69, 563, in Clark Papers, series 116, box 437; Barnouw, *The Golden Web*, p. 30.

29. See SICC, 74th Cong., 1st sess., Confirmation of the Members of the FCC (S474-4), Jan. 23–Feb. 2, 1935, p. 40.

30. Ibid. For the gifts rule see Barnouw, *The Golden Web*, p. 31.

31. Paul W. Ward, "Scandal in the Air," *Nation* 144 (Apr. 1937): 455–56.

32. Ibid. For discussion of the Connery-McFarlane resolution see *Cong. Rec.*, House, 75th Cong., 3rd sess., 1932, 83, pts. 1–12 passim.

33. McIntyre to Hodges, July 23, 1937, FDRP, OF 1059, box 1, file: "FCC 1937."

34. "How Free Is the Air?" *Nation* 143 (July 1936): 5.

35. Robert J. Landry, "Radio and Government," *Public Opinion*, Oct. 1938, p. 563, in Clark Papers, series 116, box 437.

36. See Mackey, "The Development of the National Association of Broadcasters," p. 321.

37. See Sterling and Kitross, *Stay Tuned*, pp. 154, 158, 189.

38. Quoted in Kang, "Franklin Roosevelt and James L. Fly," p. 28.

39. Barnouw, *The Golden Web*, p. 33.

40. Ibid., pp. 168–73.

41. Quoted in Sterling and Kitross, *Stay Tuned*, p. 190.

42. *National Broadcasting Company* v. *United States* 319 U.S. 138 (1943).

43. Fly, "Regulation of Radio in the Pubic Interest," *Annals* 213 (Jan. 1941): 106–7.
44. Ernst, *The First Freedom*, p. 177.
45. Koppes, "The Social Destiny of Radio," p. 375.
46. Sterling and Kitross, *Stay Tuned*, pp. 197, 243.
47. McChesney, *Telecommunications, Mass Media, and Democracy*, p. 261.

7 | *The Sellers*

1. "Radio Makes Better Citizens," *Wireless Age*, Oct. 1922, p. 26, in Clark Papers, series 14, box 197.

2. Archer, *History of Radio*, p. 352; *New York Times*, Oct. 19, 1924, p. 7, and Sept. 5, 1925, p. 1; *Radio Broadcast* 7 (Oct. 1925): 740.

3. Dunlap, *Talking on the Radio*, p. 139, and *Education by Radio* 3 (1933): 12, 23, and 37.

4. See *Nation* 118 (Apr. 16, 1924): 413; Prostak, "Up in the Air," p. 165, Broadcast Pioneers Library, F 254; Norman Thomas to William E. Borah, Apr. 30, 1926, Borah Papers, box 217, file: "1925–1926 Radio/ Re. Leg."; *Nation* 122 (June 2, 1926): 593; *New York Times*, May 3, 1927, p. 23.

5. See chapter 3, above.

6. Section 18 of the Radio Act of 1927, with changes made in the Communications Act of 1934 in brackets: "If any licensee shall permit a person who is a legally qualified candidate for any public office to use a broadcasting station, he shall afford equal opportunities to all other such candidates for that office in the use of such broadcasting station, and the licensing authority [Commission] shall make rules and regulations to carry this provision into effect: *Provided*, That such licensee shall have no power of censorship over the material broadcast under the provisions of this paragraph [section]. No obligation is hereby imposed upon any licensee to allow the use of its station by any such candidate."

7. See David Lawrence quoted in Rose, *National Policy for Radio Broadcasting*, p. 206. See also MacNeil, *The People Machine*, pp. 281ff., and Rorty, *Order on the Air!* p. 12.

8. FRC, Regulation 178. See FRC, *Rules and Regulations*, 1934, p. 52. For Lafount's statement see *New York Times*, Sept. 2, 1932, p. 18.

9. NBC MSS, file 338, July 2 and 12, 1938.

10. *Cong. Rec.*, House, 74th Cong., 1st sess., 1935, 79, pt. 13:14399–401. For the change in 1960 see Smith, *Perspectives on Radio and Television*, p. 348.

11. *New York Times*, July 29, 1928, sec. 8, p. 12.

12. William H. Harkness, Reminiscences, Columbia University Oral History Project, Radio Pioneers, p. 59.

13. Benjamin, "Broadcast Campaign Precedents," pp. 450–52; *New York Times*, Jan. 6, 1924, p. 12.

14. James H. MacLafferty to Martin Rice, Director of Broadcasting, GEC, June 1, 1924, and Rice to MacLafferty, June 6, 1924, Young Papers, file 11-14-50, box 3.

15. See Young to Harbord, June 5, 1924, and Harbord to Young, June 10, 1924, Young Papers, file 11-14-50, box 3; *New York Times*, July 19, 1924, p. 1, and July 29, 1924, p. 4.

16. Charles Popenoe to David Sarnoff, Nov. 14, 1924, NBC MSS, file 341; *New York Times*, Oct. 17, 1924, p. 3, and Oct. 18, 1924, p. 14.

17. P. F. Peter to G. W. Johnstone, NBC Interdepartmental Correspondence, July 1, 1932, NBCR, box 13, folder 12, file: "Conventions: Democratic and Republican 1932." For convention coverage in 1924 see *New York Times*, June 8, 1924, sec. 8, p. 19, June 22, 1924, sec. 8, p. 16, and July 6, 1924, sec.8, p. 13.

18. Charles Popenoe to David Sarnoff, Nov. 14, 1924, and Nov. 19, 1924, NBC MSS, file 341, "Political Broadcasting: National Campaign 1924."

19. For RCA's policy see Charles Popenoe to David Sarnoff, Nov. 14, 1924, NBC MSS, file 341. For the unnamed Boston station's policy see *New York Times*, Aug. 7, 1924, p. 1.

20. *Nation* 119 (Oct. 1924): 446.

21. Benjamin, "Broadcast Campaign Precedents," p. 454.

22. *New York Times*, Apr. 29, 1927, p. 14, and Denison, "Editorial Policies of the Broadcasting Companies," p. 73. Aylesworth quoted in Prostak, "Up in the Air," p. 172.

23. Young to Sarnoff and Aylesworth, Oct. 16, 1934, Young Papers, file 131/2675.

24. *New York Times*, Oct. 23, 1932, sec.8, p. 6; telegram from T. F. Allen of NBC to John Biggs, Oct. 20, 1932, NBCR, box 9, folder 1; telegram from T. F. Allen to Sen. Kaney, Oct. 27, 1932, ibid., box 8, folder 62; Merlin Aylesworth to Clarence C. Dill, Oct. 13, 1932, ibid., box 9, folder 1.

25. NBCR, box 13, folder 14, "Political Campaign Broadcasts 1932."

26. Figures for 1928 from P. F. Peter to G. W. Johnstone, NBC Interdepartmental Correspondence, July 1, 1932, NBCR, box 13, folder 12, file: "Conventions: Democratic and Republican 1932." Figures for 1932 from NBC, "Traffic Report Covering Democratic Convention," July 19, 1932, NBCR, box 8, file 61.

27. Liebovich, *Bylines in Despair*, p. 72.

28. NBC, "Memorandum on Broadcasting of Conventions," July 14, 1932, NBCR, box 13, folder 13; telegram to NBC from P. D. Phelps and family, NBCR, box 13, folder 53.

29. See CBS flyer, "Columbia Network Mobilizes for Record Inaugural Broadcasts," Young Papers, file 134, folder 267Y.

30. See NBC, "Broadcasting of Associated Press Election Returns, Nov. 8, 1932," NBCR, box 9, folder 38: "Election Returns Broadcast 1932."

31. Avery Marks to John W. Elwood, "Election Returns," NBC Interdepartmental Correspondence, Oct. 24, 1932, NBCR, box 9, folder 38.

32. Liebovich, *Bylines in Despair*, p. 135.

33. Sweetser to John Elwood, Aug. 22, 1928. See also, H. C. Smith to Elwood, NBC internal memorandum, Aug. 25, 1928, NBCR, box 4, folder 97, file: "Political Campaign 1928."

34. Sweetser to Elwood, Sept. 25 and 28, 1928, NBCR, box 4, folder 97, file: "Political Campaign 1928."

35. See *New York Times*, Oct. 23, 1932, sec.8, p. 6.

36. A. A. Schechter, Memorandum to Station Editors, July 1, 1936, NBC MSS, file 342.

37. R. Clements, Night Program Office, memo to John F. Royal, Sept. 24, 1940, and "Williams" telegram to Royal, Sept. 25, 1940, ibid., file 342. See also Dorothy Kemble, memo to Bertha Brainard, Apr. 27, 1938, ibid., file 332.

38. Frank M. Russell to Richard C. Patterson Jr., NBC Interdepartment Correspondence, Feb. 16, 1935, and Mar. 13, 1934, NBC MSS, file 341.

39. Sabin to Richard J. Patterson Jr., Sept. 14, 1935, NBCR, box 41, folder 4, file: "Republican National Party—General 1935."

40. NAB Press Release, Aug. 7, 1940, NBC MSS, file 337.

41. See *New York Times*, Sept. 11, 1936, p. 5; Early memorandum to Michelson, Sept. 15, 1936, Early Papers, box 11, file: "Michelson, Charles."

42. *New York Times*, Aug. 30, 1936, sec. 9, p. 10; George E. Johnson to NBC, Sept. 16, 1936, NBC MSS, file 331.

43. NBC memo, "Political Broadcasts," Jan. 8, 1936, ibid., file 340; Lenox Lohr, memo to J. V. O'Connell, Sept. 2, 1936, NBC MSS, file 340. See also NBC Interdepartment Correspondence, J. V. O'Connell to Sales Staff, Aug. 11, 1938, Walter Myers Collection.

44. CBS, *Political Broadcasts.*

45. Thomas Sabin, Director, Radio Division, RNC, to Klauber, Dec. 13, 1935, and Klauber to Sabin, Dec. 27, 1935, in CBS, *Political Broadcasts*, n.p.

46. Fletcher to Paley, Jan. 13, 1936, and Paley to Fletcher, Jan. 8, 1936, ibid.

47. Klauber to Sabin, Dec. 27, 1935, ibid.

48. Fletcher to Paley, Jan. 1, 1936, and Paley to Fletcher, Jan. 2, 1936, ibid.

49. Paley to Fletcher, Jan. 13, 1936, ibid.

50. See Lohr to Fletcher, Jan. 8, 1936, NBCR, box 49, file 14: "Political Broadcasts; Republican National Committee, Jan.–June 1936."

51. *New York Times*, Jan. 14, 1936, p. 1.

52. For a transcript of these advertisements see *New York Times*, Jan. 15, 1936, p. 1.

53. See, for example, the David Sarnoff file in FDRP, PPF 3872.

54. FDR to Lohr, Feb. 12, 1936, FDRP, PPF 477, and Russell to Early, undated, Early Papers, box 34, file: "Radio—Miscellaneous Official Correspondence."

55. Butcher to Early, Nov. 4, 1936, FDRP, OF 256, box 1, file: "CBS 1936–1939."

56. Russell to Early, Oct. 13, 1937, Early Papers, box 16, file: "Russell, Frank M."

57. *New York Times*, Oct. 18, 1936, p. 1, Oct. 19, 1936, p. 1, and Oct. 20, 1936, p.

8; *Literary Digest* 122 (Oct. 1936): 17; Butcher to McIntyre, Nov. 4, 1936, FDRP, OF 256, box 1, file: "CBS, 1936–1939."

58. See Leo Keiran to Judge Kross, Oct. 25, 1940, Records of the National Committee of Independent Voters for Roosevelt and Wallace, box 1, file: "Radio."

59. See WCLO to LaFollette, Aug. 5, 1940, WTAQ to LaFollette, Sept. 10, 1940, and WTMJ to LaFollette, Oct. 29, 1940, LaFollette Papers, container 522, file: "Radio (1940)." The capitalization is WCLO's.

60. Charles Popenoe to David Sarnoff, Nov. 14, 1924, NBC MSS, file 341.

61. Aylesworth to Owen D. Young, June 2, 1928, Young Papers, 11-14-50, box 10.

62. NBCR, box 4, file 96.

63. *New York Times*, Oct. 27, 1936, p. 10.

64. See *Literary Digest* 121 (Mar. 1936): 37; *New York Times*, Mar. 5, 1936, p. 16, and Mar. 6, 1936, p. 9.

65. *New York Times*, June 24, 1936, p. 12; John F. Royal to Lenox Lohr, Interdepartment Correspondence, Mar. 6, 1936, and NBC memos, NBCR, box 49, file 3: "Political Broadcasts, Communist Party of USA, 1936."

66. NAB Press Release, May 31, 1940, NBC MSS, file 337.

67. A. L. Ashby to John F. Royal, June 1, 1940, ibid.

68. For 1932 figures see F. M. Greene to T. F. Allen, internal NBC memo, Nov. 17, 1932, NBCR, box 13, file 10: "Political Broadcasts—Election Coverage 1932." For 1936 figures see table 2.

69. John Elwood to G. F. McClelland, internal NBC memorandum, Jan. 20, 1932, NBCR, box 20, file 45: "Political Broadcasts I 1933."

70. Pratt to Elwood, NBC Interdepartment Correspondence, Aug. 9, 1932, ibid., box 13, file 52: "Republican Campaign 1932."

71. F. M. Greene to T. F. Allen, internal NBC memorandum, Nov. 17, 1932, ibid., box 13, file 10: "Political Broadcasts—Election Coverage 1932."

72. Mark Woods to John Elwood, internal NBC memorandum, Oct. 20, 1932, ibid., box 8, folder 60, file: "Democratic Campaign 1932."

73. FDRP, PSF, box 129, file: "Democratic National Committee, 1932–43."

74. Mark Woods to George F. McClelland, internal NBC memo, Jan. 23, 1933, NBCR, box 20, folder 45, file: "Political Broadcasts I 1933."

75. M. H. Aylesworth to George F. Getz, Dec. 5, 1933, ibid., box 13, folder 52, file: "Republican Campaign 1932."

76. R. C. Patterson to W. Forbes Morgan, Dec. 5, 1935, ibid., box 49, folder 11, file: "Political Broadcasts, Indebtedness."

77. See William S. Hedges to Niles Trammell, NBC Interdepartment Correspondence, Feb. 9, 1940, NBC MSS, file 337.

78. NBC Interdepartment Correspondence between Lohr and 12 NBC executives between Mar. 10 and 28, 1936, NBC MSS, file 340; Lenox Lohr to J. V. McConnell, internal NBC memorandum, Sept. 2, 1936, ibid.

79. A. L. Ashby to Niles Trammell, NBC Interdepartment Correspondence, Jan. 30, 1940, NBC MSS, file 337.

80. Royal to Trammell, NBC Interdepartment Correspondence, Feb. 13, 1940, ibid. The emphases are Royal's.

81. NBC Sales-Research Division pamphlet, "Advertisers Using NBC, CBS & MBS Network Facilities: A Month by Month Record from Jan. 1933 to Dec. 1939 Incl.," ibid., file 640.

82. Internal NBC memorandum, "Talks by Herbert Hoover, June 1928 thru 1931, and Franklin D. Roosevelt, June 1932 thru 1935," NBCR, box 49, file 17: "Political Broadcasts; Statistics 1936."

83. Frank M. Russell to John Royal, internal NBC memorandum, June 5, 1935, NBC MSS, file 341.

8 | *The Buyers*

1. *New York Times*, Mar. 31, 1922, p. 1, Apr. 1, 1922, p. 7, and Apr. 2, 1922, p. 20; *Literary Digest* 73 (Apr. 1922): 24.

2. *New York Times*, Nov. 7, 1921, p. 2, and Nov. 8, 1921, p. 1.

3. McDonald to Coolidge, Nov. 5, 1923, Coolidge Papers, reel 79, case file 136: "Radio—General."

4. Quoted in Malcolm Lee Cross, "Calvin Coolidge," in Sprague, ed., *Popular Images of American Presidents*, p. 315.

5. Edward J. Wilson to Coolidge, Mar. 27, 1924, Coolidge Papers, reel 79, case file 136. Michelson quoted in Archer, *History of Radio*, p. 346.

6. Bryan: Dunlap, *Talking on the Radio*, p. 68; Smith: *Radio Broadcast* 7 (Oct. 1925): 740; McAdoo: *New York Times*, Feb. 20, 1924, p. 6, and *New Republic*, Mar. 19, 1924, pp. 91–93.

7. Nicholson, "Keep off the Grass: A Memorandum for Governor Smith and Mr. McAdoo," *Century Magazine*, May 1927, p. 1, in Jesse H. Jones Papers, box 183, file: "Democratic Party, 1927."

8. *New York Times*, Aug. 1, 1924, p. 2; Dunlap, *Talking on the Radio*, p. 70.

9. NARA, RG 173, entry 1, box 64, file 1045: "Plan for Republican Broadcasting"; Lupton A. Wilkinson, Assistant Publicity Director, to George Barr Baker, RNC Publicity Director, June 30, 1924, and "Budget for 1924 Campaign," undated, George Barr Baker Papers, box 1, file: "Coolidge, Calvin."

10. Overacker, *Money in Elections*, p. 75.

11. Tilson to C. Bascom Slemp, Nov. 15, 1924, Coolidge Papers, reel 80, case file 136: "Radio—General."

12. Barton to George Barr Baker, July 7, 1924, Barton Papers, box 13, file: "Coolidge, Calvin."

13. For evidence of an abortive effort by Democrats to seek assistance from RCA in its campaign, see Stuart Crocker to E. E. Boucher of RCA, July 18, 1924, Young

Papers, file 15-29 (box 1 of 16). For the 1924 campaign see Burner, *Politics of Provincialism*, pp. 103–41, and Craig, *After Wilson*, pp. 51–74.

14. See John M. Nelson, Chairman and National Manager, "Financial Report of LaFollette-Wheeler Campaign as at Oct. 10, 1924," Robert LaFollette Sr. Papers, box 205, folder: "1924 LaFollette-Wheeler Campaign—Financial Papers."

15. Report of David K. Niles, Chicago, Sept. 1924, ibid., box 203, folder: "LaFollette-Wheeler Campaign: Financial Reports."

16. *Washington Evening Star*, Feb. 2, 1925, in Wile Papers, reel 2; *New York Times*, Feb. 5, 1925, p. 18.

17. Craig, *After Wilson*, p. 176.

18. Jamieson, *Packaging the Presidency*, p. 25.

19. RNC "Proposed Budget as Developed in Conference Aug. 22nd and 23rd between the Several Department Heads and the Treasurer," 1928, HHPL, Campaign and Transition, box 162, subject: "Republican National Committee." For later budgets see Ralph D. Casey, "Party Campaign Propaganda," *Annals* 179 (May 1935): 101.

20. DNC, "Democratic National Committee Budget 1928," Young Papers, file 15-29, box 3 of 16. For revisions to the DNC radio budget see *New York Times*, Sept. 1, 1928, p. 12. For RNC figures see ibid., Feb. 17, 1929, sec. 9, p. 19. The exact figures for the RNC were $435,894 for radio, and a total publicity and advertising cost of $2,016,872.

21. *New York Times*, Sept. 9, 1928, sec. 1, p. 2.

22. RNC Press Release, John Q. Tilson, Eastern Speakers Bureau, Sept. 19, 1928, HHPL, Campaign and Transition Collection, box 206, file: "Subject: Radio." See also RNC Press Release, Eastern Speakers Bureau, Oct. 11, 1928, for an example of the Minute Men's broadcast schedule, and Liebovich, *Bylines in Despair*, pp. 73–74.

23. *New York Times*, Aug. 31, 1928, p. 4, Sept. 14, 1928, p. 6, and Sept. 16, 1928, p. 7.

24. Ibid., Sept. 9, 1928, sec. 1, p. 2.

25. Diamond and Bates, *The Spot*, p. 36; Liebovich, *Bylines in Despair*, p. 73; *New York Times*, Sept. 9, 1928, sec. 1, p. 2.

26. West, *The Rape of Radio*, p. 427. For Smith's radio manner see *New York Times*, Sept. 16, 1928, sec. 12, p. 10. R. W. Rainey quoted in George H. Mayer, *The Republican Party 1854–1964* (New York: Oxford University Press, 1964), p. 409.

27. Israels to H. C. Smith, Oct. 11, 1928, NBCR, box 3, file 9.

28. *New York Times*, Nov. 8, 1928, p. 28. Turnout figures quoted in *HSUS*, pt. 2, p. 1071.

29. NBCR, box 49, file 17.

30. Liebovich, *Bylines in Despair*, p. 194.

31. Ibid., pp. 86–130, 194, and 135.

32. Charlemagne Sloan to Hoover, undated (internal evidence suggests Aug. 1932), HHPL, PPSF, box 149, file: "Federal Radio Commission Correspondence—1932, July–Aug."

33. Paley to Hoover, Dec. 17, 1929, and George Akerson, Secretary to the President, to Elwood, Sept. 13, 1930, HIA, HCHP, Presidential Files, box 34, file: "FRC: Jan.–Dec. 1929."

34. John Elwood, Vice-president of NBC, to Hoover, Aug. 6, 1930, HCHP, PSF, box 148, file: "Federal Radio Commission Correspondence 1930 July–Aug."

35. File note, Apr. 1, 1931, ibid., box 148, file: "Federal Radio Commission Correspondence 1931 Mar.–Apr."

36. For Michelson's publicity efforts see Raskob Papers, file 602.

37. Overacker, *Money in Elections*, p. 29.

38. *New York Times*, June 12, 1932, sec. 9, p. 5.

39. Peel and Donnelly, *The 1932 Campaign*, p. 121. DNC and RNC expenditures quoted in *HSUS*, 2:1081. Rickard to Gibson, Oct. 18, 1932, Gibson Papers, box 58, file: "Rickard, Edgar 1930–1939."

40. For early radio budgets see *New York Times*, Aug. 30, 1932, p. 4. For NBC's billing records see NBCR, box 8, folder 60: "Democratic Campaign 1932," and folder 63: "Democratic National Committee Nov. 1932." See also Frank C. Walker to Lloyd C. Thomas, Nov. 17, 1932, ibid., box 8, folder 63.

41. See HHPL, PSF B269.

42. Ward Gravatt to Hoover, Sept. 24, 1932, ibid., box 252, folder: "Federal Radio Commission, Correspondence, misc. 1932."

43. L. F. Strand to Hoover, Sept. 17, 1932, ibid., box 252, folder: "Federal Radio Commission, Correspondence, misc. 1932." Capitalization and punctuation are Strand's.

44. White, *FDR and the Press*, pp. 94–118; Winfield, *FDR and the News Media*, p. 107; Buhite and Levy, *FDR's Fireside Chats*, p. xvii; Chase, *Sound and Fury*, p. 107; Best, *The Critical Press and the New Deal*, p. 11; Braden and Bradenburg, "FDR's Voice and Pronunciation" and "Roosevelt's Fireside Chats"; Ryan, *Franklin D. Roosevelt's Rhetorical Presidency*, pp. 19–24.

45. Robinton to Farley, July 13, 1930, Howe Papers, box 50, file: "Radio."

46. *New York Times*, June 18, 1933, sec. 6, p. 17; Best, *The Critical Press and the New Deal*, p. 11; Buhite and Levy, *FDR's Fireside Chats*.

47. Sullivan quoted in Best, *The Critical Press and the New Deal*, p. 11. For assessments of FDR's radio voice see *New York Times*, June 18, 1933, sec. 6, p. 17; Braden and Bradenburg, "FDR's Voice and Pronunciation"; Robert E. Gilbert, "Franklin Delano Roosevelt," in Sprague, ed., *Popular Images of American Presidents*, 358–60.

48. These points are drawn from Buhite and Levy, *FDR's Fireside Chats*, pp. xvii–xviii, and Winfield, *FDR and the News Media*, p. 107.

49. Averages calculated from data provided in Winfield, *FDR and the News Media*, p. 121.

50. See White, *FDR and the Press*, pp. 69–71.

51. Roosevelt quoted in White, *FDR and the Press*, p.129. See chapter 6, above.

52. Hugh Gallagher, *FDR's Splendid Deception: The Moving Story of Roosevelt's Mas-*

sive Disability and the Intense Efforts to Conceal It (Arlington, Va.: Vandamere Press, 1994).

53. Winfield, *FDR and the News Media*, p. 79.

54. Lawrence quoted in Best, *The Critical Press and the New Deal*, p. 8. Statistics on federal government publicity efforts after 1933 cited in Winfield, *FDR and the News Media*, p. 93; Steele, *Propaganda in an Open Society*, pp. 48–49; McCamy, *Government Publicity*, pp. 223–26; Best, *The Critical Press and the New Deal*, p. 8.

55. "Script of WPA Nation-wide Radio Staff Meeting," June 22, 1936, Hopkins Papers, box 53, file: "Radio Staff Meeting—June 1936."

56. Quoted in Best, *The Critical Press and the New Deal*, p. 20.

57. For Coughlin and Long's biographies see Brinkley, *Voices of Protest.*

58. See Mitchell, *Campaign of the Century*, p. 126; Brown, "Selling Airtime," p. 202. Coughlin's money order receipts calculated from figures in Farley Papers, Private File, reel 2, July 9, 1936. For Coughlin's difficulties with CBS in 1931 see Borah Papers, box 24, file: "Radio 1930–1931."

59. Brinkley, *Voices of Protest*, pp. 93–123. Coughlin quoted in Brown, "Selling Airtime," p. 203. See also Coughlin, *Selected Discourses.*

60. Lee and Briant, eds., *The Fine Art of Propaganda: A Study of Father Coughlin's Speeches.*

61. For Long's radio activities as governor of Louisiana and then United States senator see Merriam and Gosnell, *The American Party System*, 4th ed., p. 373. For a technical description of Long's radio technique see Bormann, "This Is Huey P. Long Talking."

62. Brinkley, *Voices of Protest*, p. 72.

63. "Address of Huey P. Long, 2/4/35 over Radio Station WDSU," Howe Papers, box 91, file: "Radio—Sept. 1934–Nov. 1935."

64. Quoted in Barnouw, *The Golden Web*, p. 48.

65. NBCR, box 20, file 6: "Political Broadcasts II 1933."

66. LaFollette Papers, container C510, file: "1934 Campaign—Post Primary."

67. Mitchell, *Campaign of the Century.*

68. *New York Times*, May 10, 1936, sec. 11, p. 10.

69. "Budget for the Democratic National Campaign of 1936," FDRP, PSF, box 129, file: "DNC 1932–43"; Farley Papers, box 53, file: "DNC Receipts and Disbursements Jan. 1, 1936 to Dec. 31, 1936." The figure of $540,000 did not represent total Democratic spending on radio in 1936; large additional amounts were spent by the various state party organizations and by independent pro-Roosevelt groups.

70. See *New York Times*, June 26, 1936, p. 13.

71. Casey, "Republican Propaganda," pp. 33–34.

72. Fred S. Purnell to Lammot du Pont, Oct. 9, 1936, and William A. Hart to Purnell, Oct. 13, 1936, E. I. DuPont de Nemours and Company Records, box 3, file: "Advertising Department 1936." For the Democratic response see Stephen Early to Charles Michelson, Aug. 5, 1936, Early Papers, box 11, file: "Michelson, Charles."

73. Michelson quoted in *New York Times*, Nov. 15, 1936, sec. 4, p. 10.

74. Barnouw, *The Golden Web*, p. 144. Total expenditures for 1940 quoted in *HSUS*, 2:1081.

75. Black, *Democratic Party Publicity 1940*, p. 44.

76. See RNC Publicity Division, "Urgent Radio Notice!" Oct. 14, 1940, Sullivan Papers, box 35, file: "Presidential Election of 1940."

77. "Spot Radio Campaign—Women's Division," National Committee for Roosevelt and Wallace 1940, box 5, file: "Radio, Screen and Personal Appearances (1)."

78. For the Women's Division report for 1940 see Dewson Papers, box 2, file: "McAllister, Thomas and Dorothy, 1937–1960." See also circular letter to all state vice-chairmen of the Women's Division, June 26, 1940, and DNC Women's Division pamphlet, "The Favored State Party Set Up for Democratic Women," FDRP, PPF 603, file 1: 1933–1939; Women's Division pamphlets, "Campaigning by Radio" and "The Director of Radio," 1940, DNC—Women's Division Collection Papers, box 283, file: "1940—Radio Publicity." See also Helen Moodie, "Campaigning on the Air," *Democratic Digest*, June–July, 1940, p. 79, in FDRP, PPF 603, file 3.

79. NBC sold $3,455.28 of time to the Socialist Labor Party and $5,527.24 to the CPA. Total NBC billings to all parties in 1940 was $873,459.72: NBC Interdepartmental Correspondence, 1940 Political Sales Report, Submitted by Walter Myers, Broadcast Pioneers Library Collections, file 82: "Broadcasting in Political Campaigns."

9 | The Product

1. Merriam, *The American Party System*, 2d ed., 1929, p. 317. See also Jordan, *Machine-Age Ideology*, pp. 144–47.

2. Peel and Donnelly, *The 1932 Campaign*, p. 146.

3. *Collier's* 1 (June 1928): 54.

4. Blythe, "Political Publicity," p. 9.

5. *New York Times*, Oct. 26, 1930, sec. 5, p. 10.

6. "Spellbinding," *Saturday Evening Post*, undated, in Smith Private Papers, file 508.

7. See Helen Lowry, "Political Revolution by Radio," *New York Times*, July 20, 1924, sec. 4, p. 1.

8. Dunlap, *Speaking on the Radio*, p. 76.

9. Ibid., p. 30. See also Cantril and Allport, *The Psychology of Radio*, p. 31, and Federal Council of Churches, *Broadcasting and the Public*, p. 160.

10. Robinson, *Radio Networks and the Federal Government*, p. 85; Young to Baker, Sept. 15, 1927, Young Papers, File 1-98: "Baker, Newton D."

11. *New York Times*, Mar. 25, 1928, sec. 10, p. 16.

12. Dunlap, *Talking on the Radio*, pp. 33, 16.

13. Ibid., pp. 209–15.

14. *New York Times*, Sept. 16, 1928, sec. 12, p. 10, and Nov. 6, 1932, sec. 8, p. 6.

15. McGerr, *The Decline of Popular Politics*, pp. 40, 69–70, 130.

16. See Robert B. Westbrook, "Politics as Consumption," in Fox and Lears, eds., *The Culture of Consumption*, p. 152, and McGerr, *The Decline of Popular Politics*, pp. 144, 160.

17. For motion pictures in campaigns see Dinkin, *Campaigning in America*, p. 133; Munro, *The Invisible Government*, p. 109.

18. Sidney Arthur to Walsh, July 3, 1924, Walsh Papers, box 373, file: "1924 A-B." See also J. L. Hines to Walsh, July 10, 1924, Walsh Papers, box 374, unnamed file.

19. See "Radio Takes the Stump," *New York Times*, Mar. 9, 1924, sec. 4, p. 9.

20. McGerr, *The Decline of Popular Politics*, pp. 36ff.

21. See "Radio Takes the Bunk out of Campaigns," *New York Times*, Oct. 26, 1930, sec. 5, p. 10; HHPL, Campaign and Transition Materials, box 162, subject: "Republican National Committee—Speakers Bureau."

22. For FDR's 1936 western tour see "List of members of Party—the President's Western Trip, Oct. 8–17, 1936," Farley Papers, reel 2, private file, Oct. 1936. For RNC publicity efforts see Casey, "Republican Propaganda in the 1936 Campaign," pp. 34–43.

23. Quoted in *Literary Digest* 182 (Aug. 1924): 11.

24. *New York Times*, July 20, 1924, sec. 4, p. 1.

25. *Richmond Times-Dispatch* quoted in *Literary Digest* 99 (Dec. 1928): 13. See also Blythe, "Political Publicity," p. 141; *New York Times*, July 4, 1924, p. 12.

26. *Omaha World-Herald* quoted in *Literary Digest* 99 (Dec. 1928): 13; White quoted in *New York Times*, Oct. 28, 1928, sec.10, p. 16; Michael F. Holt, *The Political Crisis of the 1850s* (New York: W. W. Norton, 1978), p. 61.

27. *New York Times*, Oct. 26, 1930, sec. 5, p. 10; "The Big Show at Houston," *Nation* 127 (July 1928): 34; "Our Radio Battle for the Presidency," *New York Times*, Oct. 28, 1928, sec.10, p.1.

28. "Radio Politics," *New Republic*, Mar. 19, 1924, pp. 91–93, in the Moley Papers, box 197, file: "Radio."

29. Quoted in *Literary Digest* 182 (Aug. 1924): 11.

30. Lynd and Lynd, *Middletown*, pp. 416–17. Fitzgerald quoted in Leuchtenburg, *The Perils of Prosperity*, p. 83; Lippmann quoted in Ronald Steele, *Walter Lippmann and the American Century* (New York: Vintage Books, 1981), p. 257.

31. Bliven, "How Radio Is Remaking Our World," p. 155. See also "Politics by Radio," *Nation* 118 (Jan. 2, 1924): 5; Frederick Lewis Allen, *Only Yesterday: An Informal History of the 1920s* (Harper and Row, 1931), p. 137.

32. Irwin, *Propaganda and the News*, pp. 249–50.

33. See Mark Sullivan, "Radio Audience Likely to Alter Political Ethics," *New York Tribune*, July 7, 1932, NBCR, box 8, file 64: "Democratic National Convention, Chicago, 1932."

34. See *New York Times*, Oct. 29, 1932, p. 14, Sept. 26, 1932, p. 14, and Oct. 21, 1936, p. 26.

35. Ibid., Feb. 9, 1936, sec. 8, p. 3.

36. *The World*, Mar. 2, 1921, in the Wilbur Papers, box 95, file: "Political—Misc. Corr. 1921–1927."

37. *New York Times*, Aug. 12, 1928, sec. 2, p. 1.

38. Overacker, *Money in Elections*, p. 80. See also MacNeil, *The People Machine*, p. 228, and Abrams and Settle, "Broadcasting and the Political Spending 'Arms Race,'" who argue that TV, and not radio, caused campaign costs to inflate.

39. Blythe, "Political Publicity," p. 9; and Barnard, "Radio Politics," *New Republic*, Mar. 19, 1924, p. 93.

40. Pegg, *Broadcasting and Society*, pp. 186–91.

41. For the king's speech see *New York Times*, Jan. 12, 1924, p. 5. For the BBC's programming during the 1923 and 1924 elections see Eric Estorick, "British Broadcasting and Discussion of Public Issues," *Annals* 213 (Jan. 1941): 50; McIntyre, *The Expense of Glory*, p. 133. For election programming in 1929, 1931, and 1935 see Briggs, *The History of Broadcasting in the United Kingdom*, 2:133–41.

42. Chamberlain and the *Daily Express* poll quoted in ibid., pp. 132, 139.

43. Quoted in the Australian Royal Commission on Television, p. 123.

44. Hard, "Europe's Air and Ours," p. 505. For the BBC's attitude toward controversial material see Eckersley, *The Power Behind the Microphone*, pp. 157–60, and on the General Strike see Pegg, *Broadcasting and Society*, pp. 175–85; Briggs, *History of British Broadcasting*, 1:360–84; McIntyre, *The Expense of Glory*, pp.145–46; Estorick, "British Broadcasting and Discussion of Public Issues," *Annals* 213 (Jan. 1941): 49–50.

45. Scannell and Cardiff, *A Social History of British Broadcasting*, p. 55.

46. *New York Times*, July 25, 1923, p. 9, and Dec. 1, 1924, p. 12.

47. Ibid., Sept. 30, 1932, p. 18.

48. Quoted in Hale, *Radio Power*, p. 1. See also Zeman, *Nazi Propaganda*, pp. 38–53; Sington and Weidenfeld, *The Goebbels Experiment*, pp. 140–45.

49. Johnson, *The Unseen Voice*, pp. 192–93, 32–35.

50. See Inglis, *This Is the ABC*, pp. 15, 31, 61; Johnson, *The Unseen Voice*, p. 177; Jones, *Something in the Air*, pp. 43–44.

51. Australian Royal Commission on Television, p. 133.

52. Nolan, "Canadian Election Broadcasting," p. 177. King quoted in McNeil and Wolfe, *Signing On*, p. 190.

53. Nolan, "Canadian Election Broadcasting," pp. 180–85.

54. Kerwin, *The Control of Radio*, p. 14.

55. Hard, "Europe's Air and Ours," p. 501. The emphases are Hard's.

10 | The Consumers

1. Dos Passos, "The Radio Voice."

2. See Wolfe, "Some Reactions to the Advent of Campaigning by Radio," p. 306.

3. William S. Robinson, "Radio Comes to the Farmer," in Lazarsfeld and Stanton, eds., *Radio Research 1941*, p. 267.

4. NBC MSS, file 95, "NBC History: Draft by R. Chaplin 2/33"; Banks, "History of Broadcast Audience Response," p. 33.

5. *New York Times*, July 5, 1936, sec. 9, p. 10.

6. McNeil and Wolfe, *Signing On*, p. 71; Metz, *CBS*, p. 57.

7. William S. Robinson, "Radio Comes to the Farmer," in Lazarsfeld and Stanton, eds., *Radio Research 1941*, p. 272.

8. Cleon Mason to Hoover, Dec. 6, 1929, HHPL, PPSF, box 151, file: "Federal Radio Commission—Public Opinion and Relations 1929 Nov.–Dec."

9. HHPL, PPF 66.

10. Brill to Hoover, Oct. 6, 1932, HHPL, PPF 66, file: "Congratulations—Des Moines Speech Oct. 5, 1932, Br-By."

11. Barrell to Roosevelt, Mar. 13, 1933, FDRP, PPF 200B, container: "Mar. 13, 1933—B"; Anderson to Roosevelt, Mar. 24, 1933, ibid.

12. Crawford to Roosevelt, Mar. 16, 1933, ibid., container "C"; Merritt Fields to Roosevelt, Mar. 15. 1933, FDRP, OF 136, box 5, file: "Radio Broadcasts 1933 Jan.–June."

13. For responses to the Apr. 14, 1938 and Sept. 3, 1939 radio talks see FDRP, PPF 200B, container: "Apr. 14, 1938—Radio Broadcast," and "Sept. 3, 1939."

14. Joseph P. Lash, *Eleanor and Franklin: The Story of the Relationship Based on Eleanor Roosevelt's Private Papers* (New York: W. W. Norton, 1971), pp. 418–20.

15. Mrs. Eugene Burrell to Eleanor Roosevelt, Sept. 10, 1937, Eleanor Roosevelt Papers, Radio Listener Mail, box 1, file: "B, part 2"; anonymous to Eleanor Roosevelt, received July 25, 1940, Eleanor Roosevelt Papers, Radio Listener Mail, box 5, file: "Unanswered."

16. Johnson to NBC, Oct. 30, 1936, NBCR, box 49, file 3: "Political Broadcasting, Communist Party of America, 1936"; Kelly to NBC, Oct. 24, 1936, ibid.

17. Cantril, *Public Opinion 1935–1946*, p. 710.

18. James G. Peede to NBC, Oct. 14, 1936, and Hynds to NBC, Aug. 25, 1936, NBC MSS, file 331.

19. NBC Memorandum, Anita Barnard to Frank E. Mason, "Information Division Analysis—Election Mail—1940," Nov. 27, 1940, NBC MSS, file 337.

20. *New York Times*, Feb. 21, 1926, sec. 8, p. 17.

21. *Literary Digest* 116 (Nov. 1933): 7; 116 (Dec. 1933): 9; 116 (Dec. 1933): 8; 117 (Jan. 1934): 12.

22. Ibid. 121 (Mar. 1936): 22.

23. Banks, "A History of Broadcast Audience Research," pp. 28–30.

24. Paper, *Empire*, p. 46.

25. White, *The American Radio*, p. 115; Banks, "A History of Broadcast Audience Research," pp. 34ff.; A. M. Beville Jr., "The ABCD's of Radio Audiences," in Schramm, ed., *Mass Communication*, pp. 413–23. Crossley divided his income groups thus: Group A ($5,000 annual income and above): 6.7 percent, Group B ($3,000–$4,999): 13.3 percent, Group C ($2,000–$2,999): 26.7 percent, and Group D (below $2,000): 53.3 percent.

26. Banks, "A History of Broadcast Audience Measurement," pp. 55, 60, 115; White, *The American Radio*, p. 115.

27. *New York Times*, May 14, 1933, sec. 8, p. 6; Lumley, *Measurement in Radio;* Hettinger and Neff, *Practical Radio Advertising*.

28. John J. Karol, "Measuring Radio Audiences: A Critical Analysis of Current Techniques," *Printer's Ink*, Nov. 19, 1936, pp. 1–11.

29. Cantril, *Public Opinion 1935–1946*, pp. 710, 703, 587; *New York Times*, July 5, 1936, sec. 9, p. 10.

30. Butcher to Early, Jan. 15, 1940, FDRP, PPF 8617. See also Office of Public Opinion Research, Princeton University, "Comparison of Opinions of those who do and do not Listen to the President's Radio Talks," Sept. 17, 1941, FDRP, PSF, box 157, file: "Public Opinion Polls, 1935–1941."

31. Bryce quoted in Wallas, *Human Nature in Politics*, p. 144.

32. Bernays, *Crystallizing Public Opinion*, p. 107.

33. See Hettinger and Mead, *The Summer Radio Audience*; Lee and Lee, *The Fine Art of Propaganda*; Katz and Lazarsfeld, *Personal Influence*, pp. 17–21.

34. Lazarsfeld, *Radio and the Printed Page.* See also *The People's Choice*, p. 122.

35. Lazarsfeld, "The Change of Opinion," *Journal of Applied Psychology* 21 (Feb. 1939): 131–47.

36. Lazarsfeld et al., *The People's Choice*, pp. 94, 103. Lazarsfeld also attributed 3 percent to reconversion and 6 percent to partial conversion.

37. Ibid., pp. 65, 94, 127–28.

38. Lazarsfeld, "The Effects of Radio on Public Opinion," in Waples, ed., *Print, Radio, and Film in a Democracy*, pp. 74, 71. See also Berelson et al., *Voting: A Study of Opinion Formation in a Presidential Campaign;* Klapper, *The Effects of Mass Communication*, p. 16.

39. Katz and Lazarsfeld, *Personal Influence*, pp. 137–42.

40. Goode, *What About Radio?* pp. 39, 89–90, 208; Merton, *Mass Persuasion.*

41. Key, *Public Opinion and American Democracy*, pp. 356, 379, and 404; Smith, *Perspectives on Radio and Television*, pp. 544–60. See also see Klapper, *The Effects of Mass Media*, p. 15. For a more recent, and heavily qualified, acceptance of Lazarsfeld's theories, see McQuail, *Towards a Sociology of Mass Communications*, pp. 36, 45–46.

42. Samuel A. Stouffer, "A Sociologist Looks at Communication Research," in Waples, ed., *Print, Radio, and Film in a Democracy*, pp. 133–46; Herbert Blumer, "Suggestions for the Study of Mass-Media Effects," in Burdick and Brodbeck, eds., *American Voting Behavior*, pp. 197–208.

43. See Czitrom, *Media and the American Mind*, pp. 132, and 123–46; Denis McQuail, "The Influence and Effects of Mass Media," in Graber, ed., *Media Power in Politics*, pp. 21–22; Horkheimer and Adorno, *The Dialectic of Enlightenment*, pp. 120–67.

44. McQuail, *Towards a Sociology of Mass Communications*, p. 36. For his views on the superiority of the "American system" of broadcasting see Lazarsfeld, "The Effects

of Radio on Public Opinion," in Waples, ed., *Print, Radio, and Film in a Democracy*, 77; Czitrom, *Media and the American Mind*, p. 132.

45. Robert B. Westbrook, "Politics as Consumption: Managing the Modern American Election," in Fox and Lears, eds., *The Culture of Consumption*, p. 162. See also Meyrowitz, *No Sense of Place*, p. 73; Carey, *Communication as Culture*, pp. 147–48; Thompson, *Media and Modernity*, p. 38.

46. Seymour-Ure, *The Political Impact of the Mass Media*, p. 42. For similar views see Bigsby, *Approaches to Popular Culture*, p. 20; Lang and Lang, *Politics and Television*, p. 16; Allen, *Speaking about Soap Operas*, p. 22.

47. McQuail, "The Influence and Effects of Mass Media," in Graber, ed., *Media Power in Politics*, pp. 22–23. See also Curran et al., eds., *Mass Communication and Society;* De Fleur, *Theories of Mass Communication*, pp. 121ff.

11 | Radio and the Problem of Citizenship

1. Marvin, *When Old Technologies Were New*, p. 199; Fischer, *America Calling*, pp. 25ff.; Spigel, *Make Room for TV.* For de Tocqueville on technology and republicanism see *Democracy in America* (New York: New American Library, 1956), 2:163–68. For the most famous discussion of the problem facing geographically expansive republics, see James Madison, "Paper Number 10," in *The Federalist Papers*, ed. Roy P. Fairfield, 2d ed. (New York: Anchor Books, 1966), pp. 16–23. For technological utopianism see Leo Marx, *The Machine in the Garden: Technology and the Pastoral Ideal in America* (New York: Oxford University Press, 1964); Segal, *Technological Utopianism*; Nye, *American Technological Sublime*; John F. Kasson, *Civilizing the Machine: Technology and Republican Values in America, 1776–1900* (Harmondsworth: Penguin Books, 1976); Carey and Quirk, "The *Mythos* of the Electronic Revolution."

2. Louis Galambos, *The Public Image of Big Business in America, 1880–1940: A Quantitative Study in Social Change* (Baltimore: Johns Hopkins University Press, 1975).

3. Lippmann, *The Phantom Public*, p. 13; Dewey, "The New Paternalism," *New Republic*, Dec. 21, 1918, p. 216. See also T. J. Jackson Lears, "From Salvation to Self-Realization," in Fox and Lears, eds., *The Culture of Consumption*, p. 8; Robert M. Crunden, *From Self to Society, 1919–1941* (Englewood Cliffs: Prentice-Hall, 1972), p. x.

4. McGerr, *The Decline of Popular Politics*, pp. 185–87; Paul F. Bourke, "The Pluralist Reading of James Madison's Tenth *Federalist*," *Perspectives in American History* 9 (1975): 290.

5. Lippmann, *Public Opinion*, pp. 29–30, 16, 31, and *Liberty and the News*, pp. 4, 47.

6. Michael Kirkhorn, "This Curious Existence: Journalistic Identity in the Interwar Period," in Covert and Stevens, eds., *Mass Media between the Wars*, p. 136; Lippmann, *The Phantom Public*, p. 151.

7. Ibid., p. 43.

8. Eldridge, *The New Citizenship*, pp. 3, 44, 314.

9. Dewey, "The New Paternalism," pp. 216, 217, and *The Public and Its Problems*, pp. 135, 167.

10. Dewey, *Individualism Old and New*, pp. 41, 142; Carey, *Communication as Culture*, pp. 22, 82.

11. Ross quoted in Thomas Bender, *Community and Social Change in America* (New Brunswick: Rutgers University Press, 1978), p. 17.

12. Ibid., pp. 24, 45–120.

13. Leon Bramson, *The Political Context of Sociology* (Princeton, N.J.: Princeton University Press, 1961), pp. 27ff.; Martin, *The Behavior of Crowds*, pp. 48–50, 1; Cooley, *Social Organization*, p. 150; Young, *Source Book for Social Psychology*, pp. 722–37.

14. Lipsky, *Man the Puppet*, p. 58; Bent, *Machine-Made Man*, p. 10.

15. Ortega y Gasset, *Revolt of the Masses*, p. 76.

16. Nash, *Spectatoritis*, pp. 119, 122. See also Lipsky, *Man the Puppet*, pp. 65, 254; Martin, *The Behavior of Crowds*, pp. 287, 261; Mumford, *Technics and Civilization*, pp. 4, 241.

17. Cooley, *Social Organization*, pp. 81, 87.

18. William J. Donovan, "What Does the Future Hold?" in Tyson and Donovan, eds., *Retrospect and Forecast in Radio Education*, pp. 18, 28. See also Louis E. Kirstein, "Radio and Social Welfare," *Annals* 177 (Jan. 1935): 129–35; "Radio as a Crowd-Cure," *Literary Digest* 83 (Nov. 8, 1924): 80; West, *The Rape of Radio*, p. 286.

19. Kern, *The Culture of Time and Space;* Blondheim, *News over the Wires.*

20. Rothafel and Yates, *Broadcasting: Its New Day*, p. 66; Goldsmith and Lescarboura, *This Thing Called Broadcasting*, pp. 296, 207.

21. Dewey, *Democracy and Education*, p. 101; Donovan, "What Does the Future Hold?" in Tyson and Donovan, eds., *Retrospect and Forecast in Radio Education*, p. 23.

22. McChesney, *Telecommunications, Mass Media, and Democracy*, p. 261; Prostak, "Up in the Air," p. 138.

23. McChesney, *Telecommunications, Mass Media, and Democracy*, p. 14.

24. Prall quoted in *Cong. Rec.*, Senate, 74th Cong. 1st sess., 1935, 79, pt. 7:7792–93.

25. *Report of the Advisory Committee on Education by Radio*, pp. 30, 70.

26. Prostak, "Up in the Air," p. 134.

27. McChesney, *Telecommunications, Mass Media, and Democracy*, p. 52.

28. Armstrong Perry in *Education by Radio* 1 (Mar. 1931): 20; Rorty, "Educational Radio Stations," *Education by Radio* 1 (Nov. 1931): 139.

29. See William J. Donovan, "What Does the Future Hold?" in Tyson and Donovan, eds., *Retrospect and Forecast in Radio Education*, p. 23; *New York Times*, May 12, 1935, p. 11; McChesney, *Telecommunications, Mass Media, and Democracy*, p. 97.

30. Paley, *Radio as a Cultural Force*, pp. 6, 15; Paley, "Radio and the Humanities," *Annals* 177 (Jan. 1935): 103.

31. Waller, *Radio: The Fifth Estate*, p. 133, and "Achievements in Educational Radio," in Tyson and Waller, eds., *The Future of Radio:* 22–32, , p. 30; Arnold, *Broad-*

cast Advertising, p. 33. See also William Hard, "William Hard Has a Few Words to Say," in NAB, *Broadcasting in the United States*, p. 93.

32. Horowitz, *Understanding Toscanini*, p. 202 and pp. 150–270. De Forest quoted in Henderson, *On the Air*, p. 52.

33. Joan Shelley Rubin, "Swift's Premium Ham: William Lyon Phelps and the Redefinition of Culture," in Covert and Stevens, eds., *Mass Media between the Wars*, p. 7; Hilmes, *Radio Voices*, p. 189; Rubin, *The Making of Middlebrow Culture*, pp. 266–329; *Report of the Advisory Committee on Education by Radio*, p. 70.

34. Overstreet and Overstreet, *Town Meeting Comes to Town*, pp. 211, 24.

35. Armstrong Perry, *Report to the Advisory Committee on Education by Radio*, Dec. 30, 1929, in *Cong. Rec.*, Senate, 71st Cong., 2nd sess., 1930, 72, pt. 9:9418.

36. *Report of the Advisory Committee on Education by Radio*, p. 40.

37. Lazarsfeld, *Radio and the Printed Page*, pp. 23, 94ff.

38. *New York Times*, Aug. 11, 1922, p. 3.

39. Cantril, *Public Opinion 1935–1946*, p. 706; NBC Memorandum, "Effect of News Broadcasts," Aug. 3, 1936, NBC MSS, file 297.

40. White, *News on the Air*, p. 33. Figures and Rorty quoted in Schiffer, *The Portable Radio in American Life*, p. 118. See also Rosen, "Review Essay: The Marvel of Radio," p. 580.

41. NBC, "Analysis of NBC Network Programs, 1938," Young Papers, file 11-14-50 (box 33 of 41).

42. Charnley, *News by Radio*, p. 31; Lazarsfeld and Kendall, *Radio Listening in America*, p. 34.

43. Stott, *Documentary Expression and Thirties America*, pp. 79–82; Charnley, *News by Radio*, p. 49.

44. Herbert J. Gans, *Deciding What's News: A Study of "CBS Evening News," "Newsweek," and "Time"* (New York: Pantheon, 1983), p. 145; Lazarsfeld, "The Effects of Radio on Public Opinion," in Waples, *Print, Radio, and Film in a Democracy*, p. 72.

45. Culbert, *News for Everyman*, pp. 5–6; Charnley, *News by Radio*, pp. 58–60.

46. Schudson, *Discovering the News*, p. 147.

47. See Culbert, *News for Everyman*, pp. 34–200, for biographies of prominent commentators.

48. For the AIPO survey see Cantril, *Public Opinion 1935–1946*, p. 706, and for Cantril's survey see Cantril, "The Role of the Radio Commentator," p. 658.

49. AT&T quoted in Barnouw, *A Tower in Babel*, p. 138. See Kaltenborn, "News and News Interpretation," *American Heritage* (undated), p. 84: Broadcast Pioneers Library, file 254, "Early Days of Radio."

50. Catholic priest quoted in Clark, "Hans V. Kaltenborn and His Sponsors," in Lichty and Topping, eds., *American Broadcasting*, p. 237.

51. Paper, *Empire*, p. 63; Culbert, *News for Everyman*, pp. 47–59.

52. NBC MSS, file 59.

53. White, *FDR and the Press*, p. 29; Steele, *Propaganda in an Open Society*, p. 141.

54. See chapter 2, above.

55. Barton quoted in *New York Times*, June 17, 1931, p. 16. Circulation figures from Doeden, "The Press-Radio War," p. 64.

56. *New York Times*, Apr. 23, 1931, p. 14.

57. T. R. Carskadon, "The Press-Radio War," *New Republic*, Mar. 11, 1936, p. 133.

58. See Doeden, "The Press-Radio War," pp. 33, 34.

59. See Paper, *Empire*, p. 67; *New York Times*, Apr. 23, 1931, p. 14. For the press-radio war see T. R. Carskadon, "The Press-Radio War," *New Republic*, Mar. 11, 1936, pp. 132–35; Charnley, *News by Radio*, pp. 15–26; Doeden, "The Press-Radio War"; Sammy Danna, "The Press-Radio War," in Lichty and Topping, eds., *American Broadcasting*, pp. 344–50; Lott, "The Press-Radio War of the 1930s"; Roberts, "Paul H. White," pp. 26–33.

60. Paper, *Empire*, p. 67.

61. Quoted in *New York Times*, Apr. 25, 1931, p. 11.

62. Schechter, "Reminiscences," *New York Times* Oral History Program, Columbia University Oral History Collection, pt. 4, "Radio Pioneers, No. 177."

63. See Lott, "The Press-Radio War," p. 277; Aylesworth to NBC Board of Directors, Apr. 19, 1935, NBC MSS, file 298.

64. *New York Times*, Apr. 23, 1931, p. 14, and Apr. 24, 1931, p. 16

65. Mason to David Rosenblum, NBC Interdepartment Correspondence, Mar. 14, 1935, NBC MSS, file 298.

66. Paley quoted in Paper, *Empire*, p. 69. See also Lott, "The Press-Radio War," p. 282; T. R. Carskadon, "The Press-Radio War," *New Republic*, Mar. 11, 1936, p. 133.

67. See Paper, *Empire*, p. 70; White, *News on the Air*, pp. 43ff.

68. These letters were orchestrated by independent and affiliated broadcasters: Guy C. Earl Jr. to Aylesworth, Dec. 19, 1933, and Mason to Aylesworth, NBC Interdepartment Correspondence, Dec. 29, 1933, NBC MSS, file 298.

69. Theodore C. Streibert and Fulton Lewis, "Radio as a News Medium," *Annals* 213 (Jan. 1941): 54; Lott, "The Press-Radio War," p. 282.

70. See Aylesworth to NBC Board of Directors, Apr. 19, 1935, NBC MSS, file 298; T. R. Carskadon, "The Press-Radio War," *New Republic*, Mar. 11, 1936, p. 135. For the demise of the Press-Radio Bureau see a succession of internal NBC memos: E. G. Prime to Frank Mason, Jan. 6, 1939, "Press-Radio Bureau: Draft of Letter from Mason to Friendly," Jan. 9 1939, and E. G. Prime to Frank Mason, Jan. 9, 1939, NBC MSS, file 298.

71. Doeden, "The Press-Radio War," p. 179; Carskadon, "The Press-Radio War," *New Republic*, Mar. 11, 1936, p. 134.

72. See Aylesworth to Guy C. Earl Jr., Dec. 19, 1933, NBC MSS, file 298.

73. For the Mayflower doctrine see Thomas J. Swafford of CBS, speech to Rotary Club of New York, Dec. 1, 1966, Broadcast Pioneers Library collection, file 82, "Broadcasting in Political Campaigns."

74. Bartlett, *Political Propaganda,* p. 5.

75. "Radio's 'Butt-In'," *New York Times,* Mar. 5, 1922, p. 2; CMMF, Hearings on H.R. 15430 (H515-1-A), Jan. 8–19, 1929, p. 317.

76. Young and Lawrence, *Bibliography on Censorship and Propaganda,* p. 12.

77. Bernays, *Propaganda,* pp. 9, 20, 92. See also Bernays, *The Engineering of Consent,* pp. 7–10.

78. See Murphy, *The Meaning of Freedom of Speech,* p. 176.

79. Lasswell, *Propaganda Techniques in World War I,* pp. 4, 222. See also Lasswell, "The Person: Subject and Object of Propaganda," *Annals* 179 (May 1935): 188.

80. Lumley, *The Propaganda Menace,* pp. 187–89, 431.

81. Lumley, *Means of Social Control,* p. 151; Doob, *Propaganda,* p. 408; Miller, "Radio and Propaganda," *Annals* 213 (Jan. 1941): 70.

82. Riegel, *Mobilizing for Chaos,* p. 87; Irwin, *Propaganda and the News,* p. 252. See also Malcolm L. Willey, "Communication Agencies and the Volume of Propaganda," *Annals* 179 (May 1935): 195–96.

83. Arnheim, *Radio,* p. 264.

84. *New York Times,* Jan. 31, 1934, p. 13.

85. See *Cong. Rec.*, House, 75th Cong., 1st sess., 1937, 81, pt. 8:8557–58, for a list of German shortwave programs. See also *New York Times,* Oct. 11, 1936, sec. 10, p. 12; *New York World Telegram,* Dec. 21, 1938, in Clark Papers, series 116, box 439; Grandin, "The Political Use of the Radio."

86. Welles quoted in Cantril, *The Invasion from Mars,* p. 42.

87. Quoted ibid., p. 97.

88. *New York Daily News,* Oct. 31, 1938, Clark Papers, series 144, box 554.

89. Welles quoted in Henderson, *On the Air,* p. 150. *New York Post,* Oct. 31, 1938, p. 1, Clark Papers, series 144, box 554; *New York Times,* Oct. 31 and Nov. 1, 1938.

90. *New York Herald Tribune,* Nov. 6, 1938, p. 11, Clark Papers, series 144, box 554.

91. Cantril, *The Invasion from Mars,* pp. 55–57, 70, 204.

12 | Radio at the Margins

1. Bradford to Davis, undated, Young Papers, file 87.2,129, folder 267H.

2. See Willey and Rice, "Communication," in *RST,* p. 215.

3. Cohen, *Making a New Deal,* pp. 142–43, 157–58.

4. Savage, *Broadcasting Freedom,* pp. 21–62.

5. See Edward N. Nockels, "Labor's Rights on the Air," Mar. 1931, Borah Papers, box 324, file: "Radio Legislation, 1930–1931."

6. Crosley policy quoted in "Radio Censors Labor," *Nation* 141 (Sept. 1935): 357. For NBC's attitude to strikes see L. H. Titterton to William Burke Miller, NBC Interdepartment Correspondence, Jan. 11, 1937, NBC MSS, file 332. Woods quoted in Siepmann, *Radio's Second Chance,* p. 108.

7. For the 1939 NAB Code see NBC MSS, file 396.

8. Siepmann, *Radio's Second Chance*, p. 114.

9. See Burner, *The Politics of Provincialism*; Charles W. Eagles, "Congressional Voting in the 1920s: A Test of Urban-Rural Conflict," *Journal of American History* 76 (Sept. 1989): 528–34; John L. Shover, *First Majority—Last Minority: The Transforming of Rural Life in America* (DeKalb: Northern Illinois University Press, 1976).

10. CMMF, Hearings on H.R. 15430. 70th Cong., 2d sess., Jan. 24–31, 1929, pp. 634–39.

11. Root quoted in NBC Advisory Council minutes, Feb. 18, 1927, NBCR, box 107, file 1; *New York Times*, Feb. 10, 1929, sec. 3, p. 4.

12. Bliven, "How Radio Is Remaking our World," p. 152. See also Bliven, "Will Radio Send Us 'Back to the Farm'?" *Literary Digest* 80 (Jan. 1924): 26.

13. Hettinger and Neff, *Practical Radio Advertising*, p. 39; Willey and Rice, *Communication Agencies and Social Life*, p. 191.

14. Willey and Rice, *Communication Agencies and Social Life*, p. 192; Morse Salisbury, "Radio and the Farmer," *Annals* 177 (Jan. 1935): 142.

15. For surveys of interwar rural broadcasting see Baker, *Farm Broadcasting*, and Wik, "The Radio in Rural America During the 1920s." For the National Farm and Home Hour see Rosen, *The Modern Stentors*, p. 169, and William S. Robinson, "Radio Comes to the Farmer," in Lazarsfeld and Stanton, *Radio Research 1941:* 258. Carlin, memo to Messrs. Rainey, Kelly, and Titterton, July 3, 1937: NBC MSS, file 332.

16. Smulyan, *Selling Radio*, pp. 22–30. See also Hilmes, *Radio Voices*, pp. 105–8; Lynd and Lynd, *Middletown in Transition*, p. 263.

17. Wilson, *Money at the Crossroads*, pp. 9–13.

18. T. B. Keedle (and 15 others) to Norris, Feb. 17, 1928, Norris Papers, box 27, file: "Radio, 1926–31."

19. Grundy, "We Always Tried to Be Good People," pp. 1593–1618.

20. See *The Prairie Farmer* 101 (Nov. 1929): 26 for WLS's broadcasting schedule: Young Papers, file 11-14-50, oversize collection.

21. Willey and Rice, *Communication Agencies and Social Life*, pp. 154, 213. Emphases are theirs.

22. William S. Robinson, "Radio Comes to the Farmer," in Lazarsfeld and Stanton, eds., *Radio Research 1941*, pp. 238–60.

23. Christine Frederick, "Radio for the Housekeeper," *Literary Digest* 74 (Sept. 1922): 28.

24. See Johnson, *The Unseen Voice*, p. 12; Catherine L. Covert, "We May Hear Too Much," in Covert and Stevens, eds., *Mass Media between the Wars*, p. 204; Robinson, *Broadcasting and a Changing Civilization*, p. 21.

25. Schiffer, *The Portable Radio in American Life*, p. 92; "Women and Wireless," *Literary Digest* 79 (Dec. 15, 1923): 25; Joy Elmer Morgan, "Radio and Education," in Codel, ed., *Radio and Its Future*, p. 71; Nye, *Electrifying America*, p. 282.

26. Goldsmith and Lescarboura, *This Thing Called Broadcasting*, p. 231; Pierre du

Pont, "Some Observations on Liquor Control," Nov. 11, 1933, Pierre du Pont Papers, file 1023-25, folder: "AAPA: Invitations, Meetings, Radio Talks, 1933."

27. *New York Times*, June 19, 1927, sec. 8, p. 14.

28. CBS, *Radio in 1936*, p. 14. See also Lazarsfeld, *Radio and the Printed Page*, p. 19; Lazarsfeld and Kendall, *Radio Listening in America*, p. 132.

29. Ollry and Smith, "An Index of 'Radio Mindedness' and Some Applications," *Journal of Applied Psychology* 21 (Feb. 1939): 13–14; Robinson, *Broadcasting and a Changing Civilization*, pp. 25–26.

30. Arnold, *Broadcast Advertising*, p. 65.

31. Hilmes, *Radio Voices*, p. 148.

32. Waller, *Radio: The Fifth Estate*, p. 116.

33. Thurber, "Soapland," in Susman, ed., *Culture and Commitment*, p. 152. See also Allen, *Speaking of Soap Operas*, p. 138; Hilmes, *Radio Voices*, pp. 124–29.

34. Gary Dean Best, *Nickel and Dime Decade: Popular Culture during the 1930s* (Westport, Conn.: Praeger, 1993), p. 67; Allen, *Speaking of Soap Operas*, p. 116. In 1940 NBC and CBS devoted 25 percent of their daytime programming to soap operas: "Soap Opera," *Fortune* 33 (Mar. 1941): 146.

35. Thurber, "Soapland," and Lazarsfeld, "Effects on Public Opinion," in Waples, ed., *Print, Radio, and Film in a Democracy*, 67.

36. Allen, *Speaking of Soap Operas*, p. 149. See also p. 138.

37. Quoted in Wertheim, "Relieving Social Tensions," p. 512.

38. See Waller, *Radio: The Fifth Estate*, pp. 107–8, and "Soap Opera."

39. Dunlap, *Advertising by Radio*, p. 36; Waller, *Radio: The Fifth Estate*, p. 110.

40. Lazarsfeld and Kendall, *Radio Listening in America*, p. 27.

41. Cantril and Allport, *The Psychology of Radio*, p. 91.

42. Margaret Cuthbert to John F. Royal, NBC Interdepartment Correspondence, Sept. 6, 1935, NBCR, box 41, file 16, "Roosevelt, Eleanor, 1935."

43. Katherine Ward Fisher, letter to the editor, *New York Times*, May 24, 1926, p. 18. BBC quoted ibid., Oct. 10, 1926, sec. 9, p. 19.

44. Ibid., July 29, 1926, p. 16; Goldsmith and Lescarboura, *This Thing Called Broadcasting*, p. 136; Cantril and Allport, *Psychology of Radio*, pp. 127–38. See also Heinz, "The Voice of Authority," p. 3.

45. Inglis, *This Is the ABC*, p. 32; Cantril and Allport, *The Psychology of Radio*, p. 137; Potts, *Radio in Australia*, pp. 106–7.

46. Jamieson, *Eloquence in an Electronic Age*, pp. 67–89.

47. Sanger, *Rebel in Radio*, pp. 84–86.

48. See Michael Biel, "Broadcast Announcing Styles of the 1920's," Broadcast Pioneers Library, AT 1008; Whittaker and Whittaker, "Relative Effectiveness of Male and Female Newscasters," p. 178; Jamieson, *Eloquence in an Electronic Age*, p. 81.

49. Hilmes, *Radio Voices*, pp. 132–44; Heinz, "Women Radio Pioneers"; Marzoff and Bock, "The Literature of Women in Journalism History."

50. For women in Canadian broadcasting see McNeil and Wolfe, *Signing On*, pp. 87, 150, 202. For women and the BBC see Briggs, *History of Broadcasting in the United Kingdom*, 1:254, 260; Scannell and Cardiff, *A Social History of British Broadcasting*, 1:153–55; McIntyre, *Expense of Glory*, p. 172.

51. For biographies of Brainard and Waller see Hilmes, *Radio Voices*, pp. 138–40; Williamson, "Judith Cary Waller." For examples of MacRorie's work see NBC MSS, files 65, 398; for Stone's career see Metz, *CBS*, pp. 69–74.

52. Lawrence W. Levine, *Black Culture and Black Consciousness: Afro-American Folk Thought from Slavery to Freedom* (Oxford: Oxford University Press, 1977), p. 318.

53. *HSUS*, vol. 1, series A 91-118, A 172-194, pp. 14, 22.

54. Ely, *The Adventures of Amos'n'Andy*, p. 164.

55. Levine, *Black Culture and Black Consciousness*, p. 228.

56. Willey and Rice, *Communication Agencies and Social Life*, p. 204.

57. MacDonald, *Don't Touch That Dial!* p. 334.

58. See Savage, *Broadcasting Freedom*, p. 65.

59. See ibid., pp. 327, 330ff.; Hilmes, *Radio Voices*, p. 96.

60. Cohen, *Making a New Deal*, pp. 135ff.

61. MacDonald, *Don't Touch That Dial!* p. 339; Hilmes, *Radio Voices*, p. 272.

62. Ely, *The Adventures of Amos'n'Andy;* Barnouw, *A Tower in Babel*, pp. 14ff.; Smulyan, "And Now a Word from our Sponsors," p. 120.

63. Ely, *The Adventures of Amos'n'Andy*, pp. 73, 153, 245.

64. Quoted in Wertheim, "Relieving Social Tensions," p. 504. See also Ely, *The Adventures of Amos'n'Andy*, p. 119.

65. See ibid., pp. 172–86, 189–240, and 215; Smulyan, "And Now a Word from Our Sponsors," p. 120.

66. *Chicago Defender*, Apr. 5, 1924, pt. 2, p. 3.

67. A. C. MacNeal to NBC, Feb. 11, 1936, NBC MSS, file 331.

68. Rev. William T. H. Hill to NBC, July 21, 1937, and Phillips Carlin to Hill, July 28, 1937, NBC MSS, file 375. For the Bailey broadcast see John F. Royal to William Burke Miller, NBC Interdepartmental Correspondence, June 18, 1939, NBC MSS, file 376.

69. See William Burke Miller to Thomas H. Belriso, NBC Interdepartmental Correspondence, Dec. 9, 1938, NBC MSS, file 332. For complaints about derogatory references to Jews see Harold Levenson to NBC, Nov. 11, 1931, Young Papers, file 24-18; Benjamin Greenberg to Henry P. Bristol, President of Bristol-Myers Company, Nov. 27, 1936, NBC MSS, file 331. Royal quoted in Rosen, *The Modern Stentors*, p. 157.

70. McFadden, "America's Boyfriend Who Can't Get a Date."

71. MacDonald, *Don't Touch That Dial!* p. 340. For slave stereotypes see John W. Blassingame, *The Slave Community: Plantation Life in the Antebellum South*, 2d ed. (New York: Oxford University Press, 1979), pp. 224–48.

72. Green to NBC, Nov. 29, 1931, Young Papers, file 24-18. Black performers became more prominent on networks only after Pearl Harbor. Paul Robeson, Richard

White, and Marian Anderson were placed on radio play lists, and some stations broadcast talks on the "race problem" and the contributions of African Americans to the war effort. See generally Savage, *Broadcasting Freedom.*

73. See Jim Smith to RCA, July ?, 1938, NBC MSS, file 376.

74. For the jazz controversy on radio see Douglas, *The Early Days of Radio Broadcasting*, pp. 173ff.; Hilmes, *Radio Voices*, p. 46.

75. Hilmes, *Radio Voices*, p. 93. Capitalization and emphasis are Hilmes's.

13 | Radio and the Politics of Good Taste

1. Quoted in *The Literary Digest* 106 (Jan. 1930): 26.

2. See Stanley Coben, *Rebellion against Victorianism: The Impetus for Cultural Change in 1920s America* (New York: Oxford University Press, 1991); Lears, "From Salvation to Self-Realization," in Fox and Lears, eds., *Culture of Consumption*, p. 3.

3. Susman, *Culture as History*, p. 160.

4. Levine, *Highbrow/Lowbrow*, pp. 233–34. See also Paul DiMaggio, "Cultural Entrepreneurship in Nineteenth-Century Boston," in Mukerji and Schudson, eds., *Rethinking Popular Culture*, p. 374.

5. Williams, *Television*, p. 26.

6. Quoted in Rubin, *The Making of Middlebrow Culture*, p. 269.

7. Hettinger, "Broadcasting in the United States," *Annals* 177 (Jan. 1935): 11. See also William S. Paley, "Radio and the Humanities," *Annals* 177 (Jan. 1935): 94–96.

8. Carlin to Royal, NBC Interdepartmental Correspondence, May 11, 1939, NBC MSS, file 376.

9. See Douglas, *The Early Days of Radio Broadcasting*, p. 153; Czitrom, *Media and the American Mind*, p. 85; Sherwood Gates, "Radio in Relation to Recreation and Culture," *Annals* 213 (Jan. 1941): 11.

10. Bliven, "How Radio Is Remaking Our World," p. 154. Wheeler quoted in Robinson, *Radio Networks and the Federal Government*, p. 81. Atkinson, "A European View of American Radio Programs," *Annals* 177 (Jan. 1935): 86.

11. For a discussion of the origins, theory, and practice of cultural hegemony, see Lears, "The Concept of Cultural Hegemony"; Mukerji and Schudson, "Introduction," in *Rethinking Popular Culture*, pp. 15, 38; Raymond Williams, "Base and Superstructure in Marxist Cultural Theory," in Mukerji and Schudson, eds., *Rethinking Popular Culture, pp. 412–13*. See also Lears, "Making Fun of Popular Culture"; MacDonald, "Masscult and Midcult," pt. 1, pp. 212, 228, and pt. 2, p. 592.

12. Amos quoted in Levine, "American Culture in the Great Depression," p. 211. See also Levine, "The Folklore of Industrial Society"; Wertheim, "Relieving Social Tensions."

13. McFadden, "America's Boyfriend Who Can't Get a Date," pp. 113–25.

14. Hilmes, *Radio Voices*, p. 46.

15. For the Hays Office and the Lord-Quigley Code see Black, *Hollywood Censored*,

pp. 1–4, 31–40; Mark Fackler, "Moral Guardians of the Movies and Social Responsibility of the Press: Two Movements toward a Moral Center," in Covert and Stevens, eds., *Mass Media between the Wars*, 181–97.

16. See William S. Hedges, "The Business of Broadcasting," in Codel, ed., *Radio and Its Future*, pp. 46–49, for the full text of the NAB 1929 Code of Ethics.

17. See "A Comparison of Codes," *Education by Radio* 9 (Aug.–Sept., 1939): 26.

18. "The Code of the National Association of Broadcasters," July 11, 1939, NBC MSS, file 396.

19. Pegg, *Broadcasting and Society*, p. 96.

20. See Young Papers, 11-14-82 (1925) for letters sent to invitees on Nov. 6, 1926. See also Young's statement to the first meeting of the NBC Advisory Council, Feb. 1927, Young Papers, file 11-14-50 (folder 7 of 41), p. 23.

21. For membership lists see "NBC Advisory Council Reports 1929," NBCR, box 107, file 3.

22. Statement of M. H. Aylesworth to CMMRF, Hearings on H.R. 7986 (H672-7), Mar. 1934, pp. 133–34.

23. See Young to Aylesworth, Nov. 16, 1926, Young Papers, Copy Books—Radio, box 803, no. 4, July 31, 1925–Aug. 18, 1928; Barnouw, *A Tower in Babel*, p. 206; William F. Green, Report of the Committee on Labor, NBC Advisory Council. Minutes of 6th Meeting, Feb. 16, 1932, Young Papers, file 11-14-82 (folder 12 of 25).

24. CBS, "Broadcasting and the America Public: Report of a Forum on Radio Conducted over the Facilities of the Columbia Broadcasting System, Feb. 1936," Young Papers, file 11-14-50, folder 22.

25. NAB, *Broadcasting in the United States*, p. 66.

26. Hettinger and Mead, *The Summer Radio Audience*, p. 31; H. M. Beville Jr., "The ABCD's of Radio Audiences," in Schramm, ed., *Mass Communications*, p. 418.

27. Data derived from Rose, *National Policy for Radio Broadcasting*, p. 142; NBC, "Yearbook of Programs 1937," Young Papers, file 11-14-50, folder 29; Lichty and Topping, eds., *American Broadcasting*, p. 526; NBC, "The First Ten Years: A Study of the Growth of the National Broadcasting Company 1926 to 1936," NBC MSS, file 94; NBC, Minutes of the 10th Annual Meeting of the Advisory Council, May 7 1936," Baker Papers, box 165, file: "National Broadcasting Company: Advisory Council 1936"; Summers, ed., *A Thirty Year History of Programs.*

28. Data calculated from NAB, *Broadcasting in the United States*, p. 40; Hettinger, *A Decade of Radio Advertising*, p. 303; McNair, *Radio Advertising in Australia*, p. 119.

29. Edgar Kobak to all salesmen, NBC Interdepartment Correspondence, July 6, 1934; Henry K. Norton to R. C. Patterson Jr., NBC Interdepartment Correspondence, Oct. 24, 1934, NBC MSS, file 333.

30. "NBC Program Policies, Mar. 1936," NBC MSS, file 397. For MacRorie's activities see MacRorie, "Report of Department of Continuity Acceptance for the Year 1935," Dec. 17, 1935, NBC MSS, file 65.

31. NBC, "Working Manual for Continuity Acceptance under NBC Program Policies," 1939, NBC MSS, file 396.

32. See Roy C. Witmer to John F. Royal, NBC Interdepartment Correspondence, Apr. 8, 1932, NBC MSS, file 332; NBC Program Script, "Radio Is Human, Too," Apr. 1938, NBC MSS, file 398. See also Kobak, "Address before National Association of Broadcasters," June 14, 1938, p. 4, Kobak Papers, box 4, file: "Speech, Article, and Public Statement file, 1936–1949."

33. CBS, "New Policies: A Statement to the Public, to Advertisers, and to Advertising Agencies," May 15, 1935, FDRP, OF 256, box 1, file: "CBS 1933–1935." See also Denison, "Editorial Policies of Broadcast Companies," pp. 77ff.

34. *Literary Digest* 112 (Jan. 1932): 23.

35. For CBS and venereal disease see the Federal Council of Churches, *Broadcasting and the Public*, p. 163. For the Al Jolson joke see MacRorie to John F. Royal, NBC Interdepartment Correspondence, Apr. 24, 1935; for NBC and "screwy" see Don E. Gilman to Janet MacRorie, NBC Memo, Mar. 16, 1938, NBC MSS, file 332.

36. For the outcry against the Mae West sketch see *Cong. Rec.*, House, 75th Cong., 3rd sess., 1938, vol. 83, pt. 9, App., p. 357; for NBC's attitude to divorce see Bertha Brainard to F. M. Thrower, NBC memo, Feb. 14, 1939. See also "Proposed Memorandum from Major Lohr to the Department Heads Regarding Good Taste for Programs," 1938, NBC MSS, file 398.

37. For discussion about effeminate characters see a series of memos between Sidney Strotz, Philips Carlin, Janet MacRorie, and C. L. Menser dated between Dec. 16 and 21, 1940, NBC MSS, file 332. For homoerotic subtexts in the Jack Benny show see McFadden, "America's Boyfriend Who Can't Get a Date."

38. For NBC and the birth control conference see Owen D. Young to Harry F. Ward, Dec. 3, 1929; for the ACLU's response see Ward to Elwood, Nov. 22, 1929, and Ward to Young, Dec. 10, 1929, Young Papers, file 11-14-101. For the American Birth Control League's protest against NBC policy see *New York Times*, Jan. 17, 1930, p. 18.

39. Memorandum of Minutes of the Fourth Meeting of the Advisory Council of the National Broadcasting Company, Jan. 29, 1930, Young Papers, file 11-14-82, folder 9 of 25.

40. Ward to John Elwood, Nov. 22, 1929, Young Papers, file 11-14-101. For NBC policies during Prohibition see *New York Times*, Apr. 4, 1927, p. 22. For drunkenness in programs see Janet MacRorie to A. C. Love, NBC Memo, Aug. 18, 1937, NBC MSS, file 332.

41. For CBS and hard liquor see CBS News Release, "Columbia Bars Liquor," Nov. 1, 1933, NBC MSS, file 168, p. 4. For NBC policy see Frank M. Russell to R. C. Patterson, NBC Interdepartment Correspondence, Feb. 13, 1934, NBC MSS, file 168.

42. For McNinch's statement see John H. Norton to I. E. Showerman, NBC Interdepartment Correspondence, Feb. 28, 1938. For debates within NBC see Edgar Kobak to Frank E. Mullen, NBC Interdepartment Correspondence, June 24, 1941,

and R. C. Witmer to Frank Mullen, NBC Interdepartment Correspondence, Nov. 4, 1941. For the 1949 change see James V. O'Connell to national Spot Sales Staff, July 21, 1949, NBC MSS, file 168.

43. See Spencer Miller Jr., "Radio and Religion," *Annals* 177 (Jan. 1935): 140.

44. Quoted in *New York Times*, Jan. 25, 1923, p. 10.

45. Straton quoted in Schultze, "Evangelical Radio and the Rise of the Electronic Church," p. 291. See Federal Council of Churches, *Broadcasting and the Public*, p. 141, for a tabulation of broadcast hours by denomination in 1939.

46. Young quoted in *New York Times*, Aug. 3, 1924, sec. 8, p. 10. Cantril and Allport, *The Psychology of Radio*, p. 5. See also *Literary Digest* 82 (Aug. 1924): 31.

47. Schultze, "Evangelical Radio and the Rise of the Electronic Church," pp. 291–95.

48. See CMMF, Hearings on H. R. 15430 (H515-1-B), Jan. 1929, p. 545.

49. See Statement of M. H. Aylesworth to CMMF, ibid., pp. 549–50; Spencer Miller, "Radio and Religion," *Annals* 177 (Jan. 1935): 137; Schultze, "Evangelical Radio and the Rise of the Electronic Church," p. 298.

50. E. S. Wertz to CMMF, Hearings on H. R. 7986 (H672-7) Mar. 1934, pp. 26–32.

51. See Statement of Henry L. Caravati, Statement of Henry A. Bellows, and Statement of M. H. Aylesworth to CMMF, Hearings on H. R. 7986 (H672-7), Mar. 1934, pp. 178–84, pp. 158–77, and p. 139.

52. See chapter 8, above.

53. Henry A. Bellows to CMMF, Hearings on H. R. 7986 (H672-7), Mar. 1934, pp. 164ff. 161.

Conclusion

1. For radio and World War II see NBC, "Interpretation of NBC Policies As Applied to Broadcasts during the Current European War," Sept. 7, 1939, Wilbur Papers, box 87, file: "Radio—Gen'l: Broadcasting and War"; Office of Censorship—War-time Code of Practices for Radio Broadcasters," Jan. 15, 1942, FDRP, OF 4695, box 1, file: "Office of Censorship 1941–42." See also Steele, *Propaganda in an Open Society*, pp. 134ff.; Hilmes, *Radio Voices*, pp. 230ff.; Savage, *Broadcasting Freedom*, pp. 106–53.

2. *New York Herald Tribune*, May 4, 1941, p. 2, in Clark Papers, series 116, box 439.

3. Baughman, *Republic of Mass Culture*, pp. 30–58, 65–74.

4. See Richard A. Schwarzlose, "Technology and the Individual," in Covert and Stevens, eds., *Mass Media between the Wars*, p. 101.

5. See Carey and Quirk, "The *Mythos* of the Electronic Revolution"; Czitrom, *Media and the American Mind*, p. 11; Marvin, *When Old Technologies Were New*, pp. 184–86, 215; Abbot, *Seeking Many Inventions*, p. 23; Nye, *Electrifying America*, pp. 142–57; Blondheim, *News over the Wires*, pp. 32, 190–93.

6. Sarnoff, "Probable Influences of Television on Society," *Journal of Applied Physics* 10 (July 1939): 426–3, in Young Papers, file 1-101, "Sarnoff, David, Aug. 15, 1937–Jan. 1940." For similar views see *Education by Radio* 1 (Apr. 1931): 35.

7. Grossman, *The Electronic Republic*, p. 6. The editor of *Wired* magazine even promised "social changes so profound their only parallel is probably the discovery of fire." Quoted in Rosenzweig, "Wizards, Bureaucrats, Warriors, and Hackers," p. 1530. See also *Washington Post*, June 12, 1996, p. 16; *Australian*, Aug. 13, 1996, p. 49; Davis, *The Web of Politics*, pp. 5, 114, 122.

8. *New York Times*, "Familiarity Soon Is Acquired," June 23, 1923, p. 10. See also ibid., Nov. 4, 1928, sec. 3, p. 5; Hettinger, *A Decade of Radio Advertising*, p. 3; Fischer, *America Calling*, p. 254.

Bibliography

Manuscript Collections

ALBANY, NEW YORK

New York State Archives

Alfred E. Smith Papers

CANTON, NEW YORK

Owen D. Young Library, St. Lawrence University

Owen D. Young Papers

GREENVILLE, DELAWARE

Hagley Museum and Library

E. I. Du Pont de Nemours and Company Records

Pierre du Pont Papers

John J. Raskob Papers

HYDE PARK, NEW YORK

Franklin D. Roosevelt Library

Mary W. Dewson Papers

Stephen T. Early Papers

James A. Farley Papers

Harry L. Hopkins Papers

Louis McHenry Howe Papers

National Committee of the Democratic Party, 1928–1948 Records

National Committee of Independent Voters for Roosevelt and Wallace, 1940 Records

Eleanor Roosevelt Papers

Franklin D. Roosevelt Papers

Papers as Governor of New York State, 1929–1932

Papers as President

Official File, 1933–1945

President's Personal File, 1933–1945

President's Secretary's File, 1933–1945

Women's Division of the Democratic National Committee Records

MADISON, WISCONSIN

State Historical Society of Wisconsin

Bruce Barton Papers

National Broadcasting Company Records

STANFORD, CALIFORNIA

Hoover Institution Archives

George Barr Baker Papers

James Ford Bell Papers

Hugh S. Gibson Papers

Herbert C. Hoover Papers

Addresses, Letters, Magazine Articles, and Press Releases, 1898–1960

Commerce Department Files

Presidential Files

William Henry Irwin Papers

Annie G. Lyle Papers

Raymond Moley Papers

Mark Sullivan Papers

Ray Lyman Wilbur Papers

Hubert Work Papers

WASHINGTON, D.C.

Broadcast Pioneers Library

Joseph E. Baudino Collection

Phillips Carlin Collection

William S. Hedges Collection

Walter Myers Collection

Library of Congress Manuscript Division

Newton D. Baker Papers

William E. Borah Papers

Calvin Coolidge Papers

Josephus Daniels Papers

Lee De Forest Papers

Henry Prather Fletcher Papers

Stanford C. Hooper Papers

Jesse Jones Papers

Edgar Kobak Papers

Robert M. LaFollette Sr. Papers

Robert M. LaFollette Jr. Papers

George W. Norris Papers

John Callan O'Loughlin Papers
Everett Sanders Papers
Joseph P. Tumulty Papers
Thomas Walsh Papers
Wallace H. White Jr. Papers
Frederick W. Wile Papers
Library of Congress Recorded Sound Division
National Broadcasting Company Manuscript Collection
Museum of American History
George H. Clark Papers
National Archives and Records Administration
Federal Communication Commission Records

WEST BRANCH, IOWA
Herbert Hoover Presidential Library
Campaign and Transition Materials
President's Personal File
Presidential Papers—Subject File

Government Documents

Annual Reports of the Federal Radio Commission to the Congress of the United States. Washington, D.C.: U.S. Government Printing Office, 1927–1933.

Australian Royal Commission on Television, "Control of Political Broadcasting in English-Speaking Countries." *Journal of Broadcasting* 2 (Spring 1958): 123–36.

The Congressional Record, 1911–1938.

Federal Radio Commission Publications. Washington, D.C.: U.S. Government Printing Office.
Broadcasting Radio Stations of the United States (1931)
Federal Radio Commission Rules and Regulations (1931)
Federal Radio Commission Rules and Regulations (1934)
Practice and Procedure before the Federal Radio Commission (1930)
Radio Broadcast Stations in the United States (1932)
Radio Broadcast Stations in the United States (1934)
Radio Facts and Principles Limiting the Total Number of Broadcasting Stations Which May Operate Simultaneously in the United States (1928)

Hearings before the Committee on Interstate Commerce—U.S. Senate on S.4937: 70th Congress, 2d session. Feb. 4–8, 1929 (S316-11)

on S.2910: 73d Congress, 2d session. Mar. 9–15, 1934 (S434-3)
on Confirmation of Members of FCC: 74th Congress, 1st session. Jan. 23–29, Feb. 2, 1935 (S474-4)

Hearings before the Committee on Rules—U.S. Senate
on S.Res.28 and S.Res.71: 72d Congress, 1st session. Mar. 22, 1932 (S376-12)

Hearings before the Committee on Interstate and Foreign Commerce—U.S. House of Representatives
on H.R. 8301: 73d Congress, 2d session. Apr. 10–11, 1934, May 8–16, 1934 (H677-3)

Hearings before the Committee on the Merchant Marine and Fisheries—U.S. House of Representatives
on H.R. 13159: 65th Congress, 3d session. Dec. 12–19, 1918 (H210-1)
on H.R. 7357: 68th Congress, 1st session. Mar. 11–14, 1924 (H346-4)
on H.R. 5589: 69th Congress, 1st session. Jan. 6–15, 1926 (H406-6)
on H.R. 15430: 70th Congress, 2d session. Part 1: Jan. 8–19, 1929 (H515-1-A), part 2: Jan. 24-31, 1929 (H515-1-B)
on H.R. 7986: 73d Congress, 2d session. Mar. 15–20, 1934 (H672-7)

Report of the Advisory Committee on Education by Radio, United States Department of the Interior. Washington, D.C., United States Office of Education, 1930.

Report of the President's Research Committee on Social Trends. *Recent Social Trends in the United States.* 2 parts. New York: McGraw-Hill, 1933.

United States Department of Commerce, Bureau of the Census. *Historical Statistics of the United States: Colonial Times to 1970.* Bicentennial Edition, 2 parts. Washington, D.C.: U.S. Government Printing Office, 1975.

Other Primary Sources

Bernays, Edward L. *Biography of an Idea: Memoirs of Public Relations Counsel Edward L. Bernays.* New York: Simon and Schuster, 1965.

Buhite, Russell D., and David W. Levy, eds. *FDR's Fireside Chats.* Norman: University of Oklahoma Press, 1992.

Columbia University Oral History Project, Radio Pioneers Project. Butler Library, Columbia University, New York.

Coughlin, Charles E. *Selected Discourses.* Chicago: The Educational Guild, 1932.

De Forest, Lee. *Father of Radio: The Autobiography of Lee De Forest.* Chicago: Wilcox and Follett Co., 1950.

Eckersley, Peter P. *The Power behind the Microphone.* London: Jonathan Cape, 1941.

Long, Huey P. *Every Man a King: The Autobiography of Huey P. Long.* New York: Da Capo Press, 1996.

Maxwell, Perriton, ed. "Is Radio a Blessing or a Menace? A Symposium by 32 Famous Americans." Collated 1931. Library of Congress Manuscript Division, Accession #9,041.

Michelson, Charles. *The Ghost Talks.* New York: Putnam's, 1944.

Roosevelt, Eleanor. *This Is My Story.* New York: Harper and Brothers, 1937.

Sanger, Elliott M. *Rebel in Radio: The Story of WQXR.* New York: Hastings House Publishers, 1973.

Shechter, Abel Alan. Reminiscences. Radio Pioneers, No. 177, *New York Times* Oral History Program, Columbia University Oral History Collection, Part 4 (1–219). Lamont Library, Harvard University.

Magazines, Newspapers, and Periodicals

American Review of Reviews, 1922, 1924

Annals of the American Academy of Political and Social Sciences, 1929–1941

Chicago Defender, 1924–1925

Colliers: The National Weekly, 1928, 1932

Education by Radio, National Committee on Education by Radio, 1931–1941

Fortune, 1941

The Journal of Applied Psychology 21 (Feb. 1939), 24 (Dec. 1940)

Journal of Broadcasting, 1957–1980

Journal of Broadcasting and Electronic Media, 1982–1985

The Literary Digest, 1920–1937

The Nation, 1920–1937

New York Times, 1920–1936

Printers' Ink, 1930–1940

Radio Broadcast, 1925

Pamphets and Miscellaneous Materials

American Civil Liberties Union. Minna F. Kassner and Lucien Zacharoff, colls. "Radio Is Censored! A Study of Cases Prepared to Show the Need of Federal Legislation for Freedom of the Air." New York: American Civil Liberties Union, 1936.

Columbia Broadcasting System. *Broadcasting and the American Public.* New York: Columbia Broadcasting System, 1936.

———. *Political Broadcasts: A Series of Letters Exchanged between the Columbia Broadcasting System, Inc. and the Republican National Committee.* New York: Columbia Broadcasting System, 1936.

———. *Radio in 1936.* New York: Columbia Broadcasting System, 1936.

Grandin, Thomas. "The Political Use of Radio." *Geneva Studies* 10 (Aug. 1939): n.p.

Starch, Daniel. "A Study of Radio Broadcasting Based Exclusively on Personal Interviews with Families in the United States East of the Rocky Mountains." National Broadcasting Company, 1928.

Wilson, Charles Morrow. *Money at the Crossroads: An Intimate Study of Radio's Influence upon a Great Market of 60,000,000 People.* Radio City, N.Y.: National Broadcasting Company, 1937.

Books and Articles Prior to 1945

Archer, Gleason L. *Big Business and Radio.* New York: American Historical Company, 1939.

———. *History of Radio: To 1926.* New York: American Historical Company, 1938.

Arnheim, Rudolf. *Radio.* Trans. Margaret Ludwig and Herbert Read. London: Faber and Faber, 1936.

Arnold, Frank A. *Broadcast Advertising: The Fourth Dimension.* New York: John Wiley and Sons, 1933.

Bartlett, F. C. *Political Propaganda.* Cambridge: Cambridge University Press, 1940.

Bent, Silas. *Ballyhoo: The Voice of the Press.* New York: Boni and Liveright, 1927.

———. *Machine Made Man.* New York: Farrar and Rinehart, 1930.

Bernays, Edward L. *Crystallizing Public Opinion.* New York: Liveright, 1961. First published 1923.

———. *Propaganda.* New York: Horace Liveright, 1928.

Bickel, Karl A. *New Empires: The Newspaper and the Radio.* Philadelphia: Lippincott, 1930.

Black, Theodore Milton. *Democratic Party Publicity in the 1940 Campaign.* New York: Plymouth Publishing Co., 1941.

Bliven, Bruce. "How Radio Is Remaking Our World." *Century Magazine* 108 (June 1924): 147–54.

Blythe, Samuel G. "Political Publicity." *Saturday Evening Post* 201 (Feb. 2, 1929): 9, 141–43.

Brindze, Ruth. *Not to Be Broadcast: The Truth about Radio.* New York: Da Capo Press, 1974. First published 1937.

Bruce, Harold R. *American Parties and Politics: History and Role of Political Parties in the United States.* New York: Henry Holt and Co., 1937.

Cantril, Hadley. "The Role of the Radio Commentator." *Public Opinion Quarterly* 3 (Oct. 1939): 654-62.

Cantril, Hadley, and Gordon W. Allport, *The Psychology of Radio.* New York: Harper and Brothers, 1935.

Casey, Ralph D. "Republican Propaganda in the 1936 Campaign." *Public Opinion Quarterly* 1 (Apr. 1937): 27–44.

Chase, Francis, Jr. *Sound and Fury: An Informal History of Broadcasting.* New York: Harper and Brothers, 1942.

Codel, Martin, ed. *Radio and Its Future.* New York: Harper and Brothers, 1930.

Cooley, Charles Horton. *Social Organization: A Study of the Larger Mind.* New York: Charles Scribner's Sons, 1924.

Creel, George. *How We Advertised America: The First Telling of the Amazing Story of the Committee on Public Information That Carried the Gospel of Americanism to Every Corner of the Globe.* New York: Harper and Brothers, 1920.

Davis, H. O. *The Empire of the Air: The Story of the Exploitation of Radio for Private Profit, with a Plan for the Reorganization of Broadcasting.* Ventura,Calif. : Ventura Free Press, 1932.

Davis, Stephen. *The Law of Radio Communication.* New York: McGraw-Hill, 1927.

Denison, Merrill. "Editorial Policies of Broadcast Companies." *Public Opinion Quarterly* 1 (Jan. 1937): 64–82.

Dewey, John. *Democracy and Education: An Introduction to the Philosophy of Education.* New York: Macmillan, 1926.

———. *Individualism Old and New.* New York: Balch and Co., 1930.

———. "The New Paternalism." *New Republic,* Dec. 21, 1918, pp. 216–17.

———. *The Public and Its Problems: An Essay in Political Inquiry.* Chicago: Gateway Books, 1946. First published 1927.

Dill, Clarence C. *Radio Law: Practice and Procedure.* Washington, D.C.: National Law Book Co., 1938.

Doob, Leonard W. *Propaganda: Its Psychology and Technique.* New York: Henry Holt and Co., 1935.

Dos Passos, John. "The Radio Voice." *Common Sense* 3 (Feb. 1934): 17.

Dunlap, Orrin E. *Advertising by Radio.* New York: Ronald Press, 1929.

———. *The Story of Radio.* New York: Dial Press, 1927.

———. *Talking on the Radio: A Practical Guide for Writing and Broadcasting a Speech.* New York: Greenberg, 1936.

Dygert, Warren B. *Radio as an Advertising Medium.* New York: McGraw-Hill, 1939.

Elder, Robert F. "Measuring Radio Advertising Sales Power." *Broadcasting* 1 (Nov. 1, 1931): 11, 32.

Eldridge, Seba. *The New Citizenship: A Study of American Politics.* New York: Thomas Y. Crowell Co., 1929.

Federal Council of the Churches of Christ in America, Department of Research and Education. *Broadcasting and the Public: A Case Study in Social Ethics.* New York: Abingdon Press, 1939.

Felix, Edgar H. *Using Radio in Sales Promotion.* New York: McGraw-Hill, 1927.

Frost, S. E., Jr. *Is American Radio Democratic?* Chicago: University of Chicago Press, 1937.

Gernsback, Hugo S. *Radio for All.* Philadelphia: Lippincott, 1922.

Goldsmith, Alfred N., and Austin C. Lescarboura. *This Thing Called Broadcasting.* New York: Henry Holt and Co., 1930.

Goode, Kenneth M. *What About Radio?* New York: Harper and Brothers, 1937.

Hard, William. "Europe's Air and Ours." *Atlantic Monthly* 150 (Oct. 1932): 499–509.

Hettinger, Herman S. *A Decade of Radio Advertising.* New York: Arno Press, 1971. First published 1933.

Hettinger, Herman S., and Richard R. Mead. *The Summer Radio Audience: A Study of the Habits and Preferences of Summer Radio Audiences in Philadelphia and Vicinity.* Philadelphia: Universal Broadcasting Company, 1931.

Hettinger, Herman S., and Walter J. Neff. *Practical Radio Advertising.* New York: Prentice-Hall, 1938.

Hines, Walter D. *War History of American Railroads.* New Haven: Yale University Press, 1928.

Horkheimer, Max, and Theodor Adorno. *The Dialectic of Enlightenment.* Trans. John Cumming. London: Verso Editions, 1979. First published 1944.

Irwin, Will. *Propaganda and the News: Or, What Makes You Think So?* New York: Whittlesey House, 1936.

Janowitz, Morris. "The Techniques of Propaganda for Reaction: Gerald L. K. Smith's Radio Speeches." *Public Opinion Quarterly* 8 (Spring 1944): 84–93.

Jome, Hiram L. *Economics of the Radio Industry.* Chicago: A. W. Shaw Co., 1925.

Kerwin, Jerome G. *The Control of Radio.* Chicago: University of Chicago Press, 1934.

Lasswell, Harold D. *Democracy through Public Opinion.* Menasha, Wis.: George Banta Publishing, 1941.

———. *Propaganda Techniques in World War I.* Cambridge, Mass.: Harvard University Press, 1971. First published 1927.

Lazarsfeld, Paul F. *Radio and the Printed Page.* New York: Arno Press, 1971. First published 1940.

Lazarsfeld, Paul F., Bernard Berelson, and Hazel Gaudet. *The People's Choice: How the Voter Makes Up His Mind in a Presidential Campaign.* 3d ed. New York: Columbia University Press, 1948. First published 1944.

Lazarsfeld, Paul F., and Frank N. Stanton, eds. *Radio Research 1941.* New York: Duell, Sloan, and Pearce, 1941.

———. *Radio Research 1942-1943.* New York: Duell, Sloan, and Pearce, 1944.

Lee, Alfred McClung, and Elizabeth Briant Lee, eds. *The Fine Art of Propaganda: A Study of Father Coughlin's Speeches.* New York: Harcourt, Brace, 1939.

Lee, Ivy L. *Publicity: Some of the Things It Is and Is Not.* New York: Industries Publishing Co., 1925.

Lippmann, Walter. *Liberty and the News.* New York: Harcourt, Brace, and Howe, 1920.

———. *A Preface to Morals.* New York: Macmillan, 1947. First published 1929.

———. *Public Opinion.* New York: Macmillan, 1947. First published 1922.

———. *The Phantom Public.* New York: Harcourt, Brace, 1925.

Lipsky, Abram. *Man the Puppet: The Art of Controlling Minds.* New York: Frank-Maurice, 1925.

Lumley, Frederick Elmore. *Means of Social Control.* New York: Century, 1925.

———. *Measurement in Radio.* Columbus: Ohio State University Press, 1934.

———. *The Propaganda Menace.* New York: Century, 1933.

Lynd, Robert S., and Helen Merrell Lynd. *Middletown: A Study in American Culture.* New York: Harcourt, Brace, and World, 1956. First published 1927.

———. *Middletown in Transition: A Study in Cultural Conflicts.* New York: Harcourt, Brace, 1937.

McCamy, James L. *Government Publicity: Its Practice in Federal Administration.* Chicago: University of Chicago Press, 1939.

McNair, W. A. *Radio Advertising in Australia.* Sydney: Angus and Robertson, 1937.

Martin, Everett Dean. *The Behavior of Crowds: A Psychological Study.* New York: Harper and Brothers, 1920.

Merriam, Charles E. *The American Party System: An Introduction to the Study of Political Parties in the United States.* 1st ed. New York: Macmillan, 1922. 2nd ed., 1929; 3d ed., 1940; 4th ed. (with H. F. Gosnel), 1949.

———. *The Making of Citizens: A Comparative Study of Methods of Civic Training.* Chicago: University of Chicago Press, 1931.

———. *New Aspects of Politics.* 3d ed. Chicago: University of Chicago Press, 1970. First published 1925.

Morgan, Alfred P. *The Pageant of Electricity.* New York: D. Appleton-Century, 1939.

Mott, Frank Luther. "Newspapers in Presidential Campaigns." *Public Opinion Quarterly* 8 (Fall 1944): 348–67.

Mumford, Lewis. *Technics and Civilization.* New York: Harcourt, Brace, 1934.

Munro, William B. "The Campaign in Retrospect." *Yale Review* 18 (1928–1929): 246–61.

———. *The Invisible Government.* New York: Arno Press, 1974. First published 1928.

Nash, Jay B. *Spectatoritis.* New York: A. S. Burns and Co., 1938.

National Association of Broadcasters. *Broadcasting in the United States.* Washington, D.C.: National Association of Broadcasters, 1933.

Ortega y Gasset, José. *The Revolt of the Masses.* London: George Allen and Unwin, 1932. First published 1930.

Overacker, Louise. *Money in Elections.* New York: Macmillan, 1932.

Overstreet, Harry A., and Bonaro W. Overstreet. *Town Meeting Comes to Town.* New York: Harper and Brothers, 1938.

Paley, William S. *Radio as a Cultural Force.* New York: Columbia System, 1934.

Pear, Thomas H. *Voice and Personality.* London: Chapman and Hall, 1931.

Peel, Roy V., and Thomas C. Donnelly. *The 1928 Campaign: An Analysis.* New York: Richard R. Smith, 1931.

———. *The 1932 Campaign: An Analysis.* New York: Farrar and Rinehart, 1935.

Peter, Paul F. "The American Listener in 1940." *Annals* 213 (Jan. 1941): 1–8.

Quiett, Glenn C., and Ralph D. Casey. *Principles of Publicity.* New York: D. Appleton and Co., 1926.

Riegel, O. W. *Mobilizing for Chaos: The Story of the New Propaganda.* New York: Arno Press, 1972. First published 1934.

Robinson, Ernest H. *Broadcasting and a Changing Civilization.* London: John Lane, the Bodley Head, 1935.

Robinson, Thomas Porter. *Radio Networks and the Federal Government.* New York: Columbia University Press, 1943.

Rogerson, Sidney. *Propaganda in the Next War.* London: Geoffrey Bles, 1938.

Rorty, James. *Order on the Air!* New York: John Day Co., 1934.

———. *Our Master's Voice: Advertising.* New York: John Day Co., 1934.

Rose, C. B., Jr. *A National Policy for Radio Broadcasting.* New York: Harper and Brothers, 1940.

Rothafel, Samuel I., and Raymond F. Yates. *Broadcasting: Its New Day.* New York: Century, 1925.

Schmeckebier, Laurence F. *The Federal Radio Commission: Its History, Activities, and Organization.* Institute for Government Research Service Monographs of the United States Government No. 65. Washington, D.C.: Brookings Institution, 1932.

Schubert, Paul. *The Electric Word: The Rise of Radio.* New York: Macmillan, 1928.

Shaw, George Bernard. "The Telltale Microphone." *Political Quarterly* 6 (Oct.–Dec. 1935): 463–67.

Sington, Derrick, and Arthur Weidenfeld. *The Goebbels Experiment: A Study of the Nazi Propaganda Machine.* New Haven: Yale University Press, 1943.

Starch, Daniel. *Principles of Advertising.* Chicago: A. W. Shaw Co., 1923.

Thompson, David Cleghorn. *Radio Is Changing Us: A Survey of Radio Development and Its Problems in Our Changing World.* London: Watts and Co., 1937.

Tyson, Levering, ed. *Radio and Education 1934.* Chicago: University of Chicago Press, 1935.

Tyson, Levering, and William J. Donovan. *Retrospect and Forecast in Radio Education.* Chicago: University of Chicago Press, 1936.

———. *What to Read About Radio.* Chicago: University of Chicago Press, 1933.

Tyson, Levering, and Judith Waller. *The Future of Radio and Educational Broadcasting.* Chicago: University of Chicago Press, 1934.

Wallas, Graham. *Human Nature in Politics.* New Brunswick, N.J.: Transaction Books, 1981. First published 1908.

Waples, Douglas, ed. *Print, Radio, and Film in a Democracy.* Chicago: University of Chicago Press, 1942.

West, Robert. *The Rape of Radio.* New York: Rodin Publishing Co., 1941.

Wiley, Philip. *Generation of Vipers.* New York: Rinehart and Co., 1942.

Wilke, Walter H. "An Experimental Comparison of the Speech, the Radio, and the Printed Page as Propaganda Devices." *Archives of Psychology* 25 (June 1934): 5–27.

Willey, Malcolm L., and Stuart A. Rice. *Communication Agencies and Social Life.* New York: McGraw-Hill, 1933.

Yates, Raymond Francis, and Louis Gerard Pacent. *The Complete Radio Book.* Popular Science Library vol. 17. London: Everleigh, Nash, and Grayson, 1922.

Young, Kimball. *Source Book for Social Psychology.* New York: Alfred A. Knopf, 1927.

Young, Kimball, and Raymond D. Lawrence. *Bibliography on Censorship and Propaganda.* Eugene: University of Oregon, 1928.

Zimmerman, Carle C. *The Changing Community.* New York: Harper and Brothers, 1938.

Books and Articles since 1945

Abbot, Philip. *Seeking Many Inventions: The Idea of Community in America.* Knoxville: University of Tennessee Press, 1987.

Abrams, Burton A., and Russell F. Settle. "Broadcasting and the Political Campaign Spending 'Arms Race.'" *Journal of Broadcasting* 21 (Spring 1977): 153–62.

Aitken, Hugh G. J. *The Continuous Wave: Technology and the American Radio, 1900–1932.* Princeton: Princeton University Press, 1985.

———. *Syntony and Spark: The Origins of Radio.* New York: John Wiley and Sons, 1976.

Allen, Robert C. *Speaking about Soap Operas.* Chapel Hill: University of North Carolina Press, 1985.

Baker, John C. *Farm Broadcasting: The First Sixty Years.* Ames: Iowa State University Press, 1981.

Banning, William Peck. *Commercial Broadcasting Pioneer: The WEAF Experiment, 1922–1926.* Cambridge, Mass.: Harvard University Press, 1946.

Barnouw, Erik. *A History of Broadcasting in the United States.* 3 vols. Vol. 1, *A Tower in Babel: To 1933.* Vol. 2, *The Golden Web: 1933 to 1953.* New York: Oxford University Press, 1966–68.

Baughman, James L. *The Republic of Mass Culture: Journalism, Filmmaking, and Broadcasting in America since 1941.* Baltimore: Johns Hopkins University Press, 1992.

Becker, Samuel L. "Presidential Power: The Influence of Broadcasting." *Quarterly Journal of Speech* 47 (Feb. 1961): 10–18.

Benjamin, Louise. "Broadcast Campaign Precedents from the 1924 Presidential Election." *Journal of Broadcasting and Electronic Media* 31 (Fall 1987): 449–60.

Bensman, Marvin R. "The Zenith-WJAZ Case and the Chaos of 1926–27." *Journal of Broadcasting* 14 (Fall 1970): 423–37.

Berelson, Bernard, and Morris Janowitz, eds. *Reader in Public Opinion and Communication.* 2d ed. New York: Free Press, 1966.

Berelson, Bernard, Paul F. Lazarsfeld, and William N. McPhee. *Voting: A Study of Opinion Formation in a Presidential Election.* Chicago: University of Chicago Press, 1954.

Bernays, Edward L. *The Engineering of Consent.* Norman: University of Oklahoma Press, 1955.

Best, Gary Dean. *The Critical Press and the New Deal: The Press versus Presidential Power, 1933–1938.* Westport, Conn.: Praeger, 1993.

Bigsby, C. W. E., ed. *Approaches to Popular Culture.* Bowling Green, Ky.: Bowling Green University Popular Press, 1976.

Black, Gregory D. *Hollywood Censored: Morality Codes, Catholics, and the Movies.* Cambridge: Cambridge University Press, 1994.

Blondheim, Menahem. *News over the Wires: The Telegraph and the Flow of Public Information in America, 1844–1897.* Cambridge, Mass.: Harvard University Press, 1994.

Bormann, Ernest G. "This Is Huey P. Long Talking." *Journal of Broadcasting* 2 (Spring 1958): 111–22.

Bowden, Sue, and Avner Offer. "Household Appliances and the Use of Time: The United States and Britain since the 1920s." *Economic History Review* 47, no. 4 (1994): 725–48.

Braden, Waldo W., and Earnest Bradenburg. "Roosevelt's Fireside Chats." *Speech Monographs* 22 (Nov. 1955): 290–302.

———. "Franklin D. Roosevelt's Voice and Pronunciation." *Quarterly Journal of Speech* 38 (Feb. 1952): 23–30.

Branyan, Helen B. "Medical Charlatanism: The Goat Gland Wizard of Milford, Kansas." *Journal of Popular Culture* 25 (Summer 1991): 31–37.

Briggs, Asa. *The BBC: The First Fifty Years.* Oxford: Oxford University Press, 1985.

———. *The History of Broadcasting in the United Kingdom.* 2 vols. Vol. 1, *The Birth of Broadcasting.* Vol. 2, *The Golden Age of Wireless.* London: Oxford University Press, 1961–65.

Brinkley, Alan. *Voices of Protest: Huey Long, Father Coughlin, and the Great Depression.* New York: Vintage Books, 1983.

Brown, James A. "Selling Airtime for Controversy: NAB Self-Regulation and Father Coughlin." *Journal of Broadcasting* 24 (Spring 1980): 199–224.

Burdick, Eugene, and Arthur J. Brodbeck, eds. *American Voting Behavior.* New York: Free Press, 1959.

Burner, David. *The Politics of Provincialism: The Democratic Party in Transition, 1918–1932.* New York: Alfred A. Knopf, 1968.

Campbell, Angus. "Has Television Reshaped Politics?" *Columbian Journalism Review* 1 (Fall 1962): 10–13.

Cantril, Hadley. *The Invasion from Mars: A Study in the Psychology of Panic.* Princeton: Princeton University Press, 1947.

———. ed. *Public Opinion 1935–1946.* Prepared by Mildred Strunk. Princeton: Princeton University Press, 1951.

Carey, James W. *Communication as Culture: Essays on Media and Society.* Boston: Unwin Hyman, 1989.

Carey, James W., and John J. Quirk. "The *Mythos* of the Electronic Revolution." *American Scholar* 39 (Spring, Summer 1970): 219–41, 395–424.

Charnley, Mitchell V. *News by Radio.* New York: Macmillan, 1948.

Chester, Edward W. *Radio, Television, and American Politics.* New York: Sheed and Ward, 1969.

Clark, David G. "Radio in Presidential Campaigns: The Early Years (1921–1932)." *Journal of Broadcasting* 6 (Summer 1962): 229–38.

Cohen, Lizabeth. *Making a New Deal: Industrial Workers in Chicago, 1918–1939.* Cambridge: Cambridge University Press, 1990.

Counihan, Nick. "The Formation of a Broadcasting Audience: Australian Radio in the Twenties." *Meanjin* 41 (Winter 1982): 196–209.

Covert, Catherine L., and John D. Stevens, eds. *Mass Media between the Wars: Perceptions of Cultural Tension, 1918–1941.* Syracuse: Syracuse University Press, 1984.

Craig, Douglas B. *After Wilson: The Struggle for the Democratic Party, 1920–1934.* Chapel Hill: University of North Carolina Press, 1992.

Culbert, David Holbrook. *News for Everyman: Radio and Foreign Affairs in Thirties America.* Westport, Conn.: Greenwood Press, 1976.

Curran, James, Michael Gurevitch, and Janet Woollacott, eds. *Mass Communication and Society.* London: Edward Arnold, 1977.

Czitrom, Daniel J. *Media and the American Mind: From Morse to McLuhan.* Chapel Hill: University of North Carolina Press, 1982.

Davis, Richard. *The Web of Politics: The Internet's Impact on the American Political System.* New York: Oxford University Press, 1999.

De Fleur, Melvin L. *Theories of Mass Communication.* New York: David McKay Co., 1970.

Diamond, Edwin, and Stephen Bates. *The Spot: The Rise of Political Advertising on Television.* 2d ed. Cambridge: MIT Press, 1992.

Dinkin, Robert J. *Campaigning in America: A History of Election Practices.* New York: Greenwood Press, 1989.

Donovan, Robert J., and Ray Scherer. *Unsilent Revolution: Television News and American Public Life.* Cambridge: Cambridge University Press, 1992.

Doob, Leonard W. "Goebbels' Principles of Propaganda." *Public Opinion Quarterly* 14 (Fall 1950): 419–42.

———. *Public Opinion and Propaganda.* 2d ed. Hamden, Conn.: Anchor Books, 1966. First published 1948.

Douglas, George H. *The Early Days of Radio Broadcasting.* Jefferson, N.C.: McFarland and Co., 1987.

Douglas, Susan J. *Inventing American Broadcasting, 1899–1922.* Baltimore: Johns Hopkins University Press, 1987.

Ellul, Jacques. *Propaganda: The Formation of Men's Attitudes.* Trans. Konrad Keller and Jean Lerner. New York: Alfred A. Knopf, 1965.

———. *The Technological Society.* Trans. John Wilkinson. London: Jonathan Cape, 1965. First published 1954.

Ely, Melvin Patrick. *The Adventures of Amos'n'Andy: A Social History of an American Phenomenon.* New York: Free Press, 1991.

Erickson, Don V. *Armstrong's Fight for FM Broadcasting: One Man vs. Big Business and Bureaucracy.* University, Ala.: University of Alabama Press, 1973.

Ernst, Morris L. *The First Freedom.* New York: Macmillan, 1946.

Ewen, Stuart. *Captains of Consciousness: Advertising and the Social Roots of the Consumer Culture.* New York: McGraw-Hill, 1976.

Farber, David. "Political Culture and the Therapeutic Ideal." *Reviews in American History* 23 (Dec. 1995): 681–86.

Fischer, Claude S. *America Calling: The Social History of the Telephone to 1940.* Berkeley: University of California Press, 1992.

Fleming, Raymond. *The American Newsreel, 1911–1967.* Norman: University of Oklahoma Press, 1972.

Ford, Frederick W. "The Meaning of 'Public Interest, Convenience or Necessity.'" *Journal of Broadcasting* 5 (Summer 1961): 205–18.

Fox, Richard Wightman, and T. J. Jackson Lears, eds. *The Culture of Consumption: Critical Essays in American History, 1880–1980.* New York: Pantheon Books, 1983.

Garvey, Daniel E. "Secretary Hoover and the Quest for Broadcast Regulation." *Broadcast History* 3, no. 3 (Autumn 1976): 66–70, 85.

Godfrey, Donald G. "Senator Dill and the 1927 Radio Act." *Journal of Broadcasting* 23 (Fall 1979): 477–90.

———. "The 1927 Radio Act: People and Politics." *Journalism History* 4, no. 3 (Autumn 1977): 75–78.

Graber, Doris A., ed. *Media Power in Politics,* 2d ed. Washington, D.C.: Congressional Quarterly, 1990.

Grossman, Lawrence K. *The Electronic Republic: Reshaping Democracy in the Information Age.* New York: Penguin Books, 1995.

Grundy, Pamela. "'We Always Tried to Be Good People': Respectability, Crazy Water Crystals, and Hillbilly Music on the Air, 1933–1935." *Journal of American History* 81 (Mar. 1995): 1591–1620.

Hale, Julian. *Radio Power: Propaganda and International Broadcasting.* Philadelphia: Temple University Press, 1975.

Hawley, Ellis W. *The Great War and the Search for a Modern Order: A History of the American People and Their Institutions, 1917–1933.* 2d ed. New York: St. Martin's Press, 1992.

———, ed. *Herbert Hoover as Secretary of Commerce: Studies in New Era Thought and Practice.* Iowa City: University of Iowa Press, 1981.

Head, Sydney W., and Christopher H. Sterling. *Broadcasting in America: A Survey of Electronic Media.* Boston: Houghton Mifflin, 1991.

Heinz, Catherine. "The Voice of Authority, or, Hurrah for Christine Craft." *Feedback* 25 (Spring 1984): 3–6.

———. "Women Radio Pioneers." *Journal of Popular Culture* 12 (Fall 1978): 305–14.

Henderson, Amy. *On the Air: Pioneers of American Broadcasting.* Washington, D.C.: Smithsonian Institution Press, 1988.

Herman, Edward S., and Noam Chomsky. *Manufacturing Consent: The Political Economy of the Mass Media.* New York: Pantheon Books, 1988.

Higgins, C. S., and P. D. Moss. *Sounds Real: Radio in Everyday Life.* St. Lucia: University of Queensland Press, 1982.

Hijiya, James A. *Lee de Forest and the Fatherhood of Radio.* Bethlehem, Pa.: Lehigh University Press, 1992.

Hilmes, Michele. *Radio Voices: American Broadcasting, 1922–1952.* Minneapolis: University of Minnesota Press, 1997.

Horowitz, Joseph. *Understanding Toscanini: How He Became an American Culture-God and Helped Create a New Audience for Old Music.* New York: Alfred A. Knopf, 1987.

Huyssen, Andreas. *After the Great Divide: Modernism, Mass Culture, Postmodernism.* Bloomington: Indiana University Press, 1986.

Hynes, Terry. "Media Manipulation and Political Campaigns: Bruce Barton and the Presidential Elections of the Jazz Age." *Journalism History* 4, no. 3 (Autumn 1977): 93–98.

Inglis, K. S. *This Is the ABC: The Australian Broadcasting Commission, 1932–1983.* Melbourne: Melbourne University Press, 1983.

Innis, Harold A. *The Bias of Communication.* Toronto: University of Toronto Press, 1951.

Israel, Paul. *From Machine Shop to Industrial Laboratory: Telegraphy and the Changing Context of American Invention, 1830–1920.* Baltimore: Johns Hopkins University Press, 1992.

Jamieson, Kathleen Hall. *Eloquence in an Electronic Age: The Transformation of Political Speechmaking.* New York: Oxford University Press, 1988.

———. *Packaging the Presidency: A History and Criticism of Presidential Campaign Advertising.* Oxford: Oxford University Press, 1984.

Johnson, Lesley. "'Sing 'Em Muck, Clara": Highbrow versus Lowbrow on Early Australian Radio." *Meanjin* 41 (Winter 1982): 210–22.

———. *The Unseen Voice: A Cultural Study of Early Australian Radio.* London: Routledge, 1988.

Jones, Colin. *Something in the Air: A History of Radio in Australia.* Sydney: Kangaroo Press, 1995.

Jordan, John M. *Machine-Age Ideology: Social Engineering and American Liberalism, 1911–1939.* Chapel Hill: University of North Carolina Press, 1994.

Kang, Joon-Mann. "Franklin Roosevelt and James L. Fly: The Politics of Broadcast Regulation, 1941-1944." *Journal of American Culture* 10 (Summer 1987): 23–33.

Katz, Elihu, and Paul F. Lazarsfeld. *Personal Influence: The Part Played by People in the Flow of Mass Communications.* Glencoe, Ill.: Free Press, 1949.

Kern, Stephen. *The Culture of Time and Space, 1880–1918.* Cambridge, Mass.: Harvard University Press, 1983.

Key, V. O., Jr. *Public Opinion and American Democracy.* New York: Alfred A. Knopf, 1961.

Klapper, Joseph T. *The Effects of Mass Communication.* Glencoe, Ill.: Free Press, 1960.

———. "Mass Media and the Engineering of Consent." *American Scholar* 17 (Autumn 1948): 419–29.

Koch, Howard. *The Panic Broadcast: Portrait of an Event.* Boston: Little, Brown and Co., 1970.

Koppes, Clayton R. "The Social Destiny of Radio." *South Atlantic Quarterly* 48 (1969): 363–76.

Krasnow, Erwin G., and Lawrence D. Longley. *Politics of Broadcast Regulation.* New York: St. Martin's Press, 1978.

Lang, Kurt, and Gladys Engel Lang. *Politics and Television.* Chicago: Quadrangle Books, 1968.

Lazarsfeld, Paul F., and Patricia L. Kendall. *Listening in America: The People Look at Radio—Again.* New York: Prentice-Hall, 1948.

Lears, T. J. Jackson. "The Concept of Cultural Hegemony: Problems and Possibilities." *American Historical Review* 90 (June 1985): 567–93.

———. *Fables of Abundance: A Cultural History of Advertising in America.* New York: Basic Books, 1994.

———. "Making Fun of Popular Culture." *American Historical Review* 97 (Dec. 1992): 1417–26.

———. *No Place of Grace: Antimodernism and the Transformation of American Culture, 1880–1920.* Chicago: University of Chicago Press, 1981.

Le Duc, Don R., and Thomas A. McCain. "The Federal Radio Commission in Federal Court: Origins of Broadcast Regulatory Doctrines." *Journal of Broadcasting* 14 (Fall 1970): 393–410.

Levine, Lawrence W. "American Culture and the Great Depression." *Yale Review* 74 (Winter 1985): 196–223.

———. "The Folklore of Industrial Society: Popular Culture and Its Audiences." *American Historical Review* 97 (Dec. 1992): 1369–99.

———. *Highbrow/Lowbrow: The Emergence of Cultural Hierarchy in America.* Cambridge, Mass.: Harvard University Press, 1988.

Lewis, Tom. *Empire of the Air: The Men Who Made Radio.* New York: Edward Burlingame Books, 1991.

Lichty, Lawrence W., and Malachi C. Topping, eds. *American Broadcasting: A Source Book on the History of Radio and Television.* New York: Hastings House, 1975.

Liebovich, Louis W. *Bylines in Despair: Herbert Hoover, the Great Depression, and the U.S. News Media.* Westport, Conn.: Praeger, 1994.

Loevinger, Lee. "The Ambiguous Mirror: The Reflective-Projective Theory of Broadcasting and Mass Communications." *Journal of Broadcasting* 12 (Spring 1968): 97–116.

Lott, George E. "The Press-Radio War of the 1930s." *Journal of Broadcasting* 14 (Summer 1970): 275–86.

Lyons, Eugene. *David Sarnoff: A Biography.* New York: Harper and Row, 1966.

McChesney, Robert W. *Telecommunications, Mass Media, and Democracy: The Battle for the Control of U.S. Broadcasting, 1928–1935.* New York: Oxford University Press, 1993.

MacDonald, Dwight. "Masscult and Midcult." Part 1, *Partisan Review* 27 (Spring 1960): 203–33. Part 2, *Partisan Review* 27 (Fall 1960): 589–631.

MacDonald, J. Fred. *Don't Touch That Dial! Radio Programming in American Life, 1920–1960.* Chicago: Nelson-Hall, 1979.

McFadden, Margaret T. "'America's Boyfriend Who Can't Get a Date': Gender, Race, and the Cultural Work of the Jack Benny Program, 1932–1946." *Journal of American History* 80 (June 1993): 113–34.

McGerr, Michael E. *The Decline of Popular Politics: The American North, 1865–1928.* New York: Oxford University Press, 1986.

McIntyre, Ian. *The Expense of Glory: A Life of John Reith.* London: HarperCollins, 1993.

McKerns, Joseph P. "Industry Skeptics and the Radio Act of 1927." *Journalism History* 3, no. 4 (Winter 1976–77): 128–31, 136.

Mackey, David R. "The Development of the National Association of Broadcasters." *Journal of Broadcasting* 1 (Fall 1957): 305–25.

McLuhan, Herbert Marshall. *Understanding Media: The Extensions of Man.* London: Art Paperbacks, 1964.

McNeil, Bill, and Morris Wolfe. *Signing On: The Birth of Radio in Canada.* Toronto: Doubleday Canada, 1982.

MacNeil, Robert. *The People Machine: The Influence of Television on American Politics.* New York: Harper and Row, 1968.

McQuail, Denis. *Towards a Sociology of Mass Communications.* London: Collier-Macmillan, 1969.

Mander, Mary S. "The Public Debate About Broadcasting in the Twenties: An Interpretative History." *Journal of Broadcasting* 28 (Spring 1984): 167–85.

Marchand, Roland. *Advertising the American Dream: Making Way for Modernity, 1920–1940.* Berkeley: University of California Press, 1985.

Marvin, Carolyn. *When Old Technologies Were New: Thinking About Electric Communication in the Late Nineteenth Century.* New York: Oxford University Press, 1988.

Marzoff, Marion, and Bock, Nancy. "The Literature of Women in Journalism History: A Supplement." *Journalism History* 3, no. 4 (Winter 1976–77): 116–20.

Meehan, Eileen R. "Critical Theorizing on Broadcast History." *Journal of Broadcasting and Electronic Media* 30 (Fall 1986): 393–411.

Merriam, Charles E., and Harold Foote Gosnell. *The American Party System.* 4th ed. New York: Johnson Reprint Corporation, 1969. First published 1949.

Merton, Robert K. *Mass Persuasion: The Social Psychology of a War Bond Drive.* Westport, Conn.: Greenwood Press, 1971.

Metz, Robert. *CBS: Reflections in a Bloodshot Eye.* Chicago: Playboy Press, 1975.

Meyrowitz, Joshua. *No Sense of Place: The Impact of Electronic Media on Social Behavior.* New York: Oxford University Press, 1985.

Mitchell, Greg. *The Campaign of the Century: Upton Sinclair's Race for Governor of California and the Birth of Media Politics.* New York: Random House, 1992.

Mukerji, Chandra, and Michael Schudson, eds. *Rethinking Popular Culture: Contemporary Perspectives in Cultural Studies.* Berkeley: University of California Press, 1991.

Murphy, Paul L. *The Meaning of Freedom of Speech: First Amendment Freedoms from Wilson to FDR.* Westport, Conn.: Greenwood Press, 1972.

Nolan, Michael. "Canadian Election Broadcasting: Political Practices and Radio Regulation, 1919–1939." *Journal of Broadcasting and Electronic Media* 29 (Spring 1985): 175–88.

Nye, David E. *American Technological Sublime.* Cambridge, Mass.: MIT Press, 1996.

———. *Electrifying America: Social Meanings of a New Technology, 1880–1940.* Cambridge, Mass.: MIT Press, 1990.

Orbison, Charley. "'Fighting Bob' Shuler: Early Radio Crusader." *Journal of Broadcasting* 21 (Fall 1977): 459–72.

Ostroff, David H. "Equal Time: Origins of Section 18 of the Radio Act of 1927." *Journal of Broadcasting* 24 (Spring 1980): 367–80.

Page, Leslie J., Jr. "The Nature of the Broadcast Receiver and Its Market in the United States from 1922 to 1927." *Journal of Broadcasting* 4 (Spring 1960): 174–82.

Paper, Lewis J. *Empire: William S. Paley and the Making of CBS.* New York: St. Martin's Press, 1987.

Pegg, Mark. *Broadcasting and Society.* London: Croom Helm, 1983.

Peterson, Theodore, Jay W. Jensen, and William L. Rivers. *The Mass Media and Modern Society.* New York: Holt, Rinehart, and Winston, 1966.

Pool, Ithiel de Sola. *Technologies of Freedom.* Cambridge, Mass.: Belknap Press of Harvard University Press, 1983.

Potts, John. *Radio in Australia.* Sydney: New South Wales University Press, 1989.

Pusateri, C. Joseph. "FDR, Huey Long, and the Politics of Radio Regulation." *Journal of Broadcasting* 21 (Winter 1977): 85–95.

Ribuffo, Leo P. "Jesus Christ as Business Statesman: Bruce Barton and the Selling of Corporate Capitalism." *American Quarterly* 33 (Summer 1981): 206–31.

Ronnie, Art. "First Convention on Radio." *Journal of Broadcasting* 8 (Winter 1963–64): 245–46.

Rosen, Philip T. *The Modern Stentors: Radio Broadcasters and the Federal Government, 1920–1934.* Westport, Conn.: Greenwood Press, 1980.

———. "Review Essay: The Marvel of Radio." *American Quarterly* 31 (Fall 1979): 572–81.

Rosenzweig, Roy. "Wizards, Bureaucrats, Warriors, and Hackers: Writing the History of the Internet." *American Historical Review* 103 (Dec. 1998): 1530–52.

Rubin, Joan Shelley. *The Making of Middlebrow Culture.* Chapel Hill: University of North Carolina Press, 1992.

Ryan, Halford R. *Franklin D. Roosevelt's Rhetorical Presidency.* New York: Greenwood Press, 1988.

Sarno, Edward F. "The National Radio Conferences." *Journal of Broadcasting* 13 (Spring 1969): 189–202.

Savage, Barbara Dianne. *Broadcasting Freedom: Radio, War, and the Politics of Race, 1938–1948.* Chapel Hill: University of North Carolina Press, 1999.

Savan, Leslie. *The Sponsored Life: Ads, TV, and American Culture.* Philadelphia: Temple University Press, 1994.

Scannell, Paddy, and David Cardiff. *A Social History of British Broadcasting.* 2 vols. Vol. 1, *1922–1939: Serving the Nation.* Oxford: Basil Blackwell, 1991–93.

Schiffer, Michael Brian. *The Portable Radio in American Life.* Tucson: University of Arizona Press, 1991.

Schramm, Wilbur L., ed. *Mass Communications.* Urbana: University of Illinois Press, 1949.

Schudson, Michael. *Advertising, the Uneasy Persuasion: Its Dubious Impact on American Society.* New York: Basic Books, 1984.

———. *Discovering the News: A Social History of American Newspapers.* New York: Basic Books, 1978.

Schultze, Quentin J. "Evangelical Radio and the Rise of the Electronic Church, 1921–1948." *Journal of Broadcasting and Electronic Media* 32 (Summer 1988): 289–306.

Segal, Howard P. *Technological Utopianism in American Culture.* Chicago: University of Chicago Press, 1985.

Severin, Werner J. "Commercial vs. Non-Commercial Radio during Broadcasting's Early Years." *Journal of Broadcasting* 22 (Fall 1978): 491–503.

Seymour-Ure, Colin. *The Political Impact of the Mass Media.* London: Constable and Co., 1974.

Siepmann, Charles A. *Radio's Second Chance.* Boston: Brown and Co., 1946.

———. *Radio, Television, and Society.* New York: Oxford University Press, 1950.

Skornia, Harry J., and Jack William Kitson, eds. *Problems and Controversies in Television and Radio.* Palo Alto, Calif.: Pacific Books, 1968.

Smith, F. Leslie. *Perspectives on Radio and Television: Telecommunications in the United States.* 3d ed. New York: Harper and Row, 1990.

Smulyan, Susan. *Selling Radio: The Commercialization of American Broadcasting, 1920–1934.* Washington, D.C.: Smithsonian Institution Press, 1994.

Spigel, Lynn. *Make Room for TV: Television and the Family Ideal in Postwar America.* Chicago: University of Chicago Press, 1992.

Sprague, William C., ed. *Popular Images of American Presidents.* New York: Greenwood Press, 1988.

Spring, Joel. *Images of American Life: A History of Ideological Management in Schools, Movies, Radio, and Television.* Albany: State University of New York Press, 1992.

Steele, Richard W. *Propaganda in an Open Society: The Roosevelt Administration and the Media, 1933–1941.* Westport, Conn.: Greenwood Press, 1985.

Sterling, Christopher H., and John M. Kitross. *Stay Tuned: A Concise History of American Broadcasting.* Belmont, Calif.: Wadsworth Publishing Co., 1978.

Stott, William. *Documentary Expression and Thirties America.* New York: Oxford University Press, 1973.

Summers, Harrison B., ed. *A Thirty Year History of Programs Carried on the National Radio Networks in the United States, 1926–1956.* New York: Arno Press, 1971. First published 1958.

Summers, Mark Wahlgren. *The Press Gang: Newspapers and Politics, 1865–1878.* Chapel Hill: University of North Carolina Press, 1994.

Susman, Warren, ed. *Culture and Commitment, 1929–1945.* New York: George Braziller, 1973.

———. *Culture as History: The Transformation of American Society in the Twentieth Century.* New York: Pantheon Books, 1984.

Thompson, John B. *The Media and Modernity: A Social Theory of the Media.* Cambridge: Polity Press, 1995.

Thompson, Robert Luther. *Wiring a Continent: The History of the Telegraph Industry in the United States, 1832–1866.* Princeton, N.J.: Princeton University Press, 1947.

Turner, Henry A. "Woodrow Wilson and Public Opinion." *Public Opinion Quarterly* 21 (Winter 1957–58): 505–20.

Waller, Judith C. *Radio: The Fifth Estate.* 2d ed. Boston: Houghton Mifflin, 1950.

Weeks, Lewis E. "The Radio Election of 1924." *Journal of Broadcasting* 8 (Winter 1963–64): 233–43.

Wertheim, Arthur Frank. "Relieving Social Tensions: Radio Comedy and the Great Depression." *Journal of Popular Culture* 10 (Winter 1976): 501–19.

Whale, John. *The Half-Shut Eye: Television and Politics in Britain and America.* London: Macmillan, 1969.

White, Graham J. *FDR and the Press.* Chicago: University of Chicago Press, 1979.

White, Llewellyn. *The American Radio: A Report on the Broadcasting Industry in the United States from the Commission on Freedom of the Press.* Chicago: University of Chicago Press, 1947.

White, Paul W. *News on the Air.* New York: Harcourt, Brace, 1947.

Whittaker, Susan, and Ron Whittaker. "Relative Effectiveness of Male and Female Newscasters." *Journal of Broadcasting* 20 (Spring 1976): 177–83.

Wik, Reynold M. "The Radio in Rural America during the 1920s." *Agricultural History* 55 (Oct. 1981): 339–50.

Williams, Raymond L. *Communications.* 3d ed. Harmondsworth: Penguin Books, 1976.

———. *Television: Technology and Cultural Form.* London: Fontana, 1974.

Williamson, Mary E. "Judith Cary Waller: Chicago Broadcasting Pioneer." *Journalism History* 3, no. 4 (Winter 1976–77): 111–115.

Winfield, Betty Houchin. *FDR and the News Media.* Urbana and Chicago: University of Illinois Press, 1990.

Wolfe, G. Joseph. "Norman Baker and KTNT." *Journal of Broadcasting* 12 (Fall 1968): 389–99.

———. "Some Reactions to the Advent of Campaigning by Radio." *Journal of Broadcasting* 13 (Summer 1969): 304–14.

Zeman, Z. A. B. *Nazi Propaganda.* London: Oxford University Press, 1964.

Unpublished Dissertations

Banks, Mark James. "A History of Broadcast Audience Research in the United States, 1920–1980 with an Emphasis on the Rating Services." Ph.D., University of Tennessee, 1981.

Benjamin, Louise Margaret. "Radio Regulation in the 1920s: Free Speech Issues in the Development of Radio and the Radio Act of 1927." Ph.D., University of Iowa, 1985.

Doeden, Daniel Lee. "The Press-Radio War: A Historical Analysis of Press-Radio Competition, 1920–1940." Ph.D., Northwestern University, 1975.

Prostak, Elaine J. "Up in the Air: The Debates over Radio Use during the 1920s." Ph.D., University of Kansas, 1983.

Roberts, Frank Thomas, III. "Paul H. White: Broadcast Journalism Pioneer." M.A., University of Kansas, 1981.

Smulyan, Susan Renee. "And Now a Word from our Sponsors . . . : Commercialization of American Broadcast Radio, 1920–1934." Ph.D., Yale University, 1985.

Index

Abernethy, Charles, 69
Addams, Jane, 265
Adorno, Theodor, 200. *See also* Frankfurt School
advertising: development on radio, 19–27, 258; newspaper, 26 (fig. 6), 223–4, 227. *See also* networks; newspapers; press-radio war; toll broadcasting
African Americans, 63, 237, 265; discrimination against, in radio industry, 253; portrayal of, 253–7; programs for, 252–3; protests against radio portrayals, 255–7; radio ownership, 251–2; and World War II, 322 n. 72
Agricultural Adjustment Administration (AAA), 82
Agriculture, Department of, 44, 81, 157, 240
alcoholic beverages, 243, 272–3
Alderman, Edwin A., 265
Alexanderson alternator, 4, 7
All Colored Program, 256
Allen, Frederick Lewis, 178
Allen, Henry, 133
Allen, Robert, 246
All Negro Hour, 253
Allport, Gordon, xii, 247–8, 274
Ameche, Don, 246
American Association of Advertising Agencies (AAAA), 193
American Broadcasting Company, 106, 279. *See also* networks
American Civil Liberties Union (ACLU), 84, 101, 107, 271
American Education Week, 253
American exceptionalism, 260
American Federation of Labor, 236, 266
American Institute of Public Opinion (AIPO), 27, 190, 194–5, 217, 220
American Legion, 80
American Liberty League, 129
American Marconi Company, 5, 7
American Medical Association, 74
American Newspaper Publishers Association (ANPA), 225–6
American Party System, The, 167
American School of the Air, The, 214
American Society of Composers, Authors, and Publishers (ASCAP), 18, 35
Americans All, Immigrants All, 235
"American system" of broadcasting, xvi, 27, 41, 47, 79, 90, 108–9, 261, 266–7
America's Town Meeting of the Air, 215
Amos'n'Andy, xiv, 94, 122, 256; content of, 254, 262, 268; creation of, 253–4; portrayal of African Americans, 254–5; protests against, 255
Anderson, Eddie, 256
Annals of the American Academy of Political and Social Science, 106
Archer, Gleason, 21
Armstrong, Louis, 256
Arnheim, Rudolf, 231
Arnold, Frank, 22, 214, 245
Associated Clubs for Willkie, 164
Associated Press (AP), 157, 225
associationalism: collapse of, 48–9; defined, 42; and radio, 45–8, 108
Association for Tax Equality, 137
Atkinson, C. F., 261
audience measurement, 267; early forms of, 187–91; by electricity consumption, 192; by questionnaires, 191–2; ratings systems, 191–5; relative merits, 194; use of listener mail, 187–91
audion tube, 4,
Australia, 183, 249; broadcasting system, 42–3; radio ownership rate, 12, 43; U.S. reaction to, 44–5, 70, 106, 185

Australian Broadcasting Company (later Commission) (ABC): and controversy, 183; creation of, 43–4; and political broadcasting, 183; program priorities, 269
Australian Labor Party, 183
automobile registrations, 16 (fig. 5)
Aylesworth, Merlin, 79, 121–2, 131, 134, 225, 237, 275–6

Babson, Roger, 274
Baer, Max, 192
Bagby, William Chandler, 215
Bailey, Carl E., 255
Baker, Newton D., 147, 171–3, 265
Baldwin, Stanley, 181
Barnouw, Erik, 100, 105, 164
Bartlett, Frederick, 228
Barton, Bruce, 144–6, 151, 223
Batten, Barton, Durstine, and Osborn (BBD&O), 24
Bellows, Henry A., 60, 66, 69, 80, 89, 221, 275–6
Bender, Thomas, 209
Bennetts, The, 162
Benny, Jack, 214, 256, 262, 268, 271. See also *Jack Benny Show, The*
Berger, Robert, 96
Berger, Victor, 114
Berle, Adolph, 86
Bernays, Edward, 22–3, 195, 229
Beveridge, Albert, 140
Biltmore agreement, 226. *See also* press-radio war
Bingham, Hiram, 55
birth control, 271–2
Black, Hugo, 197
Blanton, Thomas, 55
Bliven, Bruce, 178, 237, 260
Blondheim, Menahem, 211
Blythe, Samuel, 168
Borah, William E., 54, 78, 103, 113, 149
Borden, Richard, 149
Brainard, Bertha, 249
Briggs, Clay, 229
Brinkley, John, 62, 73
British Broadcasting Company (later Commission) (BBC), 27, 265; and controversy, 181–2; creation of, 40; and cultural uplift, 40, 260; and female announcers, 248; and female employees, 249; and political programming, 180–2; program priorities, 269. *See also* Great Britain
"British system" of broadcasting, 39; U.S. reaction to, 41–2, 180, 185. *See also* Great Britain
Broadcasting and the American Public, 266
broadcast licenses, 99, 104. *See also* Davis amendment; Federal Radio Commission
Brookings Institution, 157
Brooklyn Eagle, 30, 175
Browder, Earl, 132. *See also* Communist Party of America
Brown, Thad, 93
Bruning, Heinrich, 182
Bryan, William Jennings, 143, 175, 179
Bryce, James, 195
Bullard, William, 7, 60
Bureau of Applied Social Research, 197
Burns and Allen, 271
Butcher, Harry, 129–30, 195
Byrd, Richard E., 258

Caldwell, Louis, 75
Caldwell, Orestes, 27, 60, 69, 71, 229
Cameron, William J., 222
Canada: broadcasting system, 43–4, 249; radio ownership rate, 12; U.S. reaction to, 44–5, 106, 185; women in broadcasting, 322 n. 50
Canadian Broadcasting Commission (CBC), 43–4, 184
Canadian Radio Broadcasting Commission (CRBC), 43, 184
Cantril, Hadley, xii, 220, 233, 247–8, 274
Cardiff, David, 182
Carlin, Phillips, 240, 260, 271
Carter, Boake, 220, 222
Case, Norman, 93
campaign styles, changes in, 173–7
Celler, Emanuel, 63
censorship, 73–5, 100–1, 114. *See also* First Amendment
Century Magazine, 143
Chamberlain, Neville, 181, 218
Chicago Federation of Labor, 68, 203
Chicago Tribune, 129
children's programs, 264, 269
Church of the Air, 276
citizenship, interwar problems of, 206–11. *See also* radio citizenship

Clancy, Robert H., 237
Clark, David G., 222
Clark, Lloyd, 193
Clark-Hooper, Inc., 193
Clayton Anti-Trust Act of 1914, 52
Cohen, Lizabeth, 235
Collier's, 168
Coltrane, Eugene, 78
Columbia Broadcasting System (CBS), 62, 68, 79, 99, 105, 151, 206, 235; advertising charges, 122; advertising policies, 270, 272–3; and affiliates, 33 (map 3), 227; and alcoholic beverages, 272–3; audience measurement, 193–5; and Charles E. Coughlin, 159; and cultural uplift, 260–2; debt collection policies, 133–7; and educational broadcasting, 212–6; farm programs, 240; and female employees, 249–50; and female listeners, 244–7; formation of, 32–3; and jazz, 256–7; listener mail, 192; news broadcasts, 218–9; and news commentators, 220–3; and political programming, 119–33; and press-radio war, 223–8; program priorities, 268–9; and Prohibition, 272; relationship with socialists and CPA, 131–3; and religious broadcasting, 273–7; and *War of the Worlds*, 232–3. *See also* networks
Columbia News Service (CNS), 225–7
Columbia Phonograph Corporation, 32
Commerce, Department of, 8, 36, 44, 46, 51, 83–4
Commercial Democratic Business Men for Willkie, 164
Committee to Investigate Duplication of Government Communications Facilities, 84
common carrier principles, and radio, 49, 53, 56–7, 101
Commonwealth Club of San Francisco, 215
Communications Act of 1934, 93, 99; origins of, 83, 86–8; provisions of, 88–90; *vs.* Radio Act of 1927, 89, 302 n. 6; section 4, 88–9; section 303(i), 104; section 307(b), 94; section 307(c), 89, 95; section 311, 90; section 313, 90; section 315, 89, 115–6, 131, 135–6, 144, 190–1; section 326, 100
Communist Party of America (CPA): radio spending, 132, 165, 190–1; relationship with networks, 131–3, 136. *See also* Browder, Earl
Connery, Lawrence, 103
Cooke, James Francis, 267
Cooley, Charles Horton, 210
Coolidge, Calvin, 45, 52, 54, 63, 141, 150, 154; use of radio, 142–6
Coolidge, Marcus, 152
Cooper, Jack L., 253
Cooperative Analysis of Broadcasting (CAB), 193
Correll, Charles, 253–4
Coughlin, Charles E., 101, 168, 172, 178, 188, 222, 264, 276; radio style, 159–61; relationship with CBS, 159
Couzens, James, 61, 70–1, 83, 96
Couzens-Dill Resolution, 70–1, 78, 84, 95
Cox, James M., 175, 179
Crosby, Bing, 257, 270
Crosley Corporation, 236
Crossley, Archibald, 156, 193
Crossley ratings, 193, 197
"crowd mind," 209–11, 231
Crystallizing Public Opinion, 22, 195
crystal sets, 10
cultural hegemony, 261–2
cultural hierarchy, 259–62. *See also* middlebrow culture
Cummins, Albert, 55
Curran, Henry F., 141
Czitrom, Daniel, 200

Daily Express (U.K.), 181
Damrosch, Walter, 265–6
Daniels, Josephus, 6–7, 85–6
Davis, Elmer, 220
Davis, Ewin, 55, 63, 237. *See also* Davis Amendment
Davis, George, 7
Davis, Harry P., 234
Davis, John W., 145, 265
Davis, Manton, 31
Davis Amendment, 60, 63–6, 89, 94, 97, 108. *See also* Federal Radio Commission
Debs Memorial Radio Fund, 74
Defense Test Day, 28
de Forest, Lee, 4, 20, 94, 214
De Forest Company, 141

Democratic National Committee (DNC): as debtors, 133–7; and elections of 1924, 118–9, 144–5; —1928, 146–9, 179; —1932, 152–4; —1936, 162–3; —1940, 163–6; relationship with broadcasters, 118–38; Women's Division, 164–5. *See also* elections
Democratic Party, 143, 237; legislators' appearances on NBC, 138. *See also* elections
Denmark, radio ownership rate, 12
Depression, economic, 62, 124, 130, 133, 151–2, 159, 178, 218, 220, 223, 254, 262; and advertising styles, 25; and radio sales, 14–7, 43
Dewey, John, 206, 208–9; and education, 211
Dewey, Thomas E., 188
Dewson, Mary (Molly) W., 164–5
Dieterich, William, 98
Dill, Clarence C., 12, 49, 57, 69–71, 83, 86, 116; radio bill (1927), 53–4; and Wagner-Hatfield amendment, 88. *See also* Radio Act of 1927
Dillon, John F., 60
Donnelly, Thomas, 167
Donovan, William, 210–1
Doob, Leonard, 230–1
Dos Passos, John, 186
Dunlap, Orrin E., 170–2, 247
du Pont, Irénée, 146
du Pont, Pierre, 146, 243
DuPont Company, 146, 163

Early, Stephen, 80, 127, 129–30, 195
Economy Act, 80
Editor and Publisher, 159
educational broadcasting, 9, 67–8, 90, 104, 211–6, 267–8
Eighteenth Amendment, 272
Eldridge, Seba, 207–8
election funding, radio's effect on, 179–80
elections: of 1860, 179; of 1896, 173, 175, 179; of 1912, 175; of 1920, 118, 179, 282; of 1924, 118–9, 143–5; of 1928, 122–4, 133, 170, 175; of 1932, 134, 179, 188; of 1936, 135, 162–3, 175, 190; of 1940, 136, 163–6, 191, 198; of 1952, 199; of 1960, 116. *See also* Democratic party; Democratic National Committee; Republican party; Republican National Committee
Ellwood, John, 133–4, 272
El Paso Times, 177
Ely, Joseph, 152, 254
Ely, Richard, xiv
Emergency Unemployment Relief Committee, 256
End Poverty in California (EPIC), 161–2, 174
Ernst, Morris, 1, 48, 107
Erskine, John, 259
ethnic broadcasting, 235–6, 253
executive regulation, 51–3

Farber, David, xv
Farley, James A., 85, 93, 95–6, 266
farmers, 237, 250, 257; and cultural isolation, 237–8, 240; listening preferences, 242; programming for, 240–2; and radio ownership, 13, 238–40
Federal Communications Commission (FCC), 48, 115, 130, 212, 228, 236, 279; and alcoholic beverages, 273; and censorship, 103–4; creation of, 87–9; and Mayflower doctrine, 228; and networks, 104–6; policies and procedures, 104; and political advertising, 115; and politics, 95–7; "revolving door," 102; and stations, 97–102; unpopularity of, 102–6. *See also* Communications Act of 1934; *Report on Chain Broadcasting*
Federal Power Commission, 86
Federal Radio Commission (FRC), 48, 56, 82, 89, 92, 130, 212, 225, 237; and censorship, 71–5; and court decisions, 75–6, 98, 298 n. 52; early history, 59–62; engineering standards, 67; General Order No. 43, 69; policies toward stations, 66–71; powers under 1927 Act, 56–7; and religious broadcasters, 275; size and cost of, 60; unpopularity of, 59, 77. *See also* Davis Amendment; Radio Act of 1927
Federal Radio Education Committee (FREC), 95
Federal Trade Commission (FTC), 28, 35, 39
Federal Trade Commission Act of 1914, 52
Fess, Simeon, 213
Fessenden, Reginald, 4

fireside chats (FDR), 80, 126–7, 151, 154–6, 188–9; audience size, 195
First Amendment, 21, 37, 42, 52, 73, 75, 97, 107, 280. *See also* censorship
Fish, Hamilton, 132
Fitzgerald, F. Scott, 178
Fitzgerald, John, 203
Fleischmann's Yeast, 256
Fleming, John Ambrose, 4
Fletcher, Henry, 128
Fly, James Lawrence, 97, 104–7
Flynn, Ed, 62
FM broadcasting and stations, 96
Ford, Mary, 114
Ford Motor Company, 222
foreign broadcasts, 103
foreign-language broadcasts, 236. *See also* Germany; Italy
Fortune Magazine, 194, 219
France, political programming in, 182
Franco, Francisco, 221
Frankfurter, Felix, 106
Frankfurt School, 200, 261
Franklin, Ben, 205
Frederick, Christine, 242

Gallagher, Hugh, 157
Gans, Herbert, 219
Gary, Hampson, 93
Gascoigne, Paul, 124
Gates, Sherwood, 260
General Electric Company (GEC), 27–8, 141, 256; and early radio, 4–8; and political advertising, 117–9, 144
General Mills, 221, 225
General Motors Corporation, 146, 236
George V, 181
Germany: broadcasts to U.S., 231; political programming, 182–3; and radio in World War I, 6; radio ownership rate, 12; Reichs-Rundfunk, 269
Gershwin, George, 258
Getz, George, 134
Gibson, Hugh, 152
Gilman, Don, 271
Goebbels, Josef, 183, 231
Goldsmith, Alfred, 211, 243
Gold Star Radio and TV Corporation, 252
Goode, Kenneth, 199
Gosden, Freeman, 253–4
Gramsci, Antonio, 261
Great Britain: early radio, 39, licensing system, 12, 39; radio ownership rate, 12. *See also* British Broadcasting Company; "British system" of broadcasting
Green, William F., 265–6
Grossman, Lawrence, 92, 282
Grundy, Pamela, xiv, 241

Hammer v. *Dagenhart* (1918), 75
Hanley, James, 73, 83
"Happiness Boys," 19
Harbord, James, 79, 265
Hard, William, 42, 182, 185
Harding, Warren G., 39, 45, 47, 106, 115, 140, 142, 175
Hare, Ernie, 19
Harkness, William, 20, 116
Harlem Broadcasting Corporation, 252
Harney, John, 87
Hatfield, Henry, 87
Hauptmann, Bruno, 227
Hays, Will, 263
Hearst, William Randolph, 227
Heflin, Tom, 55
Heinz, Catherine, 249
Hertz, Heinrich, 3
Hettinger, Herman, 24, 194, 196, 260, 268
High, Stanley, 129
hillbilly music, xiv, 240–1, 257, 260
Hilmes, Michele, xiii, 249, 257, 262
Hindenburg, Paul von, 182
Hitler, Adolf, xiii, 160, 168, 178, 182, 218, 221–2, 230–1
Hodges, Wetmore, 103
Holt, Michael, 176
Holt, Thad, 159
Hooper, Claude, 156
Hoover, Herbert, 38, 54, 79, 106, 123, 154, 175, 182, 188; appearances on NBC, 138; philosophy, 45; and radio advertising, 46–7; as radio candidate, 146–54, 172–3; and radio regulation, 45–58, 83, 108, 114; relationship with media, 150
Hoover v. *Intercity Radio Company* (1922), 48
Hope, Bob, 124, 271
Hopkins, Harry, 158
Horkheimer, Max, 200. *See also* Frankfurt School
House of David, 74

Howe, Louis, 62, 81, 86, 96
Hudson, Grant M., 59
Hughes, Charles Evans, 114, 175, 221, 265, 272
Hylan, John F., 114, 141

Ickes, Harold, xi
immigrants, and radio, 235–6
Individualism Old and New, 208
Information Please, 188
Insull, Samuel, 68
Interior, Department of, 235
International Harvester, 241
Interstate Commerce Commission (ICC), 83, 86
Irwin, Will, 178, 230–1
Israels, Josef, 124, 147–8
Italy, broadcasts to U.S., 232

Jack Benny Show, The, xiv, 262
Jamieson, Kathleen Hall, 248
Janis, Elsie, 249
jazz, 240, 243, 256–8, 260, 270
Jefferson, Thomas, 205
Jehovah's Witnesses, 275–6
Jewett, E. H., 21
Johnny Muskrat Fur Talk, 241
Johnson, Hugh, 130, 161
Jolson, Al, 271
Jome, Hiram L., 44
Jones, Billy, 19

Kaltenborn, Hans, 114, 220–2
Katz, Elihu, 199
Kern, Stephen, 211
Kerwin, Jerome, 44
Key, V. O., 92, 199
King, Mackenzie, 184
Kirkhorn, Michael, 207
Klauber, Edward, 128, 130
Kobak, Edgar, 22, 135
Kolko, Gabriel, 58
Koppes, Clayton, 108
Ku Klux Klan, 197

LaFollette, Robert M., Jr., 130, 161
LaFollette, Robert M., Sr., 117, 145, 175
Lafount, Harold, 60, 71, 80, 82, 115
Landon, Alfred M., 127, 162–3, 166, 191
Landry, Robert, 100
Lasswell, Harold, 230
laxatives, 264, 270
Lazarsfeld, Paul, xiii, 187, 193, 219, 231, 242, 247; biography, 197; criticism of, 200–1; radio research, 197–201, 215–6
League for Political Education, 215
League of Women Voters, 66
Le Duc, Don, 75–6
Lee, Alfred and Elizabeth, 197
Lee, Ivy, 22
Lescarboura, Austin, 211, 243
Levine, Lawrence, 250
licenses, radio listening, 12. *See also* "British system" of broadcasting
Liebovich, Louis, 150
Lindbergh, Charles A., 218, 225, 258
Lippmann, Walter, 178, 220; and modern citizenship, 206–8
Lipsky, Abram, 209
listener mail, 187–91
listener sovereignty, 20, 23, 44, 69–71, 172, 229, 259, 261, 267, 283; defined, xvii
Listerine, 24
Literary Digest, 90, 191–3
Littlepage and Littlepage, 102
Lodge, Henry Cabot, 113
Lohr, Lenox, 129, 132, 134
Long, Huey, 126, 168, 172, 178; radio style, 159–61
Lord and Thomas, 161
Lord-Quigley Code, 263
Louis, Joe, 192
Lowry, Helen, 176
Lucky Strike cigarettes, 27
Lumley, Frederick, 194, 230–1
Lynd, Robert and Helen, 15, 177–8

McAdoo, William G., 143, 237
McAllister, Dorothy, 164
McCain, Thomas, 75–6
McCarthy, Charlie, 100, 232
McChesney, Robert, xiii, 21, 69, 90, 109, 211, 213
McCosker, Alfred, 85
McDonald, Eugene, 49, 55, 141–2
McDonald, J. Fred, xiii, 253, 256
McFadden, Louis T., 88
McFadden, Margaret, xiv, 262
McFarlane, William, 103
McGerr, Michael, 173–4

McGugin, Harold, 88
McIntyre, Marvin, 103, 129–30
McKerns, Joseph P., 57
MacLafferty, James, 117
McLuhan, Marshall, xiii
MacNeal, A. C., 255
MacNeil, Robert, 92
McNinch, Frank, 97, 100, 104, 273
McQuail, Dennis, 200–1
MacRorie, Janet, 135, 249, 269–73
Marchand, Roland, 23, 25
Marconi, Guglielmo, 3, 39
Mason, Frank, 226
Matheson, Hilda, 249
Maxim, Hudson, 111
Maxwell, James Clerk, 3
Maxwell House Coffee, 25
May, Earl, 62
Mayflower doctrine, 228
Mead, Richard, 196, 268
Melba, Dame Nellie, 39
Merriam, Charles, 166–7
Merton, Robert, 199
Meyrowitz, Joshua, xiv
Michelson, Charles, 127, 142, 152, 163
middlebrow culture, 260–2, 265, 270–1, 279
Miller, Clyde, 230
Mills, E. C., 18
Morgan, Joy Elmer, 213
Morrow, Dwight, 265
Morse, Samuel, 42
Moskowitz, Belle, 124
motion pictures, 208, 243; attendance figures, 16 (fig. 5); censorship of, 73, 76, 263; and cultural hierarchy, 259; use in political campaigns, 174
Motion Pictures Producers and Distributors Association (MPPDA), 263–4
Mullen, Frank, 81
Munich crisis, 218, 232
Murrow, Edward R., 227
Mussolini, Benito, 231–2
Mutual Broadcasting System (MBS), 33, 99, 129. *See also* networks

Nash, Jay, 210
Nation, 41, 99, 103, 177
National Advisory Council on Radio in Education (NACRE), 212–5
National Americanization League, 132
National Association for the Advancement of Colored People (NAACP), 255
National Association of Broadcasters (NAB), 41, 48, 69, 71, 85, 104–5, 127, 141, 268, 273; and censorship, 100–1; Codes of Ethics, 236, 263–4; formation of, 35; and section 315, 132
National Association of Manufacturers, 236
National Barn Dance, 268
National Broadcasting Company (NBC), 21, 23, 26, 54, 63, 68, 79, 99, 106, 161, 206, 235, 237–8, 246–7; advertising charges, 30, 122; advertising policies, 268–70; and affiliates, 31 (map 2), 227; and African Americans, 255–7; and alcoholic beverages, 272–3; attitude toward Advisory Council, 266; audience surveys, 192–5; and birth control, 271–2; and censorship, 100; and cultural uplift, 260–1; debt collection policies, 133–7; Department of Continuity Acceptance, 219–23; divestiture of Blue network, 105–6, 279; and early New Deal, 80–3; and educational broadcasting, 212–6; and elections of 1928, 122–4; farm programs, 240–2; and female employees, 249–50; and female listeners, 244–7; financial performance, 31–2, 41; formation of, 29–30; and jazz, 256–7; listener mail, 187–91; news broadcasts, 217–9; and news commentators, 220–3; operations of, 29–31; political party billings (1936, 1940), 136 (table 2), 165 (fig. 9); and political programming, 119–33; and press-radio war, 223–8; and Prohibition, 272–3; relationship with Socialists and CPA, 131–3, 165; and religious broadcasting, 273–7; as role model, 264–5; and sexual innuendo, 272. *See also* networks
National Broadcasting System, 28, 118
National Committee for Education by Radio (NCER), 78, 94; and educational broadcasting, 212–5
National Committee of Independent Voters for Roosevelt and Wallace, 164
National Council of Catholic Men, 276
National Farm and Home Hour, 240–2
National Hoover Minute Men, 148
National Industrial Recovery Act, 80

National Race Congress of America, 255
National Recovery Administration (NRA), 80, 82, 157, 160; broadcasting code, 90
NBC Advisory Council, 238, 264–6, 275
NBC Symphony Orchestra, 214, 253
Neilson, Arthur C., 193
"netizens," 282
networked computer, 282
networks: advertising charges, 122, 146, 162; advertising on, 25–7; and affiliates, 105; control over industry, 34; and early New Deal, 79–83, and elections of 1924, 118–9; and FCC, 104–6; formation of, 27–35; and middlebrow culture, 262; party billings (1932), 153; and political programming, 119–33; relationship with Socialists and CPA, 131–3. *See also individual networks*
New, Harry S., 140
New Deal, 106, 109, 129, 178, 218, 222, 225, 230, 233, 236, 239, 242, 266; Hundred Days, 79–83, 125, 254; network treatment of, 78–83, publicity campaign of, 157–9
"New Paternalism, The," 208
New Republic, 177
news broadcasting, 253; development of, 216–9, 264; listeners' attitudes toward, 217 (fig.11), 218, 268; nature of, 219. *See also* press-radio war
news commentators, 219–23; relations with sponsors, 220–3
newspapers, 198; advertising, 223–4; criticism of radio, 82; ownership of stations, 9, 96, 105–7, 225, 227; partisanship of, 143, 156, 219; and press-radio war, 223–8
newsreels, 174
Newton, Walter, 61–2,
New York Daily News, 232
New York Edison Company, 192
New York Herald Tribune, 82, 233
New York Post, 232
New York Times, 9, 13, 20, 32, 41, 42, 116, 149, 154, 162, 171–2, 179, 182, 229, 238, 274, 282
Nicholson, Meredith, 143
Noble, Edward J., 106
nominating conventions: of 1844, 281; of 1924, 117, 119, 149, 174, 178; of 1928, 177, 237; of 1932, 153; of 1936, 163, 194
nonprofit broadcasting, 67–8. *See also* educational broadcasting; religious broadcasting
Norris, George W., 54, 241
No Third Term Democrats, 164
Nutt, J. R., 134

O'Connell, William H., 270
Office of Radio Research, 197, 233
Ohio School of the Air, 212
Ollry, Francis, 244
Omaha World-Herald, 176
O'Neill, Eugene, 100
Only Yesterday, 178
oratory, radio's effect on, 168–72, 178
Ortega y Gasset, José, 210
Overacker, Louise, 144
Overstreet, Harry and Bonaro, 215

Paley, William S., 32, 79, 128–9, 132, 150, 260; and educational broadcasting, 213–4
Payne, George Henry, 93, 97, 266
Peel, Roy, 166
People's Choice, The, 198
Pepsodent, 254
Perilla, Jack, 131
Personal Influence, 199
Pettey, Herbert, 62, 82, 89, 93, 96
Phantom Public, The, 207
Phelps, George Harrison, 22
Phelps, William Lyon, 214
phonographs, 174, 259
Pickard, Sam, 60, 69, 250
Pittman, Key, 61
Pittsburgh Courier, 255
political advertising, 53, 115–9; on local stations, 116, 130–1; on networks, 137. *See also* Columbia Broadcasting System; elections; National Broadcasting Company
political culture, xv
political programs, 114, 139; popularity with listeners, 194–5
Poponoe, Charles, 118
Post Office, 44, 281
Potts, John, 248
Prairie Farmer, 241
Prairie President, The, 241

Prall, Anning S., 93, 96–7, 103; and educational broadcasting, 212
Pratt, Benson, 133
President's Research Committee on Social Trends, xi–xii
Press Radio Bureau, 226–7
press-radio war, 223–8. *See also* advertising; news broadcasting
Printer's Ink, 21
Procter and Gamble, 246
Progressive Party, 117; publicity budget (1924), 145; use of radio (1924), 145
Prohibition, 243, 272–3
propaganda, 103, 160, 228–33
Propaganda, 229
Propaganda and the News, 178
Propaganda Menace, The, 230
Prostak, Elaine, 211
"public interest, convenience or necessity," 52, 56, 66–72, 75–6, 98, 273
public opinion, 206–11
public utility theory, and radio, 49–50, 56–7
Public Works Administration, 81
Pure Oil, 221–2
Purnell, Fred, 163

radio: amateurs and, 4–5, 37–8; average daily listening time, 279; diffusion of, 9–17; in domestic architecture, 243, 259; and immigrants, 236; invention of, 3–5; and labor activism, 236–7; listening, by income group, 268; news broadcasts, 216–8; and propaganda, 228–33; and public opinion, 243; and religiosity, 274–7; set sales and types, 10–1; and social problems, 205–6; and voter behavior, 195–201; and World War I, 5–7
Radio Act of 1912, 36, 49, 114; inadequacies of, 46; provisions of, 5, 45–6
Radio Act of 1927, 93, 99, 114, 131, 276; *vs.* Communications Act, 302 n. 6; passage of, 55–8; provisions of, 56–7; reaction to, 57–8; section 4(h), 69; section 18, 89–90, 115, 119, 121, 137, 144; section 29, 71–2, 75
radio advertising, 109, 223–4, 227, 279; birth of, 18–25, 46; growth of, 25–7; of liquor, 72; *vs.* other media, 26 (fig. 6). *See also* Dill, Clarence C.; White, Wallace H.
Radio and Amusement Guide, 172–3
Radio and the Printed Page, 215–6
radio audience meter, 194
Radio Broadcast, 21, 114
radio campaigning, 167–8; changes in, 173–7; early history, 140–3; against End Poverty in California, 161–2; in local politics, 161; in 1924, 143–6; in 1928, 146–9; in 1932, 154; in 1933–36, 159–62; in 1936, 162–3; in 1940, 163–6
radio citizenship, 206, 209–11, 233, 234–7, 257, 281, 283; defined, xvii
Radio Conferences, 47–8, 51
Radio Corporation of America (RCA), 20, 27, 32, 35, 54, 69, 79, 141; formation of, 6–8; and political advertising, 117–9, 144; and Socialist Party, 131
radio exceptionalism, 23, 38, 51, 64, 133, 139, 141, 195, 198, 219, 235, 252, 262, 280–2; defined, xvii
radio fundraising, 149
Radio Homemakers Club, 245
Radio League of America, 37
Radio Manufacturers' Association, 54
Radio Retailing, 54
radio revolution, xvi; limits of, 281–3; proponents of, 175–7; skeptics of, 177–80
radio stations: affiliated and networked, 34 (fig. 7); distribution of, 10 (map 1), 64–6; KDKA, xi, 8, 27, 41, 118, 229; KECA, 127; KFI, 127; KFKB, 73–4; KGEF, 75; KGO, 117; KXO, 131; 2KY (Australia), 183; WBAY (later WEAF), 19, 22, 27–9, 114, 118, 131, 217, 220–1; WBT, 241; WBZ, 80; WCAP, 28; WCFL, 68, 74, 236; WCLO, 131; WDSU, 160; WEVD, 74, 236; WGL, 114; WGN, 129, 253; WGY, 154; WHA, 114; WHAP, 75; WJAR, 28; WJAZ, 48; WJTL, 253; WJY, 9; WJZ, 29, 114, 188, 191, 248; WLBL, 114; WLS, 241; WLWL, 62; WMAC, 28; WMAL, 96; WMAQ, 253; WNYC, 21, 114; WOR, 119, 221; WPG, 62; WQXR, 23, 249; WSBC, 253; WTAQ, 131; WTMJ, 131; XER (Mexico), 74
radio telegraphy, 3–4, 6
radio telephony, 4, 8
Radio Today, 239
Raskob, John J., 146–7, 152
Rayburn, Sam, 85–6
Reconstruction Finance Commission, 81

Reichs-Rundfunk, program priorities of, 269
Reid, Ogden, 82
Reith, Lord John, 40, 249; and political programming, 180–2
religious broadcasting, 68, 273–7
Report on Chain Broadcasting, 104–8
Republican National Committee (RNC), 79, 117; as debtors, 133–7; and elections of 1924, 118–9, 144–5; —1928, 146–9; —1932, 152–4; —1936, 162–3, 175; —1940, 163–6; relationship with broadcasters, 118–38. *See also* elections
Republican Party, 101; broadcasts of, 81–3; legislators' appearances on NBC, 138; relationship with networks, 124, 127–31. *See also* elections; Republican National Committee; Republican party
Revolt of the Masses, The, 210
Ribbentrop, Joachim von, 222
Rice, Stuart, 241, 252
Richmond Times-Despatch, 176
Rickard, Edgar, 152
Riegel, O. W., 230
Robeson, Paul, 256
Robinson, Ernest, 244
Robinson, Ira, 60–1
Robinson, Joseph T., 53, 147
Robinson, Thomas, 171
Robinson, William S., 241
Robinton, Alexander, 154
Rogers, Will, 30, 262
Roosevelt, Eleanor, 81, 147; ideas on women's programs, 247; radio activities, 189–90
Roosevelt, Franklin D., xv, 62, 78, 81, 85, 93, 96, 105, 122–4, 126, 128–9, 147, 150–1, 160, 175, 182, 187, 192, 222, 233, 254–5; appearances on NBC, 138; audience monitoring, 156, 195; and cross-ownership, 96–7, 228; disability, 157; and FRC, 83; listener mail, 188–9; radio strategy as governor, 154; radio style, 154–7, 172–3; relationship with press, 156. *See also* fireside chats
Roosevelt, Theodore, 175
Root, Elihu, 238, 265
Roper, Daniel, 85
Rorty, James, 3
Rose, C. B., 73
Rosen, Philip, xiii, 46, 83, 90
Ross, Edward A., 209
Rothafel, Samuel, 211
Royal, John F., 132, 137, 222, 256, 260
Rural Electrification Administration (REA), 239, 242
Russell, Frank, 126, 129–30
Rutherford, Joseph, 275

Sabin, Thomas, 126
Sam'n'Henry, 253. See also *Amos'n'Andy*
Sarnoff, David, 8, 20, 27–9, 83, 87, 129, 282
Saturday Evening Post, 170
Scannell, Paddy, 182
Scharfield, Arthur W., 72
Schechter, Abel A., 225
Schudson, Michael, 220
Scopes trial, 237
Scott, Byron, 116
Sears, Roebuck, 241
Senate Interstate Commerce Committee, 84, 87, 89
Sergio, Lisa, 249
sexual innuendo, 271
Seymour-Ure, Colin, 201
Sherman, Mrs. John, 265
Shuler, Bob, 75–6
"shut-ins," 189, 242, 246, 250, 273; defined, 234
Siepmann, Charles, 92, 236
Sinclair, Upton, 161–2
Sirovich, William, 265
Smith, Alfred E., 75, 124, 143, 174, 192, 237, 265; as radio candidate, 146–9, 168–70, 172–3
Smith, Elias, 244
Smith, F. Leslie, 200
Smith, Kate, 199
Smulyan, Susan, xiii, 21, 24, 90, 240
"Soapland," 245
soap operas, 245–6
Socialist Party of America, 191; radio spending, 132, 165; relationship with networks, 131–3, 136
social scientists, on voter behavior, 195–201
Spigel, Lynn, 205
spot advertising, 24, 148, 162, 164
Stanton, Frank, 193
Starch, Daniel, 193
Steinbeck, John, 271

Stewart, Irvin, 93
Stimson, Henry, 62, 182
Stone, Peggy, 250
Straton, Joan Roach, 274
Strong, James, 62
Sullivan, Lawrence, 157
Sullivan, Mark, 155
"superpower," 20, 27, 44
Supreme Court, U.S., 73–6, 106, 197, 272
Susman, Warren, 259
Sweden, 12
Sweetheart Soap, 190
Sweetser, Norman, 123
Swing, Raymond Gram, 220
Sykes, Eugene, 60, 83, 93, 97–9, 102

Taft, William Howard, 175
technological utopianism, 205, 282, 327 n. 7
"teledemocracy," 282, 327 n. 7
telegraph, 42, 85, 176, 205, 210–1, 259, 280–1; usage, 14
telephone, 85, 176, 205, 210–1, 259, 280–1; diffusion of, 15 (fig. 4); use in audience measurement, 194
television, 174, 176, 200, 205, 249, 255, 280; announcement of, 282; diffusion of, 279; and political culture, 282, 286 n. 5, 312 n. 38
Tennessee Valley Authority (TVA), 97
Thayer, Henry, 38
Thomas, Norman, 55, 114, 182, 266–7
Thompson, J. Walter, 256
Thompson, John B., xiv
Thurber, James, 245
Tilson, John Q., 144
Tocqueville, Alexis de, 205
toll broadcasting, 19–20, 38. *See also* advertising
Tonnies, Ferdinand, 208–9
Toscanini, Arturo, 214, 253, 260
Trammell, Niles, 81, 124
Trans-Radio Press Service, 227. *See also* press-radio war
Trinity Methodist Church v. *FRC* (1932), 76

Ullswater Committee, 181
United Fruit Company, 5, 7
United Independent Broadcasters, 32
United Press (UP), 224–5
United States Navy, and early radio, 5–7, 44

Vallee, Rudy, 257, 268, 270
Vandenburg, Arthur, 130
Vann, Robert, 255
voter turnout, 149, 176, 178, 206–8

Wagner, Robert F., 62, 87, 93
Wagner Act, 160
Wagner-Hatfield Amendment, 70, 87–9, 93–5, 213
Walker, Paul, 93
Wallas, Graham, 195
Waller, Judith, 214, 245, 247, 249
Walsh, Thomas J., 174
Walter Damrosch Musical Appreciation Hour, 214
Ward, Harry, 271–2
Ward, Paul, 103
War of the Worlds, 229, 232–3
Washington Post, 57, 96
Watson, James, 54
Weary and Willie, 162
Welles, Orson, 232–3
West, Mae, 100, 104, 246, 271
Westbrook, Robert, 200
Western Electric Company, 7
Western Union Company, 36
Westinghouse, 7, 18, 28, 141, 234; and political advertising, 117–9
Whale, John, 92
Wheeler, Burton K., 99, 102–3, 260
White, Andrew, 172, 176
White, Paul, 225
White, Wallace H., and radio bill (1927), 51–3. *See also* Radio Act of 1927
Willey, Malcolm, 241, 252
Willkie, Wendell, 124, 166, 191
Wilson, Charles Morrow, 240
Wilson, Woodrow, 6, 113, 142–3, 175, 234
Winchell, Walter, 220, 222
Wireless Age, 113
Wireless Telegraphy Act of 1904 (U.K.), 39
women, 175, 237–8, 250, 257; and Australian radio, 183; in Canadian broadcasting, 322 n. 50; discrimination against, in radio, 248–50; in election of 1928, 176; program preferences, 246–7; and public speech, 248–9; as radio advertising market, 244–6; as radio announcers, 248–9; in radio industry, 247–50; as radio listeners, 216 (fig. 10), 244; and soap operas, 245–7
Wood, C. Arthur, 37

Woodin, William H., 146
Woods, Mark, 61, 236
Works Progress Administration (WPA), 158–9
World Radio Convention (1938), xi
World War I, 42, 44, 178, 205–8; and early radio, 5–7; and propaganda, 206, 228–9
World War II, xv, 205, 209, 218, 228, 249, 268, 279–80, 283; effect on African Americans in radio, 322 n. 72
Writers' Committee for Roosevelt, 164

Yankee Network, 227
Yates, Raymond, 211
Young, Edward, 274
Young, Kimball, 229
Young, Owen D., 7, 171, 265–6, 272

Zenith Radio Corporation, 48

Library of Congress Cataloging-in-Publication Data

Craig, Douglas B.
Fireside politics : radio and political culture in the United States,
1920–1940 / Douglas B. Craig.
p. cm.
— (Reconfiguring American political history)
Includes bibliographical references (p.) and index.
ISBN 0-8018-6439-9 (alk. paper)
1. Radio broadcasting—United States—History. 2. Radio
broadcasting—Political aspects—United States—History.
3. Radio broadcasting policy—United States—History.
4. Radio in politics—United States—History. I. Title.
II. Series.
PN1991.3.U6 C73 2000
384.54'0973—dc21 00-008338